Business Milestones

Englisch für kaufmännische Berufe

Ruth Feiertag
Dr. Richard Hooton

Ernst Klett Verlag
Stuttgart · Leipzig

Business Milestones
Englisch für kaufmännische Berufe

Autoren: Ruth Feiertag; Dr. Richard Hooton

Berater: Robert Kanzog, Münster; Asiye Sezgin, Duisburg

Die Videos auf Seite 93 und 120 wurden von der Firma lingua tv
http://www.linguatv.com/ lizenziert.
Bei den Videos handelt es sich um Auszüge aus der LinguaTV-Reihe Business English.

Werkübersicht:
Schülerbuch, 978-3-12-808260-8
Lehrerhandbuch, mit Lehrer-Service-DVD-ROM und 3 Audio-CDs, 978-3-12-808267-7
Workbook mit 1 Audio-CD-ROM, 978-3-12-808265-3
Workbook mit 1 Audio-CD-ROM plus Prüfungsvorbereitung KMK-Fremdsprachenzertifikat 978-3-12-808266-0
Online-Ergänzungen unter www.klett.de/online

1. Auflage 1 13 12 11 10 9 | 24 23 22 21 20

Projektleitung: Matthias Rupp
Redaktion: Volker Wendland
Herstellung: Angelika Lindner

Gestaltung: Marion Köster, Stuttgart
Umschlaggestaltung: Ulrike Wollenberg; Angelika Lindner
Grafiken: Jörg Mair, München
Satz: Marion Köster, Stuttgart
Reproduktion: Meyle + Müller Medien-Management, Pforzheim
Druck: PASSAVIA Druckservice GmbH & Co. KG, Passau

Printed in Germany
ISBN 978-3-12-808260-8

9 783128 082608

Die vorliegende **Neubearbeitung der berufsübergreifenden Ausgabe von Business Milestones** für die Englischklassen in den kaufmännischen Berufsschulen sowie für kaufmännisch ausgerichtete Englischkurse in der Erwachsenenbildung zeichnet sich insbesondere durch folgende Elemente aus:

- Berücksichtigung der Incoterms 2010 (gültig ab 01.01.2011)
- Einbeziehung neuester Entwicklungen in der kaufmännischen Praxis, z. B. durch realitätsnahe Arbeitsaufträge wie Recherchen im Internet
- Konsequente Berücksichtigung neuester Lehrpläne (Lernfelder) sowie durchgängiges Sprachkompetenztraining nach dem Gemeinsamen Europäischen Referenzrahmen (Sprachstufen B1 / B2).
- Möglichkeit zur Binnendifferenzierung durch gekennzeichnete Aufgaben mit höherem Schwierigkeitsgrad
- Umfangreiches Seh- / Hörverstehenstraining durch u. a. Originalvideos von der BBC sowie zahlreiche Audios
- Vokabelarbeit mit der „Word Bank" und den Vokabellernlisten über Online-Link
- Vertieftes Vokabel-, Grammatik- und Hörverstehenstraining im Workbook I und II inklusive Audio-CD-ROM mit allen Schülerbuch- und Workbook-Audios
- Gezielte Prüfungsvorbereitung auf das KMK-Fremdsprachenzertifikat im Schülerbuch und im Workbook II

Workbook I:
Business Milestones Workbook mit Audio-CD-ROM,
978-3-12-808265-3

Workbook II:
Business Milestones Workbook mit Prüfungsvorbereitung KMK-Fremdsprachenzertifikat und mit Audio-CD-ROM,
978-3-12-808266-0

Lernhilfen

WORDBANK Schlüsselvokabular
Info-Box Faktenwissen
Communicating across cultures Interkulturelle Kompetenz
Language and grammar Grammatik
Video Lounge authentische Videos

Symbole

A1.27	Audioverweis
V 4	Videoverweis
Phrases	Verweis auf Phrases
P, M, I, R	Produktion, Mediation, Interaktion oder Rezeption
Example:	z. B. Beispieldialoge
Online-Link	Vokabellernlisten über Online-Link
KMK	Aufgaben zur Vorbereitung auf die Prüfung zum KMK-Fremdsprachenzertifikat Englisch
	Internet-Recherchen
*	„Advanced"-Aufgaben

New Message
Cancel
Send
H

Kodak
Purple

Unit 1
Introducing yourself

WORD BANK

I'm / my name is • I'm from • I was born in / on • to work as a … • to be a … • to work at / with / for … • to be interested in • to be into • trainee • apprentice • traineeship / apprenticeship • vocational school • to attend school • to be on a programme • to take part in • to train / to be training as a … • to train to be a … • to be training to become a … • to do a traineeship as a … • to qualify as a … • clerk • management assistant • consultant • specialist

In business it is often necessary to introduce yourself. It is therefore important to know what to say and what information to include. You may, for instance need to explain your professional role or duties in the firm. In a business situation introductions and greetings are often more formal than those among friends in a casual situation. It is important to choose the right style.

Decide which of the following phrases would be used in a formal and which in a casual situation. Match the phrases with the photos above.

1 Good afternoon, Mr Perigault. Nice to see you again.

2 Hello Janina. How's things?

3 How do you do, Mr Yamato? Pleased to meet you.

4 Hi, Ian. How are you doing?

Online-Link
808260-0001

A Talking about yourself

Students at a vocational school in Germany are asked to introduce themselves to a new English assistant who is to spend half a year at their school.

1 Take the roles of the assistant and the students and read the introductions.

Rona: Good morning. I'm Rona Mansfield. I come from Dulwich in South London and I'll be working here as an assistant teacher for the next six months. It would be good if a few of you could introduce yourselves so I can begin to learn your names. Perhaps you could tell me briefly what job you're training for and what your interests are. Hello, what's your name?

Stefanie: Hello. I'm Stefanie Krieger. I'm from Cologne but I was born in Hamburg. I'll be 17 next Monday. I'm doing a traineeship at Kabel AG in Leverkusen to become an office administration clerk. I'm very interested in computers and enjoy designing websites. I do quite a lot of sport, including aerobics and badminton.

Rona: Thank you, Stefanie, I'll remember the birthday! And what's your name?

Haris: Hi. My name's Haris Akbar. I'm from Cologne. I am 19 years old. I'm training at Schulz und Schmalenbach as an export clerk. I am very interested in football and support Werder Bremen. I work out regularly at a local gym. I love music. "The Devils" are my favourite group.

Rona: Thank you, Haris. My taste in music is a touch more traditional. Can you tell me something about yourself?

Antonella: My name is Antonella Piccolino but my friends call me Nella. Like Stefanie, I also work at Kabel AG but I'm training to be an Industriekauffrau, that's an industrial clerk or industrial business management assistant. I was born in Bergheim in 1992. Originally my family comes from Sicily. I'm very interested in the Italian language and Italian cooking. I also go to a fitness centre three times a week because I'm into body-building.

Rona: Gosh, I can see we'd better watch what we say. Right, we can continue with the introductions later. Could you make a plan of the classroom where everybody's sitting with names – first names and family names.

2 Say whether the following statements from page 7 are TRUE or FALSE.

R

1. Stefanie Krieger was born in Cologne.
2. She is training to be an office administration clerk.
3. She doesn't like working with a computer.
4. Haris Akbar is doing a traineeship to become an industrial clerk.
5. He is between 20 and 30 years old.
6. He supports a football club from Bavaria.
7. Antonella Piccolino is at the same firm as Haris Akbar.
8. Her hobby is cooking Italian dishes.
9. She tries to keep fit.

3 Complete the following introduction using the words from the box.

at • from • in (3 x) • near • to • on

I was born 1 Garforth 2 23 March 1964. Garforth is a small town 3 Leeds 4 the UK. My family comes 5 the West Indies. I work 6 an advertising agency and I'm taking part 7 a training programme for advertising assistants. I regularly go 8 a gym for a work-out.

4 Listen to the following introductions and answer the questions.

R
A1.1

Thorsten

1. Where does Thorsten come from?
2. What is he training as?
3. What is his hobby?

Ludmilla

1. How long has Ludmilla been living in Germany?
2. How old is she?

Ayshe

1. When was Ayshe born?
2. What is she training to become?
3. What does she do in her free time?

5 Work in groups and make up similar introductions with the help of the following hints.

P

Phrases

Training or working as:	industrial clerk/industrial business management assistant, office administration clerk/office management assistant, wholesale and export clerk/management assistant in wholesale and foreign trade, bank clerk/bank business management assistant, management assistant in advertising, freight forwarding and logistics services clerk/management assistant in freight forwarding, IT specialist, management assistant in retail business, publisher's assistant/management assistant in publishing, insurance clerk/insurance business management assistant
Firms:	ENKA AG, Schuster & Schneider, Taufrisch OHG, Kohlhaas & Söhne, Globistik-Transport KG, Sportsmarketing GmbH, Online-Consulting
Hobbies:	Swimming, reading fantasy novels, cycling, volleyball, Sci-Fi films, buying clothes, computer games, horses, snowboarding, clubbing

Language and grammar
Work in groups of four. Introduce yourself briefly in writing. You may use imaginary details if you wish. Read the introduction out to your group.

Phrases

Language and grammar: Introducing yourself

Antonella sagt: I **was** born in Bergheim in 1992.	Auf Deutsch hätte sie gesagt: Ich **bin** 1992 in Bergheim geboren.
Im Englischen werden Geburtszeitpunkt und Geburtsort mit simple past angegeben:	
My father **was** born in Italy. Haris **was** born on 7 July 1992.	Mein Vater ist in Italien geboren. Haris ist am 7. Juli 1992 geboren.
Außerdem wird im Englischen erst der Ort genannt und danach der Zeitpunkt: I was born **in Bergheim in 1992**.	Im Deutschen ist die Reihenfolge umgekehrt: Ich bin **1992 in Bergheim** geboren.
Haris sagt: I'm training as **an** export clerk. She's **a** travel consultant. He works as **a** programmer.	Auf Deutsch hätte er gesagt: Ich mache eine Ausbildung als Exportkaufmann. Sie ist Reiseverkehrskauffrau. Er arbeitet als Programmierer.
Im Englischen steht zur Angabe des Berufes der unbestimmte Artikel: **a travel consultant.** Im Deutschen steht kein Artikel: **Reiseverkehrskauffrau.**	
I am **a** publisher's assistant. I am training as **a** bank clerk or bank business management assistant.	Ich bin Verlagskaufmann. Ich mache eine Ausbildung als Bankkaufmann.

Communicating across cultures: Introducing and greeting people

In English-speaking countries people often give only their first name when introducing themselves - "Hi, I'm Jonathan". In more formal contexts they give their first name and surname but never just their surname as is usual in Germany - "I'm Jennifer Ashton". Often people add; "Please call me Jennifer".
"How do you do" is a formal greeting which is nowadays rarely used. The other person also says "How do you do" and will probably add "Pleased to meet you".
A usual greeting is "Hello, how are you?" The other person says something like "Fine, thanks / not so bad / so-so" and immediately adds "How are you?" Friends usually say something like "Hi, Justin. How are you doing?" or "Hello, Sarah, how's things?"
Sarah might reply: "Fine, how's things with you?"

B Young people talk about their (future) professions

Rona Mansfield meets more students at the vocational college and asks them to introduce themselves and tell her what training programme they're on:

Oliver: Hello, I'm Oliver: I'm training to become an office management assistant that's "Kaufmann für Büromanagement" in German.
Jeannine: My name's Jeannine: I'm on the trainee programme of a high street bank.
David: I'm David: I'm an insurance business management assistant.
Jennifer: Hi, I'm Jennifer: I want to train as an advertising assistant.
Antje: I'm Antje: I hope to be a restaurant manager.
Rosa: Hi, I'm Rosa: I am interested in qualifying as a foreign language correspondent.
Dennis: I'm Dennis: I want to get on to a training programme for retail management assistants.
Niko: I'm Niko: I want to train as an event management assistant.
Simone: Hi, I'm Simone: I'm applying to train as an IT specialist.
Janina: Hello, my name's Janina: I work for a wholesaler in the electrical goods industry.
Mike: I'm Mike: I'm a trainee export clerk.
Dragan: I'm Dragan: I'm training to be a management assistant in publishing.
Hasan: Good morning. I'm Hasan: I am planning to train as an industrial clerk or industrial business management assistant.

My name's Samira. I am taking part in an ITC programme.

Hello, I'm Sabrina. I'm training to be a travel consultant.

1 **Read the introductions on page 10 and match the German occupations with their English paraphrases.**

1. Kauffrau für Tourismus und Freizeit
2. Kaufmann im Einzelhandel
3. Fremdsprachenkorrespondentin
4. Kaufmann für Spedition und Logistikdienstleistung
5. Veranstaltungskauffrau
6. Industriekauffrau
7. Automobilkaufmann
8. Kaufmann für Büromanagement
9. Kauffrau für Marketingkommunikation
10. Kaufmann im Groß- und Außenhandel
11. Kauffrau für Versicherung und Finanzen
12. Informatikkaufmann
13. Bankkaufmann

a. advertising assistant/management assistant in advertising
b. bank clerk/bank business management assistant
c. automobile sales management assistant
d. management assistant in event organisation
e. management assistant for freight forwarding and logistics
f. industrial clerk/industrial business management assistant
g. insurance clerk/insurance business management assistant
h. IT consultant/management assistant in informatics
i. office management assistant/office administration clerk
j. retail business management assistant
k. secretary with foreign languages/foreign language correspondent
l. management assistant for tourism and leisure
m. wholesale and export clerk/management assistant in wholesale and foreign trade

2 **Übertragen Sie die folgenden Aussagen ins Englische.**

M

1. Ich habe eine Ausbildung als Industriekaufmann gemacht.
2. Ich möchte eine Ausbildung als Automobilkaufmann machen.
3. Ich möchte als Fremdsprachenkorrespondentin ausgebildet werden.
4. Ich will Versicherungskaufmann werden.
5. Ich nehme an einem IT-Weiterbildungsprogramm teil.
6. Ich bewerbe mich um einen Ausbildungsplatz als Kauffrau für Büromanagement.
7. Ich mache eine Ausbildung als Kauffrau im Einzelhandel.
8. Ich arbeite bei einem Großhändler.
9. Ich möchte gerne eine Ausbildung als Werbekaufmann machen.

3 I/P **Work in groups of three. Act out the following conversation, inserting your own names and training courses.**

A	B	C
Hello. My name's …	Hello. I'm … Have you met … (C)?	
No, I haven't. Hello, pleased to meet you.		Pleased to meet you, too.
Are you a trainee as well, B?	Not yet. But I'm hoping to train as a(n) … What do you want to do?	
I would like to train as a …	And what are you doing, C ?	I'm a trainee …

4 I/P **Work in groups of three. Use the phrases from the conversation above and make similar dialogues.** Phrases

5 R A1.2 **Listen to the following dialogue and say which of the following statements are true for Patrick and Janina.**

1. I'm training to become an industrial clerk.
2. I want to train as an export clerk.
3. I'm in the electrical goods industry.
4. There are good prospects of promotion.
5. I'm allowed to advise customers.
6. I get on well with the people I work with.
7. I can use my English.
8. I can work on my own.

6 I **Work in groups of two. Introduce yourselves and say what you do. Ask each other what you like or dislike in your job.** Phrases

7 **Search the Internet for two of the following international job titles. Note down the details of one job ad. Compare and discuss your findings with the group.**

freight forwarding clerk • trainee advertising assistant • insurance clerk • IT assistant • trainee assistant events • bilingual secretary / secretary or PA with foreign languages • trainee tourism assistant / tourism clerk

Communicating across cultures: The German "dual training" system

The German "dual training" system combining on the job apprenticeships / traineeships with vocational school has no direct systematic equivalent in Britain and the USA. This is also true of the large number of protected job titles with a prescribed course of training in Germany. However, in Britain, for example, there are many training programmes, traineeships and apprenticeships in more traditional skilled occupations (plumber, electrician, etc.), also vocational courses leading to an NVQ (National Vocational Qualification). Most trainee programmes (except traditional apprentices) are shorter than in Germany and people often do additional courses later (e.g. in CLAIT = computer literacy and information technology) leading to a national or international qualification.
As a result of these differences German job titles can often not be translated literally. It is necessary to paraphrase them in such a way that a foreign employer can get a realistic idea of the range of activity covered.
The statement "Ich mache eine Ausbildung zum Industriekaufmann bei der ENCOR AG" could be paraphrased as follows: "I am on a 3-year training programme with ENCOR AG to qualify as an industrial clerk / industrial business management assistant specialising in the commercial side of an industrial business. During the training programme I have to attend courses at vocational school either two days a week or in blocks of several weeks at a time. At the end of the training period I sit for an examination before the local chamber of commerce."

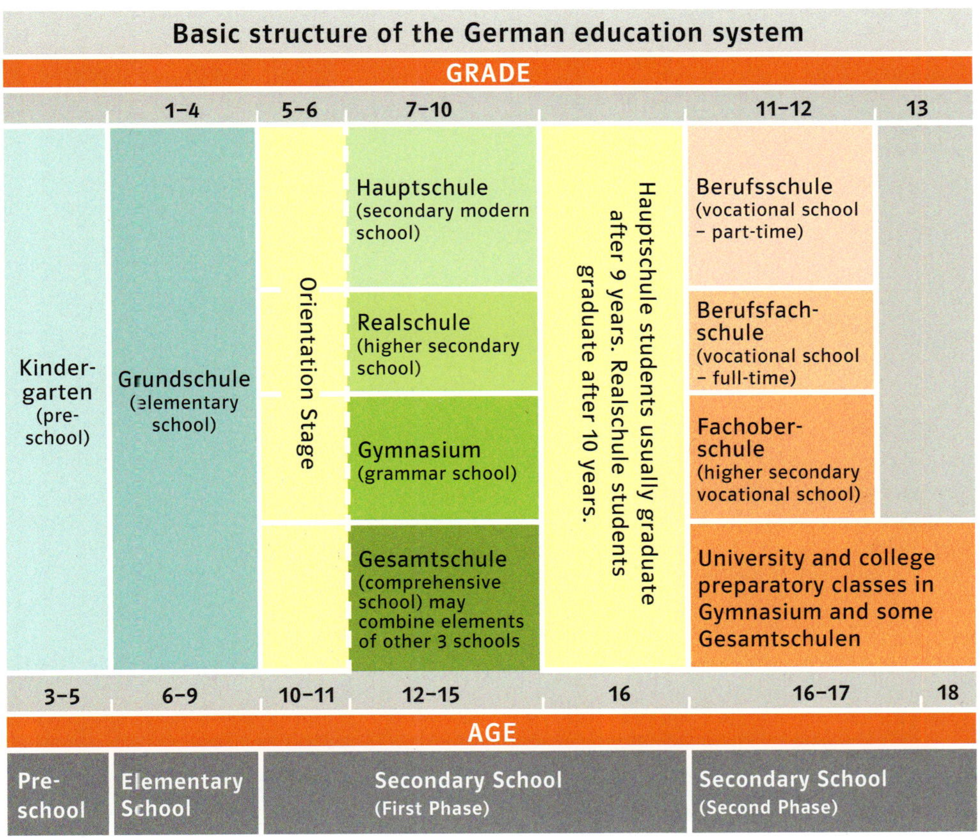

Phrases: Introducing yourself and others

To introduce yourself

I'm Peter. / My name is Henry Myers.	Ich heiße Peter. / Ich heiße Henry Myers.
Please call me Henry.	Nennen Sie mich doch Henry.
My surname is Hillary, my first name is Tom.	Mein Familienname ist Hillary, mein Vorname Tom.
How are you? (How are you doing?)	Wie geht es Ihnen / Dir? (informelle Begrüßung)
I'm from Berlin, and I am 20 years old.	Ich stamme aus Berlin und bin 20 Jahre alt.
I'm British / Irish.	Ich bin Brite / Ire.
I **was** born in Cyprus on 7 August 1982.	Ich bin am 7. August 1982 in Zypern geboren.
Have you met Mr Martens?	Kennen Sie Herrn Martens?
May I introduce Dr. Bolt to you?	Darf ich Ihnen Herrn Dr. Bolt vorstellen?
Pleased / Nice to meet you.	Ich freue mich, Sie kennen zu lernen.
And how are you?	Und (wie geht es) Ihnen?
Didn't we meet at the Boat Fair?	Haben wir uns nicht schon auf der Boot-Messe kennen gelernt?
I've heard a lot **about** you **from** Mr Winter.	Herr Winter hat mir schon viel von Ihnen erzählt.

To talk about your hobbies and interests

I am interested in computers.	Ich interessiere mich für Computer.
I love travelling more than anything else.	Ich reise schrecklich gern.
I like to go clubbing.	Ich gehe gern in die Disco.
I'm **into** body-building.	Ich interessiere mich für Bodybuilding.
I do a lot of diving.	Ich gehe oft tauchen.

To talk about your training or your work

I'm a trainee export clerk.	Ich mache eine Ausbildung zum Exportkaufmann.
I'm training to become	Ich mache eine Lehre als
an industrial clerk / industrial business management assistant	Industriekaufmann / -frau
a wholesale and export clerk / management assistant in wholesale and foreign trade	Kaufmann / -frau im Groß- und Außenhandel

an office administration clerk/office management assistant	Kaufmann/-frau für Bürokommunikation
a freight forwarding and logistics services clerk/management assistant in freight forwarding and logistics	Kaufmann/-frau für Spedition und Logistikdienstleistung
a bank clerk/bank business management assistant	Bankkaufmann/-frau
a retail clerk/management assistant in retail business	Kaufmann/-frau im Einzelhandel
a management assistant for tourism and leisure	Kaufmann/-frau für Tourismus und Freizeit
a publisher's assistant	Verlags-/Medienkaufmann/-frau
an insurance clerk/insurance business management assistant	Kaufmann/-frau für Versicherungen und Finanzen
a management assistant in advertising	Kaufmann/-frau für Marketing-kommunikation
a management assistant in event organisation	Veranstaltungskaufmann/-frau
an automobile sales management assistant	Automobilkaufmann/-frau
I'm taking part in an ITC programme.	Ich nehme an einem ITC-Ausbildungsprogramm teil.
I'm in the catering **industry**.	Ich bin in der Cateringbranche.
I work **at** SITCOM Ltd.	Ich arbeite bei SITCOM Ltd.
I **attend** vocational school.	Ich besuche die Berufsschule.
What are you doing job-wise, Nina?	Nina, was machst du beruflich?
What are you training to be, Timo?	Was machst du für eine Ausbildung, Timo?
What do you like **about** your job?	Was gefällt dir an deiner Arbeit?
What industry are you in?	In welcher Branche arbeitest du?

To say what you like or dislike about your training or your work

I like my job because I get on well with the people I work with.	Ich mag meine Arbeit, weil ich mich mit meinen Kollegen gut verstehe.
I can work **on** my own.	Ich kann selbstständig arbeiten.
There are good prospects **of** promotion.	Die Aufstiegschancen sind gut.
I have to key in data all day long.	Den ganzen Tag muss ich Daten eingeben.
I have to work a lot of overtime.	Ich muss viele Überstunden machen.

A

B

C

D

Unit 2
Taking care of visitors

WORD BANK

visitor • visit • refreshments • to greet • to receive • to welcome • to meet • flight • hotel • weather • hobbies • sports • to entertain • to chat • directions • floor plan • map • layout • premises • to go • to turn • to follow • restaurant • menu • meal • dish • to invite • to choose

Greeting visitors to your company and making them feel welcome may be an important part of your job. You should always be friendly and helpful as first impressions are often very important. You may have to entertain them until the person they want to see appears. The language in which both you and they can communicate will often be English, even when the visitors do not come from an English-speaking country. English is rapidly becoming a lingua franca in Europe.

1 Match the phrases with the photos above.

1 Welcome to Schneider GmbH. Did you have any trouble finding us?

2 Have you met Ms Reuter? She is our marketing manager.

3 Go along the corridor. The conference room is the second door on the right.

4 Did you have a pleasant flight?

Online-Link
808260-0002

2 M **Translate the following statements from the introductory text into German.**

1. Greeting visitors may be an important part of your job.
2. First impressions are often very important.
3. You may have to entertain visitors until the person they want to see appears.
4. The language in which both you and they can communicate will often be English.

A Greeting visitors

Marcel Krenz, an export clerk at International Snacks GmbH, a German food processing company, has been asked by his boss, Markus Diepholz, to receive Kirsty Burnham and Kevin Sears who represent a major British catering chain. They are interested in the wide range of snacks and lunch boxes the company produces.

1 R A1.3 **Read the above text, listen to the dialogue and answer the following questions.**

1. Who is Marcel Krenz?
2. What are his visitors from Britain interested in?
3. What refreshments do Kirsty Burnham and Kevin Sears prefer?
4. What is Kevin's position?
5. What is Frau Wieland in charge of?
6. Where have Kirsty Burnham and Frau Wieland met before?
7. Why has Marcel Krenz been asked to receive the visitors?

2 **Match the expressions on the left with those on the right.**

1. a food processing company	a. a large assortment of snacks
2. a major chain	b. she is responsible for sales to the EU
3. a wide range of snacks	c. a few minutes
4. I'll let him know you're here	d. we already know each other
5. a couple of minutes	e. water with gas bubbles
6. a sparkling mineral water	f. a company using raw materials to make food products
7. she's on the export staff	g. an important company with many branches
8. she's in charge of sales to the EU	h. I would like to introduce you to Frau Wieland
9. I'd like you to meet Frau Wieland	i. she is a member of the export sales personnel
10. we've already met	j. I will inform him that you have arrived

B Making conversation

Marcel and the visitors from Britain chat while waiting for Herr Diepholz.

1 R A1.4 **Listen to the CD and complete the following dialogue on a separate sheet of paper.**

Marcel: Did you have a pleasant flight?
Kirsty: Oh yes, the flight was very straightforward – **1**. There was a bit of turbulence, though. I'm afraid I don't like that.
Marcel: **2** does the flight from Manchester take?
Kevin: It only takes about one and a half hours. But we **3** as a result of the time difference.
Marcel: Of course. What was **4** in Manchester? Was it as good as it is here?
Kirsty: Surprisingly, yes. We have been having **5** lately. It's almost like summer. But generally Manchester gets a lot of rain. From the Atlantic – it's on the west side, you know.
Marcel: Yes, I've heard it gets a lot of rain. **6** is Manchester United doing?
Kitsty: No idea, I'm afraid. I'm **7** a football person. Kevin is, aren't you? Ask him.
Kevin: They're still among the top teams and **8** in the Champions' League quarter finals.
Marcel: I know, they may be playing Bayern Munich next … ! I've heard that Manchester is a very vibrant place.
Kirsty: It certainly is. It's become a **9** city. Lots of gigs and clubs. All the old industry has gone and the old buildings have been renovated. You'd like it. You ought to come some time.
Marcel: I'd like to. Are there any **10**?
Kevin: Definitely. It's amazing how cheap they are if you book **11**. If you search the internet you can save a lot of money.
Marcel: Well, that's really … Ah, here comes Herr Diepholz …

2 **Complete the following conversations with the words from the boxes.**

Dialogue 1

afraid • doing • flight • like • proud • time

You: How was your **1**?
Visitor: Rather bumpy, I'm **2**.
You: I'm sorry to hear that. What was the weather **3** in Glasgow?
Visitor: Oh, it was the same as here, overcast and windy. But that's nothing unusual for this **4** of the year.
You: How are Glasgow Rangers **5**?
Visitor: They play in the UEFA Cup, we're rather **6** of them. I support Celtic, though.

Dialogue 2

apart • by • for • from • how • there

You: Where do you come **1**, Miss Spears?
Visitor: I'm from South Africa. Just now I've come from Berlin **2** train.
You: **3** was the train ride? Was the train punctual?
Visitor: Actually, the train was 10 minutes late, **4** from that the ride was quite pleasant, though.
You: South Africa must be a wonderful country. At least that's what everybody here says who's been **5**.
Visitor: You should come and see **6** yourself. There's a lot to see and do for tourists.

3 Match the questions with the answers.

1. Can I offer you a cold drink?
2. Is this your first visit to Germany?
3. Did you have a good flight?
4. Would you like something to read?
5. What was the weather like in Portugal?
6. May I take your coat?
7. Do you take milk and sugar?
8. Are you interested in tennis?

a. No, thank you. I'll keep it on. I'm cold.
b. No, thanks. I'm on a diet.
c. Yes, please. Perhaps your company brochure?
d. Very sunny. We could do with some rain.
e. No, it's not my thing. I prefer cycling.
f. Yes, it is.
g. Oh no. There was a lot of turbulence.
h. Thank you. An apple juice would be fine.

4 Restore the correct order of this jumbled dialogue.

1. Barmaid (in pub): Yes, it's freezing, isn't it? And this awful drizzle.
2. Customer: It's not like June at all.
3. Barmaid: They say its going to improve for the weekend, though.
4. Customer: Isn't the weather dreadful!

Communicating across cultures: Small Talk

In Britain the weather is very changeable, which makes it a constant topic of conversation:

The weather is wonderful, superb, lovely, very good. The weather is awful, ghastly, dreadful, terrible.

Example:
Newsagent: Good morning. How are you today?
Customer: Fine. Isn't it a beautiful day?
Newsagent: Wonderful. Let's hope it stays like this.
Customer: I'm afraid the weather forecast says rain.

5 Role play: Work in pairs. Make up dialogues using the following prompts and the phrases at the end of the Unit.

Phrases

Student A:
How was your trip?

Student B:
Rather tedious, there was a tailback on the motorway from Frankfurt.

Student A asks about:		Student B replies using these expressions:
flight/trip/journey	→	pleasant, rather tedious, lots of turbulence, tailback on the motorway, long delay at the airport, etc.
weather	→	sunny, overcast, slight drizzle, fog, gale-force winds, snow, is going to improve, cold for the time of the year, quite warm, pouring rain, windy, etc.
first visit to …	→	oh yes, many times, once before, but not much time to see anything, no never, long been wanting to visit …, etc.
hotel	→	nice and quiet, service first-class, a bit far from the exhibition centre, rather noisy, excellent restaurant, etc.
visitor's home town	→	small place in Wisconsin, has changed a lot in recent years, many tourists visit it, has vibrant business centre, scenic village in the mountains, busy port in India, etc.
sports events	→	not very interested in golf, watch as many tournaments as possible, would like to see the match, support XYZ club, etc.

C Giving directions

Kirsty Burnham has lost her way in the office building. She is standing at the reception desk. The receptionist directs her to Herr Diepholz' – the managing director's – office.

1 **Take the role of the receptionist. Use the floor plan, the phrases below and the phrases at the end of the unit.**

Phrases

Herr Diepholz' office is on the right / left hand side.

The ladies' room / restroom is on your left / right.

Go down the stairs.

Go up the stairs.

Take the lift to the first / second floor.

Go down to the ground floor.

Go along the corridor.

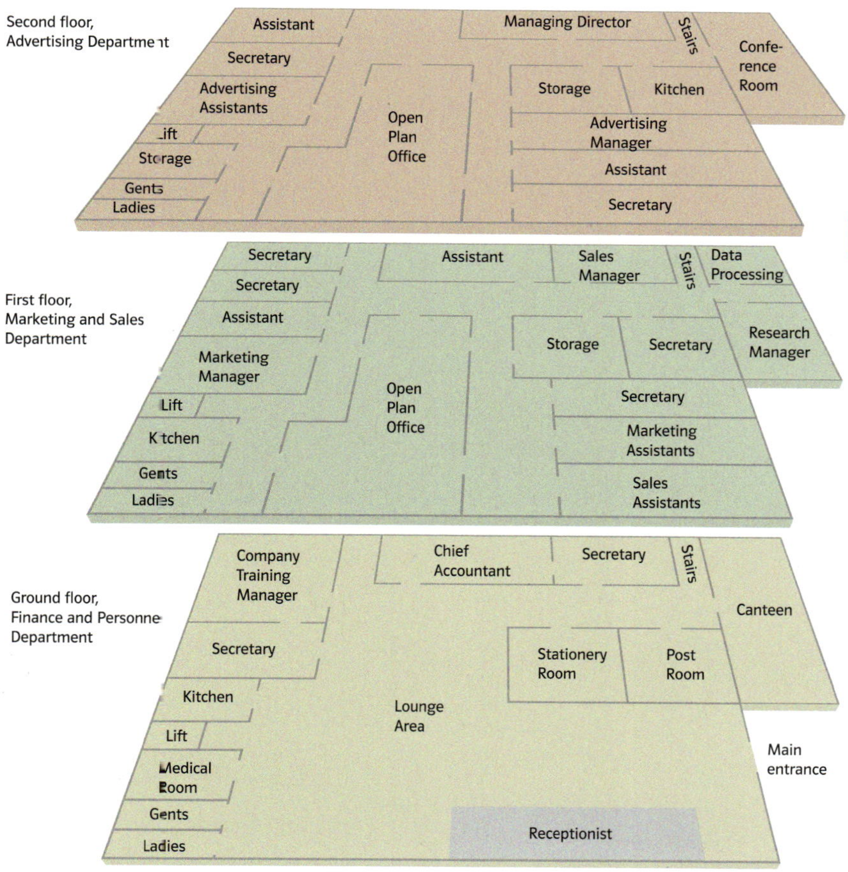

If you turn left / right you will see Mr / Ms … office on your right / left.

Take the first entrance to the right / left.

Go across the hall.

2 Work in pairs. Explain to each other the way to certain rooms.

I

1. Your partner is at the main entrance. He asks you: "Could you tell me the way to the Sales Manager's office?"
2. You are in the canteen. You ask your partner:" Where is the conference room, please?"
3. Your partner is leaving the Advertising Manager's office. He asks you: "Would you mind telling me where the medical room is?"
4. You are in the Marketing Assistants' room. You ask your partner: "I need to freshen up a bit. Could you tell me the way to the ladies'/the men's toilets/restroom (Am)?"

3 The visitors from England want to see some of the famous sights in Munich. Use the map on page 23 and direct them from the station (Hauptbahnhof) to the following destinations: Hofbräuhaus [1], Frauenkirche [2], Englischer Garten [3].

P

Phrases

Go along XYZ Street as far as the sharp bend

Follow the main road up the hill

Take the second street to the right

Go down this street till you come to the church

At the T-junction turn left

Opposite the park turn left

Turn right at the second junction

When you come to the roundabout, take the third exit

After 200 metres you will see the town hall on your left

No. 24 is the building to the right of the supermarket

4 R A1.5 **Listen to the explanations given by the Tourist Information assistant and find out which famous sights the visitors will be seeing during their stroll through the town centre of Munich.**

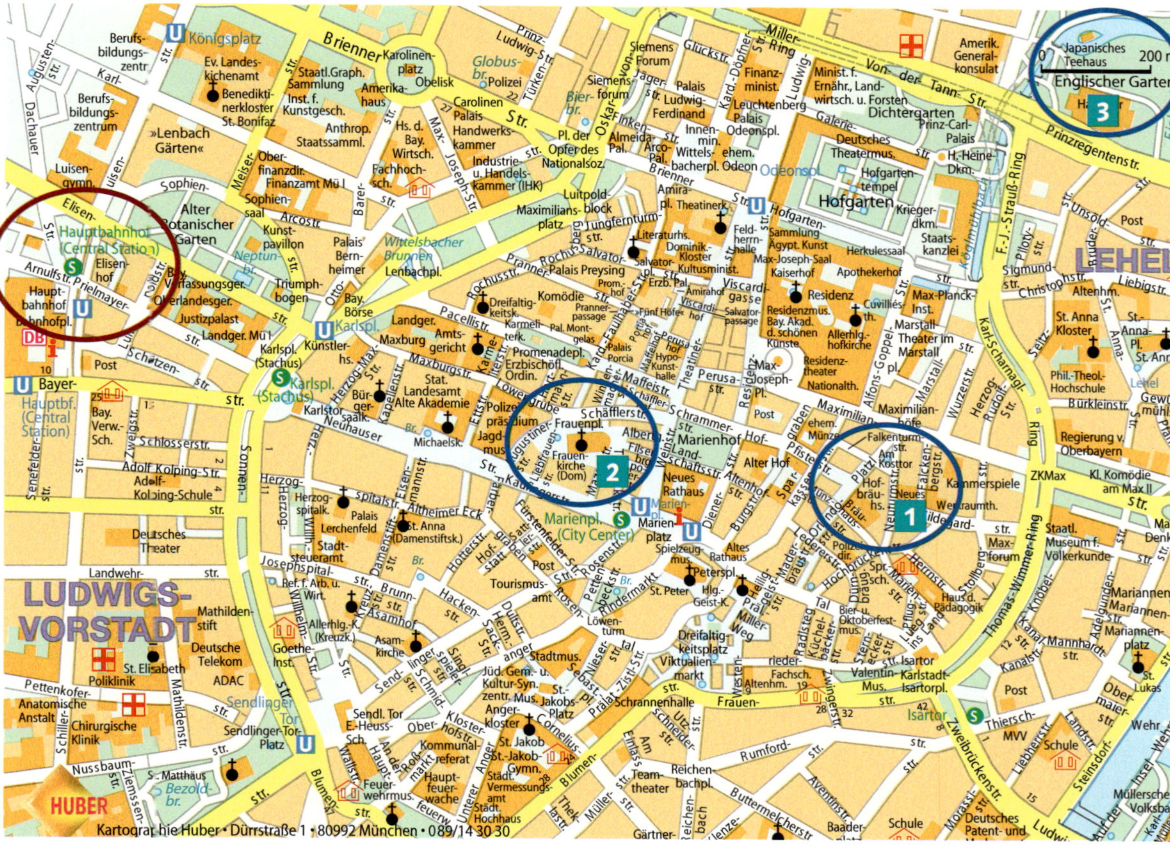

1

2

3

5 David Stedman has been visiting your headquarters in Berlin. He now has an appointment at your offices in Inselstraße, Düsseldorf. He has been told that the office is within walking distance of the main station. As he has some time on his hands before his appointment he would like to have instructions how to get there on foot.

Click on to a map of Düsseldorf on the internet and e-mail the instructions to him (davidstedman@aol.com).

D Describing the layout of the premises and carrying out a tour of the firm for visitors

Markus Diepholz and Marcel Krenz take Kirsty Burnham and Kevin Sears on a tour of the company's premises.

1 R A1.6 **Listen to the dialogue and decide whether the following statements are TRUE or FALSE.**

1. All the administrative work is dealt with at the offices.
2. The senior staff also work in the open-plan offices.
3. Marcel Krenz' office has a nice view of the surrounding countryside.
4. The canteen also provides vegetarian snacks.
5. Herr Diepholz and his visitors cross the car park to reach the kitchen facilities.
6. Freshness and hygiene are the most important considerations.
7. International Snacks are planning to do some market research on what people feel about their packaging.

2 P **You are Kevin Sears. Write a memo in English on the tour of the premises of International Snacks.**
Remember: A memo has to be brief, clear and to the point.

+ + MEMO + + MEMO + + MEMO + + MEMO + + MEMO + +

To:	Michael Kent, General Manager
From:	Kevin Sears, Assistant to Kirsty Burnham
Date:	Wednesday, 23 March 200_
Subject:	Our tour of the Premises of International Snacks, Düsseldorf

3 KMK **Sie sind Marcel Krenz. Verfassen Sie eine kurze Aktennotiz in Deutsch über die Betriebsbesichtigung und die Reaktionen der britischen Besucher.**

MEMO

Für:	Geschäftsleitung
Von:	Marcel Krenz, Exportsachbearbeiter
Datum:	20.03.201_
Betreff:	Betriebsbesichtigung mit Kirsty Burnham und Kevin Sears von Global Catering, Manchester, UK

E Taking foreign visitors to a restaurant

Herr Diepholz invites Kirsty and Kevin to lunch and asks Marcel to join them and interpret.

1 R A1.7 **Listen to the dialogue and write down what Kirsty and Kevin order (starter, main course, dessert, drinks).**

Speisekarte

Vorspeisen

Pikante Brokkoli-Pastetchen
Gefüllte Steinpilze
Kraftbrühe mit Ei
Lauchcremesuppe
Avocado-Kaltschale

Hauptgerichte

Schweinebraten mit Rotkohl und Salzkartoffeln
Rinderrouladen mit Blumenkohl und Kartoffelpüree
Rheinischer Sauerbraten mit Rotkohl und Kartoffelklößen
Wiener Schnitzel mit Pommes frites und Salat
Wildgulasch mit Speckknödeln und Preiselbeeren
Forelle Müllerin-Art
Lauch-Soufflé
Gemüsebratlinge

Nachspeisen

Gemischtes Eis
Rote Grütze mit Sahne
Bayerische Creme
Käseplatte

2 Find the correct equivalents.

1. Bockwurst	a. beef broth
2. Bratkartoffeln	b. chocolate pudding
3. Bratwurst	c. cucumber salad
4. Erbsensuppe	d. French fries
5. Frikadellen	e. fried potatoes
6. Gurkensalat	f. grilled sausage
7. Kartoffelbrei	g. mashed potatoes
8. Kartoffelsuppe	h. meatballs
9. Pommes frites	i. pea soup
10. Rinderbraten	j. potato soup
11. Rindfleischbrühe	k. roast beef
12. Schokoladenpudding	l. roast pork
13. Schweinebraten	m. large frankfurter

Communicating across cultures: Describing dishes

For a number of typical German dishes there are no direct translations. You will have to describe them to your visitors from abroad. These expressions may help you:

Which part of the meal is it?
It's a starter.
It's the main course.
It's a dessert.
What kind of food is it?
It's meat (pork, beef, veal, lamb).
It's poultry (chicken, turkey).
It's fish (salmon, trout, plaice, haddock).
It's game (venison, rabbit).
It's a sort of pasta (spaghetti, noodles).
It's a vegetable (peas, beans, carrots, green peppers, cauliflower, cabbage, Brussels sprouts, asparagus).

How is it made?
It's made of mashed potatoes, ground / minced meat, chopped onions.
It's filled / stuffed with (rice, minced meat, vegetables).
It's boiled (baked, stewed, grilled, fried, smoked).
What does it taste like?
It's hot / spicy.
It's sweet / sour.
It's tart.
It's savoury.
It tastes a bit like (yoghurt, veal, mousse au chocolat).

3 R **Study the explanations below and find out which of the German dishes they refer to.**

Jägerschnitzel • Kopfsalat • Rote Grütze • Semmelknödel • Spätzle

1. It's a dessert. It's a jelly made of red berries thickened with corn starch. It's not too sweet. Quite tart, in fact.
2. They go with a main course. They're dumplings made of white bread with eggs and parsley. They're rather filling, though.
3. It's a schnitzel, a sort of pork escalope with sauce and mushrooms.
4. It's a kind of home-made pasta, typical of the South West of Germany.
5. It's lettuce with oil and vinegar dressing.

4 M **Ask the amateur chefs among you to explain two of the following dishes in English to your group. Use the expressions at the end of the unit.**

Phrases

Wiener Schnitzel • Sauerkraut • gemischter Salat • gefüllte Paprikaschoten • Milchreis • Hackbraten • Linseneintopf

5 M **Choose a starter, a main course and a dessert from the menu on page 25 and explain it to a foreign visitor. Use the phrases at the end of the unit.**

Phrases

6 P **Work in groups. Explain your favourite dishes to the group.**

Communicating across cultures:
Going to restaurants in Britain

You may have to wait to be seated. A waiter will ask how many you are and indicate a table. Of course, you can say something like: "Couldn't we sit over there in the window?"

The waiter / waitress may ask you whether you want to order drinks straight away. After you have had time to study the menu, the waiter or waitress will say: "Are you ready to order, madam?" If you are not, you could say: "We're not quite ready. We need a moment or two."

When the food comes, he / she will probably say: "Enjoy your meal" or sometimes just "Enjoy!" However, there is nothing like "Guten Appetit" that you can say to your companions / guests.

Complaining is very difficult. You should at all costs avoid being aggressive or loud – this will not get you anywhere. Be nice, understanding, humorous if possible.

Finally, when you want to pay, you say: "Could I have the bill, please."

Language and grammar 1
Choose the correct form of the verbs.

1. I **give** you a ring towards the end of the week.
2. We **let** you **know** as soon as possible.
3. If you **wash** the dishes, I **dry**.
4. I **ask** Joanna if she **want** to come.
5. You **chop** the mushrooms and I **cook** the pasta.
6. I **pass** on the message when I **see** her on Friday.
7. I **pick** him up at the station if you **want**.
8. He **help** you with your move if you **give** him a ring on Wednesday.
9. I **give** you a lift if you like.
10. David **stand** in for you if necessary.

Language and grammar 2
Translate the following text.

Wir übergeben die Sendung morgen früh der Spedition Fuhrmann Logistik und hoffen, dass die Ware übermorgen wohlbehalten bei Ihnen ankommt. Wir helfen Ihnen gerne, wenn Sie noch weitere Fragen haben. Wir sind sicher, dass unsere exquisiten Schuhe Ihren Kunden gefallen und dass sich diese Artikel in Großbritannien gut verkaufen lassen.

Language and grammar: Will-future

Die "will"-Zukunftsform (meistens in der abgeschwächten Form I'll, we'll) wird im Englischen bei spontanen Entscheidungen benutzt und entspricht dem Präsens im Deutschen.	
Marcel Krenz says:	I'll give Herr Diepholz a ring and let him know you're here.
Kevin Sears says:	I'll have black coffee.
Marcel Krenz says:	I'll just ring through and order them.
Sit down and I'll make some coffee.	= Setz dich hin. Ich koche Kaffee.
You keep an eye on the spaghetti and I'll make the salad.	= Pass du auf die Spaghetti auf. Ich mache den Salat.
Allerdings wird "will" nicht in Nebensätzen der Bedingung und der Zeit verwendet.	
I'll fetch the newspapers if you make the tea.	= Ich hole die Zeitungen, wenn du Tee machst.
I'll tell him as soon as he arrives.	= Ich sage es ihm, sobald er ankommt.

Phrases: Taking care of visitors

To welcome visitors

Good afternoon. Can I help you?/What can I do for you?	Guten Tag. Was kann ich für Sie tun?
Please take **a seat**.	Bitte nehmen Sie Platz.
Can I offer you some refreshments?	Darf ich Ihnen etwas anbieten?
Coffee with milk and sugar, tea, herbal tea, fruit juice, sparkling/still mineral water, coke?	Kaffee mit Milch und Zucker, schwarzer Tee, Kräutertee, Fruchtsaft, Mineralwasser mit/ohne Kohlensäure, Cola?
Frau Sievers **is expecting** you.	Frau Sievers erwartet Sie.
I'm afraid, Frau Sievers is still in a meeting.	Frau Sievers ist leider noch in einer Besprechung.
She will be **with** you in a few minutes.	Sie wird in ein paar Minuten da sein.

To make conversation

Did you have a pleasant flight?	Hatten Sie einen angenehmen Flug?
How was the **journey**?	Wie war die Fahrt?
Have you ever been to Oldenburg before?	Waren Sie schon einmal in Oldenburg?
Where do you come **from**?	Wo kommen Sie her?
What was the weather **like** in Belfast?	Wie war das Wetter in Belfast?
Would you like to see something **of** Bonn?	Möchten Sie in Bonn etwas besichtigen?
Are you satisfied with your hotel?	Sind Sie mit dem Hotel zufrieden?
I'll have an orange juice.	Ich nehme einen Orangensaft.
No thanks, I don't take milk or sugar.	Nein danke, ich nehme weder Milch noch Zucker.
The flight was rather bumpy.	Der Flug war ziemlich unruhig.
The trip was very pleasant. Thank you.	Danke. Die Fahrt war sehr angenehm.
Actually, I have been to Oldenburg twice, in 1999 and in 2002.	Ich war tatsächlich schon zweimal in Oldenburg, 1999 und 2002.
The weather was fine. Not a cloud **in** the sky.	Das Wetter war schön. Kein Wölkchen am Himmel.
We've had a lot of rain lately.	In der letzten Zeit hat es bei uns viel geregnet.
I'd like to visit Beethoven's house.	Ich möchte mir gerne das Beethoven-Haus ansehen.

The hotel will do. It's **on** a rather noisy street, though.	Das Hotel geht einigermaßen. Es liegt allerdings an einer ziemlich lauten Straße.
The hotel is excellent. Very quiet.	Das Hotel ist ausgezeichnet. Sehr ruhig.

To give directions

GB	**USA**	**Germany**
second floor	third floor	2. Etage
first floor	second floor	1. Etage
ground floor	first floor	Erdgeschoss
basement	basement	Untergeschoss/Keller

Take the lift to the third floor.	Fahren Sie mit dem Aufzug in den dritten Stock.
Go up/down (the stairs) to the 2nd floor.	Gehen Sie (die Treppe) hinauf/hinunter zum 2. Stock.
Herr Diepholz' office is on the **right hand** side.	Das Büro von Herrn Diepholz ist auf der rechten Seite.
At the junction **turn** right/left.	Gehen/Fahren Sie an der Kreuzung nach rechts/links.
Go **straight ahead** to …	Gehen/Fahren Sie gerade aus bis …
Go down this street till you come to the …	Gehen/Fahren Sie auf dieser Straße weiter bis Sie zu … kommen.
When you come to the roundabout, take the 3rd exit.	Am Kreisverkehr nehmen Sie die dritte Ausfahrt.
Follow the main road up the hill.	Fahren Sie die Hauptstraße weiter bergauf.
After 200 yards you will see the church **to** your left.	Nach (ca.) 200 m sehen Sie die Kirche auf der linken Seite.

To take visitors on a tour of your firm's premises

We would like to show you **round** the company's premises.	Wir möchten Ihnen unsere Firma auf einem Rundgang zeigen.
We have two open-plan offices.	Wir haben zwei Großraumbüros.
These are our production facilities.	Hier sehen Sie unsere Fertigungsanlagen.
We'll go through this door which leads to the canteen.	Wir gehen durch diese Türe, die zur Kantine führt.

The canteen looks very modern and airy.	Die Kantine wirkt sehr modern und luftig.
We leave this building and **cross** the car park.	Wir verlassen jetzt dieses Gebäude und gehen über den Parkplatz.
I think we had better be getting back to our office now.	Ich glaube wir sollten jetzt lieber ins Büro zurückgehen.
Our visit has certainly been very interesting.	Unser Besuch war wirklich sehr interessant.

To take visitors to a restaurant

This is a typical German restaurant.	Das ist ein typisch deutsches Restaurant.
Let's have a look **at** the menu?	Wollen wir uns die Speisekarte ansehen?
What **about** you? What are you having?	Wie ist es mit Ihnen/Dir? Was nehmen Sie/was nimmst Du?
Are you having a starter?	Nimmst Du/Nehmen Sie eine Vorspeise?
I think I'll just have a main course.	Ich nehme nur ein Hauptgericht.
Could I have a starter as a main course?	Kann ich eine Vorspeise als Hauptgericht nehmen?
It's a sort of pasta.	Es sind Teigwaren.
It's cabbage stuffed with minced meat.	Es ist Kohl mit einer Hackfleischfüllung.
It tastes a bit like mushrooms.	Es schmeckt ein bisschen wie Pilze.
I'm not hungry enough for a 3-course meal.	Ein Menü mit 3 Gängen ist mir zuviel.
I'd like a German beer.	Ich möchte ein deutsches Bier.
Would you like a salad as a starter?	Möchten Sie einen Salat als Vorspeise?
I'll have the lamb cutlets with beans.	Ich nehme die Lammkoteletts mit Bohnen.
I prefer chicken **to** fish.	Ich esse lieber Geflügel als Fisch.
I'm **a** vegetarian.	Ich bin Vegetarier/in.
My wife would like the trout with almonds.	Meine Frau möchte die Forelle mit Mandeln.
What about some ice cream as a dessert?	Wie wär's mit Eis als Nachtisch?
I'd **rather** have some cheese.	Ich hätte lieber etwas Käse.
It was delicious but I'm afraid I can't eat any more.	Es hat sehr gut geschmeckt, aber ich bin leider schon satt.
I'm going to do without a dessert.	Ich verzichte auf eine Nachspeise.

A

B

UNIT 3
The company and its products and services

WORD BANK

image • history • range of products • company brochure • global player • start-up business • family-owned firm • workforce • manufacturing • provision of services • business idea • stock corporation • public limited company • private limited company • to found • to establish • to manufacture • to provide • old-established • modern • traditional • leading • small • medium-sized • state-of-the-art

When companies describe themselves in their sales literature they generally attempt to create a particular image. They may refer to the firm's history to emphasise qualities such as experience and reliability. If they do not have a long history behind them, they may prefer to emphasise that they are a young, dynamic, forward-looking company, providing new products and services.

1 **List the adjectives and expressions from the box under the categories given below:**

old-established • flexible • dynamic • reliable • with many years' experience • young • forward-looking • taking advantage of the new media • solid • state-of-the-art

Example:

traditional	modern
old-established	state-of-the-art

Online-Link
808260-0003

2 **Find examples of traditional and young companies in Germany and other countries.**

3 **Choose the adjectives from the box on page 32 which best describe the company you are training at. Is it a traditional or a young company? Give details.**

A Introducing a firm and giving a brief history

While waiting for an interview at Herkules AG, Sandra Kohl studies the company brochure in English. It begins with an article on the history of the firm.

Herkules
the global sports brand

Back in 1922 the shoemaker Heinrich Schuster made the first sports shoes for the local sports club, the TSV Neustadt. Very soon sportsmen from neighbouring clubs ordered sports shoes from Mr. Schuster and two years later he employed a staff of 25. In 1927 he rented a factory building and bought the machinery required for industrial manufacturing. The company continued to prosper until World War II. In 1948 Heinrich Schuster's son Helmut took over and changed the company's name to Herkules. At the Olympic Games in Melbourne in 1956 several of the athletes competing wore Herkules shoes.

A few years later Helmut Schuster added footballs and other types of ball to Herkules's range of products and in the early 70s took up the production of sports bags. Meanwhile Herkules employed 3400 people and its products featured in all the Olympic Games and World Championships.

Olympic Games

By 2014 the workforce had risen to 12,500 and Herkules had become the market leader in the EU and a global player with production sites in Germany, Portugal, Morocco, Malaysia and Taiwan.

1 Read the text on page 33 and ask the questions which would produce the following answers.

R

Example:
Question:
1. Who founded the company?

Answers:
1. The company was founded by **Heinrich Schuster**.
2. Mass production began **in 1927**.
3. **Olympic Games and World Championships** are of particular importance for the company.
4. Apart from shoes the company produces **bags and balls**.
5. Herkules has got production sites in **Germany, Portugal, Morocco, Malaysia and Taiwan**.

2 Find the missing prepositions from the box with the help of the text on page 33.

R

by • from • in (2x) • of • over • until • up • to (2x) • with

Back 1 1922 Heinrich Schuster made the first sports shoes.
Sportsmen 2 neighbouring clubs ordered sports shoes.
Two years later he was employing a staff 3 25.
The company prospered 4 World War II.
In 1948 Schuster's son Helmut took 5 and changed the name 6 Herkules.
In the early 70s Herkules took 7 the production of bags.
Herkules' products featured 8 all the Olympic Games.
9 1990 the number of staff had risen 10 9,500.
Herkules is a global player 11 production sites in several countries.

3 Read the text on Herkules again and find words or phrases that mean the same as the following expressions.

R

1. people employed by a firm
2. production on a large scale
3. an assortment of articles
4. the company that has a dominant position in a given market
5. a company that is active worldwide

* 4 Sandra Kohl informiert eine Freundin über die Firma Herkules. Verfassen Sie hierfür eine schriftliche Zusammenfassung der wichtigsten Fakten in Deutsch, die ca. 80 Wörter umfasst. Gehen Sie dabei kurz auf folgende Punkte ein:

KMK

- Entwicklung des Unternehmens
- Produkte
- gegenwärtige Stellung des Unternehmens

5 R A1.8 **Read the introduction below, then listen to Martha Dinsdale describing her firm and complete the following text.**

Christian Kleine, an IT specialist, is interested in doing a short practical abroad. At a job fair he meets Martha Dinsdale, managing director of Smartmart Ltd, who describes the development of her firm.

"Our company, Smartmart Ltd., was **1** in 1999. Our business **2** was to provide an online market for private individuals or **3** companies with something to **4** who do not want to spend a lot of **5** online selling it themselves. This, as we all **6**, can be very time-consuming! It's not everybody's idea of an **7** way to spend an evening! Some people do not feel sufficiently secure with the **8** to do their own buying and selling. But, it is amazing how many **9** have things to sell and how many potential **10** there are. After we had completed a feasibility study, we **11** through the local chamber of commerce for financial and other **12** in establishing a start-up business. Our **13** expenditure was for designing and setting up an attractive and efficient **14** which would be capable of dealing with a large **15** of hits. There's no point in opening up **16** on the internet with an inadequate or badly designed website. We were quite overwhelmed by the amount of **17**. Our business has grown in line with the other big **18** marts. We charge a commission of 10% on sales completed, i.e. the **19** pays. We are now making a healthy **20** and in two or three years' time we will be thinking in terms of going public."

6 **Match the English expressions with their German equivalents.**

1. private individuals	a. 10% Provision verlangen
2. time-consuming	b. Auslagen, Ausgaben
3. sufficient	c. ausreichend, genügend
4. amazing	d. bei der örtlichen IHK beantragen
5. feasibility study	e. erstaunlich
6. apply through the local chamber of commerce	f. finanzielle Unterstützung
7. financial support	g. Machbarkeitsstudie
8. start-up business	h. neugegründetes Unternehmen
9. expenditure	i. Online-Markt
10. inadequate	j. Privatpersonen
11. overwhelmed	k. sich in eine Aktiengesellschaft umwandeln
12. online mart	l. überwältigt
13. charge a commission of 10%	m. unzureichend, unzulänglich
14. go public	n. zeitraubend

7 R **Answer the following questions on Martha's talk.**

1. When was the company founded?
2. What was their business idea?
3. Why did they think people would use their services?
4. What was their most expensive investment?
5. How does the company earn its living?

8 KMK **Christian Kleine fasst die Informationen, die ihm Martha Dinsdale über ihre Firma gegeben hat, auf Deutsch in einer Gesprächsnotiz für seine Personalabteilung zusammen. Bitte übernehmen Sie seine Rolle.**

Gesprächsnotiz

Empfänger: *Personalabteilung*

Verfasser: *Christian Kleine, IT-Support* Datum: ____________

Gesprächspartner: *Martha Dinsdale von Smartmart Ltd.*

Betreff: *Vorstellung von Smartmart Ltd.*

* **9** P **Describe your own company in writing. Model your description on the descriptions of other companies in this unit.**

Communicating across cultures:
Joint stock companies *(Kapitalgesellschaften)* in the USA and Britain

The British **Public Limited Company** (abbreviated to **PLC** or **plc** after the company name) and the American **Stock Corporation** (abbreviated to **Inc.** or **Corp.**) are roughly comparable to the German Aktiengesellschaft. The British **Private Limited Company** (abbreviated to **Ltd**) and the American **Closed Corporation** are approximately equivalent to the German GmbH. British and American joint stock companies are managed by a **Board of Directors** under the leadership of a Chief Executive Officer (CEO) (chairman of the board or managing director), who may also hold the title of Chairman or President. The head of a **Private Limited Company** is generally called the Managing Director.

10 **Search the Internet for some of the following global players. Make notes on their products or services in English. Compare your notes with the group.**

Tata Group • GlaxoSmithKline • Arcelormittal • Antofagasta • RWE Group • Berkshire Hathaway • Verizon • De Beers • China Mobile • Rio Tinto Zinc • HSBC • Selesio AG • Sir Robert McAlpine

B Describing products and services

At home Sandra Kohl looks at Herkules' homepage on the internet. Sandra clicks on the button "about us" to learn more about the company. The following website appears.

about us | back

Herkules
the global sports brand
www.herkules.com

Herkules is Europe's leading manufacturer of state-of-the-art sports shoes, balls and bags. Innovative technology and minute attention to detail provide products that successfully fuse the creative energies of the world of sport, lifestyle and fashion.

Herkules concentrates its efforts on the three big fields of football, athletics and tennis. For decades our superb shoes, balls and bags have helped world-class athletes to win gold medals at Olympic Games and prestigious cups at World Championships and Tournaments.

www.herkules.com

about us | login | join | shopping cart | track your order | delivery | contact | customer service | FAQ | imprint | disclaimer

Herkules
ALL PRODUCTS
FOOTBALL
BAGS
TENNIS
RUNNING

NEW! Wimbledon II — NEW! Sports Mate — NEW! Turbostar — NEW! Air Lift 2000

We accept Visa, Mastercard and Switch / Delivery is free for orders worth € 250 or more.

For further information click here

1 Which buttons do you click on if you want to find out more about the following?

1. the firm
2. all their products
3. particular product groups
4. individual products
5. details about delivery
6. frequently asked questions
7. how to place an order
8. repairs

2 Replace the adjectives in brackets with appropriate expressions from the box.

excellent • the most modern • very careful • highly regarded

1. Herkules is Europe's leading manufacturer of (state-of-the-art) **1** sports shoes.
2. Innovative technology and (minute) **2** attention to detail provide products that fuse the creative energies of the world of sport, lifestyle and fashion.
3. For decades our (superb) **3** shoes and bags have helped world-class athletes to win gold medals at Olympic Games and (prestigious) **4** Cups at World Championships and Tournaments.

3 R/M **Match the German statements on the next page with the following English statements.**

Janine: I work for a small upmarket advertising agency. We specialise in media companies.

Patrizia: I work for a medium-sized company manufacturing organic cosmetic preparations.

Tatjana: The company I work for is a leading manufacturer of precision instruments.

Sinan: I work for a small family firm making a wide range of high quality furniture.

Markus: My company are IT consultants providing customised solutions for corporate clients.

Holger: I work for a small catering company specialising in providing lunches for local companies. We offer a lot of vegetarian dishes. We're basically a small start-up.

Jörg: My company is a whole-saler stocking a wide range of electrical products.

Claudia: The company I work for is a major retailer of food and some non-food products. I work in the admin section.

V1 Video Lounge Sport and leisure

BBC Motion Gallery

You are about to see a video on the sport and leisure industry. While watching the video, keep the following questions in mind:

1. How are the three presenters dressed? Which do you find most natural and convincing? Why?
2. Which different fitness club products does the video mention?
3. What does the first presenter mean when she says fitness has become a lifestyle business?
4. According to the video what is the overall economic situation of the fitness and leisure club industry?

Discuss your answers with the class.

1. Ich arbeite für ein mittelständisches Unternehmen, das Biokosmetik herstellt.
2. Meine Firma ist eine IT-Beratungsgesellschaft und bietet Firmenkunden maßgeschneiderte Lösungen an.
3. Die Firma, bei der ich arbeite, ist ein bedeutender Einzelhändler für Lebensmittel und Non-Food-Produkte.
4. Ich arbeite bei einem kleinen Partyservice, der sich auf Mittagessen für die Firmen in der Umgebung spezialisiert hat.
5. Meine Firma ist ein führender Hersteller von Präzisionsinstrumenten.
6. Ich arbeite bei einem Familienunternehmen, das hochwertige Möbel herstellt.
7. Ich arbeite bei einer kleinen exklusiven Werbeagentur.
8. Bei meiner Firma handelt es sich um eine Großhandlung mit einem breiten Sortiment von Elektroartikeln.

4 P **Write similar descriptions of two firms' products or services with the help of the following hints.**

Types of firms	medium-sized enterprise, import/export company, large manufacturer, start-up company, wholesaler, retail chain, family-owned firm, IT consultancy, publishing house, advertising agency, catering firm, Public Limited Company, Private Limited Company, Stock Corporation
Products / services	household appliances, IT services, exotic fruit, steel tubes, creation of advertising material, groceries, silk fabrics, audio books, clocks and watches, cleaning services, office software
Descriptions	modern, upmarket, high-quality, fresh, in demand, excellent, unique, interesting, attractive, reliable, thorough, long-lasting, state-of-the-art, customised, inexpensive

We specialise in …

Our products / services are …

We are …

We offer …

I work for …

Example:
I work for a family-owned firm specializing in the manufacture of state-of-the-art steel tubes.

5 P **Work in groups. Describe the firm you are training at and its products and / or services to your group. Use the phrases at the end of the unit.**

Phrases

6 Dolmetschen Sie folgende Aussagen:
M

1. „Ich arbeite bei einer mittelgroßen Werbeagentur. Wir stellen attraktives Werbematerial für eine Lebensmittel-Einzelhandelskette her."

2. „Meine Firma ist auf die Herstellung einzigartiger Seidenstoffe höchster Qualität spezialisiert."

3. „Wir bieten maßgeschneiderte Lösungen für Bürosoftware an."

4. „Wir sind ein junger Musikverlag mit einem anspruchsvollen Sortiment von Titeln."

* 7 Project work: Work together with two other students to set up your own company. See Exercise 5 for useful expressions.
I/P

Phrases

Step 1: Discuss the following questions:
- What is your business idea?
- How can you find out whether your idea is any good?
- Where can you get help, financial or otherwise?
- What are the most essential investments to enable you to begin trading?

Step 2: Think up a good name for your company.

Step 3: Divide the work among yourselves:
- Student A creates an eye-catching logo.
- Student B designs a business card incorporating the logo.
- Student C designs a company letterhead also incorporating the logo.

Step 4: Present the result to the class.

Language and grammar 1

Find out whether the periods of time mentioned in the following sentences are entirely in the past or whether they continue to the present. Then choose the correct tense for the verbs in brackets.

1. It all (begin) in 1975.
2. Two years later he (launch) the new product.
3. The company (be successful) for many years now.
4. Since 2002 we (offer) these unique marketing services.
5. By now Herkules (become) a global player.
6. Last September Robert Hanks (start) a new business in the USA.
7. In the past there (be) a big demand for such systems.
8. But in the meantime they (be replaced) by faster systems.
9. So far we (have) no complaints.
10. I (speak) to him only yesterday.

Language and grammar: Simple Past and Present Perfect

Wird ein Zeitraum genannt, der vollständig in der Vergangenheit liegt, steht "simple past".

Back **in 1922** Heinrich Schuster **made** the first sports shoes.
At the Olympic Games several athletes **competed** wearing Herkules shoes.
A few years later he **added** footballs to the range of products.
Our company **was founded in 1999**.

Wenn ein Zeitraum genannt wird, der bis in die Gegenwart reicht, steht "present perfect".

For decades our superb shoes **have helped** athletes to win gold medals.
In the meantime ACE **has become** the market leader in Germany.
Since the beginning of the 90s **we have specialised** in real-time solutions.
I **have been** in my present department **for three months**.

Language and grammar 2
Decide which of the alternatives in brackets are correct.

1. I (am/have been) a trainee (for/since) 4 months.
2. We (see/have seen) a number of employees leave (for/since) 1998.
3. We (have specialised/specialise) in providing networking systems (for/since) more than a year.
4. She (wants/has wanted) to live in Berlin (since/for) she was 17 years old.
5. We (have known/know) the company (since/for) it was founded in 1983.
6. I (am thinking/have been thinking) of changing my job (since/for) a long time.
7. We (place/have placed) orders with this company (since/for) its foundation.

Language and grammar: "since" and "for"

"since" bezieht sich auf den Anfang des Zeitraums
since Christmas
since 24 June
since my last report

"for" bezieht sich auf den Zeitraum selbst
for 3 weeks
for several days
for a couple of years

Merke: **Im Deutschen wird „seit" mit der Gegenwart verwendet, "since" und "for" stehen im Englischen mit "present perfect".**

Ich **bin seit** drei Jahren bei Topline-Computers beschäftigt.
Seit Januar **bin** ich der Abteilungsleiter.

I **have been** employed with Topline-Computers **for three years** now.
Since January I have been head of the department.

Phrases: The company and its products and services

To introduce your firm

Our company was founded in 1972.	Unsere Firma wurde 1972 gegründet.
Our business idea was …	Unsere Geschäftsidee bestand darin …
In 1998 we were taken over by …	1998 wurden wir von … übernommen.
We are a leading manufacturer **of** …	Wir sind ein führender Hersteller von …
I work for an upmarket advertising agency.	Ich arbeite bei einer exklusiven Werbeagentur.
We are a **medium-sized** family firm.	Wir sind ein mittelständisches Familienunternehmen.
We are a wholesaler **specializing in** …	Wir sind ein Großhandelsunternehmen und sind spezialisiert auf …
My company is a major food retailer.	Meine Firma ist ein bedeutender Lebensmitteleinzelhändler.
We are a start-up company offering customized solutions.	Wir sind ein junges Unternehmen, das maßgeschneiderte Lösungen anbietet.
We are a chain of organic cosmetics suppliers.	Wir sind eine Kette von Anbietern biologischer Kosmetikprodukte.
The legal form of our company is a public limited company.	Juristisch gesehen ist unsere Firma eine (britische) Kapitalgesellschaft, vergleichbar einer deutschen Aktiengesellschaft.
FastTrack Inc. is a stock corporation.	FastTrack Inc. ist eine (US-)Kapitalgesellschaft.

To describe your firm's products / services

We manufacture state-of-the-art solutions.	Wir bieten Lösungen nach dem neuesten Stand der Technik an.
Our high-quality products are well-known **all over** the world. They are unique.	Unsere erstklassigen Produkte sind weltbekannt. Sie sind einzigartig.
Our instruments are both reliable and long-lasting.	Unsere Instrumente sind zuverlässig und haben eine lange Lebensdauer.
The software we offer is carefully adapted to suit your requirements.	Unsere Software wird Ihren Bedürfnissen sorgfältig angepasst.
We make a wide range of high-quality furniture.	Wir stellen ein breites Sortiment hochwertiger Möbel her.
We import exotic fruit **from** South America.	Wir importieren tropische Früchte aus Südamerika.
The travel agency I work for **specialises in** upmarket package tours.	Das Reisebüro, bei dem ich arbeite, ist auf exklusive Pauschalreisen spezialisiert.

Unit 4
The office

WORD BANK

front office • back office • open-plan office • office supplies • furniture • electronic equipment • internet access • catering equipment • organization chart • department • business unit • head • assistant • superior • colleague • to be in charge of • to be responsible for • to report to

Offices may be spacious open-plan, purpose-built areas in a major company, individual small rooms to accommodate two to three people, or elegant premises at a prestigious address in a converted building. They may be back offices where employees have no contact with the public, or front offices to which the public have access.

1 **Match the following types of office with the pictures above.**

1. front office
2. back office
3. manager's office
4. open plan

2 **Tell your group in which type of office you would prefer to work and give reasons for your preferences.**

I'd like to work in a(n) … office because …

I'd prefer to work in a(n) … office because …

Online-Link
808260-0004

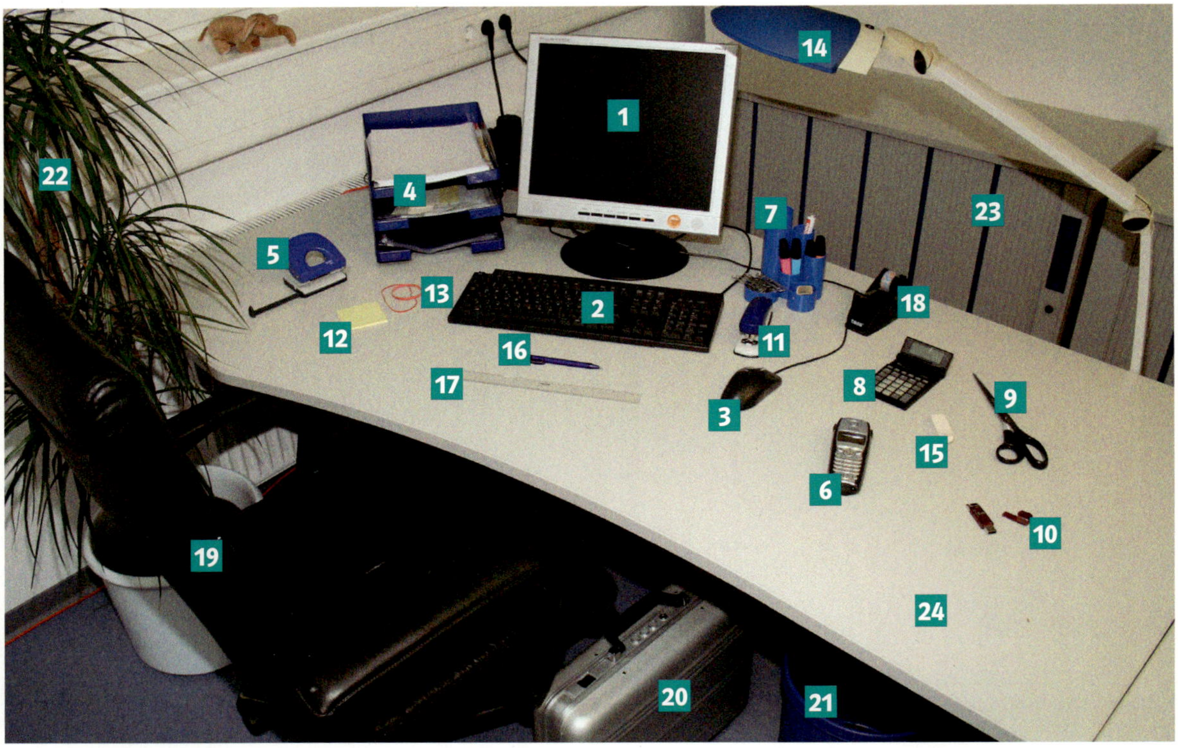

A The office environment

1 Match the following pieces of office equipment with the numbered items above.

a. calculator	j. memory stick	r. pot plant
b. scotch tape/sellotape	k. monitor	s. desk lamp
c. biro	l. desk tidy	t. mobile phone
d. desk	m. pair of scissors	u. stapling machine/stapler
e. note pad	n. wastepaper bin	v. swivel chair
f. trays	o. ruler	w. mouse
g. filing cabinet	p. punch	x. elastic band
h. aluminium briefcase	q. rubber/eraser	
i. keyboard		

2 Use the following prepositions and describe the position of the equipment you see in the picture.

The keyboard is The …	on • under • behind • between • in front of • next to • on the right of • opposite • near • on top of	the desk. the …

3 List the items shown on page 44 under the following categories:

Office supplies / Stationery	Furniture	Electrical equipment / Hardware
rubber	desk	computer

4 How many computer terms and abbreviations can you find in the puzzle below? Make a list. Compare your lists in class.

Computer terms puzzle

	A	B	C	D	E	F	G	H	I	J
1	I	B	M	O	D	E	M	Q	R	H
2	T	O	E	S	L	A	N	P	X	A
3	D	C	M	T	C	D	R	O	M	R
4	E	T	O	O	L	B	A	R	O	D
5	S	E	R	O	W	S	E	T	N	D
6	K	E	Y	B	O	A	R	D	I	I
7	T	E	R	M	I	N	A	L	T	S
8	O	S	C	A	N	N	E	R	O	K
9	P	C	C	C	U	R	S	O	R	M
10	D	O	W	N	L	O	A	D	X	B

5 P/I Work in groups. Make up similar puzzles with other computer terms and abbreviations. Ask the other groups to find the terms and abbreviations.

6 Listen to Anita, Ali and Nadine describing the office environment in which they work and take notes. Work in pairs and compare your notes.
R
A1.9

7 Draw a grid like the following. Use your notes and fill in the grid. Then listen to the dialogue again, complete the grid and answer the questions below.
R
A1.9

	Office (front office – open plan or back office?)	**Office equipment** (PC? Photocopier? Scanner? …?)
Anita	…	…
Ali	…	…
Nadine	…	…

1. What does Anita like about her office?
2. What does Ali like about his office?
3. What does Nadine like about her office?

8 Translate the following statements from the dialogue into German.
M

1. I work in a large open-plan office with about 20 other people. It is spacious and airy with large windows. Fortunately, there is air-conditioning.
2. Our offices are situated in an old villa in the centre of Hanover. The office I work in is a front office.
3. The view from the windows is not very exciting – the office looks out on to the car park.
4. Our office has a wide range of equipment. We all have PCs with internet access.
5. I like the privacy of a small office – you don't get the feeling there's somebody looking over your shoulder the whole time. We all get on very well together.

9 Describe your own office.
P

10 Check out the latest products of three manufacturers of photocopiers and scanners, including any innovative features. Make notes and compare your findings with the group.

B Catering in the office

* **1** Übertragen Sie die Aussagen von Anita, Nadine und Ali ins Deutsche.

KMK

Anita We have a small kitchen attached to the office with a fridge and tea and coffee making facilities. Our official coffee break is a quarter of an hour at 10.30 am and 3 pm.
At lunchtime we go to the canteen. There is quite a good range of hot and cold snacks, some of them vegetarian. My friend Alexandra is a vegetarian so we usually have a fresh vegetable soup and a salad with fruit as a dessert. We both watch our figures and the canteen is very good about giving calorie counts.

Nadine We have a tea and coffee machine in the office and a kitchen at the end of the corridor with a microwave. We don't have a set coffee break but lunch is from 12.30 to 1.15 pm.
Our company is too small to have a canteen so we either bring sandwiches or convenience food that we can warm up in the microwave. There is an upmarket supermarket nearby with an interesting range of good quality convenience food with things like fresh soups and Chinese and Thai dishes. We sometimes go out to a pub but the lunch break is really too short for that.

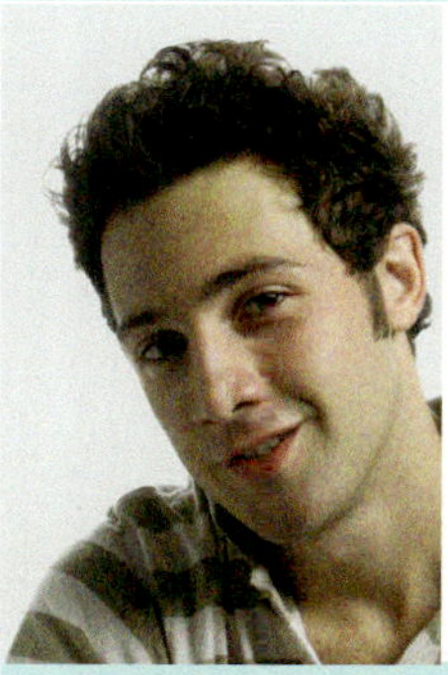

Ali We have a small kitchen with a coffee machine and fridge. Only Amelie is allowed to touch it. We have an hour lunch break.
We don't have a canteen either. So we usually bring sandwiches or go out. There's a snack bar nearby that has quite an interesting range of snacks and a pub with not very appetising meatballs and filled rolls. Quite often, when we're working to a deadline, we just eat a sandwich at our desks and an apple.

2 Match the words on the left with the explanations on the right.

1. calorie count
2. coffee making facilities
3. convenience food
4. snack bar
5. upmarket supermarket

a. equipment for making coffee
b. pre-prepared food
c. small restaurant/shop producing light/quick food
d. high-quality supermarket
e. energy content

3 What are the catering arrangements like at your firm? Work in pairs to produce a brief description in writing that you can read out to the other students.
P

Phrases

C The company's organization chart

1 Study the organization chart below and complete the following text.
R

Nadine works for a car sales company. The [1] is Jochen Küppers who is one of the two owners of the firm. His personal assistant is his elderly [2] Eva Cebulla. Nadine's superior, Jessica Rathsmann, a trained accountant, is the head of the [3] Department, and a motor-car mechanic, Markus Nehring, is in charge of [4]. The [5] manager is Natalie Hoffmann, the managing director's sister-in-law. Eddy Gerstenberg, an engineer, is the head of the [6] Department. André Fontaine, who is training to become a car sales management assistant, reports to him.

The car sales company is organized like this:

Managing Director
Jochen Küppers

Secretary
Eva Cebulla

Administration and Finance	**Purchasing**	**Sales**	**Customer Service**
Jessica Rathsmann	Natalie Hoffmann	Eddy Gerstenberg	Markus Nehring
Nadine Boedeker		André Fontaine	

Info: Large companies

The larger a company is the more complex its organisation tends to be. Large companies are headed by a chief executive officer (CEO) or a chairman of the board. They have many different business units and departments, such as a personnel, legal or marketing department. The scope of an individual employee's responsibilities will also be smaller and his or her duties more specialised in a large company than in a small one.

2 Study the above texts and find the equivalents of the German titles.
R

Geschäftsführer • Einkaufsleiter • Vorstandsvorsitzender • Automobilkaufmann • Leiter des Kundendienstes • Personalchef • Leiter des Rechnungswesens • Persönliche Assistentin

3 I **Work in pairs. Partner A asks Partner B about his current department. Then change roles.**

Phrases

Which department are you in?

I work in the … department.

Partner A	Partner B
Who is your boss?	The head of our department is …
What is he/she responsible for?	She is in charge of …
Who does she report to?	Her superior is …
What's your general manager's name?	Our general manager is called …
Who are your colleagues?	My colleagues are …
What are you responsible for?	I process/I'm in charge of …

4 R A 1.10 **Listen to five trainees describing to their friends what they or their colleagues do in the departments they are in. Find out which departments they are working in.**

	Christine	Harun	Annette	Simon	Christos
Department?	…	…	…	…	…

Language and grammar 1
Translate the following sentences.

1. Unsere Firma ist zu klein für einen eigenen Parkplatz.
2. Diese Frage zu beantworten ist für mich zu kompliziert.
3. Nun ist es zu spät für eine Bewerbung.
4. Es ist noch zu früh, darüber zu entscheiden.
5. Sie kam als Letzte zu der Besprechung.
6. Unser Unternehmen ist das einzige, das diese Lösung anbietet.

Language and grammar 2
Choose the correct form of the verbs in brackets.

1. We are having problems (find) qualified programmers.
2. We look forward to (get) your comments on this matter.
3. It is no use (buy) a new one, if it is still the same model.
4. They are having difficulties (meet) the deadline.
5. I am not used to (drive) big cars like this.
6. I object to (have) my work criticised when it's not justified.

Language and grammar: Infinitive and gerund

Nach "too ...", "the first", "the last", "the only one" steht im Englischen der Infinitiv:

Our company is	too small	**to have** a canteen.
This problem is	too difficult for us	**to solve** without help.
It is	too late for you	**to apply** for the job.
She was	the first	**to come.**
He was	the last	**to arrive.**
He was	the only one	**to take part.**

In folgenden Fällen sind deutsche Sprecher auch versucht, einen Infinitiv zu benutzen.
Es steht aber das Gerund:
I am looking forward **to receiving** your reply.
I am looking forward **to being shown** their new flat.
I am not used **to speaking** in public.
I object **to being forced** to work overtime.
I am having problems **understanding** him.
We had no difficulty **persuading** him.
It is no use **waiting** for the new regulations.

Communicating across cultures: Addressing people

In English-speaking countries hierarchical differences may be less pronounced than in German companies. Certainly, they are not so obvious from the way people address each other as first names are generally used. Immediate superiors are also usually addressed by their first name. Where there is a considerable difference in status the titles Mr / Mrs / Miss and surname may be used when addressing a superior.

In Britain or the USA business contacts will very quickly address you by your first name and try to establish an informal atmosphere. When introducing yourself to English-speaking people, always give both your first name and your surname. If they firstname you, you should, of course, do the same.

In schools students usually address teachers with the title (Mr / Mrs / Miss) and surname and in shops and restaurants customers may be addressed as sir / madam, e.g.: Are you ready to order, sir? Can I help you, madam? It is important simply to recognise this – you will not have to use it yourself.

Note:
As we have already seen there is often no one-to-one equivalent to German job titles. Similarly there is no direct equivalent to the much used German word "Sachbearbeiter". It may correspond to "the person dealing with the case / our order" or "the person in charge of ...".

Phrases: The office

To describe the office

I work in an open-plan office.	Ich arbeite in einem Großraumbüro.
I work in a small office for two people. She works in the back office.	Ich arbeite in einem kleinen Büro für zwei Personen. Sie arbeitet in einem Büro ohne Publikumsverkehr.
I prefer working in a front office.	Ich arbeite lieber in einem Büro mit Publikumsverkehr.
My office is spacious and airy.	Mein Büro ist geräumig und luftig.
The office looks **out on to** the car park.	Vom Büro sieht man auf den Parkplatz.
We all have PCs with internet access.	Wir haben alle einen PC mit Zugang zum Internet.
There is a photocopier, a fax machine and file shredders.	Wir haben einen Kopierer, ein Faxgerät und Aktenvernichter.
The senior staff use the computer projectors for presentations.	Die leitenden Angestellten verwenden die Beamer für ihre Präsentationen.

To introduce the people in the office

He is the overall **boss**, the managing director.	Er ist der oberste Chef, der Geschäftsführer.
Mr Kent is the chief executive.	Herr Kent ist der Vorstandsvorsitzende.
She is **head** of department.	Sie ist die Abteilungsleiterin.
He **reports to** Frau Niemeyer.	Er untersteht Frau Niemeyer.
Frau Niemeyer is our superior.	Frau Niemeyer ist unsere Vorgesetzte.
She is assistant/secretary **to** Mr Kent.	Sie ist Herrn Kents Assistentin/Sekretärin.
I am **in charge of** exports.	Ich bin Exportsachbearbeiterin.
I am responsible for sales to the EU.	Ich bearbeite/bin zuständig für den Verkauf in die EU-Länder.
He deals with/processes/handles complaints.	Er bearbeitet Mängelrügen.
He makes sure that instalments are paid **on** time.	Er kümmert sich um den pünktlichen Eingang der Ratenzahlungen.
Robert is one of the partners of our firm.	Robert ist einer der Partner in unserer Firma.
I hope to be **taken on** after I've finished my course.	Ich hoffe nach der Ausbildung übernommen zu werden.

To talk about catering in the office

Our official coffee break is a quarter of an hour.	Offiziell haben wir eine Viertelstunde Kaffeepause.
We have a small kitchen with a fridge, a coffee machine and a microwave.	Wir haben eine kleine Küche mit Kühlschrank, Kaffeemaschine und Mikrowelle.
At lunchtime we go to the canteen.	Zum Mittagessen gehen wir in die Kantine.
We either bring sandwiches or convenience food.	Wir bringen entweder belegte Brote oder ein Fertiggericht mit.
The canteen caters for vegetarians, too.	Die Kantine bietet auch Gerichte für Vegetarier.

To describe your company's organization chart

He is our **chief executive officer**.	Er ist der Chef unserer Firma.
The department Administration and Finance is subdivided into five units.	Die Abteilung Verwaltung und Finanzen besteht aus fünf Bereichen.
The Marketing Department is part of Sales.	Die Marketing-Abteilung gehört zum Verkauf.
IT Support is responsible for all our IT equipment.	IT-Support ist zuständig für alle IT-Anlagen.
We are an international company and our **personnel** department is called "human resources".	Wir sind ein internationales Unternehmen und unsere Personalabteilung heißt „Human Resources".
The head of our legal department is a lawyer specializing in company law.	Der Leiter unserer Rechtsabteilung ist ein Fachanwalt für Gesellschaftsrecht.
Our company is divided **into** five business units.	Unsere Firma ist in fünf Geschäftsfelder unterteilt.

Unit 5
Telephoning

WORD BANK
telephone • number • extension • handset • landline • answering machine • mobile / cell phone • mailbox • text message • telephone alphabet • symbols • codes • to put through • to hold • to catch • to spell • to repeat • to take down • to read back • slowly • clearly • precisely

The telephone has long been an essential tool of business communication but in the past few years it has been revolutionised by the advent of mobile telephony. People can call and be called wherever they happen to be. Even if a person is not available to take calls a text message can be sent or a message can be left on their voice-mail.

1 R **Read the text and match the expressions on the left with the explanations on the right.**

1. essential tool	a. telephoning without fixed lines
2. participant	b. arrival
3. advent	c. person taking part
4. mobile telephony	d. mailbox
5. voice-mail	e. important instrument

2 P **Describe the telephone situations above.**

Online-Link
808260-0005

A Appliances and components

1 **Read the following sentences and translate them into German. Use the words**
M **below.**

Handy

Telefonbuch

Festnetztelefonanlage

Besetztzeichen

Hörer

Onlineverzeichnis

Telefonauskunft

Anrufbeantworter

Freizeichen

Festnetzleitung

1. My fixed line handset includes an answering machine.
2. It is important to replace the receiver carefully otherwise anyone ringing will get the engaged signal.
3. When you pick up the receiver you hear the dialling tone.
4. The latest innovation is to combine landline and mobile phones – when you leave your home the landline becomes a mobile.
5. My telephone handset can also be used to send and receive fax messages.
6. Most people use a copy of the old-fashioned local telephone directory with a business section. Sometimes the Yellow Pages are in a separate book.
7. However, post offices no longer keep a complete nationwide set of telephone directories.
8. Many people use online directories.
9. The traditional Directory Enquiries has been replaced by a number of competing companies.
10. The applications of mobile phones / cell(ular) phones are increasing all the time.

2 **Work in groups. Describe to your group the telephoning equipment you have at**
P **the office, at home and for mobile communication.**

B Receiving and redirecting calls

1 R **Restore the correct order of the two jumbled dialogues and write them out.**

Dialogue 1

1. Receptionist: Delphi Materials. Good afternoon. How can I help you?
2. Caller: No, thanks. I'll call back later.
3. Receptionist: Just a moment, Mr Martin. I'll put you through to Louisa Bates …
   Oh, I'm sorry, her extension is engaged at the moment. Would you like to hold?
4. Caller: Hello. This is Robert Martin from Komplettbau in Erfurt, Germany. I'd like to speak to someone in accounts, please.

Dialogue 2

1. Receptionist: May I ask what it's about?
2. Caller: It's about the dreadful beds we had to sleep in. My back is still aching.
3. Receptionist: Could you give me your name please?
4. Caller: My name is Jakob Grailing and I need to speak to your general manager.
5. Receptionist: Just a second. I'll connect you to Customer Relations.
6. Caller: Hi. The reason I'm calling is …
7. Receptionist: Florida Leisure Park. Good morning. What can I do for you?

2 R A1.11 **Listen to the following telephone conversation between Marcel Krenz of International Snacks GmbH and Jennifer Glover, a receptionist at Global Catering in Manchester and say whether the following statements are TRUE or FALSE.**

1. Jonathan Ashley works for Omnipolis Research Consultants Ltd.
2. Marcel Krenz wishes to speak to Jennifer Glover.
3. Jennifer Glover knows for certain that Kirsty Burnham is not in.
4. Marcel Krenz prefers to be put on hold.
5. Marcel Krenz has got Kirsty Burnham's mobile phone number.
6. Marcel Krenz does not want to be put through to Kevin Sears.

3 Hören Sie sich die Dialoge noch einmal an und finden Sie heraus, wie Folgendes auf Englisch formuliert wird.

KMK
A1.11

1. Was sagt Jonathan Ashley, als das Telefon klingelt?
2. Was sagt Marcel Krenz, als er sich verwählt hat?
3. Wie stellt sich Marcel Krenz bei Ms Glover vor?
4. Was sagt Jennifer Glover, während Sie Marcel Krenz durchzustellen versucht?
5. Was antwortet Marcel Krenz auf die Frage, ob er jemand anderen sprechen möchte?
6. Was sagt Jennifer Glover, als sie wissen will, ob Marcel warten möchte oder ob sie zurückrufen soll?
7. Mit welchen Worten schlägt Jennifer Glover vor, Kirsty auf ihrem Handy anzurufen?
8. Wie formuliert Marcel die Bitte, zu Kevin Sears durchgestellt zu werden?

4 Beantworten Sie die Fragen zu nachstehendem Text schriftlich auf Deutsch.

KMK

1. Warum schicken viele Menschen einem Geschäftspartner lieber eine E-Mail als ihn anzurufen?
2. Wovor haben wir Angst, wenn wir ein Auslandsgespräch führen sollen?
3. Welche Aspekte der Kommunikation fehlen bei einem Telefongespräch?
4. Was soll man tun, wenn man nicht versteht, was der Gesprächspartner sagt?

Info:
Telephoning in a foreign language

Telephoning in a foreign language can be rather frightening. No wonder people often prefer to send an e-mail where they can plan what they want to say and need not fear immediate comeback. However, a telephone call is sometimes unavoidable and one wonders: Will I understand what they are saying? What do I say if I can't? Can I just hang up in embarrassment? Will I be able to express what I want to say? Will they laugh if I make some awful mistake? We all know these kinds of fears when we have to ring someone abroad. And, to some extent, the fears are justified. The non-verbal side of communication is missing. We can't see the person's face, their lips and gestures. They can't see our gestures and the look of despair on our faces! It's best to remain calm and ask them to speak slowly and repeat anything that is not clear.

5 R A1.12 In her first week at Herkules Sandra Kohl finds herself alone in the office and it is precisely then that the telephone rings.

Work with a partner. Listen to the telephone conversation twice. Partner A makes a note of the phrases Sandra uses to ensure that she understands what Jim Farquhar is saying. Partner B makes a note of the strategies and phrases Jim Farquhar uses to make Sandra understand him and feel good about her English. Then compare your findings.

6 R / M **Complete the telephone phrases below using words from the box. Then translate the phrases into German.**

cut • get • line • repeat • slowly • speak • quite • what

- I'm sorry this is a bad **1**.
- Could you **2** a bit louder?
- Could you speak a bit more **3**, please?
- I'm sorry I didn't **4** that.
- I'm sorry we were **5** off.
- I'm afraid, I didn't **6** catch that.
- Could you **7** that, please?
- **8** was the number again?

7 Roleplay this telephone conversation with a partner. Use the phrases at the end of the unit. Phrases

Firma: Heinz GmbH, Dresden

Company: Baltic Car Supplies, Tallinn, Estonia

Nehmen Sie den Anruf entgegen.

Nennen Sie Ihren Namen und den Namen der Firma. Sie möchten Frau Lange sprechen.

Sagen Sie, dass Sie den Anrufer schlecht verstehen und bitten Sie ihn, etwas lauter zu sprechen.

Sprechen Sie etwas lauter und fragen Sie, ob Sie jetzt besser zu verstehen sind.

Es ist jetzt besser. Fragen Sie, worum es geht.

Es geht um eine Rechnung.

Bitten Sie den Anrufer einen Moment zu warten und verbinden Sie ihn mit Frau Lange.

Bedanken Sie sich.

Sagen Sie, dass die Leitung leider im Moment besetzt ist und fragen Sie, ob der Anrufer warten möchte.

Sagen Sie, dass Sie lieber später zurückrufen möchten und fragen Sie nach der Durchwahl.

Die Durchwahl ist 23. Frau Lange wird bis 16 Uhr im Büro sein.

Sie haben das nicht richtig verstanden und bitten um Wiederholung.

Wiederholen Sie die vorherige Information.

Bedanken Sie sich und verabschieden Sie sich.

Antworten Sie und verabschieden Sie sich.

8 Work in pairs. Sit back to back. Use your notes from Exercise 5 and the phrases at the end of the unit. Then act out a similar dialogue. Phrases

C Taking messages

1 KMK **Übertragen Sie den folgenden Text ins Deutsche.**

Info: How to take a message

When taking messages it is important to make sure that you take down all the relevant details. You should first make sure that you take down the name of the caller. It is usually necessary to ask him / her to spell names and addresses. Be sure to get the postcode.

It is essential to note down telephone numbers accurately. Failure to do so will lead to a lot of problems. Read back telephone numbers to check that you have got them right. Telephone numbers are often read differently in different countries. In Britain numbers are simply given in the order they occur, eg: 0044 020 363 2991 = oh oh four four – oh two oh - three six three – two nine nine one. Instead of **oh** Americans usually say **zero**. People often say: double oh or: two double nine one. If necessary, ask the caller to repeat the number more slowly.

Get callers to spell e-mail addresses precisely. Even the slightest mistake results in e-mails being sent back. @ is pronounced at, (.) is read as dot, (cf "dotcoms" = internet companies), (/) is pronounced slash and (–) is read as hyphen or dash or minus.

Your company may have a special form for recording telephone messages.

2 R A1.13 **There are different international telephone alphabets but people very often make up their own as they go along. Spell the following names and addresses using the international telephone alphabet on page 60. Then listen and check.**

Brian Urquart • Jonathan McEwan • Trevelyan Networking Ltd • Peterborough • Heidi Schlösser • Detlev Jaegermeyer • Jörg Eyrich • Silberstein • Chemnitz • Ditzhuizen • Mbamali • Werchojansk • Ian McWhirter • Appletreewick in Wharfedale • Georg Süsterhenn • Bad Oeynhausen

3 **Spell the following names and addresses using your own telephone alphabet.**

Mississippi • Philadelphia • Rhondda • Le Havre • Eyjafiallajökull • Energize Ltd. • Joachim • Fort Myers • Wolfgang Somborn • Kiel • Mississauga Enterprises Inc. • Maldives Travel Lounge

International telephone alphabet

S for Sierra
C for Charlie
H for …
U … …
L … …
Z … …

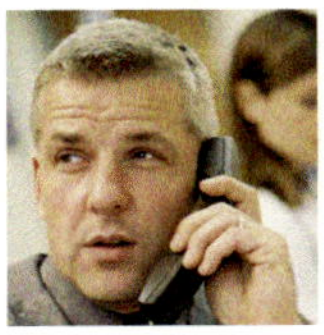

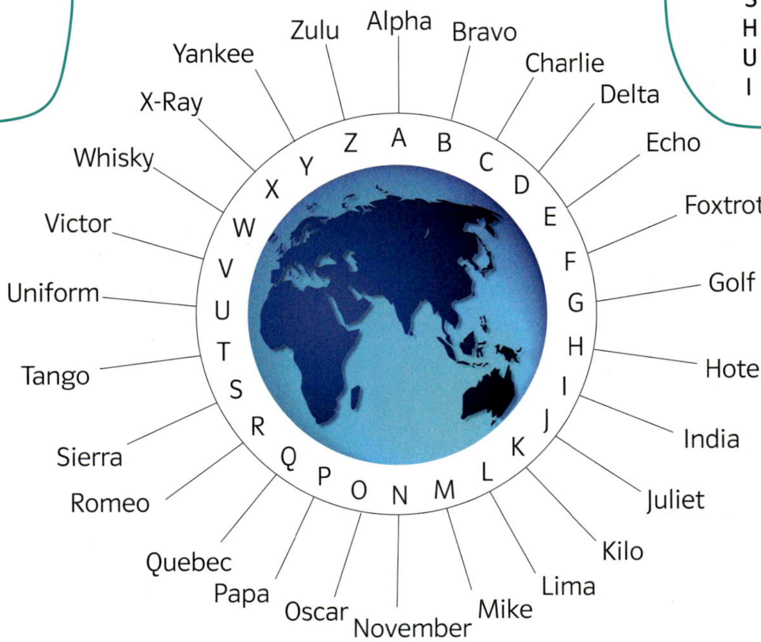

H for Hotel
E for Echo
N for …
S … …
H … …
U … …
I … …

4 **Work in pairs: Sit back to back and spell your name and the name and address of your company using the international telephone alphabet. Then change roles and check the results.**

I

Phrases

Symbol:	Name:	Example:
‘	apostrophe	O’Connor
@	at	info@
A/a	capital letters/small letters	USA/asap
-	hyphen/dash/minus	t-online
Ö	o-umlaut/oe/o with 2 dots	Möller
:	colon	http:
/	slash/stroke	org/gla/
\	backslash	\docs.nt\
.	dot	.de
_	understroke	tourist_org.

Codes / numbers:

+49	(0)711	664376-0	34
country code	**area code**	**office number**	**extension**
04275	Leipzig		
post/zip code	**city**		

5 KMK Work in groups. Group A uses the role card below and dictates the following telephone numbers, e-mail addresses and websites. Group B uses the role card on page 228 and dictates the information given there. Then check your results.

Role card: Partner A Role card partner B ⇨ page 228

1. +44 (1234) 687791
2. (0203) 4670976
3. (051) 27 81 13 - 12
4. (0171) 25333980
5. info@terstegen.com
6. dieter.wilhelmsen@abconsulting.de
7. www.mittelpunkt.de/abo
8. info@sykescottages.com

6 R/P A1.14 First copy the form below. Then listen to the conversation and take the message.

TELEPHONE MESSAGE

Message for:

Message taken by: Date:

Caller:

Subject:

7 R/P A1.15 You are David Verhoeven. You receive a telephone call from the UK. See on page 62 for what you yourself say in the conversation with Mr Jones.

First copy the form below. Then listen to the conversation and make a note of the message in German.

TELEFONNOTIZ

Nachricht für:

aufgenommen von: am:

Anrufer:

Betreff:

David Verhoeven: Anton Hein GmbH, Erkelenz, guten Tag.

David Verhoeven: Good morning, Mr Jones. I'm afraid Mrs van Steuben is away on a business trip. She is not due back before the beginning of next week. Is there anyone else you'd like to speak to?

David Verhoeven: Certainly. No problem.

David Verhoeven: Right. Could you give me your name and your boss's name again, please?

David Verhoeven: It's David Verhoeven. I'd better spell my second name: V for Victoria, E for egg, R for Richard, H for happy, O for ox, E for Egg, V for Victoria, E for egg and N for nice. I hope you got that alright.

David Verhoeven: I'll make sure she gets your message. The name of your company was CyberWorld, wasn't it? I didn't catch the name of the town, though.

David Verhoeven: Thank you and thank you very much for ringing. Goodbye.

8 | **Work in pairs. Copy the English and the German forms for telephone messages. Sit back to back. Partner A "rings" partner B and leaves a short message. Partner B takes down the message, either in German or in English – depending on the recipient. Then change roles. Use the role card on page 228.** Phrases

Example:

Partner A: "This is Pavel Banka speaking. I've got a message for Herr Meister, your purchasing manager. Please tell him that the MP3 Player C27 is again in stock and that I could ship them tomorrow morning. Ask Herr Meister to ring me as soon as possible."

Partner B takes down the message on a form.

TELEFONNOTIZ

Nachricht für: *Herrn Meister, Einkauf*

aufgenommen von: *(Ihr Name)* am:

Anrufer: *Pavel Banka*

Betreff: *MP3 Player C27 wieder vorrätig*

Herr Banka könnte die C27-Player morgen früh absenden.

Bittet möglichst bald um Rückruf.

9 | **Work in pairs. Sit back to back and practise taking messages. Use the phrases at the end of the unit.** Phrases

D Making telephone calls

Communicating across cultures:
Telephoning in English-speaking countries

It is important to use suitable polite phrases when ringing people in English-speaking countries. If you know the person you are ringing it is usual to ask how they are getting on etc. before you get down to business (Example: How are you doing? I haven't spoken to you for a long time etc.).

If you are about to mention a problem or difficulty, you should begin with "I'm afraid ..."
A request often begins with "Could you possibly ...?" (Could you possibly repeat the address?) or "I would be grateful if you would / could …".

When someone does you a service, it is usual to say something like: "Excellent!", or "Brilliant!"

When someone thanks you for your help you can say, "You're welcome" or "Not at all".

Don't just say "yes" or "no". Say: "Yes, I think so"; "No, I'm afraid not".

! The problem for German speakers is that short answers which are NOT impolite in German come across in English as unfriendly or impolite.

1 **Listen to the conversation and note down the missing expressions on a separate sheet of paper.**
R
A1.16

Voice:	Good morning. Cardboard Box Company, John Hough speaking.
Nadine Pfeiffer:	Good morning. **1** your packaging materials. My boss **2** your sales literature.
John Hough:	Certainly, **3** you our literature. **4** the name and address of your company.
Nadine Pfeiffer:	The name of the company is Hülshoff GmbH.
John Hough:	**5**, please.
Nadine Pfeiffer:	H for Harry, **6**, L for lemon, S for sugar, H for Harry, O for Otto, double F for Frederick, and then G m b H. The street is Zülpicher Str 131, 50001 Köln, that's Cologne and it's spelt K for knock, O for Otto with two dots, L for lovely and N for nice.
John Hough:	Oh dear, **7** the street as well.
Nadine Pfeiffer:	Z for Zoe; U for ugly with two dots; L for lovely; P for princess; **8**; C for carrot; H for Henrietta; E for egg and R for Ritz.
John Hough:	Brilliant. I will send you the sales literature immediately and **9** you again. By the way, **10** name?
Nadine Pfeiffer:	Yes, Huff. **11**?

John Hough: I'm afraid not. It's spelt H O U G H, that is H for Henry, O for orange, U for united, G for Green and H for Henry again. My first name's John 12!

Nadine Pfeiffer: Thank you very much. Goodbye.

John Hough: Thank you. 13 the literature in a couple of days. Goodbye.

2 R A1.17 **First copy the form below. Then listen to the telephone conversation between Lucy Batt and Chloe Stott and fill in the form Chloe has prepared for her boss's information.**

Contact person:
Days of arrival and departure:
Size and location of the cottage:
Charge per week:
Additional charges:
Half the total rent plus booking charges to be paid by:
Balance to be paid by:
Modes of payment:
Mode of booking:

3 KMK **Roleplay this telephone conversation with a partner.**

Phrases

Employee at Form und Raum GmbH (eigener Name)	British customer John Willoughby, Exclusive Interiors, London
Melden Sie sich am Telefon. →	
	Stellen Sie sich vor. Sie haben die neuen Lampen der deutschen Firma auf einer Ausstellung gesehen und möchten eventuell einige bestellen.
← Sie sind gerade allein im Büro. Fragen Sie, ob der Anrufer eine Nachricht hinterlassen möchte. →	
	Sie möchten, dass jemand so bald wie möglich zurückruft. Sie geben Ihre Telefonnummer in London an: (020 897 3884).
← Sie bitten den Anrufer, die Telefonnummer langsam zu wiederholen. Den Namen haben Sie auch nicht verstanden. Er soll ihn bitte buchstabieren. →	
	Buchstabieren Sie den Namen und wiederholen Sie die Telefonnummer langsam und deutlich. Sie sind heute bis 18.00 Uhr britischer Zeit im Büro.
← Es wird auf jeden Fall jemand im Laufe des Nachmittags anrufen. →	
	Sie bedanken sich und verabschieden sich.
← Sie verabschieden sich ebenfalls.	

4 **Work in pairs. Search the Internet for suggestions for role plays. (Search words: "Telephoning in English".) Sit back to back and practise telephone dialogues with your partner. Use the phrases at the end of the unit.**

E Formulating messages for the answering machine and the mailbox

1 Leaving a message on an answering machine

Info: A message on an answering machine

1. Begin by saying "Good morning" etc. Do not say your name first as the first few words may get "lost".
2. Pronounce your name very clearly, give your company's name as well and mention the place / country you are calling from, if necessary.
3. Be as clear and concise as possible when leaving the message.
4. Be polite and friendly.
5. Repeat figures and spell names, if necessary.
6. At the end repeat your name and telephone number.
7. Dictate the telephone number slowly, pausing between each number.

1 KMK A1.18 **Kopieren Sie den Vordruck, hören Sie die Nachricht ab und fassen Sie sie auf Deutsch in einer Telefonnotiz zusammen.**

TELEFONNOTIZ

Nachricht für:

aufgenommen von: am:

Anrufer:

Betreff:

2 P **Work with a partner. Write out a message to be left on an answering machine. Use the following details.**

Arrive London • 12 January • 1 pm • Waterloo station • Eurostar from Brussels • staying Prince's Gate Hotel • Tel.: 0207 897 3998 • request appointment with Mr Chin 13 January • to discuss joint venture • exhibition Singapore • end October • suggest working lunch • contact at hotel or on mobile 0049 (0)1625 673 225 • suggest place to meet • possibly restaurant • or this hotel • Best regards

2 Text messaging

Texting or text-messaging has also become an important method of communication and networking. Millions of messages are sent that only a few years ago could not have been sent by any other medium. Obviously, one big advantage is that text messaging is cheap. Like the e-mail it also avoids the necessity of speaking to the person directly. However, he/she can reply virtually immediately so that it is possible to have a kind of conversation with slight delays in between.

1 **Use your mobile phone and find out the messages that appear when you key in the following figures:**

Example:
733 968 46 566366 reads See you in London.

1. 843 87246 9455 23 46 8463
2. 74255 93 46 86 843 782 23837 9675
3. 733 968 7666
4. 93 273 65

2 P **Write text messages using the abbreviations below. Compare your messages in class.**

Example:
C U 2MORO = See you tomorrow.

Info:
Abbreviations used in e-mails and text messages

1	one
2	to or too (it's up 2 U = It's up to you)
2DAY	today
2MORO	tomorrow
2NITE	tonight
4	for (4U = for you)
B4	before
8	ate or eat (GR8 = great; C U L8R = see you later)
BFN	bye for now
AFAIK	as far as I know
ASAP	as soon as possible
ATB	all the best
BTW	by the way
C U 2MORO	see you tomorrow
CID	consider it done
CUL8R	see you later
D8	date
EZ	easy
FAO	for the attention of
FAQ	frequently asked questions
FYI	for your information
IMO	in my opinion
K	OK
L8	late
MSG	message
NE	any
NE1	anyone
NO1	no one
NETHING	anything
NM	no message
OTOH	on the other hand
PCM	please call me
PLS	please
PROLLY	probably
R	are
RGDS	regards
RUCMNG	are you coming?
RUOK	are you OK?
SPK	speak
SRY	sorry
THNQ	thank you
THX	thanks
W8	wait
WAN2	want to
WRK	work
XLNT	excellent
Y	why
YR	your

Language and grammar
Choose the correct prepositions.

1. The meeting will be held from 2 pm (until/to) 4 pm.
2. Thank you for your letter (from/of) 9 December.
3. We are prepared to wait (until/by) next Friday.
4. We enclose a description of our facilities (by/of) an independent expert.
5. We have received numerous enquiries (of/from) start-up companies.
6. The tickets will have to be confirmed (by/until) the middle of next week.
7. We haven't heard (of/from) him recently.
8. The book (of/by) a well-known writer is available in paperback.
9. We expect to receive the consignment (by/until) Friday at the latest.
10. I've never heard (of/from) the firm. Are you sure you've got the name right?
11. It's a study (of/by) the CBI (Confederation of British Industry).
12. He has to get to the airport (until/by) 4 pm.

Language and grammar: Tricky prepositions – getting the wrong one may change the meaning

by / until **bis**
I need the report **by** Monday means that you must get it on Monday (or sooner) because from then on you will need it for your work. Example: The goods must reach us **by** the end of next week.

I need the report **until** Monday means that you need it only until Monday and will then be finished with it.
Example: The import licence is valid **until** 31 August. (You say: until **the thirty-first of** August.)

from … to **von … bis**
This year's shoe fair will take place **from** 30 June **to** 4 August. (You say: … from **the thirtieth of** June to **the fourth of** August.)
Wrong: from 30 June ~~until~~ 4 August

from, of, by **von / vom**
The date of a communication is preceded by "of" or "dated":
Example: We refer to your offer **of** 2 November. (You say: … of **the second of** November.)
Wrong: We refer to your offer ~~from~~ 2 November.

Where the communication came from is expressed by "from":
Example: We received a complaint **from** one of our customers.
Wrong: We received a complaint ~~of~~ one of our customers.

The author is introduced by means of the preposition "by":
Example: This is shown in a report **by** an independent study group.
Wrong: This is shown in a report ~~of~~ an independent study group.

Phrases: Telephoning

To make friendly remarks at the beginning of a telephone conversation

Oh, hello Nadine. Nice to hear **from** you. How are things **over there**?	Hallo Nadine. Schön von Dir zu hören. Wie geht's denn so?
Good morning Mrs Glover. I hope you had a pleasant holiday.	Guten Morgen Mrs. Glover. Ich hoffe, Sie hatten einen angenehmen Urlaub.
Good afternoon Mr McEwan. **What's** the weather in Scotland **like**?	Guten Tag Mr. McEwan. Wie ist das Wetter in Schottland?

Reactions

Fine, thank you. And how are you?	Gut, vielen Dank. Und wie geht es Ihnen?
Thank you, it was really very relaxing.	Danke, es war wirklich sehr erholsam.
We've had an awful lot of rain recently, I'm afraid. What's it like in Germany?	Es hat in der letzten Zeit leider schrecklich viel geregnet. Wie ist das Wetter in Deutschland?

To ask the caller to speak more slowly, to spell sth., to repeat sth.

Oh sorry. I didn't quite catch that. Could you repeat it more slowly, please?	Es tut mir Leid, das habe ich nicht verstanden. Könnten Sie es etwas langsamer wiederholen?
Could you possibly spell that? Is that the name of the town?	Könnten Sie das vielleicht buchstabieren? Ist das der Name der Stadt?
I'm afraid I didn't get the telephone number. Could you give me it again, please?	Leider habe ich die Telefonnummer nicht mitbekommen. Würden Sie sie bitte wiederholen?

To ask for somebody

Could I speak **to** Ms Burnham, please?	Könnte ich bitte Ms. Burnham sprechen?
Could you put me **through** to Mr Hough?	Könnten Sie mich mit Mr. Hough verbinden?
Could you give me his/her extension, please?	Könnten Sie mir bitte seine/ihre Durchwahl geben?
I'd like to speak to someone from the sales department.	Ich möchte gern jemanden im Verkauf sprechen.

To say that someone is not available

I'm afraid Kirsty Burnham is not in the office at the moment.	Kirsty Burnham ist z. Zt. leider nicht in ihrem Büro.
… is in a meeting.	… ist in einer Besprechung.
… has someone **with** her.	… hat Besuch.

… is **on** a business trip.	… ist auf Geschäftsreise.
… is out **at** lunch.	… ist zu Tisch.
… is no longer **with** the company.	… ist nicht mehr bei unserer Firma.

To offer to ring back or take a message

I'm afraid Mr Hough is speaking **on** the other line. Would you prefer to hold or shall I ask him to ring back?	Mr. Hough spricht leider gerade auf der anderen Leitung. Möchten Sie warten, oder soll er Sie zurückrufen?
Can he call you back this afternoon?	Kann er Sie heute Nachmittag zurückrufen?
Can I give him a message?	Kann ich ihm etwas ausrichten?
Would you like to leave a message?	Möchten Sie eine Nachricht hinterlassen?

Reactions

Thank you. I'll ring back later.	Danke sehr. Ich rufe später zurück.
I'm afraid I won't be in the office this afternoon. I'll give you my mobile number.	Ich bedaure, ich bin heute Nachmittag außer Haus. Ich gebe Ihnen meine Handy-Nummer.
Yes, please. Could you tell him that …?	Ja bitte. Könnten Sie ihm ausrichten, dass …?

To refer someone to someone else

I'm afraid … I don't know the details. … I am not familiar **with** this order. … I am not in charge of this transaction. I'll put you through to Mr Sears.	Leider … kenne ich mich damit nicht aus. … weiß ich über diesen Auftrag nicht Bescheid. … bearbeite ich diesen Vorgang nicht. Ich stelle Sie zu Mr. Sears durch.
Shall I put you through **to** his secretary?	Soll ich Sie mit seiner Sekretärin verbinden?
Would you like to speak **to** somebody in the accounts department?	Möchten Sie mit jemandem aus der Abteilung Rechnungswesen sprechen?

Reactions

Yes, please. She may be able to help.	Ja bitte. Sie kann mir vielleicht helfen.
No thanks, I really need to speak **to** the export manager.	Nein danke. Ich muss unbedingt mit dem Exportleiter sprechen.

To ask for / about something

Would you please let me know if …?	Ich möchte gern wissen, ob …?
I'd like to ask **whether** it would be possible to …	Wäre es möglich, dass …

Could you possibly …?	Könnten Sie/Könntest Du …?
Do you think you could …?	Könnten Sie/Könntest Du vielleicht …?
You'd be doing us a great favour if you could …	Sie täten uns einen großen Gefallen, wenn Sie …
Please **make sure** that …	Bitte sorgen Sie dafür, dass …
I would really appreciate **it** if you could …	Ich wäre Ihnen sehr dankbar, wenn Sie …

Reactions

Certainly.	Ja, natürlich.
I see no reason why not.	Natürlich. Warum nicht.
Certainly. No problem.	Klar. Kein Problem.
I will certainly do my very best.	Ich werde bestimmt mein Bestes tun.
Definitely. I'll see to it myself.	Ganz bestimmt. Ich werde mich selbst darum kümmern.

To refuse something

I'm afraid we can't agree **to** your proposal.	Leider können wir uns mit Ihrem Vorschlag nicht einverstanden erklären.
We find this level of service quite unacceptable.	Für uns ist diese Art von Kundendienst absolut inakzeptabel.
This is unfortunately not what we had in mind.	Leider hatten wir uns das nicht so vorgestellt.

Reactions

That is a pity.	Das ist wirklich schade.
That is most regrettable.	Das ist überaus bedauerlich.
I can quite understand. We are trying hard to improve things.	Das kann ich verstehen. Wir bemühen uns nach Kräften um eine Verbesserung.
There must have been a misunderstanding.	Hier muss ein Missverständnis vorliegen.

To apologise

I'm terribly sorry but …	Es tut mir schrecklich Leid, aber …
I really must apologise for the inconvenience we've caused you.	Ich möchte mich für die Ihnen entstandenen Unannehmlichkeiten vielmals entschuldigen.
I'm very sorry. Thank you for being so understanding.	Es tut mir sehr Leid. Vielen Dank für Ihr Verständnis.
I can only repeat that I'm very sorry **for** the delay.	Ich kann mich nur nochmals für die Verzögerung entschuldigen.

Reactions

It could happen to anyone.	Das hätte jedem passieren können.
It's a mistake that is very easily made.	So ein Fehler kommt oft vor.
Don't worry. The main thing is that the mistake has been rectified.	Machen Sie sich keine Gedanken. Hauptsache, der Fehler ist behoben.
Well, let's just hope it doesn't happen again.	Hoffen wir nur, dass es nicht noch einmal geschieht.
It has caused us a lot of embarrassment.	Es war für uns sehr peinlich.

To play for time

Can I ring you back? I need to look **at** the file.	Kann ich Sie zurückrufen? Ich muss erst die Unterlagen einsehen.
I'll have to have a word with the line manager.	Ich muss die Sache erst mit dem Bereichsleiter besprechen.
I'm afraid I can't access the file **on** my monitor at the moment. Can I ring you back?	Leider habe ich im Moment auf meinem Computer keinen Zugriff auf die Datei. Kann ich Sie zurückrufen?
I'm afraid I can't give you a definitive answer **at** the moment. I'll get back to you this afternoon if that's OK.	Leider kann ich Ihnen z. Zt. keinen endgültigen Bescheid geben. Wenn es Ihnen recht ist, rufe ich Sie deswegen heute Nachmittag zurück.

Reactions

I'm afraid you said that the last time I rang. I'm not prepared to be put **off** again.	Das haben Sie schon beim letzten Mal gesagt. Ich lasse mich nicht noch einmal so abspeisen.
Certainly, but please give me your extension so that I can ring you direct if necessary.	Natürlich, geben Sie mir aber doch bitte Ihre Durchwahl, damit ich Sie nötigenfalls direkt anrufen kann.
I wish to settle the matter now. I should be grateful if you would put me through to the person responsible.	Ich möchte die Angelegenheit jetzt klären. Bitte stellen Sie mich zu dem entsprechenden Sachbearbeiter durch.
Fine. I look forward to hearing from you. I leave the office **at** 4pm your time.	Schön. Ich erwarte Ihren Anruf. Ich bin bis 4 Uhr Ihrer Zeit im Büro.

To insist that something is done by a certain date

We need the goods **by** Wednesday **at** the very latest.	Wir benötigen die Ware bis spätestens Mittwoch.
We definitely need the documents **by** 3 May.	Wir müssen die Unterlagen unbedingt bis zum 3. Mai erhalten.
Can we rely **on** that?	Können wir uns darauf verlassen?
Please make sure it arrives **no** later **than** the end of April.	Bitte sorgen Sie dafür, dass es spätestens Ende April eintrifft.
Monday 31 July is the final deadline.	Montag, der 31. Juli ist der letzte Termin.

To promise something

We promise you that …	Wir versprechen Ihnen, dass …
You have my word. The documents will reach you **by** Monday.	Ich gebe Ihnen mein Wort. Die Dokumente treffen spätestens Montag bei Ihnen ein.
We will certainly **ensure** that …	Wir werden bestimmt dafür sorgen, dass …
The goods will be definitely dispatched tomorrow.	Die Ware wird mit Sicherheit morgen abgeschickt.

To end the conversation

Goodbye Miss Pfeiffer. Thank you for calling.	Auf Wiederhören, Frau Pfeiffer. Vielen Dank für Ihren Anruf.
Thank you. Goodbye. Have a nice weekend.	Danke schön. Auf Wiederhören. Schönes Wochenende!
Sorry, I must have got a wrong number.	Entschuldigung, ich habe mich verwählt.

Reactions

Goodbye Mr Hough. You'll be hearing from us again soon.	Auf Wiederhören Mr. Hough. Sie werden bald wieder von uns hören.
Goodbye. You too.	Auf Wiederhören. Gleichfalls.

UNIT 6
Making arrangements

WORD BANK
arrangements • booking • reservation • flight • destination • departure • arrival • hotel • accommodation • ensuite bathroom • diary • appointment • conference • meeting • topic • agenda • minutes • fair • exhibition • application • stand • to organise • to book • to hire • to attend • to record

An important part of the job of secretarial or clerical staff is to make arrangements on behalf of management. This may include managing the boss's diary and making or rescheduling appointments, booking flights or train tickets, making hotel reservations and hiring cars.
A secretary may be required to organise meetings and conferences and to take part in order to keep a record of what is said and decided. It is her job to generally facilitate proceedings, making sure that the participants have everything they need.
Many companies take part in trade fairs and exhibitions and it may be the task of the secretary to book stand space and help organise the company's participation.
Finally, the secretary will be responsible for welcoming visitors, often from abroad.
Obviously, a good command of foreign languages is an absolute must.

Study the text and answer the following questions.

R/P

1. Why may a secretary be asked to be present at a meeting?
2. What are the various duties of a secretary as given in the text? Make a list and translate it into German.

Online-Link
808260-0006

A Flights and accommodation

1 R A1.19 Global Catering in Manchester has meanwhile taken over a German company and renamed it Global Catering München GmbH. Executives from the German, British and American companies are to meet for a conference in Munich before flying on to Madrid to attend an international food fair.

Melanie Schmiedel, personal assistant (PA) to Udo Moersen, manager of Global Catering München GmbH, has been asked to organise the conference from 5th to 7th September at the company's premises in Munich. She decides to start by ringing her opposite number at the company's headquarters in Manchester.

Listen to the dialogue and complete the following sentences:

1. The conference is to take place in 1 on 2
2. The sales manager is going 3
3. Melanie Schmiedel will book rooms for 4 at 5
4. Jackie Rowland asks whether the Munich hotel caters for 6
5. Lunch will be provided by 7
6. Jackie Rowland will book the flights from 8 to 9
7. Jackie Rowland sends Melanie Schmiedel a copy of 10

2 P **Taking the role of Melanie Schmiedel send two e-mails confirming the hotel reservation at Zum Goldenen Ochsen, Wittelsbacher Allee 57, 81220 München to Naomi Rodgers at the American company on Rodgers.GlobalCateringusa@aol.com and to Jackie Rowland on Rowland.GlobalCateringuk@aol.com answering Jackie Rowland's query and asking whether the Americans have any special wishes as far as catering is concerned. Executives will be picked up at the airport. You require flight times and the names of the American executives.**

To:	Rowland.GlobalCateringuk@aol.com	Cc:	
From:	schmiedel.GlobalCateringmunich@aol.com	Date:	
Subject:			

3 R A1.20 Melanie Schmiedel then rings the Hotel Granada in Madrid to make arrangements for the six executives attending the International Food Fair from 7 to 9 September.

Listen to the conversation twice and answer the following questions:

1. What rooms does Melanie want to book?
2. What are the special features of the rooms she is offered?
3. What are the nationalities of the executives?
4. What meal will the executives receive automatically?
5. What arrangements are there for the evening meals?
6. What special catering arrangements are necessary for Kirsty Burnham?
7. How will the executives get to the exhibition grounds?
8. Why are they advised against hiring a car?

Flight	Departure Time	Arrival Time	Destination
ZY 207	8.45 am	11.30 am	Madrid
ZY 213	6.30 pm	9.15 pm	Munich

Melanie has meanwhile booked the flights from Munich to Madrid. The flight ZY207 leaves Munich at 8.45 am on 7 September and arrives in Madrid at 11.30 am. Return flight ZY213 is at 6.30 pm on 9 September.

4 P **Taking the role of Melanie Schmiedel send an e-mail to the Granada Hotel informing them of the flight number and times and giving the names of the six executives. Ask them to confirm that the executives will be picked up at the airport.** Phrases

5 P **In your role as Melanie Schmiedel send an e-mail to Naomi Rodgers cc Jackie Rowland giving information about the flight from Munich to Madrid and the hotel booking in Madrid.** Phrases

6 Work with a partner. Act out the following dialogue with the help of the prompts.

James Critchley	Jennifer Ainsworth
SmartMart Ltd	
	Saskatchewan Airlines
book flight / O'Hare airport Chicago	
	date / one-way / return?
return / start 25 June / return 30 June	
	one moment / look monitor / flight 2pm 25 June / London Heathrow / return O'Hare 9 am 30 June
OK / price?	
	Business / Economy?
Business	
	£837 return / book? / pay credit card
book / pay Visa	
	number / expiry date
4731 5026 7100 5314 / 9 July 2014	
	address?
James Critchley 136 Brunswick Avenue Brighton BN3 1NA	
	thank you / flight SA324 / booking reference SA7XP2 / send confirmation / ticket / I forgot – aisle or window?
window	
	anything else?
book car / recommend company	
	work with Excelsior Limos / 20% discount / mention us / booking reference / telephone number / New York Office / 001.201.4338301
thank you / will ring	
	thank you / choose Saskatchewan / goodbye

7 Your boss asks you to check out times and prices of business class flights to Mumbai, India (direct flights from your nearest airport). Make notes on the options.

*** 8** Work with a partner. Act out the following dialogue with the help of the role cards.

Phrases

Role card: Partner A Role card partner B ⇨ page 230

Sie sind Ivor Friedmann von der Mietwagenfirma Excelsior Limos Inc. in Chicago und erhalten einen Anruf von James Critchley von der britischen Firma SmartMart Ltd. **Nehmen Sie den Anruf entgegen.**

- Mietwagen verschiedener Kategorien (Kompakt- bis Luxusklasse) zur Abholung am Flughafen bereit
- Preis für Kompaktklasse $200 pro Woche, Preis pro Tag $50
- keine Beschränkung der Anzahl der gefahrenen Meilen
- Versicherung im Preis enthalten, bei Unfall muss der Kunde allerdings 10% der Kosten selbst tragen
- Zusatzversicherung zur Deckung der 10% Selbstbeteiligung (excess coverage): $60 pro Woche
- 20% Rabatt für Kunden der Saskatchewan Airlines
- Gesamtpreis: $200 plus $60 Zusatzversicherung minus $40 Rabatt = $220
- Zahlung per Kreditkarte erwünscht unter Angabe der Kreditkartennummer und des Verfallsdatums sowie der Adresse des Kunden

B Meetings, conferences and fairs

1 Making an appointment

Melanie Schmiedel's boss Udo Moersen is to go to Manchester for one day to discuss the integration of the German company into the group and the new product range with Kirsty Burnham. He asks his PA to arrange a day to fit in with Ms Burnham's agenda. He would arrive about 9.30 and stay till 2.45. He would prefer Wednesday.

Melanie Schmiedel has Herr Moersen's diary in front of her and rings Jackie Rowland, who likewise refers to Ms Burnham's diary. They try to decide which day it would be possible to meet. Kirsty Burnham would like to invite Udo Moersen out to a pub for a working lunch, if he would like that.

1 Sit back to back with your partner (Role card B) and act out the dialogue between them in which they arrange an appointment in Manchester and cover the other points mentioned.

Phrases

Role card: Partner A

Role card partner B ⇨ page 229

Terminkalender von Udo Moersen

Montag **13. Juni**
9 Uhr: Treffen mit Lieferanten Pauli & Co;
11.30 Ad.Slot Internetwerbung Frau Franzen

Dienstag **14. Juni**
Einzelhändler im Großraum München ab 9 Uhr bis ca 15.30 Uhr

Mittwoch **15. Juni**

Donnerstag 16. Juni
Geburtstag meiner Frau, 20.00 Uhr Tisch bei Da Pino reserviert

Freitag 17. Juni
11 Uhr: Besprechung der Produktplanung mit Xaver;
13–14 Uhr Mitarbeiterbesprechung

Communicating across cultures: Tips for visitors to the UK

Trains:
There are no supplementary charges for faster trains in Britain (the Eurostar to Brussels and Paris is more expensive!). Trains that stop at many stations are obviously slower than those that rarely stop. How often and where they stop is given on the indicator and timetables. It is very important to make sure that the train stops where you want to get off! Do not assume that all trains will stop at the same station on your return journey. Each train may stop at a different selection of stations.

Pubs:
Pubs are an important institution in Britain and are a popular venue at lunchtime for an informal meal. Many provide food at lunchtime, less often in the evening. As a rule there is no waiter service. You go to the bar to buy drinks where turn-taking is observed although there is no visible queue. If the pub is crowded it may be a good idea to discreetly wave a 10 pound note to let the barman / barmaid know you are waiting. Often English people buy rounds, saying things like “What’s yours?” or “What are you having?”.

Everybody is in principle expected to buy a round. If you don't, there may be an embarrassed silence. Food is also ordered and paid for at the bar and is brought to the table where you are sitting. All drinks and food are paid for straight away.

Tipping (taxis and restaurants):
In Germany you frequently tip by rounding up the amount of the bill. If the taxi fare is Euro 8.10 you might say Euro 8.50 or Euro 9.00. In Britain a taxi driver would not know what you meant. If the fare is £5.30 you could give the driver a £10 pound note and say "please give me change for £6". In restaurants the bill is generally brought on a little tray. You put enough money on the tray to pay the bill. The waiter returns, takes the tray away and comes back again with your change on the tray. You then decide what to put on the tray as a tip. It does not have to be a percentage of the bill.

2 KMK **Ihr Chef muss geschäftlich zum ersten Mal nach England. Geben Sie ihm einige Tipps. Fassen Sie dazu die Informationen in der Box (Communicating across cultures) zusammen.**

2 Preparing the agenda

1 KMK **Übertragen Sie die Agenda ins Deutsche.**

Melanie Schmiedel has now received the draft agenda of the conference in Munich on 6 and 7 September as drawn up by her boss.

Agenda

1. Welcoming guests
2. Minutes of the last conference in Boston, USA
3. Report on the Munich company and its integration in the group by Xaver Ertl
4. Presentation by Kirsty Burnham on the development of Global Catering's sales
5. Report by Kevin Sears on the development of Global Catering's European business
6. Consumer health concerns – from obesity to organic food – recent market research presented by Jeanne-Anne Taylor
7. Presentation on the role of international trade fairs in Global Catering's marketing strategy by Udo Moersen
8. Other business

2 P **In your role as Melanie Schmiedel send an e-mail to Jackie Rowland at Global Catering UK and Naomi Rodgers at Global Catering USA enclosing the above draft agenda as an attachment, requesting notification of any additions or modifications in the course of the following week.** Phrases

3 Preparing a meeting

Read the following text and make a list of the most important points.

R

As PA to Udo Moersen Melanie Schmiedel has been asked to assist at the conference in Munich.

This involves supervising the preparation of the room, making sure that there is an adequate supply of tea, coffee, soft drinks and mineral water (sparkling and still) available

Any equipment required such as a computer projector, whiteboard or flip chart with a supply of board markers must be available and in working order.

Her boss may require files, additional information, or he may need to make telephone calls etc.

She must be on hand to provide any assistance necessary. Some of the German executives' English leaves much to be desired and so she may be asked to interpret or translate.

V2 Video Lounge Hospitality

BBC Motion Gallery

This video deals with the hotel and catering trade.
Keep the following questions in mind while watching the video:

1. Does Judith like her job? What are the disadvantages?
2. What problem does the sector face that is highlighted several times in the course of the video?
3. What – mentioned towards the end of the video – is the sector doing to solve this problem?
4. What is Wayne Spencer's job title? Describe his appearance.
5. What particular skills do people working in this industry require?

Discuss your answers with the class.

4 Taking the minutes

* M **Translate fhe first three paragraphs of the following text.**

The minutes

It is important for an accurate written record of the transactions of a meeting or conference to be kept. It is essential for those involved to be able to refer back to the minutes and see what was said and, in particular, what was agreed. The minutes are evidence in law of the proceedings of the meeting.

The names of those present and any apologies for non-attendance must be recorded. In this case there are the six executives with Udo Moersen acting as chairman or chair and a number of other employees of the Munich company and finally, Melanie Schmiedel.

Especially in a discussion it is difficult to keep a word for word account of what is being said. The person taking the minutes may be able to note down only the most important points. It is particularly important that any figures or dates should be recorded accurately.

The minutes have to be presented to those present at a later date for approval or corrections.

Melanie Schmiedel has also been asked to take the minutes. As most of the topics on the agenda are presentations which will be available in written form her minute-taking will be largely restricted to the questions and answers following the presentations.

5 Booking an exhibition stand

Melanie now has to ring the exhibition authorities in Madrid to check that their order for a stand is OK. After checking her records she sees that she returned the application about two months ago.

Melanie Schmiedel:	Good morning. Melanie Schmiedel from Global Catering in Munich speaking. I'm afraid I don't speak Spanish. Do you speak English or German?
Exhibition authorities:	I do speak English. What can I do for you? By the way my name's Rosa de la Fuente.
Melanie Schmiedel:	I'd like to check our stand reservation for the International Food Fair. I sent off the application form two months ago but I have not received confirmation yet.
Rosa de la Fuente:	Just a second. Let me check my monitor. Yes, here it is. Global Catering. A corner stand, $25m^2$, with kitchenette and conference area. Is that OK?
Melanie Schmiedel:	Excellent. When will you be sending out the confirmations?
Rosa de la Fuente:	In a couple of weeks at the latest, I should think. But you can assume that everything's OK.
Melanie Schmiedel:	We shall need an interpreter with English and German. Can you recommend anyone?
Rosa de la Fuente:	I would get in touch with the Multilingua Agencia by e-mail under multilinguaservices@aol.com or send them a fax. The telephone number is 0034 91 4022468 and the fax number is the same with a 9 at the end instead of the 8. I'm sure they'll be able to recommend someone suitable.
Melanie Schmiedel:	Brilliant. I'll get in touch with them right away. Thank you very much. Goodbye.
Rosa de la Fuente	Thank you for ringing. Bye.

1 R **Lesen Sie den Dialog, decken Sie den Text dann ab und drücken Sie Folgendes auf Englisch aus.**

1. Sie sprechen kein Spanisch.
2. Sie möchten die Standreservierung überprüfen.
3. Sie haben einen Eckstand von $25\,m^2$ mit Teeküche und Besprechungsraum gebucht.
4. Sie wollen wissen, wann die Bestätigungen herausgeschickt werden.
5. Sie brauchen eine Dolmetscherin für Englisch und Deutsch.

2 Write a fax as Melanie Schmiedel to the Multilingua Agencia (see page 83) giving details of your requirements. Set out your fax as in the form below.
P

TELEFAX TRANSMISSION
Global Catering München GmbH

Nymphenburger Allee 93
80335 München
Tel.: (0049) (0)89277183
Fax: (0049) (0)89277190

To:
From:
Date:
Subject:

Attention:
Fax: (0034) (91)4022469
Pages (incl. this one):

Language and grammar
Translate the following sentences.

1. Als Anhang senden wir Ihnen unsere neueste Preisliste.
2. Gestern habe ich von 13:00 Uhr bis 16:30 Uhr auf Ihren Anruf gewartet.
3. Pro Woche versenden wir zwischen 20 und 30 Angebote.
4. Wir investieren regelmäßig 5 % unseres Gewinns in neue Technologien.
5. Leider warten wir noch immer auf Ihre Überweisung.
6. Zur Zeit versuchen unsere Mitbewerber eine Firma in USA zu übernehmen.
7. Wegen des Booms in China steigen die Stahlpreise weltweit.
8. Er organisiert die Konferenz, die nächste Woche stattfindet, und wir buchen die Hotelzimmer.

Language and grammar: Continuous form (Verlaufsform)

Die Verlaufsform (he is writing an e-mail) dient zur Beschreibung einer gerade vor sich gehenden Handlung sowie einer allmählichen Entwicklung, häufig markiert durch **now, just, still, when, while, since, for** etc.	Our competitors **are trying** to undercut our prices. They **are** still **waiting** for a reply. Prices **have been rising** in the last few months. We **are thinking** of buying a house.
Da die einfache Verbform (he writes 50 e-mails a day) ausdrückt, dass etwas immer so ist oder immer wieder geschieht, ist die Verwendung der Verlaufsform in bestimmten Fällen unerlässlich, um klar zu machen, dass etwas nur von vorübergehender Natur ist.	They **are having** problems with their suppliers (= at the present time). They **have** problems with their suppliers (= often / always). I **am living** with my parents at the moment (= but I'm looking for a flat of my own). I **live** in Dresden (= permanently).
Die Verlaufsform kann für feste Planungen und Abmachungen auch für die Zukunft benutzt werden.	He is giving a presentation at the conference. I am picking him up at the airport next Friday (= this has been arranged).

Phrases: Making arrangements

To book flights or trains

Please reserve a window/aisle seat **on** the 8.30 am flight to Munich.	Bitte reservieren Sie einen Platz am Fenster/Gang für den Flug um 8:30 Uhr nach München.
Are you travelling economy or business class?	Fliegen Sie Economy- oder Business-Class?
I would like to reserve a window seat on the 9.15 ICE train to Hamburg.	Ich möchte einen Fensterplatz des ICE um 9:15 Uhr nach Hamburg reservieren lassen.
Is that first or second class, one way or return?	Erster oder zweiter Klasse? Einfach oder hin und zurück?
Is there a supplementary charge for the InterCity to Edinburgh?	Muss für den Intercity nach Edinburgh ein Zuschlag bezahlt werden?
There is no supplementary charge.	Es wird kein Zuschlag erhoben.
You are booked **on** flight no ZY 652 **on** 23 March, departing London Gatwick **at** 7.30 am, arriving Munich 10.15 am.	Sie sind am 23. März für Flug Nr. ZY 652 gebucht, Abflug London Gatwick um 7:30 Uhr, Ankunft München 10:15 Uhr.
You should check in two hours before departure to allow **for** security.	Sie sollten wegen der Sicherheitsüberprüfung zwei Stunden vor Abflug einchecken.

To book hotel or conference rooms

We require a single/double room with **ensuite** bathroom.	Wir benötigen ein Einzel-/Doppelzimmer mit Bad.
I should like to book an executive suite for three nights **from** 3 **to** 6 March with Internet access.	Ich möchte eine Präsidentensuite mit Internetzugang für drei Nächte vom 3. bis 6. März buchen.
We require a conference room **to seat** 25–30 people.	Wir brauchen ein Besprechungszimmer für 25–30 Personen.
For our annual general meeting we need an assembly hall **of** at least 500 square metres equipped with a stage and a big screen.	Für unsere Jahreshauptversammlung brauchen wir einen Versammlungssaal von mindestens 500 Quadratmetern mit Bühne und Großbildschirm.
I should be grateful if you could confirm the booking **in** writing/**by** e-mail/**by** fax.	Wir wären für eine Bestätigung der Buchung per Brief/E-Mail/Fax dankbar.
Is it possible to order a buffet lunch?	Besteht die Möglichkeit ein Mittagsbuffet zu bestellen?
We regret that we have to cancel the reservation. We realise that it is very short notice.	Wir bedauern, diese Reservierung stornieren zu müssen. Wir sind uns dessen bewusst, dass dies sehr kurzfristig geschieht.

To make appointments

I'm afraid I'm engaged all day on Wednesday.	Leider bin ich am Mittwoch den ganzen Tag besetzt.
Friday would suit me fine.	Freitag würde mir gut passen.
I'd prefer Thursday morning.	Donnerstag Morgen wäre mir lieber.
It's Monday **at** 11, then.	Also bleibt es bei Montag um 11 Uhr.
Could we meet **on** Monday 17 at 10 am?	Könnten wir uns am Montag, den 17. um 10 Uhr vormittags treffen?
– Certainly. Monday at 10 am is fine.	– Ja, sicher. Montag 10 Uhr ist o.k.
Would Tuesday suit you?	Würde Ihnen Dienstag passen?
– Not so good. My diary's full, I'm afraid. Wednesday would be better.	– Eigentlich nicht. Mein Terminkalender ist leider voll. Mittwoch wäre besser.
I'm free all day Wednesday.	Am Mittwoch geht es den ganzen Tag.

To prepare the agenda

A draft agenda has already been drawn up.	Ein Entwurf für die Tagesordnung ist bereits erstellt worden.
Notification of any additions or changes is requested within a week.	Es wird gebeten, eventuelle Zusätze oder Änderungen innerhalb einer Woche anzugeben.

To prepare and assist at a meeting

He/She is chairing the meeting.	Er/Sie leitet die Sitzung.
He is the chairman, he/She is the chairperson.	Er/Sie ist der/die Vorsitzende.
Perhaps you could each introduce **yourself** briefly indicating your role in the company.	Vielleicht könnten Sie sich kurz vorstellen und dabei auf Ihre Stellung in der Firma eingehen.
Has everyone got a copy of the agenda?	Haben alle eine Kopie der Tagesordnung bekommen?
We shall adjourn **for** lunch **at** …	Um … unterbrechen wir für das Mittagessen.
Lunch will be provided by our own caterers.	Unser eigener Versorgungsbetrieb wird das Mittagessen liefern.
Are there any further comments?	Gibt es noch Wortmeldungen?
Shall we take a vote?	Sollen wir nun abstimmen?
The proposal is accepted.	Damit ist der Vorschlag angenommen.

To book an exhibition stand

We are interested in displaying our products **at** the Madrid Motor Show.	Wir sind daran interessiert, unsere Produkte auf der Automobilmesse in Madrid auszustellen.
Our company wishes to reserve floor space for a stand **covering** 8 x 15 metres.	Unsere Firma möchte die für einen Stand von 8 x 15 Metern benötigte Ausstellungsfläche reservieren lassen.
We are interested in introducing our software solutions at this years's Computer Fair and would like to ask you to send us your information package with application forms.	Wir sind daran interessiert, unsere Software-Lösungen bei der diesjährigen Computermesse vorzustellen und möchten Sie bitten, uns Ihre Messe-Information mit Anmeldeformularen zu schicken.
We wish to book a stand in the main exhibition hall.	Wir möchten einen Stand in der Hauptausstellungshalle buchen.

To organise the necessary equipment

Our stand must have internet access and it must be equipped with telephone lines.	Unser Stand muss Internetzugang haben und er muss mit Telefonleitungen ausgestattet sein.
First-class catering services will also be required.	Wir benötigen ebenfalls erstklassigen Catering-Service.

To write invitations

The chairman will be pleased to welcome you **at** our annual dinner **at** the Park Hotel.	Der Vorsitzende gibt sich die Ehre, Sie zu unserem alljährlichen festlichen Abendessen im Park Hotel begrüßen.
The reception will be held in our main hall **between** 10 am **and** 3 pm.	Der Empfang findet zwischen 10 und 15 Uhr in unserer Haupthalle statt.

To have a stand built and dismantled

Are you in a position to design an eye-catching stand for us and erect it before 15 March?	Sind Sie in der Lage, für uns einen ins Auge fallenden Stand zu entwerfen und vor dem 15. März aufzubauen?
Can you help us remove the heavy exhibits and dismantle the stand?	Können Sie uns dabei helfen, die schweren Ausstellungsstücke zu entfernen und den Stand abzubauen?

UNIT 7
Making presentations

WORD BANK

presentation • audience • delivery • content • prompt cards • key words • points • introduction • main body • conclusion • visual aids • eye-contact • body language • handout • to prepare • to rehearse • to deliver • statistics • developments • degree • percentage • comparisons • rankings • graphs • diagrams • bar chart • line graph • pie chart • to visualise • to describe • to rise • to fall • to remain unchanged • to fluctuate • to account for • slight • steady • dramatic

You may be required to present your company and its products – either informally or on a more formal level. This may range from the introduction of a specific product or products to presenting the company as a whole. Although many may feel a bit scared of standing up before an audience, the ability to make good oral presentations is a key skill. However, it is a skill that can be acquired and improved by practice. It is important, above all, to remember that the style and manner of delivery is as important as the content.

Translate the following sentences into German.

M

1. You may feel scared of standing up before an audience.
2. Making a good oral presentation is a key skill.
3. This skill can be acquired and improved.
4. Style of delivery is as important as content.
5. You may be required to make a presentation on your company and its products.

Online-Link
808260-0007

A Preparing a presentation

You have been asked to give a presentation of your company and its products. The presentation will be brief. You have a maximum of 5 minutes at your disposal. The following hints should help you to prepare.

Start by deciding what you want to include and what your objectives are. Remember that there are limits to the number of facts your audience can absorb. The following are intended as helpful hints:

How to make a presentation

- Do not write out your presentation in full. Use numbered prompt cards with key words. They are the best way to avoid forgetting important points.
- Your presentation should have an introduction, main body and conclusion.
- First give a brief overview of points to be covered.
- Divide up the main body according to the number of important points.
- Finish with a conclusion.

Use expressions like:

"I should like to start / begin by …"

"Another important factor is ..."

"In conclusion …"

"I should like to conclude by saying …"

"First, I should like to…"

"Next, I'd like to tell you something about …"

"This brings me to my third point …"

in order to signal the different sections of your presentation.

Reinforce what you say by **visual aids**, such as powerpoint slides. Visual aids help you to explain complicated ideas more easily and arouse and hold the interest of your audience and make your presentation look more professional. If you print them out they may double as a handout.

Visual aids may take the form of slides or computer files showing graphs, pictures, flowcharts, brief statements / cues (e.g. the key words from your prompt cards). Here are a few helpful hints:

- Limit the text to six or seven lines.
- Use no more than six or seven words per line.
- Print the text in large letters, using upper and lower case letters.
- Use dark colours, such as black, blue or green.

1 KMK **Fassen Sie den Text über die Vorbereitung einer Präsentation unter Beantwortung folgender Fragen auf Deutsch zusammen.**

1. Warum soll eine Präsentation nicht schriftlich ausformuliert werden?
2. Wie soll eine Präsentation gegliedert sein?
3. Welche Vorteile bietet Anschauungsmaterial?
4. Wie müssen Folien aussehen, damit sie wirken?

2 R A1.21 **Now listen to a presentation by Udo Moersen from the German subsidiary of Global Catering and complete the following text.**

Good morning, ladies and gentlemen. [1] a few words about our company. Since last January we have been a part of Global Catering Manchester but we are an old-established Munich company producing a range of Bavarian specialities.

We have now entered the rapidly growing market for convenience foods, [2] a range of freshly prepared dishes to quality supermarkets and delicatessens and [3] the catering for company board meetings, conferences etc.

In Munich and internationally [4] of young business people (male and female) who do not have the leisure to cook but who still demand high-quality, imaginative, prepared meals which they can quickly pop into their briefcases on their way home.

Our sales figures show that this is a growth market (I don't want to bore you [5] which I hope you have all received). We are also exporting Bavarian specialities to Britain and the USA via Global Catering and its subsidiaries. At the same time we are importing British and American specialities to Germany.

[6] that we look forward to rapid growth in these markets. Catering is a modern industry with massive potential whose importance is still underestimated in Germany [7].

3 R A1.21 **Udo Moersen used the following prompt cards for his presentation. Listen again and restore the correct order of his jumbled prompt cards.**

① conclusion:
growth industry

② part of Global
Catering but old
Munich company.
Bavarian specialities!

③ target group:
busy young
professionals

④ supermarkets/
delicatessens/
corporate catering

⑤ sales figures (see
handout!) exports
to USA/UK; imports

4 P **Having studied the above information, hints and examples now start preparing your presentation of your company and its products. Write your prompt cards and decide which visual aids you are going to use.**

Content of your presentation:
- size, type, location, activities of company
- products in general, selection of products, services
- main markets, domestic/export
- sales figures
- special features of products e.g. state-of-the-art, environmentally friendly

5 **As your British boss frequently has to give presentations at changing venues, she has asked you to find information on the latest computer projectors. She is especially interested in lightweight compact models that are easy to carry and cost under $500. Use the internet to find this information and make notes for her in English.**

B Delivering a presentation

Useful tips

It is a good idea NOT to read out a prepared text. It is easy to bore your audience. You make a much more lively impression if you speak freely using prompt cards and visual aids to remind you of the various points. This also helps to ensure that your body language is natural. If you are planning to use equipment such as an interactive whiteboard or a computer projector, make sure a) they are working and b) you know how to operate them. Practise and rehearse your presentation, preferably with real people as an audience.

- Do not speak too quickly (in order to get the whole thing over as quickly as possible!)
- Speak clearly – make sure everybody can hear you.
- Do not speak monotonously – you will sound as if you are boring yourself and will bore your audience!
- Do not wave your arms around mechanically – your gestures should be appropriate.
- Look at your audience, establish eye contact.
- Look happy and confident. Smile.

It is very helpful for the person making the presentation to be given constructive, concrete and detailed feedback. Only in this way can they become aware of how they come across and how this can be changed. This is a prerequisite for developing skills in oral presentation.

1 KMK **Ein Kollege muss eine Präsentation halten und hat Sie um Rat gebeten. Schreiben Sie ihm eine E-Mail auf Deutsch und geben Sie ihm Hinweise für eine Präsentation unter Verwendung der Informationen in „Useful tips".**

*** 2** P/I **Now give your presentation on your company and its products to your fellow students. The other students listen to the presentation and assess it according to the following evaluation scheme. The audience should award points out of ten under each heading (on a separate sheet of paper).**

Evaluation of presentation / checklist:

		Points
Preparation	evidence of careful preparation	▪
Structure	introduction, main body – clear emphasis on small number of important points – conclusion	▪
Content	relevance, well-substantiated with facts and figures	▪
Visual aids	appropriate use of simple, easy-to-understand visual aids	▪
Delivery	not too fast, eye contact, appropriate body language, confident, relaxed	▪
Language	no jargon, straightforward, use of signalling expressions like: "I should like to begin / conclude by …"	▪
Overall impression	lively, humorous, easy to follow, right length	▪

*** 3** R **The following is an example of a more ambitious presentation using visual aids. At an investment seminar Daniela Webb gives a brief presentation on the Limpopo Mining Company and its products, using a computer projector. Make a list of expressions that would be useful in any presentation.**

"Good morning, ladies and gentlemen. I should like to give a brief presentation on our company and its products in the context of this investment seminar.

I'll begin by showing you a graph illustrating the rising demand for zinc and copper worldwide and the development of production at our sites in Asia and Africa. As a result of the strength of the world economy and particularly rapid growth in China and India demand for our products has soared dramatically over the last two years.

At the same time we are investing strongly in the development of our sites. This is a photograph of construction work on our new site in Kazakhstan. As you can see from this graph, production there jumped by 20% last year. We are also spending a large slice of our profits on exploration.
The pie chart shows what proportion of our expenditure goes on the construction and development of sites and the exploration of new sites.

In conclusion, I should like to emphasise that demand for our products is expected to be strong in the foreseeable future. I am sure that this brief presentation will have shown you that Limpopo Mining shares will add some excitement to your investment portfolio.

Thank you very much indeed for your time. I shall be very pleased to answer any questions you may have."

Language and grammar: Describing graphs and diagrams

Statistics are easier to read if they are presented in the form of bar charts, line graphs or pie charts. When making a presentation, you may have to describe graphs. The expressions given on the following pages will be helpful.

1 Developments over time can be visualised by **line graphs**

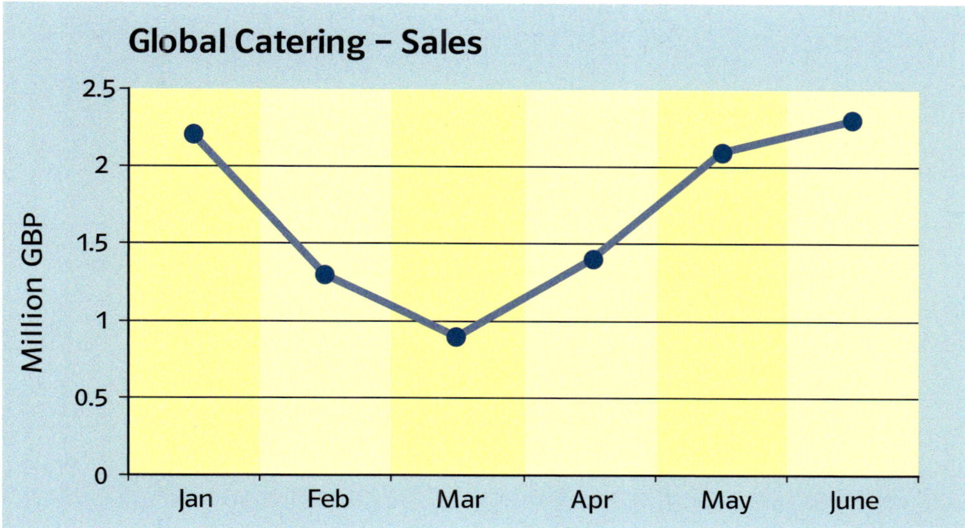

V3 Video Lounge Presentations

lingua tv

This video shows a presentation given by a senior Purple Fashion executive. After watching it answer the following questions:

1. Does the presenter make a natural impression?
2. Do you find her gestures and smile convincing?
3. Why is it not necessary to take notes?
4. When does she plan to answer questions?
5. When and where was Purple Fashion founded?
6. Is this her actual presentation?
7. What in her view is Purple Fashion's "obsession"?

To describe developments

1. upwards to rise / increase / go up / jump **by ... from ... to ...** to reach a peak / maximum of ...	Between May and July exports rose by 5% from 10,000 units to 10,050 units. In June prices reached a peak of €75.	↑
2. unchanged to remain / stay unchanged / stable / flat **at ...** to fluctuate **between ... and ...**	Sales remained unchanged at 750m units. In the second quarter oil prices fluctuated between 42 and 61 dollars per barrel.	→
3. downwards to fall / decline / go down / drop / slump **by ... from ... to ...** to reach a low / minimum **of ...** / the lowest point **at ...**	Last year the average price dropped by 2% from € 100 to €98. In March the lowest point was reached at 28 dollars.	↓

At a meeting Kirsty Burnham from Global Catering in Manchester presents her company to a gathering of potential customers. She refers to the last half year's sales and to the line graph on the preceding page.

1 Read her description and find the correct prepositions from the box.

at • by • from • of • of • to • to • to

In January sales stood **1** 2.2 million pounds. Then there was a dramatic decline **2** GBP 1.3m in February. Sales continued to fall steadily and reached the minimum **3** 0.9m in March. Between March and May, however, sales jumped **4** 0.9m **6** 2.1m. In June sales had risen **7** around 9% **6** the peak **8** 2.3 million pounds.

2 Choose the correct adjective or adverb. See *Language and grammar* in Unit 9.

1. In January imports fell (sharp/sharply).
2. Sales remained (constant/constantly) for three months.
3. A (slight/slightly) increase in prices had been expected.
4. There was a (gradual/gradually) fall in turnover.
5. Oil prices have been rising (dramatic/dramatically).

To describe the speed or degree of change

slight(ly)
slow(ly)
moderate(ly)
gradual(ly)
steady / steadily
significant(ly)
sharp(ly)
dramatic(ally)

In the second quarter there was a **dramatic** increase in sales. In June imports rose **sharply**.

2 Comparisons and rankings are visualised by means of bar charts

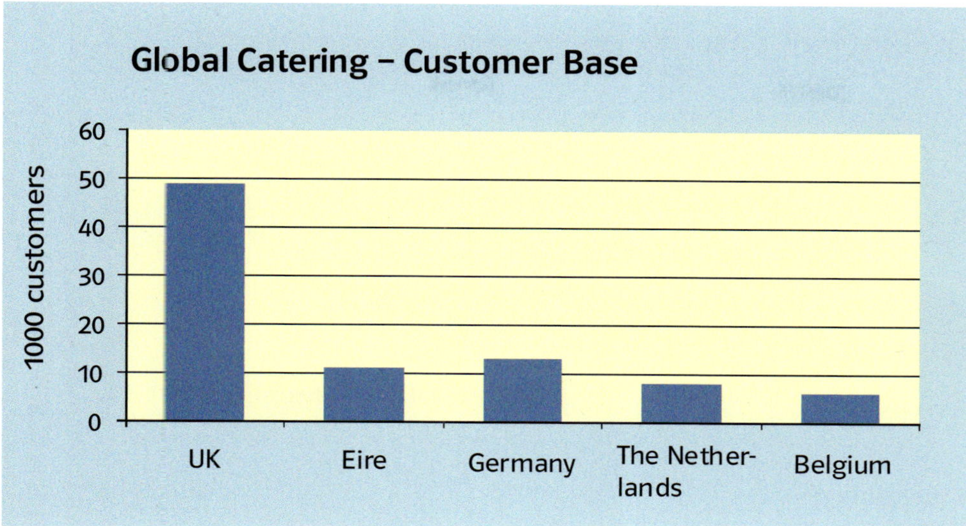

To describe comparisons and rankings

to be higher/lower/bigger/smaller/more/less expensive **than** …	Petrol prices in Germany are higher than in Austria.
to be **as** high/low/expensive **as** …	French cars are just as expensive as German cars.
to be the biggest/lowest/most expensive **of** …	This is the most expensive model of all.
to be/come first/second/last **with**	Spain comes first with 45 million tourists.
to be/follow **in** first/fifth/last place	Norway is in fourth place behind France and the UK.
to be followed **by** …	Sweden is followed by Denmark which exports 56 % of its production.
to be **at** the bottom/top/of the list/table	Germany is at the bottom of the table with just 17%.

At the same meeting Kirsty Burnham presents the above bar chart indicating the company's customer base.

Study the bar chart above and her description below and complete the description as appropriate.

Naturally most of our **1** are based in the UK, close to 50,000. Our next biggest **2** is Germany, where we have approx. 13,000 customers, closely **3** by The Irish Republic with more **4** 10,000 customers. The Netherlands and Belgium are **5** fourth and fifth place **6** around 8,000 and 6,000 customers, respectively.

3 Shares and percentages can be visualised with the help of pie charts

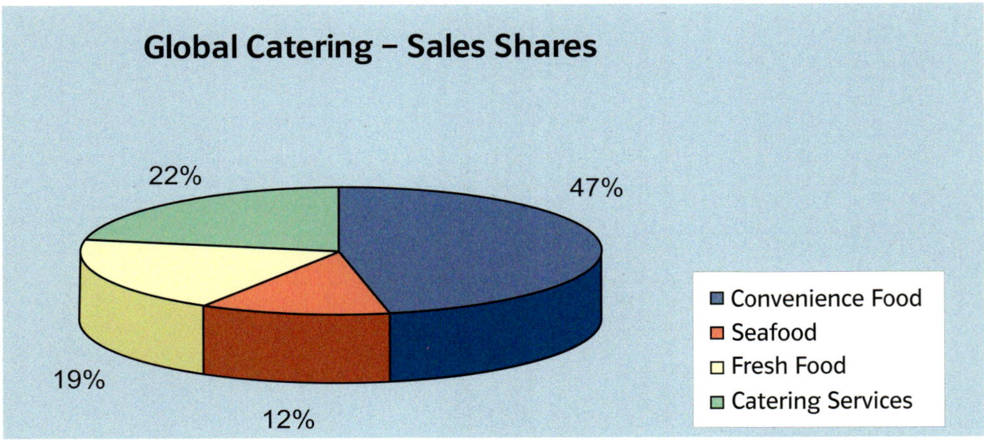

To describe shares (percentages)

to make **up** …/to account **for** …	Nail varnish makes up 20% and lipsticks account for half of the total.
to have a share/percentage/slice **of** …	Hairspray has a share of only 10 per cent.

1 P Write down what Kirsty Burnham might say to describe the above pie chart on Global Catering's sales shares.

* **2** Two years ago your company installed solar panels on the roof of an office building. As a number of your business partners are interested in this project, you are preparing a presentation in English for them. Describe the monthly electricity output in kWh generated by the solar panels in the first year. Note that in that year April was particularly sunny and July exceptionally wet.

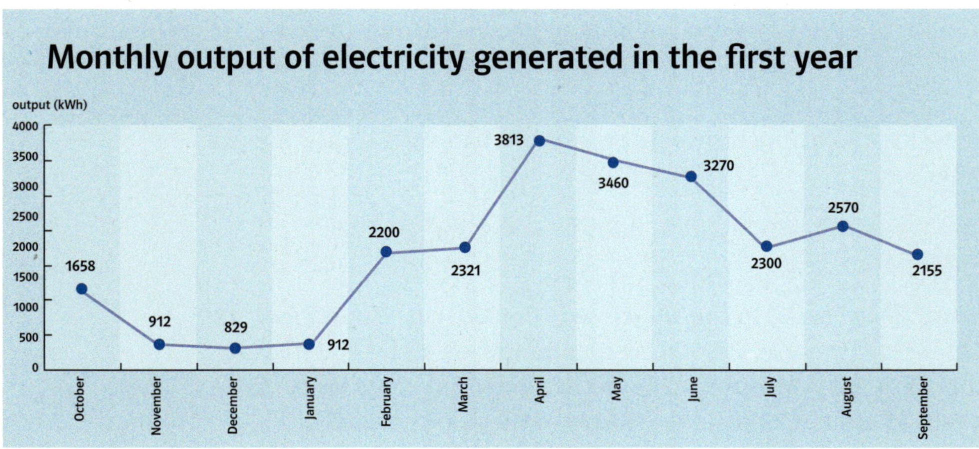

Phrases: Making presentations

To make a presentation

I should like to start **by** telling you something about my company/organisation.	Zunächst möchte ich Ihnen etwas über meine Firma/mein Unternehmen sagen.
First, I should like to introduce my company briefly.	Als Erstes möchte ich Ihnen mein Unternehmen kurz vorstellen.
My presentation will deal **with** …	Meine Präsentation behandelt …
I intend to keep my presentation as brief as possible.	Ich möchte meine Präsentation so kurz wie möglich halten.
I would like to focus **on** the following points/areas/products/services:	Ich möchte mich auf folgende Punkte/Gebiete/Produkte/Dienstleistungen konzentrieren:
I would welcome any questions **at** the end of my presentation.	Ich wäre gern bereit, etwaige Fragen am Ende meiner Präsentation zu beantworten.
Has everyone received a copy of the handout?	Haben alle den Handzettel bekommen?
The handout summarises the main points and gives an overview of the relevant figures and statistics.	Der Handzettel enthält die Hauptpunkte und gibt einen Überblick über die entsprechenden Zahlen und Statistiken.

To structure the main part of your presentation

Now my second point is …	Ich komme nun zu Punkt 2 …
Thirdly, let me give you some basic statistics.	Drittens darf ich Ihnen ein paar grundlegende Statistiken zeigen.
The gist of the matter/central issue is …	Der Kernpunkt/die zentrale Frage ist …
I should now like to move **on** to the next topic.	Ich möchte nun gern zum nächsten Thema kommen.
An excellent example **of** this is …	Ein hervorragendes Beispiel dafür ist …
I should like to give you an example to illustrate this point.	Ich möchte diesen Punkt mit einem Beispiel erläutern.
A distinct trend emerges **from** the figures.	Aus den Zahlen geht ein deutlicher Trend hervor.
In this connection it is worth mentioning …	In diesem Zusammenhang sollte man erwähnen, …

To conclude your presentation

To sum **up** we can say that …	Zusammenfassend kann man sagen, dass …
I should like to finish **by** saying/thanking the organisers/pointing out …	Ich möchte schließen mit der Bemerkung/dem Dank an die Organisatoren/dem Hinweis …

Unit 8
Form of written communication

WORD BANK

e-mail • facsimile message • letter • sender • letterhead • addressee • recipient • attention line • reference line • date • attachment • subject • salutation • initials • complimentary close • signature • covering page • enclosure • structure • paragraph • style • linking words • to attach • to delete • to forward

Written communication plays an essential role in business in cases where documentation in writing is required. It may, for instance, also be used to ensure that misunderstandings cannot arise. However, in recent years the traditional letter has increasingly been replaced by new, quicker and frequently less formal media. In business correspondence the letter has now largely been replaced by e-mails and to a lesser degree by faxes.

1 **Work with a partner. Make a grid for yourself like the one below. Then read the text that follows**
R **and fill in your grid. Compare the result with your partner's information in the grid.**

	Advantages	Disadvantages
E-mail		
Letter		
Fax		

Online-Link
808260-0008

The advantages of **e-mails** are too well-known to require explanation here. However, there are a number of disadvantages. Spam is a major time waster. According to one source 95% of e-mails sent worldwide are spam. Hence the need to install spam filters. Security is also a major issue. E-mails and attachments may be used to transfer spyware and other viruses. Privacy is also a problem – you cannot be sure that your e-mails are not being read by an unauthorised third party. Finally, authenticity – who is the e-mail really from? – is a further issue undermining the reliability and safety of e-mails which can be addressed by installing digital signatures. Sometimes one might feel it's safer to entrust one's important message to the old-fashioned snail-mail!

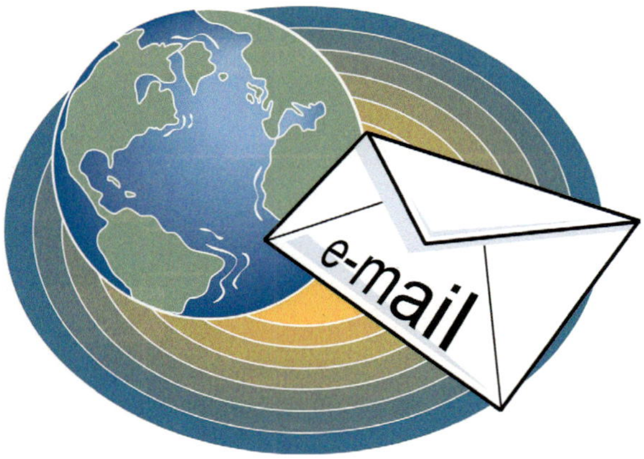

In international business transactions **faxes** are used to communicate with partners in countries where the e-mail system is still unsatisfactory or unreliable. Faxes are also preferred to e-mails whenever business people want their partners to have some written (and possibly signed) evidence of a transaction. Faxes, like e-mails, may also be used where speed is essential, e.g. for offers. Signatures on faxes are nowadays recognised as evidence even by the courts.

The business **letter** is still widely used in legal contexts, in connection with formal contracts and complaints. Such letters are often "faxed and posted", i.e. sent by fax and by post. Only a letter ensures that the communication is not read by an unauthorised person. Letters also serve as covering letters when a catalogue or similar enclosure is to be sent.

* 2 Translate the following English sentences into German.

M

1. Letters have largely been replaced by e-mails.
2. E-mails can be addressed to several people at the same time.
3. Worms and viruses may make it necessary to instal protective software.
4. It is a disadvantage that e-mails cannot easily be signed.
5. In some countries the e-mail system is unsatisfactory or unreliable.
6. It may sometimes be necessary to have written evidence of a transaction.
7. Business letters are still widely used in connection with formal contracts.
8. A letter is less likely to be read by unauthorised persons.

A Layout and components of business correspondence

1 E-mails*

From:	stella.starr@shineandsparkle-uk.com
To:	info@sunshineflights.co.uk
Cc:	f.pluto@shineandsparkle-usa.com
Sent:	201_-08-14 15:18
Attachments:	
Subject:	Package tours to the Dominican Republic

Dear Sunshine Flights — salutation

As an incentive we wish to offer a one-week package tour to the Dominican Republic to our most successful sales representatives. Please make us preliminary offers for at least three price categories. — body of e-mail

Kind regards — complimentary close

Stella Starr (Miss)
Marketing Manager — signature block

Shine and Sparkle UK Ltd.
143 High Street
Starminster
BS34 1BU
Tel. 01420 562 265 — signature footer

* Both ways of spelling are acceptable, **e-mail** and **email**.

Info: E-mails

From:	Your e-mail address will appear automatically.
To:	Be careful not to make the slightest mistake when entering the recipient's address, or else the e-mail will be returned.
Cc:	The abbreviation stands for "carbon copy". With old-style typewriters copies used to be made by inserting carbon paper between the blank sheets of paper. This is where you enter the addresses of the persons to whom you wish the message to be forwarded.
Bcc:	Addresses listed under "Blind Carbon Copy" do not appear in the message header of the other recipients.
Sent:	Instead of "Sent" you may find the word "Date". The correct date and time will be entered automatically.
Attachments:	Any kind of file, such as word documents (.doc), excel sheets (.xls), pictures (e.g. .jpg), etc. can be attached to an e-mail.
Subject:	You should always mention the precise subject matter of your correspondence. Firstly it will help your business partner to deal with your mail and secondly it will prevent him / her from deleting it for fear of viruses.
Salutation:	Very formal salutations like "Dear Sirs" or "Gentlemen:" are not used in e-mails. Use "Dear …" instead. In the English-speaking world correspondence is personalised whenever possible: Dear Fiona Dear Ms Starr or even (to avoid "Dear Sirs"): Dear Sunshine Flights
Body of the e-mail:	Note that the first word starts with a capital letter.
Complimentary close:	There is a range of expressions to choose from, like: With best / kind regards Kind / Best regards Regards Best wishes or (very formal in e-mails) Yours sincerely
Signature block:	Write your title or department below your name. In Britain women often add (Miss) or (Mrs) in brackets after their name, e.g. Janine Smith (Miss), if they wish to be addressed in this way.
Signature footer:	Add your company's full name, address and telephone number to all e-mails you send to persons or companies who may not know you or your firm. The signature footer is usually added automatically.

Do not use special characters like ß, ä, ö or ü. They may come out very strangely at the other end! Use ss, ae, oe and ue instead.

1 Choose the appropriate alternative from the brackets.

1. You may (enclose/attach) files to an e-mail.
2. You should always watch out for (viruses/germs).
3. Make sure that you (wipe out/delete) suspicious e-mails.
4. E-mails can be (passed on/forwarded) to third parties.
5. Do not forget to mention the (theme/subject) of your e-mail.
6. E-mails always start with the (complimentary close/salutation).
7. The recipient or (addressee/sender) is the person the e-mail is sent to.

2 Study the example e-mail on page 100. Then restore the correct order of the jumbled elements below and rewrite the e-mail.

(1) **Sent:** 201_-11-09

(2) **Cc:** walter-elliot@kellynchhall.ie

(3) Thank you.
Kind regards
Nancy

(4) **From:** nancy.steele@jenningsfood.com

(5) Jennings Food Ltd.
Delaford Industrial Estate
Barton
GU7 3AB
Tel. 01430 37968

(6) Sorry to inform you that the 150 picnic hampers as per yesterday's order have not yet arrived. Please make sure that we get them by tomorrow 11 a.m. at the very latest.

(7) Dear Kitty

(8) **To:** k.bennet@longbourne.co.uk

(9) **Subject:** Late delivery

3 Search the Internet and find out about "netiquette" and "texting abbreviations". Make notes and compare your findings with the group. Send a text message in English using appropriate abbreviations to one of your classmates.

Info: How to write e-mails

- Keep messages short and to the point.
- Focus on one subject per message and include a relevant subject title for the message.
- Include your signature footer when communicating with persons who may not know you personally.
- Capitalize words only to highlight an important point. Capitalizing is generally felt to be like SHOUTING!
- Be sparing in your use of exclamation marks.
- Never send chain letters through the Internet.
- Be professional and be careful what you say. E-mails are easily forwarded.
- Be careful when using sarcasm and humour.
- Never assume that your e-mails will be read only by you and the recipient.
- Emoticons like :-) for "happy" or ;-) for "only joking" should be reserved for communication with business partners with whom you are on a familiar footing.
- Use abbreviations sparingly as you cannot be sure that your partner in a foreign country is familiar with them.

* **4** Your colleague does not speak English. Explain the above information to him in German.
M

You might begin like this:
„Ich habe im Internet interessante Hinweise über das, was man bei E-Mails beachten soll, gefunden. Der Text beginnt mit der Ermahnung E-Mails kurz und präzise zu formulieren. Man soll sich auf ein Thema pro Mail beschränken und einen passenden Betreff wählen …"

2 Faxes

There is no established layout for faxes (facsimile messages). Firms are free to design their own covering page. A typical one could look like this:

Herkules
the global sports brand

Ziegelberg 8–12
89331 Neustadt
Tel. +49 8358 888-0
Fax +49 8358 88820
www.Herkules.com

Telefax Message

To: India Sports
112 Delhi Road, Meerut-250 001
Uttar Pradesh, India

Attention: Mr. Kunal Mahajan

Fax: +91 121 2512275

From: Laura Bayerle, Purchasing Department

Date: 1 Feb 201_

Pages: (incl. this page) 1

Subject: Our order No. ABF/16 of 20 January

Dear Mr. Mahajan

If it is possible, we should like to increase our order for item 345 (plain navy T-shirts) from 1750 to 2000 units for the sizes L and XL.

Please let me know by return whether you are in a position to dispatch the extra articles together with the rest of our order.

Thank you very much.

Regards

Laura Bayerle

Laura Bayerle

If you do not receive all the pages, please advise us as soon as possible.

Info: Fax

The **names, addresses, telephone** and **fax numbers** of both the sender and the addressee should be recorded on the fax. The **date** is also essential as well as an appropriate **subject line**. As fax transmissions are sometimes interrupted, the **number of pages** is mentioned to show the recipient whether any pages are missing. If you send a business letter by fax, write the recipient's fax number below the inside address and refer to the total number of pages on the first page.

1 P **Use the fax on page 104 as an example and rewrite the following fax using the correct spacing and punctuation.**

Getränke König Am Sprudelbach 17 06122 Halle Tel. 0345 785634 Fax 0345 785635 Telefax To BIG Beverages Ltd 38 Cromwell Road Chipping OX7 5SR UK Fax +44 1608 647919 Attention Ms Maggy Lane From Nicole Sachse Import Department Date 31 Jan 201_ Pages incl. this one 1 Subject Our order for 500 bottles of Tropicana Fruit Juice of 28 Jan Dear Ms Lane I am sorry to cause you trouble but our client has just informed us that he needs the fruit juice as early as Friday next week I trust you will be able to bring forward delivery by three days Thank you for your co-operation Best wishes *Nicole Sachse* Nicole Sachse

2 R/P **Study the fax on page 104. Then restore the correct order of the jumbled elements below and rewrite the fax.**

Calendars 4 U
100 Dolphin Way
San Sebastian, CA 94901
Fax (408) 635-8574
Tel. (408) 635-8584
www.calendars4U.com **1**

From: Cyrus B. Reid **2**

Sincerely yours,
Cyrus B. Reid **3**

Date: January 17, 201_ **4**

Telefax **5**

Attention : Lester P. Klein **6**

Subject: International Sales Training Program **7**

To: MAT Management Training
268 Rolling Hills
Bearsdale, PA 19508
Fax (207) 873-9562 **8**

Pages: (incl. this page) 1 **9**

Dear Mr. Klein: **10**

Could you please fax me information about your international sales training program as advertised in the January issue of the Management Magazine. Thank you very much. **11**

3 Business letters

1 **Match the numbers (1–11) in the following business letter with the letters (A–K) in the definitions given on the following pages.**
R

International Snacks GmbH (1)

Fürstenstr. 19
40547 Düsseldorf
Tel. 0211 577563
Fax 0211 577566
E-Mail info@internationalsnacks.de
www.internationalsnacks.de

MD / rf (2)

14 August 201_ (3)

Global Catering (4)
17 Nelson Square
Manchester
MA17 3DF
UK

Attention: Ms Kirsty Burnham (5)

Dear Ms Burnham (6)

Brochure on rules and regulations (7)

As promised on the occasion of your recent visit to our company I am sending you enclosed the translation of the brochure on the German rules and regulations for food processing in the catering industry.

May I take this opportunity of thanking you and Mr. Sears for your visit.
My colleagues and I greatly enjoyed meeting you in person. (8)

Yours sincerely (9)
International Snacks GmbH (10)

Markus Diepholz

Markus Diepholz
Export Manager

Enc. (11)

A Letterhead shows a company's logo, name and address, its telephone, fax and e-mail numbers and its Internet address.

B Reference line may show the initials of the signatory and the secretary or references to files or departments.

C Date

As 07/08/12 would mean 7 August 2012 for an Englishman and 8 July 2012 for an American, it is advisable to write out the month. The following ways of writing the date are recommended:

7 August 2012 or 7 Aug 2012 or August 7, 2012

Note that the year is written out in full.

Giving the year first, then the month and then the day is rapidly becoming accepted worldwide: 2012-08-07.

D Inside address

British usage	North American usage
Messrs J. McDream & Co. 91 Malvern Road Ashford Kent CA3 6AH UK	Samantha Duvet The Mattress Corporation 1386 Munras Avenue Monterey, CA 93940 USA

Note that in British business letters Messrs, Mr, Mrs, Ms and Miss are written on the same line as the name. In the USA they are often omitted altogether. Messrs is only used for smaller firms, such as partnerships. Do not write Messrs if the company's name is followed by "Ltd", Plc", "Inc." or "Corp.". Ms should be used whenever the marital status of the female addressee is not known.

Note that in Great Britain the postal code is written on its own line below the place name, whereas in USA and Canada it is placed after the place name on the same line.

When letters are written to foreign countries, the name of the country should be shown on the final line of the inside address.

E Attention line ensures that the letter is dealt with by a specific person. You may write **Attention:**, **For the attention of ...:**, or (less formal) **FAO:**
As an alternative the person's name may be included in the inside address. This is a must if the recipient is addressed by name in the salutation.

Global Catering
17 Nelson Square
Manchester
MA17 3DF
UK

Attention: Ms Kirsty Burnham

Ms Kirsty Burnham
Global Catering
17 Nelson Square
Manchester
MA17 3DF
UK

F Salutation (UK)	**G Complimentary close (UK)**
Dear Sirs, Dear Sir/Madam	Yours faithfully/sincerely (Yours faithfully is rarely used now)
Dear Ms Burnham	Yours sincerely, Kind regards
Dear Customer	Yours sincerely
Dear Margaret	Best regards, Kind regards, Best wishes
Salutation (USA and Canada)	**Complimentary close (USA and Canada)**
(Ladies and) Gentlemen:	Sincerely, Very truly yours,
To whom it may concern:	Sincerely, Sincerely yours,
Dear Mr O'Reilly:	Yours truly, Sincerely, Sincerely yours,
Dear Sean:	Regards, Cordially,

If at all possible you should address the person you are writing to by name. "Dear Sirs" or "Gentlemen:" is only used when you do not have a name to write to. Traditionally salutation and complimentary close should be in line with each other.

H Body of the letter
Note that in English the first word of a business letter starts with a capital letter.

I Subject line may be preceded by the words "Subject" or "Re" and should be as specific as possible. Do not just write **"Your offer"** but **"Your offer for mouse pads of 23 May"**. In the UK subject lines are normally written below the salutation, in the USA above the salutation. They may be either underlined or typed in capital letters or bold type.

J Enclosure
Whenever enclosures are sent with a letter, a reference to the enclosure is required at the bottom of the letter. You may write "Enclosure(s)" or "Enc(s)".

K Signature block
In the UK – but not in the USA – the signature block often begins with the company's name. The signatory's name and title (or department) are typed below the signature. If somebody signs the letter on behalf of another person, the other person's name is typed below the signature, preceded by the word **"for"** or by the abbreviation **pp.** meaning "on behalf of".

NetOrbiter Ltd.	
Maria Bertram	*Fred Parry*
pp. Henry Crawford	for Betty Bickerton
Chief Information Officer	Credit Manager

2 Work with a partner. Find the right order for these jumbled addresses. Then dictate them to your partner.

UK Woodbridge Messrs Frost & Winter 22 James Street Suffolk IP3 7KL Managerial Skills Training	Ultimate IT Solutions Inc. USA Denver, CO 80121 Barbara Goodyear 1280 Mayflower Drive	Attention: Tom Finch 4 Tamar Industrial Estate UK Finch Electronics Ltd. PL3 7CT Plymouth

3 R/P Seven elements are missing from this traditional business letter. Copy the letter and add the missing elements using your own imagination for details.

Superdress GmbH

Fritz-Walter-Str. 28, 80469 München
Tel. +49 89 4677524, Fax +49 89 4677625
www.superdress.munich.de

TS / is

Mr Tony Shaw
Wilson and Thatcher Ltd.
2 Brook Lane
Bristol
BS9 2ET

We are pleased to enclose our Spring Catalogue showing our absolutely fabulous range of shirts. We feel sure that they will appeal to your young customers. If you place an order within the next two weeks, you will be granted 3% early order discount.

We look forward to welcoming you as a customer.

Resi Martl

B Structure and style of business correspondence

1 Beginnning, main part and end

Business correspondence must be well organised. The body of the correspondence should consist of three separate parts: the beginning, the main part and the end.

The **beginning** is either a single sentence or a short paragraph that states the reason why you are writing the correspondence. Example: I am going to be in Boston on May 20, and would like to meet you, if possible.

The **main part** contains the details. There should be a separate paragraph for every new idea. Example: Every now and then the new software does not provide the degree of protection against spam that we had expected. That is why I would like to discuss the problem with you personally.
A morning meeting would be best for me. Would 9 a.m. be convenient for you?

In the **end section** the writer sums up and underlines what he/she would like the recipient to do. Alternatively he/she may add a remark designed to create goodwill. Example: If this fits in with your schedule, please leave a message with my secretary. I look forward to seeing you in Boston.

Especially when you are writing to a customer it is advisable to end the communication on a friendly note.

Business correspondence should meet the so-called ABC specifications:

Accurate	correct and complete as to facts
Brief	short sentences, simple expressions, plain English
Clear	easy, natural style, without formality or familiarity

R/P **Put the eight jumbled elements of this correspondence into the correct order and write it out.**

1 Furthermore, we would like to draw your attention to our latest development, small wind turbines for commercial and domestic use. Please see page 3 of our catalogue.

2 Yours sincerely

3 Should you need any further information please contact us at any time.

4 As an attachment we are sending you our catalogue and price list. These already include a 25% trade discount. We also offer quantity discounts for major orders. Our terms of payment are 30 days net.

5	Dear Mr Wyndham
6	We look forward to receiving your first order which will be given top priority.
7	Your e-mail enquiry of 18 June
8	Thank you for your interest in our solar panels.

2 Linking words

Business correspondence is often made up of standard phrases. In order for the correspondence to read smoothly such individual text-building blocks ought to be connected by **linking words** like **also**, **as well as**, **both** … **and**, **in addition**, **moreover**, **further**, **firstly**, **secondly**, **finally** etc. which suggest a list. Example: **Finally**, we should like to confirm the date for next year's fashion show.

Other linking words imply a contrast: **whereas**, **while**, **in contrast to**, **however**, **although** etc. Example: Last month sales of DVD players rose by 3.5 per cent **whereas** sales of TV sets fell by 2.8 percent.

The following linking words indicate that an explanation is being given: **this is why**, **therefore**, **thus**, **as**, **because** etc. Example: We are most dissatisfied with your services. **This is why** we have decided to instruct a different company.

M **Translate the following sentences into German. Note particularly the linking words in bold type.**

1. He is very unhappy with the service. **This is why** he has stopped going to that restaurant.
2. Last year wages increased **whereas** retail sales stagnated.
3. **First,** delivery by road is quicker and **second**, it is more flexible.
4. We have decided not to place further orders **as** there have been so many delays.
5. **Both** our company **and** our suppliers have experienced strong growth this year.
6. We are prepared to place an order for 1000 notebooks. **However**, we expect a substantial quantity discount.
7. There has been severe flooding in this part of the country. **In addition**, we have been faced with prolonged electricity cuts.
8. **Although** we were not entirely satisfied with the execution of our previous order, we are prepared to give your company another chance.
9. Our canteen offers three different menus. We **also** serve vegetarian dishes.
10. **Finally**, we would like to thank you once more for making this concession.

Language and grammar 1
Decide which of the alternatives in brackets is correct.

1. I suggest (that you wait/to wait) for the outcome of the inspection.
2. We would appreciate (if you could/it if you could) let us have your confirmation by return.
3. We would appreciate (receiving/to receive) your prompt reply.
4. We would like to (excuse us/apologize) for not having reacted earlier.
5. Please (excuse/apologize) the inconvenience caused by this incident.
6. We look forward (to doing/to do) business with you.
7. We hope (to be entrusted/to being entrusted) with your order.
8. I would appreciate (to hear/hearing) from you soon.
9. We would suggest (to ring/ringing) Fisher's bookshop in Cambridge.
10. I would appreciate (it if you sent/if you sent) a driver to the airport.

* Language and grammar 2
Find the English equivalents of the following German phrases.

1. Wir möchten uns für die entstandenen Unannehmlichkeiten entschuldigen.
2. Wir sehen Ihrer baldigen Antwort mit Interesse entgegen.
3. Bitte entschuldigen Sie dieses Versehen.
4. Wir hoffen, bald wieder von Ihnen zu hören.
5. Wir schlagen vor, die Teile per Luftfracht zu schicken.
6. Wir möchten Ihnen vorschlagen, die Sache mit der Geschäftsleitung zu besprechen.
7. Wir wären Ihnen für eine ausführliche Beschreibung sehr dankbar.
8. Ich würde vorschlagen, ein Taxi zu nehmen.
9. Wir freuen uns, Ihren Auftrag in Kürze zu erhalten.
10. Für diese Verzögerung bitten wir um Entschuldigung.

Language and grammar: Typical mistakes in business correspondence

Wer diese Verben korrekt verwendet, vermeidet die häufigsten Fehler, die Deutschen beim Verfassen englischer Geschäftskorrespondenz unterlaufen.

suggest (vorschlagen)
We suggest **repeating** the test.
We suggest **that you (we) repeat** the test.
falsch: We suggest ~~to repeat~~ the test.

appreciate (schätzen, begrüßen, dankbar sein, anerkennen)
(a) We would appreciate **it** if you could assist us.
(**"it"** is absolutely necessary here!)
(b) We would appreciate **receiving** the unit as soon as possible.
falsch: We would appreciate ~~to receive~~ the unit as soon as possible.

apologize (sich entschuldigen)
We **apologize for** the delay.
falsch: We ~~excuse us~~ for the delay.

excuse (verzeihen, entschuldigen)
Please **excuse** the delay.
falsch: Please ~~apologize~~ the delay.

look forward to (entgegensehen, sich freuen auf)
We look forward to **hearing** from you soon.
falsch: We look forward ~~to hear~~ from you soon.

hope (hoffen)
We hope **to hear** from you soon.
falsch: We hope ~~to hearing~~ from you soon.

Communicating across cultures: The tone of English business correspondence

What is considered polite differs in different cultures. For example, one-word answers such as "ja", "nein" are not impolite in German. If I say: "Sollen wir ins Kino gehen?", you could answer "Ja" in German. In English people would be more inclined to say "Yes, that would be nice / great". Thus, German business correspondence tends to be factual and to the point. Polite phrases are often considered superfluous. While this abrupt tone is generally accepted in Germany, it may seem rude to English-speaking people or sound as though you are not interested. That is why you ought to aim to make frequent use of expressions like: **We would like to** (inform you); **I would be grateful** (if you could help me), **I am afraid** (the system is not running smoothly); **We are very sorry** (to inform you); **Would you be so kind as** (to inform us in time) in your English correspondence. Do not forget to insert the word **please** whenever you make a request, e.g.: If we can be of further assistance **please** do not hesitate to contact us.
Note: Please do not say: ~~**We kindly ask you**~~ …, say **We would like to ask you** … instead.

Phrases: Correspondence – E-mail, Letter, Fax

To refer to previous communication

Thank you very much for your letter **of** …	Wir danken Ihnen für Ihren Brief vom …
Many thanks for your e-mail/e-mail.	Vielen Dank für Ihre E-Mail.
We refer to your fax **of** …	Wir nehmen Bezug auf Ihr Fax vom …
Further to our discussion **on** 2 May …	Im Anschluss an unser Gespräch am 2. Mai …

To ask for something

Please let us have …	Wir bitten Sie um …
Would you please send us …	Bitte schicken Sie uns …
Please be so kind **as** to send us …	Wir bitten Sie höflich uns … zu schicken.
We **would** like to ask you for …	Wir möchten Sie um … bitten.
Please make sure that …	Bitte sorgen Sie dafür, dass …

To communicate good news

We are pleased to inform you that …	Wir freuen uns Ihnen mitteilen zu können, dass …
You will be pleased to hear that …	Sie werden sich bestimmt darüber freuen, dass …
It is particularly gratifying that …	Besonders erfreulich ist, dass …

To refuse something

I'm afraid I cannot agree **to** this proposal.	Leider muss ich diesen Vorschlag ablehnen.
I'm afraid that sounds quite unacceptable **to** us.	Das ist für uns leider völlig inakzeptabel.
Much as we regret it, we have to say no.	Zu unserem großen Bedauern müssen wir eine abschlägige Antwort geben.
We regret that we are unable to assist you.	Wir bedauern, Ihnen nicht behilflich sein zu können.

To apologize

We are very sorry but …	Es tut uns sehr leid, aber …
We **would** like to apologize for the delay.	Wir möchten uns für die Verspätung entschuldigen.

Please accept our apologies for this.	Wir entschuldigen uns dafür.
Please excuse the mix-up.	Bitte entschuldigen Sie die Verwechslung.

To make a suggestion

We would suggest that you send us a copy.	Wir schlagen Ihnen vor, uns eine Kopie zu schicken.
May we suggest that you inform the supplier.	Wir möchten vorschlagen, den Lieferanten zu benachrichtigen.
It would be advisable to send the details **by** fax.	Es wäre gut, wenn Sie uns die näheren Angaben faxen könnten.

To request that something is done by a certain date

We need the components **by** Friday **at** the very latest.	Wir benötigen die Teile spätestens Freitag.
Please make sure that they arrive **no** later **than** the end of April.	Bitte sorgen Sie dafür, dass sie spätestens Ende April ankommen.
Monday, 31 July, is the final deadline.	Montag, der 31. Juli, ist der letzte Termin.

To end a correspondence on a friendly note

We **look forward to hearing** from you.	Wir sehen Ihrer Antwort mit Interesse entgegen.
We **hope to hear** from you soon.	Wir hoffen, bald von Ihnen zu hören.
We look forward to a long and fruitful business relationship.	Wir freuen uns auf lange und lohnende Geschäftsbeziehungen mit Ihrer Firma.
We look forward to serving you again.	Wir freuen uns darauf, Ihnen wieder zu Diensten sein zu können.
We look forward to welcoming you as our customers.	Wir würden Sie gerne als neuen Kunden begrüßen.
We hope this proposal will be of interest **to** you.	Wir hoffen, dieser Vorschlag findet Ihr Interesse.
We hope this information **will** help you.	Wir hoffen, dass diese Auskunft hilfreich für Sie ist.
Thank you for your assistance.	Wir danken Ihnen für Ihre Bemühungen.

Unit 9
Enquiries

WORD BANK

enquiries • transactions • supplier • source of information • website • quotation • cost estimate • brochure • price list • terms and conditions • samples • trade discount • quantity discount • cash discount • introductory discount

Business transactions often start with enquiries. **General enquiries** are requests for brochures, pricelists etc. and for information about business terms. **Specific enquiries** give particulars about the goods/services requested and ask for detailed **quotations**.

The internet is now the most convenient way of locating possible suppliers and this is facilitated by the use of search engines. Traditional sources of information, such as chambers of commerce, yellow pages and trade associations have their own websites offering links to many potential suppliers. Trade fairs and exhibitions, visits by agents and advertising campaigns also provide information on new products.

Read the text above and translate the German sentences into English.

M

1. Die Suche nach Lieferanten im Internet wird durch Suchmaschinen sehr erleichtert.
2. Industrie- und Handelskammern, Gelbe Seiten und Branchenverbände geben auch über das Internet Auskunft.
3. Auch auf Messen und Ausstellungen sowie durch Werbekampagnen und den Besuch eines Vertreters werden neue Produkte bekannt gemacht.

Online-Link
808260-0009

A Enquiries in writing

Sarah Brookfield, purchasing manager at SPORTS ISLAND, a British sports equipment chain, is interested in the latest running shoes presented by Herkules, the German manufacturers, on their website. She decides to make further enquiries by e-mail.

1 R **Study Sarah's e-mail enquiry and say which of the prepositions in brackets are correct.**

From: sarah.brookfield@sportsisland.co.uk
Sarah Brookfield, purchasing manager, SPORTS ISLAND
To: exports@herkules.com **Cc:**
Sent: 201_-09-25 **Attachments:**

Subject: Enquiry about Herkules Turbostar running shoes

Dear Sir/Madam — *appropriate salutation*

We saw your presentation of the new Turbostar On and Off Road Running Shoe (**1 on/in**) your website and would like to ask you (**2 for/of**) further details. — *source of address*

We are a chain of sports equipment retailers with outlets (**3 at/in**) 12 major cities in the UK. For further information (**4 on/of**) our firm please see our website www.sportsisland.uk. — *introduction of your company*

Please inform us (**5 of/about**) your export prices and possible discounts as well as your terms of payment and delivery. We may be placing regular orders (**6 about/for**) 300 to 400 pairs of each size. We assume that you will be able to deliver (**7 from/off**) stock.

request to send
- *catalogues and price lists*
- *a quotation or cost estimate*

request for information on
- *prices and discounts*
- *terms of payment and delivery*
- *delivery periods*

In conclusion may we ask you to send us samples (**8 for/to**) test purposes.

further requests (if applicable)
- *samples*

Thank you for your attention (**9 at/to**) our enquiry. We look forward to hearing (**10 of/from**) you. — *closing phrase*

Best regards — *complimentary close*

Sarah Brookfield
Purchasing Manager

SPORTS ISLAND
41 Bryant Road
London W7 9QB
Tel. 020 74127333
Fax 020 74127334

2 R/P Cover up Sarah Brookfield's e-mail and complete these sentences on your own sheet of paper.

1. Sarah Brookfield saw a presentation of …
2. SPORTS ISLAND is a …
3. They would like to be informed about …
4. Their regular orders might comprise …
5. For test purposes they would like to have …
6. They look forward to …

3 R/P Restore the correct order of these jumbled elements and rewrite the correspondence on your own sheet of paper.

1 We look forward to your early reply.

2 Please send us your price list and information on quantity discounts, terms of payment and delivery and indicate your shortest delivery time.

3 Subject: Topsweets Mint Bars

4 We are a German wholesaler specialising in confectionery for young people and are very interested in your Mint Bars as there is a rapidly growing market for British-type sweets here in Germany.

5 Yours sincerely
Zuckermann & Sacher GmbH

Dieter Sacher

6 We would appreciate it if you could send us samples for test purposes.

7 Dear Topsweets Ltd

8 We would then place a trial order. If the mint bars sell well, we expect to place regular orders in future.

9 We saw the advertisement for your Topsweets Mint Bars in the March issue of the International Confectionery Journal and our general manager tasted them at a reception in the British Embassy in Berlin.

4 P Copy the e-mail form below. Use the above correspondence and the phrases at the end of the unit and write a detailed e-mail enquiry about the new innovative generation of tablet PCs. You saw their advertisement in the computer journal "IT.NEWS!". Address your e-mail to IT.COM, ITcom@aol.com, using your own name and a company name of your choice. Use your imagination for any details you may need.

Phrases

From:			
To:		**Cc:**	
Sent:		**Attachments:**	
Subject:			

5 KMK Sie arbeiten bei Getränke König, Am Sprudelbach 17, 06122 Halle, Tel. 0345 785634, Fax 0345 785635 im Einkauf. Ihre Firma möchte ihren guten Kunden zu Weihnachten ein besonderes Geschenk machen. Ihre Chefin, Nicole Sachse, hat auf der Homepage des irischen Glasherstellers Wexford Crystal plc, 1 Wexford Avenue, Sanditon, County Cork, Republic of Ireland, farbige Kristallgläser für Long Drinks im Geschenkkarton zu je drei Stück gesehen.

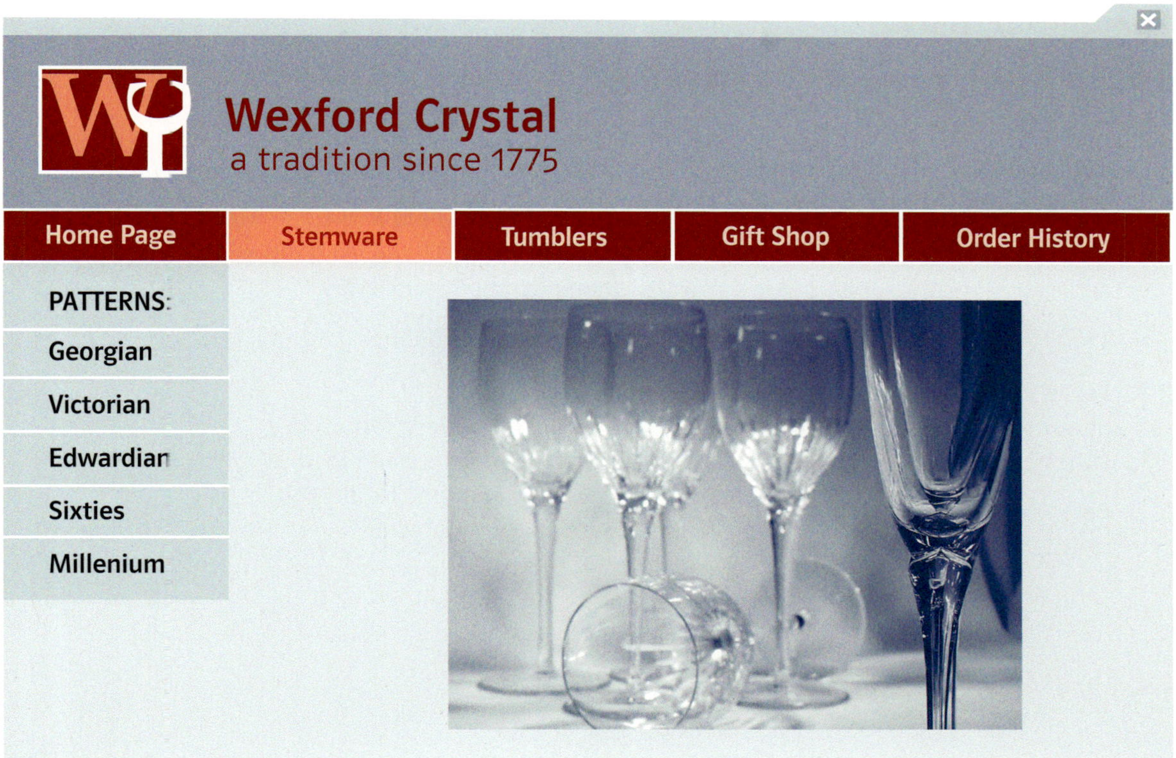

Sie bittet Sie eine Anfrage, die sie selbst unterschreiben wird, zu verfassen und dabei folgende Punkte zu berücksichtigen:

Phrases

- Datum 1. September
- Betreff
- Bezug auf Internetseiten von Wexford Crystal
- Vorstellung Ihrer Firma als einer führenden Getränkegroßhandlung, Firmenbroschüre liegt bei
- Grund Ihrer Anfrage
- Bitte um Zusendung von Prospekten und Preislisten
- Bitte um Angabe der Lieferzeit
- Bitte um Angabe der Liefer- und Zahlungsbedingungen
- Sonderwunsch: nur je zwei Gläser pro Geschenkpackung
- Umfang eines möglichen Auftrags: 3000 Sets
- Bitte um baldige Antwort
- Anlage: Firmenbroschüre

6 Your stressed out boss, a Canadian, feels he is in desperate need of a wellness holiday on a Caribbean island. Check out wellness holidays on the Caribbean Commonwealth island of Santa (or Saint) Lucia and make notes for him in English. Your boss is very demanding and only the best is good enough for him.

B Enquiries by phone

1 Restore the order of this jumbled dialogue. Match the numbers with the letters.

1. Calendars 4 U. Michael Bennet speaking. How can I help you?
2. Certainly. Please let me have your address.
3. Thank you. I'll post it today.
4. Yes of course. And full details of our generous discounts for volume orders.
5. My pleasure. Thank you for calling.

a. That's good. Thank you.
b. It's 30, Netherfield Road, Winchester SO2 9LZ. And my name is Jonathan Denny.
c. I take it the brochure contains a price list?
d. Hello. My name is Jonathan Denny. I'm interested in your animal calendars. Could you send me a brochure?
e. Goodbye.

2 Listen to the dialogue and check your work.

R
A1.22

V4 Video Lounge General enquiries

lingua tv

This video shows an enquiry by telephone. Look out for the answers to the following questions:

1. Compare the appearance of the two women. Which do you find more appropriately/appealingly dressed?
2. What seems to be the secretary's main activity apart from answering the phone?
3. What is Purple Fashion enquiring about?
4. What kind of order does she wish to place first?
5. What discount does the manufacturer offer her? What discount does she want?
6. What is the final discount offered?
7. What is the total amount of the invoice?
8. How long does delivery take?

3 I/P **Working with a partner now create and act out a similar dialogue along the following lines.**

Phrases

A	B
Linda/Larry Lawson from the British language school Business Speak in Brighton gets a call. →	The caller introduces him/herself as Stefan/Stefanie Merz from Rostock, Germany. He/she is interested in crash courses in business English in the summer.
← Linda/Larry Lawson offers to send a detailed brochure and asks for the caller's address. →	Stefan/Stefanie Merz spells his/her name and address, Ostseeallee 27, 66123 Rostock, Germany.
← Linda/Larry Lawson promises to send the brochure by post the next morning and thanks the caller for his/her interest in their courses. He/she adds that he/she is convinced that the caller will find the appropriate course. →	Stefan/Stefanie Merz thanks Linda/Larry Lawson and says Good-bye.

4 I **Work with a partner, sit back to back and act out the following telephone conversation with the help of the role cards.**

Phrases

Role card: Partner A

Role card partner B ⇨ page 230

Torsten/Tanja Kirchner, Auszubildende/r bei Hammer Werkzeughandel, Remscheid, ruft auf Bitten des Chefs bei Powertools plc, Cardiff, UK, an. Torsten/Tanja bittet um Auskunft über die Werkzeugsätze für Heimwerker (household tool kits) von Powertools.
Die E-Mail-Adresse lautet: imports@hammerwerkzeughandel.de. Vor allem möchte man Näheres über Lieferzeiten und Mengenrabatte erfahren.
Torsten/Tanja beendet das Gespräch und dankt für die Bemühungen.

Info: Discounts

Granting discounts is an effective means of winning new or retaining old customers.
Trade discounts are granted to retailers.
Introductory discounts are granted to facilitate the introduction of new products or services.
Quantity discounts are granted for volume orders.
Early order discounts are granted for bookings/purchases made well in advance.
Cash discount is granted for early payment.

5 R **Copy the sentences and complete them on your own sheet of paper, inserting the appropriate type of discount.**

1. In view of the size of your order we are prepared to grant you a **1** of 15%.
2. We are prepared to launch your new product on the Greek market, if you grant us a substantial **2**.
3. For payment within 7 days we grant 2% **3**.
4. Only registered businesses qualify for a **4**.
5. On bookings made 3 months in advance you will be granted 10% **5**.

6 I **Work with a partner. Partner A wishes to place an order with partner B, provided he/she is granted a discount. Use the ideas from the grid below to negotiate the granting of a discount. Then change roles.**

Phrases

Example:

A

I'd be quite willing to introduce your new software package CP36-97 to the German market. But I'm afraid that won't be so easy. There are a lot of competing programs. That's why I'd have to offer customers at least a 20% introductory discount.

B

Well, actually the package isn't exactly new. It's just an updated version of the previous one. So there isn't any real reason for granting an introductory discount.

A

I'm afraid we will have to offer **some** incentive to our customers. What would you say to 10% introductory discount?

B

I'd have to get back to my boss for that. I'll let you know in a few minutes.

Order for	Discount requested	Arguments for	Arguments against
Hotel room for 3 nights	20% early order discount	booking made 2 months in advance	granted on bookings made 3 months in advance
200 Topsweets Mint Bars	30% trade discount	buyer is a retailer, has a small shop	quantity too small, trade discount only for business-size volumes
50 CD/radio/cassette stereo players	3% cash discount	payment made within 10 days	normally only 2%
75 kgs of Norwegian Smoked Salmon	5% quantity discount	price high compared to competitors' prices	quantity discounts start at 100 kgs.

Language and grammar

Copy the sentences and fill in the correct form, either the adjective or the adverb, and underline the word the adjective or adverb refers to.

Example:
(clear) We wish to point out 1 that this is the deadline.
We wish to point out *clearly* that this is the deadline.

(prompt) We would be grateful for a 2 reply.
(prompt) Thank you for replying 3 to our inquiry.
(strict) This information is given in 4 confidence.
(relative) This is a 5 minor problem.
(immediate) We must insist on 6 delivery.
(immediate) Please contact our representative 7.
(comparative) Last year they placed 8 small orders with us.
(high) We are 9 dissatisfied with your services.
(fair) Their customers receive updates 10 regularly.
(considerable) Prices have increased 11 in the last few months.
(considerable) They have 12 funds at their disposal.
(approximate) What is the 13 arrival date of the vessel?
(approximate) We have received 14 seventy enquiries.
(definite) This car is 15 too small for me.
(definite) We will let you have our 16 decision by Wednesday.

Language and grammar: Adjectives and adverbs

Mit Adjektiven werden Substantive und das Verb "to be" näher bestimmt.

We expect to place **regular orders** in future.
"regular" ist ein Adjektiv und kennzeichnet das Substantiv "orders".

We **will be glad** to receive information on your discounts.
"glad" ist ein Adjektiv und gehört zu "will be", einer Form von "to be".

Mit Adverbien (adjective +ly) werden Verben, Adjektive und Adverbien näher bestimmt.

We assure you that your order **will be executed promptly**.
"prompt**ly**" ist ein Adverb und kennzeichnet das Verb "to execute".

There is a **rapidly growing** market for British sweets in Germany.
"rapid**ly**" ist ein Adverb und kennzeichnet das Adjektiv "growing".

There is an **extremely rapidly** growing market for British sweets in Germany.
"extreme**ly**" ist ein Adverb und kennzeichnet das Adverb "rapidly".

Phrases: Enquiries

To mention the source of address

We have seen your advertisement for copiers in the computer journal IT.News!.	Wir haben Ihre Anzeige für Kopiergeräte in der Computer-Zeitschrift IT.News! gesehen.
We have obtained your address **from** the Anglo-German Chamber of Commerce.	Wir erhielten Ihre Anschrift von der Deutsch-Britischen Handelskammer.
Your services have been recommended to us **by** a business partner, …	Ihre Dienstleistungen wurden uns von einem Geschäftspartner empfohlen, …
We have visited your website and …	Wir haben Ihre Webseite angeklickt und …

To introduce your company

We are a young and rapidly growing firm **specialising** in …	Wir sind ein junges, rasch wachsendes Unternehmen und sind auf … spezialisiert.
We are well-established manufacturers **of** …	Wir sind ein gut eingeführter Hersteller von …
Our firm is a leading importer of tools with excellent contacts **all over** the EU.	Unsere Firma ist ein führender Importeur von Werkzeugen mit ausgezeichneten Kontakten in der gesamten EU.

To say what you require

We are interested in …	Wir interessieren uns für …
Could you please let us have a brochure and a price list **for** the services you offer.	Wir bitten um einen Prospekt und eine Preisliste für die von Ihnen angebotenen Dienstleistungen.
Please enclose a catalogue **of** your latest products.	Bitte fügen Sie einen Katalog für Ihre neuesten Produkte bei.
Please send us a quotation **for** …	Bitte machen Sie uns ein (Preis-)Angebot über …
We would be grateful for a cost estimate **for** …	Für einen Kostenvoranschlag für … wären wir dankbar.
Please quote your lowest prices for …	Bitte nennen Sie uns Ihre günstigsten Preise für …
We need a further shipment **of** …	Wir benötigen eine weitere Lieferung …

To ask for further information

We would be grateful for information **on** your terms of payment and delivery.	Wir bitten um nähere Angaben zu Ihren Liefer- und Zahlungsbedingungen.
Do you grant any quantity discounts? ... any early order discount? ... trade discount? ... introductory discount? ... cash discount?	Gewähren Sie Mengenrabatt? ... Frühbucherrabatt? ... Wiederverkaufsrabatt? ... Einführungsrabatt? ... Skonto?
Can you deliver ex stock?	Können Sie ab Lager liefern?
Please state your earliest delivery date.	Bitte geben Sie uns Ihr frühestes Lieferdatum an.
What is the minimum quantity **for** a trial order?	Was ist die Mindestmenge für einen Probeauftrag?

To ask for other services, if applicable

We would welcome a presentation of your services on our premises.	Wir wären dankbar für eine Präsentation Ihrer Dienstleistungen in unseren Geschäftsräumen.
A visit **by** your representative would be appreciated.	Wir wären dankbar für einen Besuch Ihres Vertreters.

To close the communication with a standard phrase

We look forward to hearing from you soon.	Wir freuen uns darauf, bald wieder von Ihnen zu hören.
If your prices are competitive, we may be able to place substantial orders in future.	Wenn Ihre Preise konkurrenzfähig sind, werden wir Ihnen bald größere Aufträge erteilen können.
If the goods **meet with** our customers' approval, your products should sell well in this market.	Wenn die Ware unseren Kunden zusagt, dürften sich Ihre Erzeugnisse auf unserem Markt gut verkaufen lassen.
We hope to hear from you shortly.	Wir hoffen, bald wieder von Ihnen zu hören.

Unit 10
Offers

WORD BANK
offer • quotation • cost estimate • catalogue • brochure • price list • stock • sample • terms of delivery • INCOTERMS • terms of payment • options • solicited • unsolicited • valid • to offer • to quote • to process • to enclose • to attach

Offers are sent either in reply to an enquiry **(solicited offers)** or on the seller's own initiative in the form of sales communications to individuals or companies likely to be interested in the goods or services offered **(unsolicited offers)**. Detailed, specific offers are often called **quotations**. Offers for work to be done take the form of **cost estimates**.

By making an offer the seller declares his willingness to sell certain goods or perform certain services at a certain price and on certain terms.

Offers are binding on the person or firm making the offer unless it is expressly stated in the offer that

- the prices are subject to change without notice or that the offer is either
- without engagement or
- valid until a certain date or
- valid as long as stocks last.

Note that all enquiries should be answered, even those for goods or services your firm does not provide. Where possible, recommend an alternative supplier.

Online-Link
808260-0010

1 **Study the text on offers on page 126 and match the expressions on the left with their German equivalents on the right.**

1. solicited offer
2. unsolicited offer
3. without engagement
4. valid until 31 May
5. as long as stocks last
6. prices are subject to change without notice
7. cost estimate

a. freibleibend
b. gültig bis 31. Mai
c. Preisänderungen vorbehalten
d. Kostenvoranschlag
e. solange Vorrat reicht
f. unverlangtes Angebot
g. verlangtes Angebot

2 **Übertragen Sie folgende Sätze ins Englische.**
KMK

1. Ein verlangtes Angebot wird als Reaktion auf eine Anfrage abgegeben.
2. Viele Firmen schicken unverlangte Angebote an mögliche Interessenten für ihre Produkte.
3. Ein Kostenvoranschlag ist ein Angebot für eine Arbeit, die ausgeführt werden soll.
4. Dieses Angebot ist freibleibend.
5. Unsere Preise gelten nur bis zum 31.07.201_.
6. Preisänderungen bleiben vorbehalten.
7. Solange der Vorrat reicht, bieten wir Ihnen wie folgt an: …

Info: Successful offers

Effective offers are decisive for the success of your business. When making an offer you should

- answer an enquiry promptly
- whenever possible personalise the salutation
- thank the enquirer for his interest in your goods or services
- if you cannot provide all the information right away let the prospective customer know that his enquiry will be processed as soon as possible
- be as helpful and polite as possible
- give all the information required
- provide additional information that might be useful
- refrain from making promises you cannot keep
- say something positive about your firm and / or your products
- conclude your offer with a phrase designed to make the customer feel positive towards your firm

3 **Work in pairs. Close the book. Write down as many of the above recommendations as you remember. Then compare your list with your neighbour's list.**
P

A Offers in writing

In reply to her enquiry about running shoes Sarah Brookfield from SPORTS ISLAND has received the following e-mail offer from Herkules.

1 R **Study the e-mail offer and find the missing nouns from the box.**

attachment • business • delivery period • discount • enquiry • orders • position • sample • stock

From: exports@Herkules.com, Philipp Schäfer, export department
To: sarah.brookfield@sportsisland.co.uk, Sarah Brookfield, purchasing manager, SPORTS ISLAND
Cc:
Attachments: Price List, Test Report, Brochure
Sent: 201_-09-26

Subject: Your enquiry about Herkules Turbostar running shoes

Dear Ms Brookfield — *personal salutation*

Thank you very much for your **1** of 25 September. — *expression of thanks for the enquiry*

We are sending our brochure and price list as an **2**. On orders exceeding 200 pairs in one size we grant a quantity **3** of 5 per cent. Our prices are quoted EXW Neustadt. For orders exceeding 1000 pairs of one size each we require a **4** of 3 weeks. Smaller orders can be delivered from **5**. — *description of goods/services offered* / *prices (unit and total) and discounts* / *terms of delivery and delivery period*

Normally we do business on the basis of cash with order for first orders. For regular **6** we are prepared to grant open account terms with quarterly settlement. — *terms of payment*

We are also attaching a Test Report, published by the British Consumers' Association, which puts Herkules running shoes in top **7** in the categories of both comfort and durability. — *additional information*

Five **8** pairs of the new Turbostar have been despatched to you this morning and should reach you in the next few days. — *reference to samples, etc.*

We look forward to establishing regular **9** relations with you. — *goodwill phrase*

Yours sincerely
Herkules — *complimentary close*

Philipp Schäfer
Export Department

2 R/P **Restore the correct order of these jumbled elements and rewrite the correspondence on a piece of paper.**

1 We look forward to welcoming you as our customers.

2 Topsweets Mint Bars

3 For first orders our terms of payment are cash with order.
For regular customers our terms are 30 days net.

4 Our prices are quoted DAP to your premises. On orders for more than 100 kgs we grant 10 % discount. The mint bars can be delivered within 2–4 weeks from receipt of order, depending on the volume of the order.

5 We are pleased to send you enclosed our brochure describing our whole range of products and our special folder on Topsweets Mint Bars as well as our latest price list.

6 Dear Mr Sacher

7 To enable you to convince yourself of the superior taste of Topsweets Mint Bars we are sending you by separate post samples together with an assortment of our other products. We are sure that you will be delighted with our sweets that are very popular among discerning customers all over the world.

8 Encls. Brochure, folder, price list

9 Yours sincerely
Topsweets Ltd.

Martha Creams

10 Thank you very much for your recent enquiry.

3 P **You work in the export department of a German wholesaler for electronic equipment. Your boss, Cornelia Klinkenberg, has received the following e-mail enquiry. Reply to this enquiry taking your boss's notes into account.**

Phrases

From:	james.leigh@leigh.co.uk
To:	cornelia.klinkenberg@topelektronik.de
Cc:	
Sent:	201_-08-02 **Attachments:**
Subject:	SomeThing Mp3 Players

Dear Ms Klinkenberg

Please quote us your best prices for the following SomeThing Mp3 players:

500 units article No. 487-13, 8 GB, with backlit LCD display
vorrätig, Stückpreis EURO 83,50

700 units article No. 487-26, 16 GB 3D, USB, extremely compact in size
nur 400 vorrätig, Stückpreis EURO 32,80 Lieferzeit für die restlichen 300 Stück 6 Wochen als Ersatz Artikel 487–15 vorschlagen, gleiches Modell, aber Lebensdauer der Batterie 30 statt 24 Stunden, Stückpreis EURO 45,90

300 units article No. 487-45, 1.5 GB, with SD-card slot
vorrätig, Stückpreis EURO 85,30

20 % Mengenrabatt für gesamten Auftrag einräumen

As the goods are urgently required for a new store to be opened by the end of next month, we would ask you to indicate your earliest date of delivery.
Versand kann drei Tage nach Auftragseingang erfolgen

We assume that the usual terms of payment and delivery will apply.
richtig

Thank you for your prompt attention to our enquiry.

Yours sincerely

James Leigh
Leigh & Co. Ltd.
17 Camden Place
Bristol
BS6 6HR
Tel. 0117 4430030

bitte meinen Namen darunter setzen

Danke Klinkenberg

4 KMK Sie sind Susan/James Vernon und arbeiten im Verkauf bei Powertools plc, Snowdon Industrial Estate, Cardiff CA4 9ZB. Torsten/Tanja Kirchner von der Firma Hammer Werkzeughandel, Lehmkuhle 104, 42896 Remscheid, hat um eine schriftliche Bestätigung des Angebots gebeten, das Sie ihm/ihr heute früh telefonisch gemacht haben.

Verfassen Sie dieses Schreiben (in englischer Sprache) und berücksichtigen Sie dabei Folgendes:

- Datum von heute
- Betreff: Angebot Nr. TK/234
- Bezug auf Telefongespräch
- Angebot für 1000 Stück 9-teiliger Haushalts-Werkzeugsatz (9-piece household tool kit), Artikel Nr. HTK-9
- Listenpreis pro Stück: €4,99, FCA Cardiff, Incoterms 2010, einschließlich Verpackung, abzüglich 30% Händlerrabatt
- Gesamtpreis nach Abzug des Händlerrabatts: €3.493,00.
- Zahlungsbedingungen: innerhalb von 30 Tagen netto, innerhalb von 10 Tagen 2% Skonto (cash discount)
- Lieferzeit: 3 Wochen
- 2 Muster-Werkzeugsätze werden heute an Hammer Werkzeughandel zu Testzwecken geschickt
- Dank für das Interesse an den Produkten von Powertools plc
- Zusicherung sorgfältiger Ausführung des Auftrags

B Offers by phone

1 Edward Ferrars from Norland Industries in Southampton, Great Britain, gets a phone call from an overseas customer.
R
A1.23 Read the statements first. Then listen to the dialogue and mark on your own sheet of paper whether the statements are TRUE or FALSE.

1. Tom De Boer is calling from South America.
2. He has no Norland colour printers left in his stock.
3. He wishes to order 200 units of the colour printer CP 150.
4. The terms of delivery are FOB Durban.
5. Last year's model CP 100 cost GBP 72.50.
6. There is increasing competition from Japan.
7. 30% trade discount will be granted on all future orders.
8. The customer asks for an offer in writing.

2 Copy Mr Ferrars' quotation and insert the missing expressions from the box.
R

from receipt of order • look forward to • pleased to • Referring to • within 30 days

Dear Mr De Boer

Norland Colour Printers CP 100 and 150 – Quotation no. CP-2024

1 your enquiry of 2 Feb. 201_ we are **2** inform you that we can quote as follows

Quantity	Description	Unit Price	Total
500	Norland Colour Printer CP 100	GBP75.50	GBP 37,750.00
200	Norland Colour Printer CP 150	GBP85.20	GBP 17,040.00
			GBP 54,790.00
	less 30 % trade discount		GBP 16,437.00
TOTAL			**GBP 38,353.00**

Delivery: within four weeks **3**, CIF Durban.

Payment: net cash **4** from receipt of invoice.

We **5** receiving your order.

Yours sincerely
Edward Ferrars
Norland Industries

C Comparing options

1 **KMK** Ihre Firma plant, 5 Mitarbeiter aus dem Export für eine Woche zu einem Intensiv-Sprachkurs nach England zu schicken. Zwei Angebote wurden in die engere Wahl gezogen. Verschaffen Sie sich einen Überblick über diese beiden Angebote, indem Sie die Tabelle auf Seite 134 (kopieren und) in deutscher Sprache vervollständigen.

THE DORSET SCHOOL OF ENGLISH

The DORSET SCHOOL OF ENGLISH offers you a tailor-made study programme for your staff at any time you wish, except in August. Our offer includes a one-week intensive course, 6 hours of tuition a day (except Sundays), focussing on general business English and on specific export terminology.

Our language school is situated in Lyme Regis, the pearl of Dorset, a traditional seaside resort on the English Channel, made famous by the celebrated novelist Jane Austen.

Your staff will be placed with English business and professional families and there will never be another student of your native language in the same family.

The sports programme (tennis, swimming, surfing and sailing), which is free of charge, takes the learning experience outside the classroom.

Lyme Regis is rich in fossils. We offer fossil hunting trips as a special treat for our students.

Excursions to Exeter, Dartmoor and Bath can be booked at short notice.

Tuition fees: £400 per week
For more than 10 participants from one firm we offer a 15 % discount.
Accommodation and full board in host families: £490 per week.

Booking fee, to be paid when booking: £50.
Full payment to be made 6 weeks before the course begins.

Contact: Brian Hill, THE DORSET SCHOOL OF ENGLISH, The Cobb, Lyme Regis, EX3 5AN

BUSINESS SPEAK

BUSINESS SPEAK is an international language school for business people, located in Brighton on the South Coast. Brighton is a vibrant seaside resort and conference centre, just one hour's train journey from London.

Our business English intensive courses which take place four times a year (September 2–8, October 14–20, February 10–16 and May 21–27) would suit your staff's needs admirably. These intensive courses consist of 5 hours of tuition in the mornings and four study visits to British firms in the afternoons.

Maximum number of participants: 8.

Our students live either at an exclusive private hotel or with carefully selected English host families.

We offer a wide range of sports activities, such as golf, riding, surfing, sailing and fishing. Equipment can be hired at a small charge.

Course fees: £480 per week
Accommodation and half board:
Private hotel: £90 per day
Host family: £450 per week

To confirm the booking a deposit of £75 per person must accompany the booking form. The balance is required no later than eight weeks before the course commencement date.

Please contact:
Mrs Pam Robinson • BUSINESS SPEAK • 120, Brunswick Square • Brighton • BN1 9PH

	Anbieter A	Anbieter B
Veranstalter	Dorset School of English	
Kursort		
Teilnehmerkreis und -zahl	speziell unsere Gruppe	
Schwerpunkt		
Unterrichtsstunden pro Tag		
Unterbringung		
Exkursionen		
Freizeitangebot		
Kurstermine		
Preis für Unterkunft und Verpflegung		
Kursgebühren		
Anzahlung		
Auskunft		

* **2** P **Make up your mind which of these two offers you would prefer to accept. Then write a short memo for your US parent company's personnel department, giving at least two reasons for your choice.**

MEMO
From: (your own name) Date:
To: Personnel Department, Headquarters USA
Subject: Intensive language course in the UK

3 **Your boss has asked you to look up Business English courses in Poole / Bournemouth on the south coast of England. Make notes on two or three that seem suitable and write a memo in English giving names and important details.**

D INCOTERMS® (Terms of delivery)

The Incoterms are a set of nationally and internationally accepted rules defining the obligations of the seller and the buyer as regards the tasks, costs and risks involved in the transport of goods. They were first drawn up by the International Chamber of Commerce in Paris in 1936 and were last updated in 2010.

The Incoterms 2010 are grouped in two categories:
- rules for any mode or modes of transport
- rules for sea and inland waterway transport

The Incoterms 2010 consist of 11 rules, two of which are new:
- DAT (Delivered at Terminal) replaces the former DEQ rule
- DAP (Delivered at Place) replaces the former rules DAF, DES and DDU

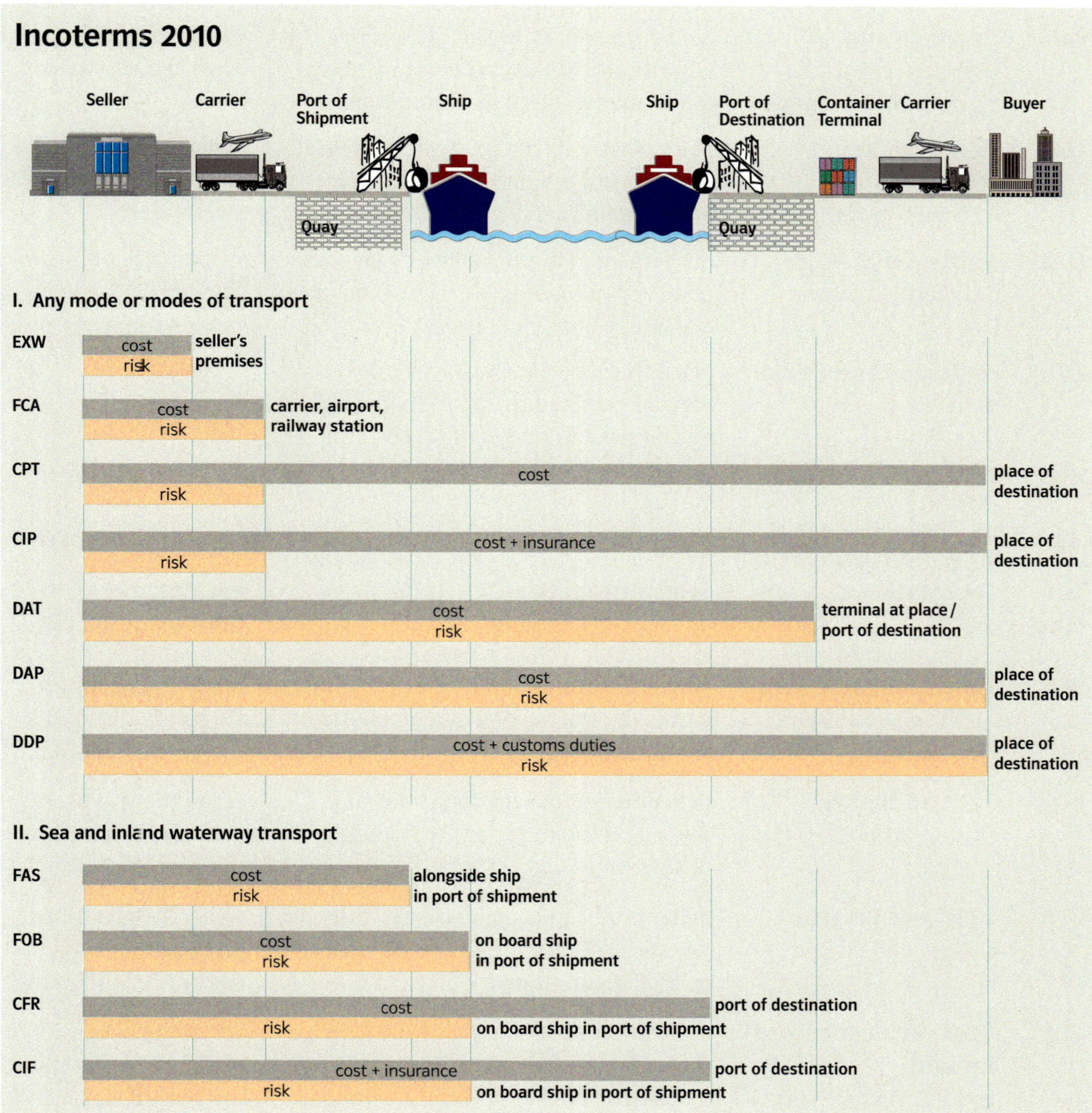

® International Chamber of Commerce, ICC

Rules for any mode or modes of transport **Incoterms® 2010**

Inco-term	Designation	Seller's obligations	Passing of risk from seller to buyer
EXW	**Ex Works** Ab Werk	place the goods at the disposal of the buyer at the seller's premises (factory, warehouse etc.)	at the seller's premises
FCA	**Free Carrier** Frei Frachtführer	deliver the goods to the carrier named by the buyer	when the goods are handed over to the carrier
CPT	**Carriage Paid to** Frachtfrei	deliver the goods to the carrier and pay the cost of carriage to the named place of destination	when the goods are handed over to the carrier
CIP	**Carriage and Insurance Paid to** Frachtfrei versichert	deliver the goods to the carrier, pay the cost of carriage and take out insurance to the named place of destination	when the goods are handed over to the carrier
DAT	**Delivered at Terminal** Geliefert Terminal	place the goods at the buyer's disposal, unloaded, at a named terminal at a named place/port	when the goods have been unloaded at the terminal
DAP	**Delivered at Place** Geliefert benannter Ort	place the goods at the buyer's disposal, ready for unloading, at the named place of destination	at the place of destination
DDP	**Delivered Duty Paid** Geliefert verzollt	place the goods at the buyer's disposal, ready for unloading, at the named place of destination, carry out all customs formalities and pay import duty, if any	at the place of destination

Rules for sea and inland waterway transport **Incoterms® 2010**

Inco-term	Designation	Seller's obligations	Passing of risk from seller to buyer
FAS	**Free Alongside Ship** Frei Längsseite Schiff	deliver the goods alongside the ship named by the buyer at the named port of shipment	when the goods are alongside the ship in the port of shipment
FOB	**Free on Board** Frei an Bord	deliver the goods on board the ship named by the buyer at the named port of shipment	when the goods are on board the ship in the port of shipment
CFR	**Cost and Freight** Kosten und Fracht	deliver the goods on board the ship and pay the costs and freight to the named port of destination	when the goods are on board the ship in the port of shipment
CIF	**Cost, Insurance and Freight** Kosten, Versicherung und Fracht	deliver the goods on board the ship; pay the costs and freight to the named port of destination and take out insurance for the transport	when the goods are on board the ship in the port of shipment

Under all clauses the seller must deliver the goods to the buyer at the named place and the buyer must take delivery of the goods *(Ware abnehmen)*. The seller must procure *(beschaffen)* or help to procure the transport documents and pack the goods, if customary *(handelsüblich)*.

Note that under the Incoterms CPT, CIP, CFR and CIF the seller bears the risks only up to the place of delivery, i.e. until the goods are handed over to the (first) carrier or have been loaded on board ship in the port of shipment. Under these terms the seller must, in addition, contract *(Vertrag abschließen)* and pay for the carriage to the place or port of destination.

1 R **Read the business transactions and complete them with the right Incoterms.**

1. Jennings Food Ltd. has bought five colour printers from Norland Industries. Jennings Food's driver picks up the colour printers at Norland Industries' production plant. The printers have been sold on the basis of …?

2. Powertools plc, Cardiff, has received a large export order from a Brazilian customer. Powertools plc pays for the goods to be taken to the docks in Cardiff and for the loading on board the vessel "Southern Cross". The terms of delivery are …?

3. International Snacks GmbH, a German food processing company, usually delivers its snacks by lorry to Global Catering's premises in Manchester, assuming all costs and risks for the entire transport and dealing with any border formalities that may arise. Their terms of delivery are most likely …?

4. Herkules is processing a major order for running shoes and tennis shoes from a Japanese customer. Herkules arranges and pays for the transport of two 20 ft containers to the container terminal at the Japanese port of Yokohama. Herkules delivers on the basis of …?

2 M Study the Incoterms 2010 on page 135 and 136 and find the English equivalents for the following German expressions.

1. Geschäftsräume des Verkäufers
2. Frachtführer
3. vom Käufer benannt
4. Gefahrenübergang
5. Beförderungskosten
6. Versicherung abschließen
7. entladebereit
8. Bestimmungsort
9. dem Käufer zur Verfügung stellen
10. Verschiffungshafen
11. sich an Bord befinden
12. Einfuhrzoll

Language and grammar
Complete these sentences with "some" or "any".

1. He says he has lived in the UK for … years.
2. Fortunately we did not have … trouble getting an import licence.
3. When we finally managed to go the cafeteria there was hardly … food left.
4. I don't think he will complete … of these tasks in time.
5. Could you lend me … of your knives and forks for the party?
6. I couldn't think of …thing else to buy.
7. Scarcely …body turned up for the meeting.
8. …body must help me with this update.
9. We doubt that …body could have solved that problem without help from the experts.
10. We will send you … samples by parcel post.
11. Has …body seen my car keys?
12. …body must have copied the data.
13. I wonder whether …body will bother to return the questionnaire.
14. There are scarcely … funds left for this project.

Language and grammar: some and any

"Some" steht • in **bejahten Aussagen** und • in Fragen, auf die eine **positive Antwort** erwartet wird.	Examples: Here are **some** brochures for you. Can you give us **some** of these folders?
"Any" steht • in **verneinten Aussagen** und • in Fragen, auf die eine **negative Antwort** erwartet wird, • bei **"hardly", "scarcely" oder "barely"** (deutsch: kaum), • in **Bedingungssätzen** und • nach Ausdrücken des **Zweifels**.	Examples: I am afraid there aren't **any** mint bars among the samples TOPSWEETS sent us. Are there **any** of those delicious ginger cookies left? There can hardly be **any** doubt about it. If you have **any** problems, let me know. I wonder whether **any** of the students will be satisfied with this reply.

Phrases: Offers

To say thank you for an enquiry

Many thanks for your enquiry **of** 2 October **about** our new range of …	Wir danken Ihnen vielmals für Ihre Anfrage vom 2. Oktober wegen unseres neuen Sortiments von …
We **were** pleased to hear that you are interested in our …	Wir freuen uns über Ihr Interesse an unseren …

To make an offer and to refer to prices and discounts

As requested, we are sending you enclosed our latest catalogue and price list.	Wie gewünscht, fügen wir unseren neuesten Katalog und unsere Preisliste bei.
We are pleased to quote as follows:	Wir freuen uns, Ihnen hiermit folgendes Angebot machen zu können:
We would now like to make the following quotation:	Wir möchten Ihnen nun folgendes Angebot unterbreiten:
… **at** a unit price of € …, including packing.	… zum Stückpreis von € … einschließlich Verpackung.
… less 30% trade discount.	… abzüglich 30% Händlerrabatt.
We can offer a 10% quantity discount **on** orders **for** at least 500 units.	Für Aufträge über mindestens 500 Stück wird 10% Mengenrabatt gewährt.
May we draw your attention **to** our special offer for …?	Dürfen wir Sie auf unser Sonderangebot für … aufmerksam machen?
We grant 2% cash discount **for** payment within 10 days.	Für Barzahlung innerhalb von 10 Tagen gewähren wir 2% Skonto.
We take pleasure **in** submitting the following cost estimate:	Wir freuen uns Ihnen folgenden Kostenvoranschlag zu unterbreiten:

To state your terms of delivery and payment

Our prices are quoted CIF Singapore.	Unsere Preise verstehen sich CIF Singapur.
Terms of delivery: EXW Neustadt	Lieferbedingungen: EXW (Ab Werk) Neustadt
Our usual terms of payment are: cash **with** order cash **on** delivery 30 days net, 10 days 2% **by** irrevocable and confirmed letter of credit	Normalerweise lauten unsere Zahlungsbedingungen: Barzahlung bei Auftragserteilung Barzahlung bei Lieferung 30 Tage netto, 10 Tage 2% Skonto durch unwiderrufliches und bestätigtes Akkreditiv

Regular customers are granted open account terms.	Unseren Stammkunden gewähren wir offenes Zahlungsziel.
We would request payment **by** bank transfer **to** our account **with** ABC bank.	Wir bitten um Zahlung per Banküberweisung auf unser Konto bei der ABC Bank.

To refer to the delivery time

The delivery period is 6 weeks.	Die Lieferzeit beträgt 6 Wochen.
Delivery can be made ex stock.	Die Lieferung kann ab Lager erfolgen.

To inform the customer how long the offer is valid

The offer is firm **until** 31 March. without engagement. valid **as long as** stocks last.	Das Angebot ist fest bis 31. März. unverbindlich. gültig solange der Vorrat reicht.
The prices are **subject to** change without notice.	Preisänderungen bleiben vorbehalten.
The offer is **subject to** prior sale.	Zwischenverkauf vorbehalten.

To create goodwill

I hope this quotation will find your approval.	Ich hoffe, dieses Angebot sagt Ihnen zu.
We look forward to welcoming you as our customers.	Wir freuen uns darauf, Sie als Kunden begrüßen zu dürfen.
We assure you that your order **will be** dealt with promptly and carefully.	Wir sichern Ihnen eine rasche und sorgfältige Erledigung Ihres Auftrags zu.
Should you have any further queries, our staff **will be** pleased to assist you **at any** time.	Sollten Sie nun weitere Fragen haben, stehen Ihnen unsere Mitarbeiter jederzeit gerne zur Verfügung.

Unit 11
Orders

WORD BANK
initial order • trial order • standing order • repeat order • order on call • order form • quantity • description • item • article • sample • pattern • terms and conditions • unit price • total price • to choose • to order • to place an order • to process • to deliver

Orders are placed either in response to an offer or on the buyer's own initiative. A first order is also called an **initial order**. A **trial order** is placed for a small quanitity to test the merchandise or service. **Repeat orders** cover goods or services ordered before. **Standing orders** ensure that identical quantities are supplied at regular intervals. **Orders on call** are placed for large quantities, called for at irregular intervals. They play an important role within the concept of just-in-time delivery.

1 **Read the text. Then cover it up and complete the sentences.**
R/P

1. A first order is also called …
2. A trial order is placed for a small quantity to test …
3. Repeat orders cover goods or services …
4. Standing orders ensure that identical quantities are supplied at …
5. Orders on call are placed for large quantities, called for at …

* **2** **Translate the text above.**
M

Online-Link
808260-0011

A Orders in writing

Sarah Brookfield has studied Herkules' offer for Turbostar running shoes and has read the attached test report. As she is favourably impressed by this report and by the results of the durability tests Sports Island conducted on the sample pairs, she decides to place a trial order.

1 R **Study Sarah Brookfield's order letter and the order form on the next page and choose the correct prepositions from the box.**

by • for • from • of • to • with (2x)

Sports Island
Quality Sports Equipment

41 Bryant Road – London W7 9QB
Tel. 020 74127333 – Fax 020 74127334 – www.sportsisland.uk

Ex/SB 5 October 201_

Mr Philipp Schäfer
Herkules
Ziegelberg 8–12
89331 Neustadt
Germany

Dear Mr Schäfer — appropriate salutation

Subject: Order for Turbostar running shoes

Thank you for your e-mail offer **1** 26 September, the attached Test Report and the five sample pairs you sent us by separate post. — reference to offer, etc.

We are favourably impressed by your products and wish to place a trial order **2** a total of 750 pairs, as per our attached Order Form No. 5347. — order on order form

Please confirm this order indicating the bank account **3** which you wish to have the sum in question transferred. We will then instruct our bankers immediately to remit the invoice amount.

The goods will be collected **4** Transeurope Hauliers who will contact you shortly. — instructions, if necessary

We look forward to receiving the consignment soon. If the shoes find our customers' approval we will be pleased to place further orders **5** you. — appropriate ending

Yours sincerely
SPORTS ISLAND — complimentary close

Sarah Brookfield
Sarah Brookfield
Purchasing Manager

Encl. Order Form No. 5347 — enclosure, if applicable

Order form

Sports Island
Quality Sports Equipment

41 Bryant Road – London W7 9QB
Tel. 020 74127333 – Fax 020 74127334 – www.sportsisland.uk

ORDER NO. 5347

5 October 201_

Herkules
Ziegelberg 8–12
89331 Neustadt
Germany

order (on order form, if appropriate)
– quantity
– description (article No.)
– unit price, total price

Please supply

Quantity	Item	Sizes	Unit Price	Total Price
25 pairs each	Turbostar Running Shoes	5, 5 ½ ,11, 12	€40.50	€4,050.00
50 pairs each		6, 6 ½, 7, 7 ½, 10	€40.50	€10,125.00
100 pairs each		8, 8 ½, 9, 9 ½	€40.50	€16,200.00

Terms of delivery: EXW Neustadt — terms of delivery

Terms of payment: Cash **6** order — terms of payment

Delivery: **7** stock — delivery time

Sarah Brookfield

Sarah Brookfield
for Sports Island

2 R/P **Restore the correct order of these jumbled elements and rewrite the correspondence on a sheet of paper.**

1 We have studied the enclosed spring catalogue and have chosen two models:

2 Dear Ms Martl

3 I would like to stress that this is a trial order. If we are satisfied with your shirts you may expect regular repeat orders.

4 Thank you very much for your letter of 11 November.

5

Quantity	Article No.	Description	Colours	Sizes	Unit price
50 each	334 053 R	Sports Shirt	Canyon Red	L and XL	€17.50
50 each	334 062 T	Dress Shirt	White	L and XL	€21.70

6 We look forward to receiving the goods as soon as possible.

7 We would like to point out that this order qualifies for 3% early order discount, as mentioned in your letter.

8 Yours sincerely
Tony Shaw

Wilson & Thatcher Ltd.

9 This order is placed subject to the terms and conditions specified in your catalogue.
Payment will be made by bank transfer on receipt of your invoice.

10 Subject: Trial order for shirts

3 P You work in the purchasing department of the German stationery shop, Papier Gehrke, Bahnhofsallee 27, 19053 Schwerin, Tel. 0385 467095, e-mail m.gerke@paper-gehrke.de. Your boss, Martin Gehrke, has put this leaflet with his handwritten notes on your desk and has asked you to e-mail an order to Calendars 4 U.

Phrases

Calendars 4 U

proudly presents its multilingual animal calendar range

Kittens
You're certain to be smitten
12″ x 12″ wall calendar

$11.99

gehen besonders gut! 30 Stück bestellen

Tigers **! new !**
Spectacular photos
12″ x 12″ wall calendar

$11.99

sehr interessant, 20 Stück bestellen

Puppies
Bright-eyed and ready to romp
8″ x 8″ wall calendar

$9.99

fragen, ob auch in '12 x 12' erhältlich, wenn ja 20 Stück, sonst nur 10 Stück

Horses
Superb photos capture their nobility
12″ x 12″ wall calendar
$11.99

nicht bestellen

We offer special rates for orders of 200+ items. Please call us: 800/752-3326.

Calendars 4 U
100 Dolphin Way
San Sebastian, CA 94901
info@calendars4U.com
www.calendars4U.com

auf sofortige Lieferung per Luftpost drängen

Zahlung, wie üblich, durch Überweisung bei Erhalt der Rechnung

um kurze Auftragsbestätigung bitten

E-Mail in meinem Namen an Cyrus B. Reid senden: cb.reid@calendars4U.com

* **4** KMK Sie arbeiten bei Getränke König, Am Sprudelbach 17, 06122 Halle, Tel. 0345 785634, Fax 0345 785635 im Einkauf. Ihre Chefin, Nicole Sachse, hat von der irischen Glashütte Wexford Crystal plc, 1 Wexford Avenue, Sanditon, County Cork, Republic of Ireland, ein Angebot über farbige Kristallgläser für Long Drinks im Geschenkkarton erhalten. Die Gläser sollen guten Kunden zu Weihnachten geschenkt werden.

Sie bittet Sie, das Auftragsschreiben, das sie selbst unterschreiben wird, zu verfassen und dabei folgende Punkte zu berücksichtigen:

- Datum 10. September
- Ansprechpartner: Sean O'Sullivan
- Betreff
- Dank für Angebot vom 5. September
- Bestellung: je 1000 Sets bestehend aus je 2 Kristallgläsern für Long Drinks in den Farben rot, blau und grün, im Geschenkkarton
- Gesamtauftragsvolumen: 3000 Sets
- Preis: € 12,50 pro Set zu 2 Gläsern
- Mengenrabatt: 10 %
- Lieferungsbedingung: DAP Am Sprudelbach 17, 06122 Halle, Germany, Incoterms 2010
- Zahlung: bei Erhalt der Ware durch Banküberweisung auf das Konto bei der Cork County Bank.
- Bitte um strikte Einhaltung der versprochenen Lieferfrist von vier Wochen
- Bestellung wird auf Grund unserer beiliegenden allgemeinen Geschäftsbedingungen erteilt
- Anlage: Geschäftsbedingungen

5 **Your boss wants "draper trestles" (Tischböcke) to furnish a factory outlet. Use the internet to find suppliers. Note down prices etc. in English and check that the supplier has an online ordering facility.**

B Orders by phone

Kirsty Burnham from Global Catering in Manchester has received an order from an upmarket chain of delicatessens. She rings International Snacks in Düsseldorf and places an order with them.

1 KMK A1.24 **Kopieren Sie das Bestellformular und füllen Sie es aus, während Sie das Telefonat zweimal hören.**

Portionen	Code-Nr.	Artikel	Preis pro Portion
	PSF 135	Schwäbischer Wurstsalat	€ 0,55
	PSF 136	Schinkenröllchen mit Spargel	€ 0,45
	PSF 137	Salami-Aufschnitt auf Roggentaler	€ 0,60
	PSF 138	kleine Frankfurter Würstchen mit Senf	€ 0,45
	PSF 139	Mini-Frikadellen mit Kartoffelsalat und fettarmer Yoghurtsoße	€ 1,05
	PSG 234	Putencocktail in Melone	€ 0,85
	PSG 235	Geflügelsalat Hawaii	€ 0,75
	PSM 311	Räucherlachs auf Pumpernickel mit Meerrettich	€ 0,95
	PSM 312	Bismarckhering, gerollt mit Gürkchen	€ 0,35
	PSM 313	Matjesfilet mit Remoulade	€ 0,65
	PSM 314	Anchovisfilet, gerollt mit gefüllten Oliven	€ 0,85
	PSM 315	Eismeerkrabben-Cocktail	€ 1,15
	PSD 408	Früchtequark	€ 0,45
	PSD 409	Rote Grütze mit Vanillecreme	€ 0,45

Transportart:	Liefertag und -zeitpunkt:	Lieferort:	Rechnung an:

2 KMK **Schreiben Sie als Marcel Krenz die im Telefonat mit Kirsty Burnham angekündigte E-Mail als Auftragsbestätigung (siehe ausgefülltes Bestellformular) mit Versandanzeige.**

Absender: marcel.krenz@internationalsnacks.de
Empfänger: burnham.globalcateringuk@aol.com
Sie haben inzwischen folgende Einzelheiten zum Versand geklärt:

- Versand per Luftfracht durch Spedition Fuhrmann & Söhne, Düsseldorf
- Flug-Nr. LH 3697, Abflug: Flughafen Düsseldorf, 13:05 Uhr deutsche Zeit
- Ankunft Manchester Airport, Freight Terminal, 13:25 Uhr britische Zeit

3 Work with a partner. Sit back to back and act out the following telephone conversation. Then change roles.

Phrases

A	B
Sie sind Nico/Nicole Sachse und arbeiten bei Getränke König in Halle. Sie hatten ihren britischen Lieferanten BIG Beverages gestern in einem Fax gebeten, einen Auftrag über 500 Flaschen Fruchtsaft, Marke Tropicana, drei Tage früher auszuliefern. →	You are Max/Maggy Lane from BIG Beverages in Chipping, UK. Yesterday you got a fax from a German customer, Getränke König from Halle requesting you to bring delivery of their order for 500 bottles of Tropicana fruit juice forward by three days. You ring them up. Begin the conversation with a few friendly personal remarks e.g. asking how the person taking the call is.
Sie nehmen den Anruf entgegen. Reagieren Sie angemessen auf die Frage, wie es Ihnen geht. →	Refer to yesterday's fax and tell your partner that you regret that it is absolutely impossible to dispatch this particular fruit juice earlier.
Drücken Sie Ihre Enttäuschung aus und erklären Sie, dass Ihr Kunde den Fruchtsaft spätestens nächsten Freitag für einen großen Empfang benötigt. →	Suggest that you send a substitute, your new fruit drink, called Tropical Sunset. The taste is very similar to that of Tropicana fruit juice.
Fragen Sie nach dem Preis dieses neuen Fruchtsafts. →	Tell your partner that you are sorry to say that the price is 5 p higher per bottle as Tropical Sunset contains no artificial flavouring.
Machen Sie Ihrem Gesprächspartner klar, dass Sie nicht in der Lage sind, so viel mehr zu bezahlen. →	To accommodate the customer offer 2.5% introductory discount on this particular order.
Zeigen Sie sich erfreut über dieses Entgegenkommen und fragen Sie, wann die 500 Flaschen abgeschickt werden können. →	Reply that the consignment will be handed over to the forwarders tomorrow morning and will reach the customer the day after tomorrow.
Danken Sie Ihrem Gesprächspartner für seine Bemühungen und beenden Sie das Gespräch. →	Close with thanks for the order.

Language and grammar

Rewrite the following text, using capital letters where necessary.

the organisation of petroleum exporting countries (opec) was formed in 1960 with five founding members: iran, kuwait, saudi arabia and venezuela. by the end of 1971 six other nations had joined the group: qatar, indonesia, libya, united arab emirates, algeria and nigeria. since then opec has been trying to control crude oil prices by setting quotas for production. some major oil exporting countries such as russia, norway and mexico have remained outside opec. the british analyst jonathan baker writing in the june edition of the trade journal "global oil" says that oil prices are highly cyclical and are supported by high demand from south east asia, especially china and india.

Language and grammar: Use of capital letters

Geographische Eigennamen werden groß geschrieben. Im Gegensatz zum Deutschen werden im Englischen auch geographische Adjektive groß geschrieben.

We have customers in **N**ew **S**outh **W**ales in **A**ustralia.
Our **B**ritish and **I**talian subsidiaries are quite successful.

Wochentage, Monate und Feiertage werden groß geschrieben.

The meeting will be held next **F**riday / in **S**eptember / before **C**hristmas.

Vorangestellte Titel, die Teil des Namens bilden, schreibt man groß. Nachgestellte Titel werden meist klein geschrieben.

The report was presented by **V**ice-**P**resident Brian Laurel.
John Hardy, chairman of Media Clusters, agreed to the proposal.

Die Namen von Ministerien, Behörden etc. werden groß geschrieben.

The **F**ederal **C**ommunications **C**ommission ruled that the deal was illegal.
The **D**epartment of **T**rade and **I**ndustry provides help for start-ups.

V5 Video Lounge Manufacturing

BBC Motion Gallery

You are about to see a video about a company based on the Isle of Wight (small island off the south coast of England). Watch the video, then answer the following questions:

1. What does the company manufacture?
2. What industry do orders for these products come from?
3. How are the products transported to customers?
4. What other industry on the Isle of Wight is mentioned?

Phrases: Orders

To refer to previous contacts and place an order

We have studied your quotation and enclose Purchase Order No. …	Wir haben Ihr Angebot genau durchgesehen und fügen unsere Bestellung Nr. … bei.
Please supply the following items **on** the terms stated below:	Bitte liefern Sie uns folgende Positionen zu den unten genannten Bedingungen:

To confirm prices and discounts

We would like to order model AC **at** the price of € … less 5 % introductory discount.	Wir möchten Modell AC zum Preis von € …, abzüglich 5 % Einführungsrabatt, bestellen.
We would like to confirm that the prices are taken **from** your price list **of** 1 September.	Wir möchten bestätigen, dass die Preise Ihrer Preisliste vom 1. September entnommen sind.

To confirm the method of payment and the terms of delivery and the delivery time

As agreed, we will effect payment **by** bank transfer 30 days **from** date of invoice.	Wie vereinbart werden wir die Zahlung 30 Tage nach Rechnungsdatum per Banküberweisung vornehmen lassen.
Payment will be made **by** irrevocable and confirmed letter of credit.	Die Zahlung erfolgt durch unwiderrufliches und bestätigtes Akkreditiv.
Your above-mentioned prices are quoted CIF Hamburg.	Ihre oben genannten Preise verstehen sich CIF Hamburg.
Delivery **is to** be made DAP Stuttgart.	Die Lieferung soll DAP Stuttgart erfolgen.
Complete delivery **by** … is a firm condition of this order.	Vollständige Lieferung bis … stellt eine feste Bedingung für diesen Auftrag dar.
Please note that the goods must reach us **by** 1 March at the latest.	Wir weisen darauf hin, dass die Ware bis spätestens 1. März hier eintreffen muss.

To give instructions and ask for confirmation

Please arrange for transportation **by** Eurotrans Ltd.	Bitte veranlassen Sie, dass der Transport von Eurotrans Ltd. durchgeführt wird.
Please make sure that the figurines are packed with the utmost care.	Bitte sorgen Sie dafür, dass die Figürchen äußerst sorgfältig verpackt werden.
Please acknowledge this order promptly.	Bitte bestätigen Sie diesen Auftrag umgehend.

To close the correspondence

We look forward to receiving the goods **in** time and to doing further business with you.	Wir sehen dem rechtzeitigen Eintreffen der Ware entgegen und freuen uns auf weitere Geschäfte mit Ihnen.

Unit 12
Transport and logistics

WORD BANK

transport • logistics • shipping • forwarding • cargo • freight • door-to-door delivery • modes of transport • types of packing • dispatch advice • waybill • consignment note • bill of lading • certificate of origin • packing list • insurance policy / certificate • to confirm • to acknowledge • to send • to ship • to transport • to pack • to wrap • to deliver

CONTAINER SHIPPING

World trade is forecast to continue growing strongly over the next decade. Today roughly 90 % of non-bulk cargo is transported in containers stacked on transport ships. Cargo is also transported via roll on / roll off (ro-ro) ferries that offer easy loading and unloading. New cars, for instance, are simply driven on and off massive car carriers that hold thousands of vehicles. Ports such as Felixstowe in East Anglia are being deepened to accommodate the new generation of massive container ships.

The fact that the average consumer appears to have no idea how running shoes, washing machines, coffee or tonnes of toys arrive in the shops from all over the world is a constant source of irritation to the shipping world. "The global economy only exists thanks to shipping, in particular container shipping," says one industry analyst. The long-term downward trend in shipping costs has facilitated economic growth worldwide.

At the present time China clearly dominates world trade flows both in terms of exports of finished goods and imports of raw materials. However, shipping is a highly cyclical business reflecting growth and stagnation in the world economy. Carriers, ship-owners and terminal operators have constantly to invest in new ships and facilities. But they do not have a good record of getting the supply / demand ratio right and have often ended up either with inadequate or excess capacity.

1 R **Beantworten Sie folgende Fragen zu vorstehendem Zeitungsartikel auf Deutsch.**

1. Welches sind die größten und wichtigsten Transportmittel für den Welthandel?
2. Weswegen ist die Schifffahrtsbranche verärgert?
3. Wodurch wurde das rasche Wachstum des Welthandels erst ermöglicht?
4. Wie zeigt sich, dass die Schifffahrtsbranche von der Konjunktur abhängt?

* **2** M **Work in groups. Each group translates one paragraph from the text on page 151 in writing. Present your result to the class.**

3 **Use the internet to find out the percentages of goods transported by a) road and b) rail in the EU.**

A Modes of transport

Tobias Krabbe from the German company Form und Raum GmbH has been asked to collect first-hand information on the various modes of transport. He interviews Marie Boucher from the freight forwarding company FranceTransports which handles most of Form und Raum's international shipments.

1 KMK A1.25 **Listen to the interview with Marie Boucher twice and complete the grid on a separate sheet of paper. Then add whatever other advantages, disadvantages and suitable cargoes you can think of. Compare your result with that of your neighbour.**

	Road 	**Rail** 	**Air** 	**Sea / Inland Waterways** 
Advantages	door-to-door delivery, flexible timetables			
Disadvantages		unless a firm has its own private siding, goods must be transported to and collected from the station		slow; seaworthy packing required
Suitable cargoes			light, urgently required, perishable or valuable goods	

2 **Work in groups. Choose one of the goods mentioned below and explain to your group which mode(s) of transport you would use, giving reasons for your choice. Use the expressions in the bubbles.**

Example: "I'd send the wine by road from Spain to Poland because door-to-door delivery by lorry is probably faster than rail transport."

"I wouldn't transport … because …"

"I'd rather send …"

"It would not be a good idea to ship … considering that …"

"I'd definitely not use … as …"

"In my opinion it would be best to choose …"

"There's no doubt that … should be transported by …"

"I think it would be better to …"

"I suggest we send … either by … or by …"

"I'd suggest sending …"

Urgent medical supplies from Leipzig, Germany, to Wellington, New Zealand

Laptops from a port in South Korea to Berlin

A large printing press from Mannheim in Germany to the port of Jeddah in Saudi Arabia

Tropical fruit from Brazil to Sweden

Designer shoes from Italy to Denmark

Furniture from a manufacturer in Westphalia to a hotel in Austria

Wine in bottles from Spain to Poland

50 cars from a plant in Munich to a car dealer in Lisbon, Portugal

B Packing

Adequate packing is essential to ensure that goods arrive in perfect condition, regardless of the distance they have travelled.

1 Match the German terms (see photos above) with their English equivalents.

1. Eisenfass, Trommel
2. Holzkiste
3. Fass
4. folienumwickelter Karton
5. Rolle, Coil auf Europalette
6. Kunststoffbox mit Formeinlagen
7. Container
8. Ballen
9. Bündel mit Stahlbandumreifung
10. Lattenkiste, -verschlag
11. Einwegpalette
12. Sack

a. bale
b. bundle with steel strapping
c. coil on euro-pallet
d. container
e. crate
f. drum
g. foil-wrapped cardboard box
h. plastic box with mouldings
i. one-way pallet
j. sack
k. wooden case
l. barrel

2 The following sentences do not make much sense. Rearrange the words to form meaningful sentences.

R/P

1. The fruit will be packed in 15 bundles with steel strapping.
2. The pure new wool will be sent in a crate.
3. The steel rods will be shipped in bales.
4. The replacement Mp3 player will come on a reusable pallet.
5. The printing machine will be packed in a cardboard box.
6. The engine will be sent in a plastic gift box with mouldings.

C Dispatch advice

As soon as the goods are ready for dispatch it may be necessary to inform the customer that the goods can either be collected at the seller's premises or that they have been handed over to the carrier – depending on the Incoterms agreed upon in the sales contract. Remember that you are communicating with a customer and be as friendly and helpful as possible.

1 Dispatch advice in writing

Topelektronik has received an order for a total of 1,500 SomeThing Mp3 players from the British company Leigh & Co. Ltd. Cornelia Klinkenberg, head of sales at Topelektronik, informs James Leigh that the goods have now been shipped to the UK.

1 R **Complete Cornelia's e-mail using the verbs from the box.**

accompanied • arrive • attached • delivered • given • packed • picked up • pleased • reach

From:	cornelia.klinkenberg@topelektronik.de		
To:	james.leigh@leigh.co.uk		
Cc:			
Sent:	201_-08-14	**Attachments:**	Invoice No. 149 / 08 / 1_
Subject:	Your order no. 134 A dated 7 August for 1,500 SomeThing Mp3 Players		

Dear Mr Leigh

We are **1** to inform you that the consignment has today been **2** by our forwarders, Transcontinental Logistik, to be **3** by road to your warehouse in Bristol.
The forwarders have **4** us the assurance that the goods will **5** you by Friday afternoon, at the latest.

The Mp3 players are **6** in 15 triple-walled cardboard boxes on one pallet.
The consignment is **7** by the required documents (consignment note, packing list and commercial invoice). A copy of the invoice is **8**.

Thank you once more for this order. We hope the goods will **9** safely and in good time.
We look forward to serving you again.

Kind regards

Cornelia Klinkenberg
Topelektronik
Am Osthang 37
09114 Chemnitz
Tel. +49 371 460873
Fax. +49 371 460874

2 P **Mr Kunal Mahajan, export manager at India Sports, has been processing an order for T-shirts from the German firm Herkules. He now sends them a dispatch advice. Write his fax, using the following prompts:**

- reference to their order of 20 Jan. and their letter of 1 Feb.
- consignment packed in one 20 ft container
- markings on the container: HKS, 3479, Antwerp
- yesterday loaded on board MV Maharani in the port of Mumbai
- expected time of arrival at Antwerp: on or about 12 March
- friendly closing phrase

India Sports

112 Delhi Road, Meerut-250 001
Uttar Pradesh, India
Fax +91 121 2512275
Tel. +91 121 2512270

Telefax

To :	Herkules Ziegelberg 8-12 89331 Neustadt, Germany	**Attention:** **Fax:**	Ms Laura Bayerle +49 8358 88820
From:	Kunal Mahajan, Export Manager		
Date:	15 Feb 201_	**Pages (incl. this one):**	1
Subject:	Your order No. ABF/16 of 20 January and 1 February		

* **3** KMK Sie (eigener Name) arbeiten bei der Münchner Firma Superdress GmbH, E-Mail: sales@superdress.munich.de. Ein britischer Kunde, Richard Knight, Einkäufer bei der Warenhauskette Hamilton's, E-Mail: richard.knight@hamiltons.co.uk, hatte bei Ihnen eine Sendung Herrenhemden bestellt, die dringend für eine Modeschau benötigt werden.

Schreiben Sie eine E-Mail als Versandanzeige und berücksichtigen Sie dabei Folgendes:

- Bezug auf Auftrag vom 18. August
- Sendung heute der Spedition Kleine zum Transport per Luftfracht übergeben
- British Airways Flug Nr. BA 777
- Abflug: Flughafen München, 22 August, 11:35 Uhr,
  Ankunft: Manchester Airport, 12:55 Uhr
- Erwartung, dass Hemden rechtzeitig für die Modeschau eintreffen
- nochmaliger Dank für den Auftrag

2 Order confirmation and inquiry concerning transport by phone

1 R A1.26 **Thomas Krabbe from Form und Raum has received an order from a British customer. He confirms the order and the transport arrangements by phone. Listen to the dialogue and answer the following questions.**

1. What is the name of Jennifer Ashley's firm?
2. Has Tobias spoken to Jennifer before?
3. When did Jennifer place the order?
4. How many Hermes standard lamps, Odin uplighters and Bauhaus coffee tables were ordered?
5. What are the first and the last order numbers, the second being O160u?
6. When is the consignment expected to arrive?

2 I Cornelia Klinkenberg from Topelektronik in Chemnitz had promised James Leigh from Leigh & Co. Ltd in Bristol, UK, that the Mp3 Players he had ordered would arrive by Friday afternoon at the latest. It is now 4 pm on Friday (local time) and the lorry has not yet arrived. James Leigh rings Cornelia Klinkenberg.

Act out their dialogue with your neighbour using the prompts below. Phrases

James Leigh	**Cornelia Klinkenberg**
	Topelektronik, Klinkenberg
James Leigh/Leigh & Co., Bristol/ Mp3 players/not yet arrived/ now 4pm	
	Try to reach driver on his mobile phone/hold line?/ring back?
hold/urgent	
	spoken to driver/driver on motorway M4/ 20 miles away
here/next half hour?	
	driver confident/arrive before 5 pm/ reason for delay/held up in Channel Tunnel/ security check/false alarm/explosives in a van on the train/took almost 3 hours
glad to hear/arrive this afternoon/thanks	
	lucky still in office/5 pm in Germany
e-mail/as soon as goods have arrived/ nice weekend/Bye	
	too/Goodbye

D Documents in foreign trade

Waybills, also called **consignment notes, (Frachtbriefe)** are used in road, rail or air transport. They are contracts between the sender of the goods and the carrier (Frachtführer) and provide detailed information about the consignment and the transportation.

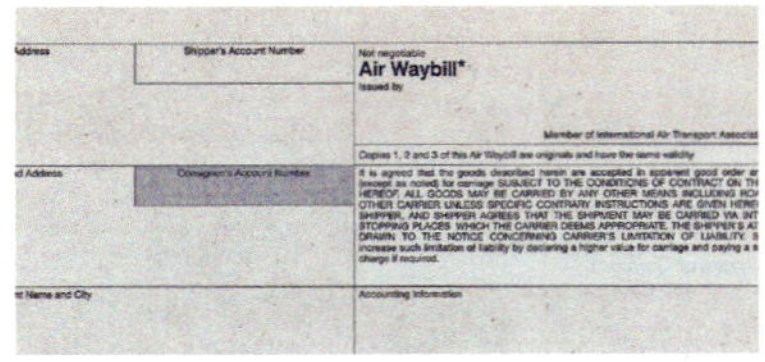

The **Bill of Lading** (B/L) **(Konnossement)** is the freight document in sea transport and when the transportation involves several modes of transport. It is a document of title (Eigentumsurkunde) , which means that any lawful holder of the B/L is the rightful owner of the goods. Bills of Lading must be **clean (rein)**, that is to say the carrier (e.g. the captain of the ship) must have signed the B/L **without** making a note on it that the consignment shows signs of a defect or damage from the outside.

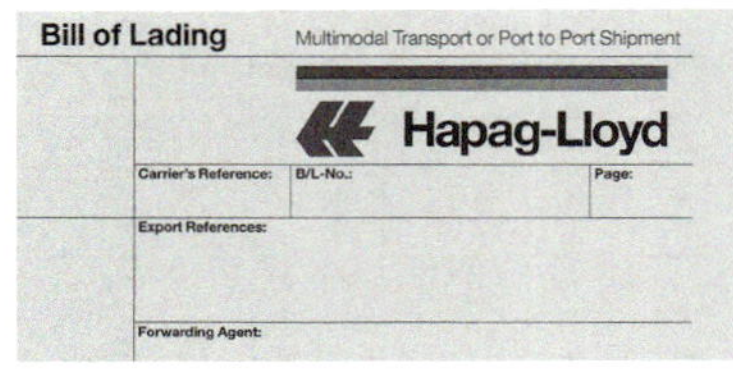

A **Certificate of Origin (Ursprungszeugnis)** shows the country of origin of the goods or the country where they were mainly produced. There is a common EU Certificate of Origin. Certificates of Origin are usually legalized by a chamber of commerce.

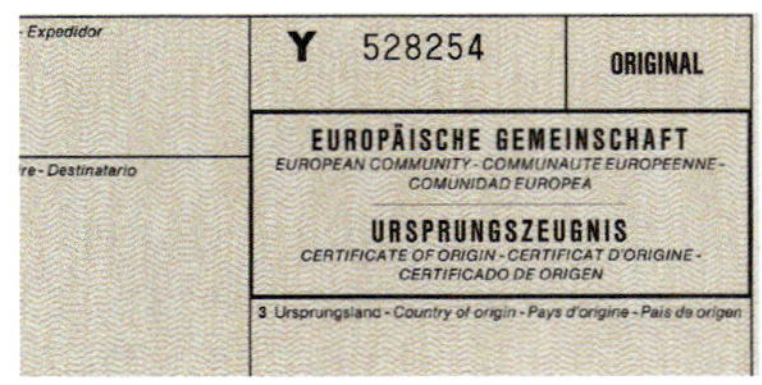

The **Packing List (Packliste)** is a detailed statement of the goods supplied in a particular consignment.

Commercial Invoice (Handelsrechnung) and Proforma Invoice (Proforma-Rechnung) see Unit 13.

Insurance Policy/Certificate (Versicherungspolice/-schein) see Info-Box on page 159.

Export documents are available as standard paper forms. Increasingly, however, such documents are created by computer software and forwarded via the internet.

1 R Compare the translation with the above text on the Bill of Lading and find the missing words from the box.

Beschädigung • Eigentümer • Kapitän • Seetransport • Sendung

Das Konnossement (B/L) ist das Frachtpapier für den **1** und für Transporte, bei denen mehrere Transportarten zum Einsatz kommen. Es ist eine Eigentumsurkunde, d.h. jeder rechtmäßige Inhaber der B/L ist rechtmäßiger **2** der Ware. Konnossemente müssen rein sein, das heißt, der Frachtführer (z.B. der **3** des Schiffes) muss die B/L unterschrieben haben, ohne einen Vermerk anzubringen, der besagt, dass die **4** äußerlich Zeichen eines Mangels oder einer **5** aufweist.

2 P **Edward Ferrars from Norland Industries in Southampton ships 700 colour printers to a customer in Durban, South Africa. Study his quotation in Unit 10 and fill in the details missing from the B / L (on a separate sheet of paper).**

SHIPPER
Norland Industries,
39 Marchwood Industrial Park,
Southampton SO11 3DG

CUSTOMER NO.	REF. NO.	B/L NO.
MSA-24	CP 100 / 150	428 379 421

LINER BILL OF LADING

568 HARBOUR STREET, SOUTHAMPTON, SO4 3DL
UNITED KINGDOM

GENERAL AGENTS WORLD WIDE
WORLDCARGO

CONSIGNEE

NOTIFY
De Boer Office Equipment Pty.,
422 Drakens Road,
Durban 4051, SA

LOCAL VESSEL	FROM
	Southampton
OCEAN VESSEL	**PORT OF LOADING**
Santa Maria	
PORT OF DISCHARGE	**FINAL DESTINATION**

FREIGHT PAYABLE AT	NUMBER OF ORIGINAL B/L
Southampton	three

MARKS & NUMBERS	NUMBER OF PACKAGES/DESCRIPTION OF GOODS	GROSS WEIGHT Kos.	MEASUREMENT Cbm.
MOE, 18/18 Durban	18 pallets containing	6.1 t	600 x 1200 x 215 each

FREIGHT AND CHARGES
GBP 1145.30

Shipped on board in apparent good order and condition, weight, measure, marks, numbers, quality, contents and value unknown, for carriage to the port of discharge or so near thereunto as the Vessel may safely get and lie always a oat, to be delivered in the like good order and condition at the aforesaid Port unto Consignee or their Assigns they paying freight as per note on the margin plus other charges incurred in accordance with the provisions contained in this Bill of Lading.
In accepting this Bill of Lading the Merchant expressly accepts and agrees to all its stipulations on both pages, whether written, printed, stamped or otherwise incorporated as fully as if they were all signed by the Merchant.
One original Bill of Lading must be surrendered duly endorsed in exchange for the goods or delivery order.
IN WITNESS whereof the Master of the said Vessel has signed the number of the original Bills of Lading stated above, all of this tenor and date, one of which being accomplished, the others to stand void.

PLACE AND DATE OF ISSUE
SOUTHAMPTON

SIGNED FOR THE MASTER BY:

Info: Insurance Policy / Certificate

Exports shipments are usually insured **"against all risks"**, which covers a wide range of risks, from sinking to theft. The contract between the sender and the insurance company is called a **policy**. Whenever an open policy, covering a certain lump sum or valid for a certain period, has been taken out, the insurance company issues an insurance **certificate** for an individual shipment. The **premium** is the sum payable by the insured to the insurance company at regular intervals.

3 M **Translate the text above into German. Use the words from the box.**

abdecken • abschließen • ausstellen • Diebstahl • Generalpolice • Pauschalsumme • Police • Prämie • Untergang • Versicherungsnehmer • Versicherungszertifikat

Language and grammar
Translate the statements into English.

1. Ich arbeite in einem Warenhaus und möchte Einzelhandelskaufmann werden.
2. Mein Chef ist leider ziemlich selbstbewusst und nicht sehr sympathisch.
3. Auf Seite 3 unseres Prospekts finden Sie Berichte unserer Kunden, die den Erfolg unserer Methode beweisen.
4. Ich bekomme ungefähr 50 E-Mails pro Tag.
5. Unsere Firma beobachtet die aktuellen Trends auf dem Markt sehr genau.
6. Diese Rechnungen müssen noch einmal geprüft werden.
7. Dieses System wird eventuell in unserem Büro eingeführt.

Language and grammar: False friends

Einige deutsche Wörter werden oft mit englischen Wörtern verwechselt, die etwas ganz anderes bedeuten

deutsches Wort	englische Bedeutung	nicht zu verwechseln mit	deutsche Bedeutung
aktuell	current(ly), topical	actual	tatsächlich, wirklich
bekommen	to get	to become	werden
Billion	trillion	billion	Milliarde
Chef*	boss	chef, chief	(Chef-)koch, Häuptling
eventuell	perhaps, possibly	eventual	schließlich
Fabrik	factory, works	fabric	Stoff
Gymnasium	grammar school	gym(nasium)	Sporthalle
Prospekt	brochure	prospect	Aussicht
Provision	commission	provision	Vorsorge
prüfen	to check, examine	to prove	beweisen
übersehen	to overlook	to oversee	überwachen
Warenhaus	department store	warehouse	Lagerhaus

*Ausnahme: Zusammengesetzte Begriffe wie chief accountant, chief executive officer

V6 Video Lounge IT

BBC Motion Gallery

**This video illustrates important IT applications.
Look out for the answers to the following questions:**

1. What are the duties of the three staff members shown in the video?
2. Give a brief description of any one of them.
3. Why is it important to check everything carefully?
4. What possible problems do they have to watch out for?

Phrases: Transport and logistics

To give particulars about packing

The goods are packed in …	Die Ware ist verpackt in …
• polythene bags.	• Plastikbeutel.
• 20 bales weighing 50 kgs per bale.	• 20 Ballen zu je 50 kg.
• one 20 ft container.	• einem 20-Fuß-Container.
• fibreboard boxes with steel bands.	• Hartfaserkisten mit Stahlbändern.
The goods will be shipped …	Die Ware wird …
• **in** sturdy crates.	• in stabilen Lattenkisten
• **on** reusable pallets.	• auf Mehrwegpaletten
	versandt.

To say that the goods are ready for collection

We are pleased to inform you that the keyboards can now be collected **at** our plant in Leeds.	Wir freuen uns Ihnen mitteilen zu können, dass die Keyboards jetzt in unserem Werk in Leeds abgeholt werden können.

To give particulars about the transport

The consignment has today been handed over to the freight forwarders **for** transportation **to** Warsaw by lorry.	Die Sendung wurde heute der Spedition zur Beförderung nach Warschau per LKW übergeben.
Yesterday the machine was loaded **on board** MS Seagull in Bremerhaven.	Die Maschine wurde gestern in Bremerhaven auf die MS Seagull verladen.
The spare parts will be sent **by** air freight **on** Air Canada flight No. AC 442, arriving **at** Toronto airport at 11:55 **on** 25 September.	Die Ersatzteile werden per Luftfracht mit Air Canada, Flug Nr. AC 442 verschickt. Ankunft: Flughafen Toronto, 25. Sept., 11:55 Uhr.

To close on a friendly note

We hope the goods will arrive punctually and in good condition.	Wir hoffen, die Ware kommt pünktlich und in gutem Zustand bei Ihnen an.
We trust that the quality of our garments will meet your expectations.	Wir sind überzeugt, dass die Qualität unserer Bekleidungsartikel Ihren Erwartungen entspricht.
We feel sure that your customers will be pleased with our new range of …	Wir sind sicher, dass unser neues Sortiment von … Ihren Kunden gefallen wird.

Unit 13
Payment and reminders

WORD BANK

currency • commercial invoice • proforma invoice • IBAN • BIC • bank account • unit price • subtotal • total price • cash • credit card • debit card • cheque • bill of exchange • payment in advance • cash on delivery • open credit • open account • letter of credit • reminder • statement of account • amount due • settlement • to make out an invoice • to transfer • to delay • to collect • to take legal steps

CURRENCY QUIZ

Questions:

1. Which is the youngest of the currencies shown above?
2. Which is the oldest of these currencies?
3. Which of these currencies is the most widely used in international business transactions?
4. Which of these currencies do most individuals use for their daily purchases?

1. The Euro. Euro banknotes and coins replaced 12 former European currencies on 1 January 2002.
2. The Pound Sterling. It has been in use since the Middle Ages. The US Dollar was introduced in 1785, (the Swiss Frank in 1798 and the Yen in 1871).
3. The US Dollar. On a global scale the US-Dollar is still the most widely used currency in business transactions.
4. The Euro. The number of inhabitants in the Euro zone (at present comprising 18 out of 28 EU member countries) is estimated at 335,1 million, approx. 316,1 million people live in the USA.

Online-Link
808260-0013

A The Invoice

The **commercial invoice** (Handelsrechnung) is sent by the seller to the buyer and provides full details on the transaction, such as names, dates, numbers, descriptions, quantities, prices, discounts, terms, taxes (VAT) etc. When making out an export invoice you should make sure that it includes your company's IBAN and your bank's BIC.
A **proforma invoice** (Proformarechnung) contains all the details of the eventual commercial invoice. It may serve as a quotation or be required to apply for an import licence.

1 R **The above text contains three abbreviations. Study their German translations and find the words that have been left out in the full English expressions.**

VAT	Value-added 1 = Mehrwert**steuer**
IBAN	International Bank 2 Number = Internationale **Konto**nummer
BIC	Bank Identifier 3 = Internationaler Bank-**Code**.

2 R Philipp Schäfer is processing the trial order for Turbostar Running shoes which his company, Herkules, has received from Sports Island, a major British chain of sports equipment retailers. (See Unit 11, A). The necessary arrangements for transportation having been made Philipp Schäfer now confirms the order by e-mail and sends the invoice as an attachment.

Study Philipp Schäfer's e-mail and decide which of the tenses in brackets is correct.

Dear Ms Brookfield

Thank you very much for your above-mentioned order.

We are pleased to inform you that the consignment 1 **is picked up / will be picked up** by Transeurope Hauliers for transportation to the UK in two days' time, that is to say on Wednesday, 10 October. The forwarders 2 **have given / had given** us the assurance that the running shoes 3 **will be delivered / will have been delivered** to your premises in London on the following Friday, 12 October, between 9 and 11 a.m. your time.

Since this is a first order we 4 **were sending / are sending** you our invoice No. GB113-14 as an attachment and would appreciate it if you 5 **instructed / have instructed** your bankers at your earliest convenience to remit the sum of €30,375.00 to our account with Bayernbank. For particulars see the attached invoice.

We 6 **feel / felt** sure that your customers 7 **will be pleased / are pleased** with the Turbostar running shoes as they are not merely comfortable, serviceable and durable but stylish as well. We look forward to receiving further orders from you in the near future.

Herkules
the global sports brand
Ziegelberg 8–12
89331 Neustadt
Tel. +49 8358 888-0
Fax +49 8358 88820
www.Herkules.com

USt. ID No. DE 812 039 979

Customer No. UK 22267

INVOICE No. GB113-14

Date: 8 Oct 201_
Your Order No. 5347 of 5 Oct 201_

Sports Island
41 Bryant Road
London W7 9QB
UK

VAT No. 186 4405 32

Person in charge: Mike Kappler
Tel.: +49 8358 888 317
Fax: +49 8358 888 300
E-Mail: accounts@herkules.com

Quantity	**Item**	**Sizes**	**Unit Price**	**Subtotal**
25 pairs each	Turbostar Running Shoes	5, 5 ½ ,11, 12	€ 40.50	€ 4,050.00
50 pairs each		6, 6 ½, 7, 7 ½, 10	€ 40.50	€ 10,125.00
100 pairs each		8, 8 ½, 9, 9 ½	€ 40.50	€ 16,200.00

Total Price € 30,375.00

tax-exempt intra-Community delivery

Terms of delivery: EXW Neustadt
Terms of payment: Cash on receipt of invoice

Please instruct your bank to forward the payment order through

Bank:	Bayernbank AG
BIC:	BABADET TS08
In favour of:	Herkules AG
Bank account number:	214365987
IBAN:	DE49 2006 0460 0214 3659 87

3 R **Study the invoice and find words and expressions for the following German equivalents.**

1. Gesamtpreis
2. Preis pro Einheit/Stückpreis
3. Zahlungsbedingungen
4. Artikel
5. Lieferbedingungen
6. Größen
7. Menge
8. Rechnung
9. Zwischensumme

* **4** P **Study the invoice again and draw up the invoice Cornelia Klinkenberg sent James Leigh on 14 August. Use your imagination for the missing details and refer back to**

1. the enquiry James Leigh sent Cornelia Klinkenberg (Unit 10, A)
2. the dispatch advice Cornelia Klinkenberg sent James Leigh (Unit 12, C)
3. James Leigh's reply to Cornelia Klinkenberg's reminder (Unit 13, C).

B Means and terms of payment

1 Means of payment in trade

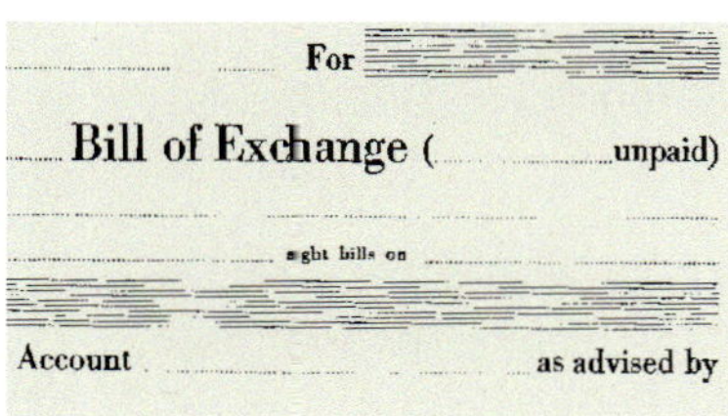

A **credit card** (Kreditkarte) issued by a major credit card company is widely accepted as a means of payment all over the world. The amount to be paid is advanced by the credit card company and debited to the cardholder's account at a later date.

A **debit (or bank) card** (Bankkarte) is issued by a bank. The account-holder may use it to pay for goods and services in shops without handling cash. It differs from credit cards in that the customer's account is immediately debited with the amount of the transaction. Bank cards can also be used to withdraw money from cash points (ATMs). The German EC card is a debit card.

A **cheque** (Scheck) is a written order to a bank to pay a sum of money to a named person or to the bearer (Überbringer) of the cheque. Crossed cheques (Verrechnungsschecks) require the sum to be paid into a bank account. In the UK cheques are still widely used in private and business transactions.

A **bill of exchange** (Wechsel) is a written order telling one person to pay a certain sum of money to a named person on demand or at a certain time in the future. Nowadays bills of exchange are used mainly in foreign trade. If the exporter wishes payment to be made immediately, he orders the importer to pay the invoice amount on demand, or "at sight", that means on presentation of the bill of exchange (B/E). Should the exporter be obliged to grant the importer credit, he will order him to pay the invoice amount at a certain time in the future, e.g. 60 days after the date of the B/E.

1 Match the following expressions with their German equivalents.

1. to accept a credit card	a. Geld abheben
2. to advance an amount	b. eine Kreditkarte annehmen
3. to debit an account	c. eine Bankkarte ausstellen
4. to grant credit	d. ein Konto belasten
5. to issue a bank card	e. Kredit gewähren
6. to withdraw money	f. einen Betrag vorschießen

* 2 Study the text on the bill of exchange on page 165 and translate the following text.

M

Mittels eines Wechsels kann der Verkäufer den Käufer auffordern, eine bestimmte Summe zu einem bestimmten Zeitpunkt an eine bestimmte Person zu zahlen. Der Verkäufer könnte auf dem Wechsel auch vorschreiben, dass der Käufer den Betrag „auf Verlangen" zahlt. Die entsprechende Formulierung wäre dann „zahlbar bei Sicht", d. h. bei Vorlage des Wechsels.

* 3 Übersetzen Sie nachstehenden Text zum Einsatz von Kreditkarten in Großbritannien ins Deutsche. Im Internet haben Sie Übersetzungen für folgende Ausdrücke gefunden:

KMK

overindebted – überschuldet; to turn down an application – einen Antrag ablehnen; debit card – Bankkarte; cashback – Auszahlung von Bargeld; debt levels – Ausmaß der Verschuldung; check-out – Ladenkasse

Payment by plastic cards

In the UK payment by plastic cards overtook cash payments several years ago as consumers use credit or debit cards more frequently. The vast majority of retail outlets accept these cards as a matter of course and supermarkets offer cashback*. Adults now have an average of 4 cards each and this is expected to rise to 5 cards by 2013. Last year the number of credit cards issued rose by 13 per cent and the number of debit cards rose by 6 per cent. Well over half of all debit card holders use their cards on a regular basis when shopping.

Recently banks and other credit card providers have come in for criticism because of fears that consumers are becoming over-indebted. A spokesman for the banks said that between 40 and 50 per cent of all credit card applications were turned down. Debt levels were a problem only for 4 per cent of households.

Plastic cards are essential for e-commerce. Four out of five adults who have access use the internet for online shopping. A third of all online purchases are made from work and top sites include major supermarkets and a well-known young people's fashion chain.

* If the customer wishes, they provide a sum in cash at the check-out, as stipulated by the customer.

4 Use the internet to find statistics on the preferred payment methods – cash, credit card, debit card, cheque, bank transfer – in Germany and the UK.

2 Terms of payment in foreign trade

The terms of payment chosen in an international transaction will depend on the size of the order, the creditworthiness of the customer and the banking system and political situation in the customer's country.
Payment in advance (Vorauszahlung) provides maximum security for the seller, e.g. when the goods have to be manufactured to the buyer's specifications. Payment in advance may also be part of staggered payment, e.g. ⅓ with order, ⅓ on delivery, ⅓ 30 days after delivery.
If **Cash on delivery (COD)** (Zahlung durch Nachnahme) has been agreed upon, the carrier (e.g. the postman) will hand over the goods to the buyer against payment or against written proof by the bank that payment has been effected.
Open credit (Zahlung gegen einfache Rechnung) terms are terms like "30 days net, 10 days 2 %", which means that the buyer has to remit the invoice amount within 30 days. If he pays the amount within 10 days he will be entitled to deduct 2 % cash discount from the invoice amount. Open credit terms provide little security for the seller but are widely used in transactions involving comparatively small sums and/or trusted customers.
In long-standing business relations it is customary to trade on **open account** terms (offenes Zahlungsziel). This means that the buyer does not pay individual invoices, but waits for the monthly statement of account.
A **letter of credit (L/C)** (Akkreditiv) is a promise made by the importer's bank to pay a certain sum to the exporter on presentation of specified documents, the most important of which is a clean bill of lading (see Unit 12). Nowadays L/Cs are irrevocable (unwiderruflich) that means they cannot be revoked without the consent of all parties concerned. As the L/C offers maximum security for both buyer and seller it has become one of the most widely used methods of payment in foreign trade. The exporter can be sure to receive payment as he can rely on the promise made by the importer's bank (the opening bank) – and in the case of a confirmed (bestätigtes) L/C – also on the promise of a bank in his own country (the confirming bank). The importer can be sure to receive the goods as the bank(s) will only advance the money against presentation of the shipping documents which prove that shipment has been effected.

1 R/M **Study the paragraph on the Letter of Credit on page 167. Choose the correct prepositions from the box for the following text. Then translate the text into German.**

at • by • in • until

In a major export transaction the terms of payment may read as follows: **Terms of payment:** Payment **1** irrevocable and confirmed letter of credit, to be opened **2** our favour, payable **3** a German bank and valid **4** 31 July.

2 R **Complete the following business transactions by matching the terms of payment from the box with the numbers.**

cash on delivery • letter of credit • open account terms • open credit • payment in advance

Wilson & Thatcher Ltd, a British retailer, also sells its high-quality shirts and blouses via the Internet. As a means of payment the firm accepts all major credit cards. For customers who refuse to disclose their credit card details on the internet, the retailer's terms of payment are **1** which means that the postman will collect the amount due.

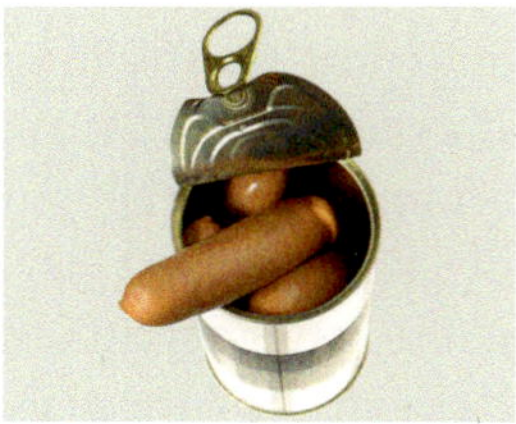

International Snacks GmbH, a German food processing company, gets a phone call from its long-standing customer, Global Catering in Manchester, asking for another 500 tins of mini smoked sausages. These two business partners most likely trade on **2**.

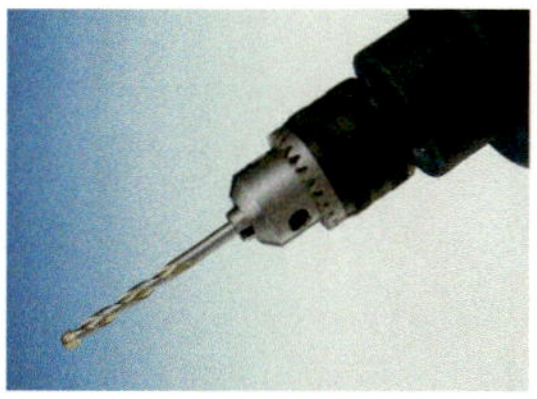

Powertools plc from Cardiff has received an enquiry from a new German customer who wishes to have 10,000 drill heads (Bohrköpfe) manufactured to the German firm's specifications. As Powertools would be unable to sell these drill heads to another customer if the deal broke down, Powertools will insist on **3**.

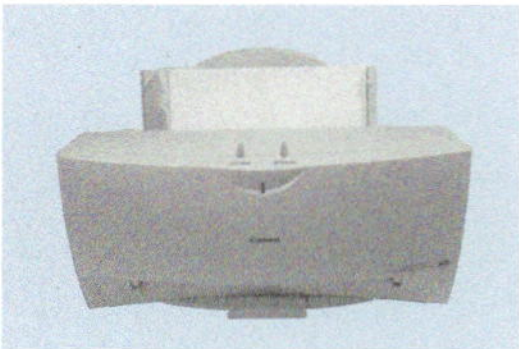

Norland Industries made an offer for colour printers to De Boer Office Equipment in Durban, South Africa. The terms of payment stipulated were: net cash within 30 days from receipt of invoice. Such terms of payment are referred to as **4**.

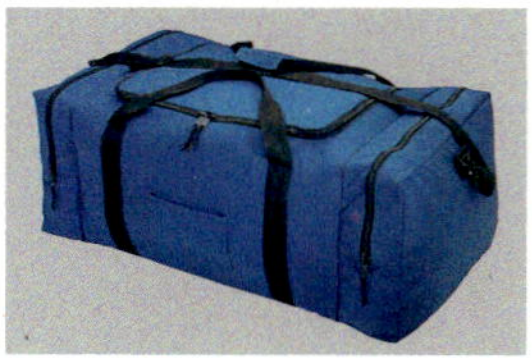

At Herkules, a German manufacturer of sports shoes and bags, the managers in charge of exports are discussing the terms of payment for a substantial order for sports bags from a firm in Bolivia they do not know. They decide to demand payment by **5**.

C Reminders

There are times when bills go unpaid and steps must be taken to collect the invoice amount. One or several reminders may have to be sent, with the requests for payment becoming increasingly insistent. At first a copy of the invoice or statement of account is sent suggesting that the invoice may have been overlooked. If further reminders by telephone, e-mail, fax, or letter have failed to produce the desired reaction, the seller will threaten to charge interest on arrears and to take legal steps unless payment is received by a certain deadline.

1 Reminders in writing

On 18 August the British department stores Hamilton's placed an urgent order for men's shirts with Superdress GmbH. Payment was to be effected 30 days after date of invoice. The goods were shipped by air and must have arrived at Manchester Airport on 22 August. It is now 10 October and no communication from Hamilton's has been received. Bastian Schneider, who is in charge of accounts at Superdress GmbH, decides to send a first polite reminder by fax.

1 R **Complete Bastian Schneider's fax using the words from the box.**

above • aware • dated • due • grateful • immediate

Superdress GmbH

Fritz-Walter-Str. 28, 80469 München
Tel. +49 89 4677524, Fax +49 89 4677625
www.superdress.munich.de

Telefax Message

Date: 10 Oct 201_

Sender: Bastian Schneider, Accounts

To: Hamilton's Department Stores
Hamilton House
Beaumont Rd
Bolton
BL3 4TA

Attention: Richard Knight

Fax : +44 161 234 57799

Pages : 1 (including this)

Re: Our invoice no. OHGB / 42778 **1** 21 August

reference to invoice

Dear Mr. Knight

According to our records the **2** invoice, which was **3** on 21 September, has not been settled.

I wonder whether the invoice has been overlooked or if there has been a problem with this order of which we are not **4** ?

request for explanation

We should be **5** for an **6** settlement and look forward to serving you again.

request for settlement

Yours sincerely
Superdress GmbH

2
P

You are Richard Knight, purchasing manager at Hamilton's Department Stores, e-mail: richard.knight@hamiltons.co.uk. You have just received the fax on page 169 from Superdress GmbH.

Send Mr Schneider, whose e-mail address is b.schneider@superdress.munich.de, an e-mail:

- thanks for fax
- apologize for the delay in payment
- reason: new software in accounts department faulty
- operations now running smoothly at last
- bank instructed to remit invoice amount
- further orders probably next month

3
R

Restore the correct order of these jumbled elements of a final request for payment.

1 I still hope that you will make this action unnecessary by remitting the amount in full within the next seven days.

2 Dear Mr Clarke

3 This account has now remained unpaid for eight weeks and I cannot allow this state of affairs to continue. I regret that I will have to take legal steps unless payment is received in the course of one week.

4 Yours sincerely

Barbara Bruno
Legal Department

5 I am surprised to have received no reply to our previous e-mails and faxes asking for immediate settlement of the attached statement of account.

6 Re: Our statement of account number NZ / 7034 of 9 December 201_

4 KMK Sie arbeiten bei Topelektronik in der Exportabteilung. Ihre Chefin hat gestern nachstehende E-Mail eines britischen Kunden erhalten.

Bitte beantworten Sie die E-Mail und berücksichtigen Sie dabei die handschriftlichen Anweisungen Ihrer Chefin.

From: james.leigh@leigh.co.uk
To: cornelia.klinkenberg@topelektronik.de
Cc:
Sent: 201_-09-27 **Attachments:**
Subject: Your invoice No. 149 / 08 / 14

Dear Ms Klinkenberg

We have received your fax of 15 September concerning the above invoice and would like to apologize for the delay in payment.

Today we have instructed our bank to transfer €30,000 to your account. Much to our regret we have to ask you to grant us a respite of eight weeks for the rest of the invoice amount.

Dank für Überweisung

You may have heard of the severe gale that devastated the South of England two weeks ago. Unfortunately our warehouse was severely hit by the storm, parts of the roof were taken off and much of our stock was soaked by the rain. As the insurance company will take some time to assess the damage and compensate us, we are having to advance considerable sums for the repairs to our warehouse and for the replacement of the damaged stock. This is why we must ask you for the extension.

Bedauern über Sturmschäden, im Fernsehen Bilder gesehen

We hope you will understand our difficulties and grant us this concession.

Mit Aufschub grundsätzlich einverstanden

We are very sorry for the inconvenience caused and look forward to your comments.

Dennoch Bitte um Überweisung des Restbetrags sobald Leigh dazu in der Lage

Yours sincerely

Grußformel: Best wishes
(Setzen Sie meinen Namen darunter)

James Leigh
Leigh & Co. Ltd.
17 Camden Place
Bristol
BS6 6HR
Tel. 0117 4430030

Klinkenberg

*** 5** KMK Sie (eigener Name) arbeiten im Rechnungswesen des Reisebüros Ferne Horizonte, Erfurt, Fax. +49 361 476903, Tel. +49 361 476900. Für den britischen Reiseveranstalter Sunshine Flights Ltd., Fax +44 1233 443006, hatten Sie für eine Gruppe eine Mountainbike-Tour im Thüringer Wald organisiert. Die Rechnung hierfür ist seit 6 Wochen überfällig. Eine erste Erinnerung war ohne Reaktion geblieben.

Schreiben Sie eine Mahnung unter Berücksichtigung folgender Punkte:

- Datum: 28. November
- Ansprechpartner: Margaret Allen
- Bezug auf Rechnung Nr. 009575 vom 04. Oktober
- Verweis auf Ihr Schreiben vom 14. November
- Rechnung inzwischen 6 Wochen überfällig
- Frage nach möglichen Gründen für Zahlungsverzug, da früher pünktlich gezahlt
- Bitte um sofortige Überweisung des Rechnungsbetrags, sonst Rücknahme der günstigen Zahlungsbedingungen
- Erwartung einer umgehenden Reaktion

2 Reminders and replies to reminders by telephone

1 R A1.27 Angela Schirmer from Digitaldruck GmbH in Wiesbaden rings their Spanish customer Imago S.A.

Listen to the dialogue and mark on your own sheet of paper whether the following statements are TRUE or FALSE.

1. Carmen Gonzales is the best person to talk to.
2. Olivia Rubio works in accounts.
3. The reference number is Z2P 7900.
4. Olivia Rubio transferred the amount of €13,723 five weeks ago.
5. This is the first time this year that there has been a delay in payment.
6. Olivia Rubio is going to transfer the amount immediately.

2 KMK A1.27 Sie sind Angela Schirmer und überwachen bei Digitaldruck GmbH den Rechnungseingang. Sie haben soeben einen spanischen Kunden wegen einer überfälligen Rechnung angerufen und das Gespräch aufgezeichnet.

Hören Sie sich das Gespräch noch einmal an und verfassen Sie darüber eine Aktennotiz für den Abteilungsleiter Dr. Klaus Werner.

MEMO

Für:

Verfasser / in: Datum:

Gesprächspartner / in:

Betreff:

3 **Work with a partner. Sit back to back and act out the telephone conversation using the prompts on the role cards on pages 229 and 230. Then change roles.**

Language and grammar
Translate the following sentences.

1. Wir machen Sie darauf aufmerksam, dass die Zahlung per Kreditkarte erfolgen soll.
2. Das Unternehmen soll in 5 selbstständige Geschäftseinheiten aufgeteilt werden.
3. Sollen wir Ihnen die Preisliste per E-Mail zukommen lassen?
4. Soll die Rechnung Nr. ABC/1234 storniert werden?
5. Die neue Geschäftsleitung soll weiteren Stellenabbau planen.
6. Die neue Autobahn soll von einem privaten Unternehmen betrieben werden.
7. Der neue Exportleiter soll sehr tüchtig sein.

Language and grammar:
How to translate the German word "sollen"

Wendungen mit **sollen** werden von Deutschen häufig ungeschickt wiedergegeben.

Die direkte Entsprechung **shall** passt nur bei • Fragen • und juristischen Texten	Shall I help you? The parties to this contract shall notify the administrator within 24 hours.
should bedeutet **sollte (eigentlich)**:	You should put more emphasis on this point.
sollen kann im Geschäftskontext in Fragen mit **do you want me / us to ...?** übersetzt werden: Sollen wir diese Teile zurückschicken?	Do you want us to return these components?
to be to ... ist eine passende Übersetzung für **sollen** im Sinne einer Anordnung oder einer Absicht bzw. eines festen Planes: Die Bauarbeiter sollen sofort anfangen. Das Problem soll durch weitere Verhandlungen gelöst werden.	The builders are to start work immediately. The problem is to be solved by further negotiations.
Im Falle einer Absicht / eines Plans kann **to be to ...** durch **to be intended to / planned to ...** präzisiert werden: Die Erhöhung der Mehrwertsteuer soll den Haushalt ausgleichen. Die Ausstellung soll Anfang nächsten Jahres stattfinden.	The increase in VAT is intended to balance the budget. The exhibition is planned to take place early next year.
to be said to ... bedeutet **sollen** im Sinne von **es heißt, man sagt**: Die Firma soll sich in Schwierigkeiten befinden.	The company is said to be in trouble.

Phrases: Invoices and reminders

To refer to the invoice or statement of account

We are sending you our invoice No. 43-298 **amounting to** €304.75 as an attachment.	Als Anhang senden wir Ihnen unsere Rechnung Nr. 43-298 in Höhe von €304,75.
The enclosed statement of account shows a balance of €5,402.90 **in** our favour.	Der beiliegende Kontoauszug weist einen Saldo von €5.402,90 zu unseren Gunsten auf.
The invoice was due **on** 31 July.	Die Rechnung war am 31. Juli fällig.
The invoice amount is now four weeks overdue.	Der Rechnungsbetrag ist nun vier Wochen überfällig.

To suggest an oversight or demand an explanation

I wonder whether the invoice has been overlooked.	Ich frage mich, ob die Rechnung übersehen wurde.
You have not given us any explanation for the delay **in** payment.	Sie haben uns keinerlei Erklärung für den Zahlungsverzug gegeben.

To demand payment and to point out consequences of non-payment

Please remit the amount due immediately.	Bitte überweisen Sie den fälligen Betrag umgehend.
We should be grateful for an early settlement of our statement of account.	Für baldigen Ausgleich unseres Kontoauszugs wären wir dankbar.
We would ask you to clear the balance without further delay.	Wir möchten Sie bitten, den Saldo unverzüglich auszugleichen.
We must insist that you make payment **by** 5 May at the latest.	Wir müssen darauf bestehen, dass Sie die Zahlung bis spätestens 5. Mai vornehmen.
Should you fail to meet this deadline we shall have no option **but** to change our terms of payment.	Sollten Sie diese Frist nicht einhalten, bleibt uns keine andere Wahl als unsere Zahlungsbedingungen zu ändern.
If we do not receive payment **by** the end of the week, we will have to stop further deliveries.	Wenn Ihre Zahlung nicht bis Ende der Woche hier eingeht, müssen wir die Belieferung einstellen.
I will have to take legal steps if you do not settle the account within 7 days.	Ich werde juristische Schritte einleiten müssen, falls Sie die Rechnung nicht innerhalb von 7 Tagen begleichen.
Unless you remit the amount **in** time, we will hand the matter over to a collection agency.	Wenn Sie den Betrag nicht rechtzeitig überweisen, übergeben wir die Angelegenheit einem Inkassounternehmen.

To close the reminder

If payment has already been effected in the meantime, please disregard this letter.	Sollte die Zahlung inzwischen erfolgt sein, betrachten Sie diesen Brief bitte als gegenstandslos.
We should be sorry to lose a long-standing customer and would ask you to contact us immediately.	Wir würden einen langjährigen Kunden nur ungern verlieren, setzen Sie sich deshalb bitte sofort mit uns in Verbindung.
We are looking forward to an early settlement.	Wir erwarten Ihre baldige Zahlung.

To reply to a reminder

We have instructed our bank to transfer the sum of €7,455 **to** your account **with** Sachsenbank.	Wir haben unsere Bank angewiesen, den Betrag von €7.455 auf Ihr Konto bei der Sachsenbank zu überweisen.
We have received your letter **of** 2 July and thank you for your patience.	Wir haben Ihr Schreiben vom 2. Juli erhalten und danken Ihnen für Ihre Geduld.
We assure you that payment will be effected in full as soon as our computers are operational again.	Wir versichern Ihnen, dass die Zahlung in voller Höhe erfolgt, sobald unsere Rechner wieder funktionieren.
We are deeply sorry that the invoice has become overdue.	Es tut uns sehr leid, dass die Rechnung überfällig wurde.
We apologize for the delay **in** payment.	Wir entschuldigen uns für den Zahlungsverzug.
The delay was due to • an oversight. • a breakdown of our computer system. • an error **by** our bank.	Der Grund für den Zahlungsverzug war • ein Versehen. • eine Störung unserer EDV-Anlage. • ein Irrtum unserer Bank.
We are afraid we must ask you **for** an extension of 4 weeks.	Wir müssen Sie leider um einen Aufschub von 4 Wochen bitten.
We suggest that we pay **in** 3 instalments **of** $30,330.	Wir schlagen vor, dass wir in 3 Raten von $30.330 zahlen.
We are prepared to pay 7% interest on arrears.	Wir erklären uns bereit, Verzugszinsen in Höhe von 7% zu entrichten.
We hope you will understand our difficult situation and grant us this concession.	Wir hoffen, Sie haben Verständnis für unsere schwierige Lage und machen uns dieses Zugeständnis.

UNIT 14
Complaints and adjustments

WORD BANK
complaint • inconvenience • transaction • explanation • adjustment • solution • replacement • substitute • discount • compromise • faulty • damaged • too late • defective • wrong • justified • unjustified • to complain • to insist on • to cancel • to return • to apologize • to grant • to repair • to replace • to take back

A Making complaints

Even though in business transactions not "everything that can go wrong, will" – as the saying goes – it will sometimes be necessary to make a complaint. Goods or services may have been supplied too late, goods may be faulty or damaged, services may prove unsatisfactory, the wrong goods or the wrong quantities may have been delivered etc. In such cases the customer must promptly notify the seller of the problem in writing, especially if a complaint by telephone has not brought the desired result. A complaint should not be written to express anger, but to get results. It should be calm and polite but also firm. In your written complaint you should

- give all the necessary details of the transaction (order No., date of delivery, etc.)
- describe the problem clearly (327 mugs broken, hotel noisy, etc.)
- stress the inconvenience caused
- suggest a solution (replacement, discount, etc.)
- ask for immediate action

Online-Link
808260-0014

1 KMK **Übertragen Sie den Text auf Seite 176 ins Deutsche.**

2 **Match the causes for complaint on the left with the suggested solutions on the right. Sometimes several solutions may be appropriate.**

1. delay in delivery	a. grant a price reduction
2. faulty goods	b. improve the service rendered
3. goods damaged	c. repair the goods
4. services unsatisfactory	d. replace the goods
5. the wrong goods	e. send the goods by air freight
6. wrong quantity	f. send the missing quantity
	g. take back the goods
	h. take back the surplus goods
	i. send a credit note

3 P **Describe to your class a recent experience when you had reason to complain or actually made a complaint. If you can't think of any, use the prompts below.**

- flight overbooked
- hairdresser ruined your hair
- noisy building site next to the beach
- had to wait 50 minutes for a meal at a restaurant
- beetle found in soft drinks bottle
- car repair costs not refunded by insurance company
- pages in detective novel were missing
- new camera did not work
- soles came off new shoes after 4 weeks
- bank debited your account with the wrong amount

1 Complaints in writing

The British chain of sports equipment, SPORTS ISLAND, has just received a consignment of polo shirts from a new supplier in India. Unfortunately their Incoming Goods Control has found that most of the polo shirts are not correctly labelled. Sarah Brookfield, the purchasing manager, decides to complain by e-mail.

From: sarah.brookfield@sportsisland.co.uk
To: mahajan@indiasports.id
Cc:
Sent: 201_-01-31 **Attachments:**
Subject: Polo shirts, our purchase order No. PH / 346 / 06 of 18 Dec 201_

detailed reference to order

Dear Mr Mahajan

The consignment of 5,000 polo shirts under our above-mentioned purchase order arrived yesterday in due course.

However, when our Incoming Goods Control checked the merchandise we were dismayed to find that most of the polo shirts are not labelled correctly. The sizes printed on the inside tags sewn onto the shirts do not correspond to the actual sizes of the garments. Needless to say, the polo shirts cannot be sold with these incorrect tags.

description of problem

As it would be rather time-consuming to return the goods to you at your expense and wait for a replacement delivery, I would like to suggest that we commission a local firm to remove the tags and replace them with the right ones. You would, of course, have to bear the costs for the reworking and send us the required number of tags by air as soon as possible.

solution suggested

We are disappointed at the way you have handled our first order and look forward to receiving your comments on this matter in the very near future.

request for prompt adjustment

Best regards

Sarah Brookfield
Purchasing Manager

SPORTS ISLAND
41 Bryant Road
London W7 9QB
Tel. 020 74127333
Fax 020 74127334

1 R **Read Sarah Brookfield's e-mail several times. Then cover it up and complete these sentences on your own sheet of paper.**

1. The consignment of polo shirts arrived yesterday **1**.
2. We were dismayed to find that most of the polo shirts **2**.
3. **3** the polo shirts cannot be sold with these incorrect tags.
4. As it would be **4** to return the goods to you at your expense …
5. You would, of course, **5** for the reworking …
6. We are disappointed **6** our first order …

2 R **Restore the correct order of these jumbled elements of a complaint about a delay in delivery.**

1 This matter is causing us great inconvenience and we hope you will do your utmost to deliver the tool kits without any further delay.

2 On 31 July we placed the above mentioned order with you which you confirmed the next day assuring us of delivery within 3 weeks.

3 Subject: Delay in delivery of our order No. W-549 / 07 for 1000 household tool kits

4 We hope to receive your comments by return.

5 Dear Mr Vernon

6 Since then 5 weeks have passed and we have neither received the tool kits nor heard anything from you.

7 Yours sincerely
Hammer Werkzeughandel

8 Tanja Kirchner
Purchasing Department

9 As our own customers are getting impatient we must insist on immediate delivery. Should you fail to deliver by the end of next week we are afraid that we shall have no option but to cancel the order and seek another supplier.

3
P

You (Markus Reber) work in the personnel department of Otto Greiling GmbH (e-mail: personnel@ottogreiling.aol.com), a major supplier to the car industry. For several years your firm has been sending junior executives to a language school in Brighton, UK, for intensive coaching in business English. This year's two participants were, however, not completely satisfied with the language school's services when they attended the course from October 14 to 20.

Send the principal an e-mail. (E-mail: pam.robinson@businessspeak.co.uk)

- Point out the following shortcomings:
  - accommodation at private hotel inadequate – central heating system out of order
  - participants' needs (the language of export procedures) not properly taken into account
  - one morning teacher did not turn up, took school three hours to organise replacement
  - golf course closed for refurbishment.
- Ask for refund of part of the course fees.
- Ask the school to take up the matter with the hotel.
- Close on a friendly note considering your long business relationship.

* **4**
KMK

Sie sind Christiane Sauer und sind bei Ihrer Firma, Zuckermann & Sacher, Farinweg 19, 73979 Suessen, für den Einkauf von Büromaterial zuständig. Seit 4 Jahren beziehen Sie jedes Quartal Drucker- und Kopierpapier sowie Umschläge aller Art von der britischen Firma East Anglia Stationery Ltd., 6 Malvern Business Park, Ely, CB6 4JR, UK. In der letzten Zeit hat Ihnen dieser Lieferant wiederholt Anlass zur Unzufriedenheit gegeben.

Schreiben Sie einen förmlichen Beschwerdebrief an den Geschäftsführer, Charles Bingley, und führen Sie dabei Folgendes an:

- Datum: 30 Juli
- In den ersten Jahren keine Beanstandungen
- Seit letztem Jahr allmähliche Verschlechterung des Service:
  - Ware häufig nicht vorrätig
  - Lieferzeiten immer länger
  - keine prompte Reaktion auf E-Mails und Faxe
  - stets wechselnde Ansprechpartner am Telefon
  - dieses Jahr schon einmal zu viel und einmal zu wenig geliefert
- Mängel bei der heutigen Lieferung:
  - 150 000 Umschläge DIN A3 nicht selbstklebend (self-adhesive), (Auftrag Nr. 200-5437 vom 23. Juni)
  - Muster der beanstandeten Umschläge beigefügt
  - Bitte um Abholung der beanstandeten Umschläge bei nächster Gelegenheit
  - sofortiger Ersatz erforderlich
- Drei Monate Frist für Verbesserung des Service
- Andernfalls keine Verlängerung des Liefervertrags
- Anlage

2 Complaints by telephone

1 R Maria Sanchez from Papier Gehrke in Schwerin has placed an order for multilingual wall calendars with the US firm Calendars 4 U. Two weeks after the date the calendars should have arrived in Germany she rings Joan Reid at Calendars 4 U whom she knows very well from numerous previous transactions.

Restore the order of their jumbled dialogue. Match the numbers with the letters.

Joan	Maria
1. Calendars 4U. Joan speaking. How can I help you? 2. Hi Maria. Can you give me the order number and date? 3. Here it is on my monitor. Is there a problem? 4. I see that they should arrive in Germany any day now. We dispatched them a week ago by air-mail. 5. I am very sorry about this. I was going to call you but whenever I got around to it, it seemed to be the wrong time of day in Europe. 6. That's true. I am so sorry. I promise it won't happen again. 7. Thank you very much for your patience. 8. Bye Maria.	a. Certainly. It is 4900/312 dated 18 July. b. You're welcome. Good bye Joan. c. Yes, there certainly is. The calendars have not arrived yet. They ought to have been here two weeks ago. d. You could have mailed me. e. Hello Joan, this is Maria Sanchez from Papier Gehrke in Schwerin, Germany. I'm calling about our order for calendars. f. Well, as long as the calendars arrive in the next few days, no harm will be done. g. Why didn't you let us know that delivery would be made two weeks later?

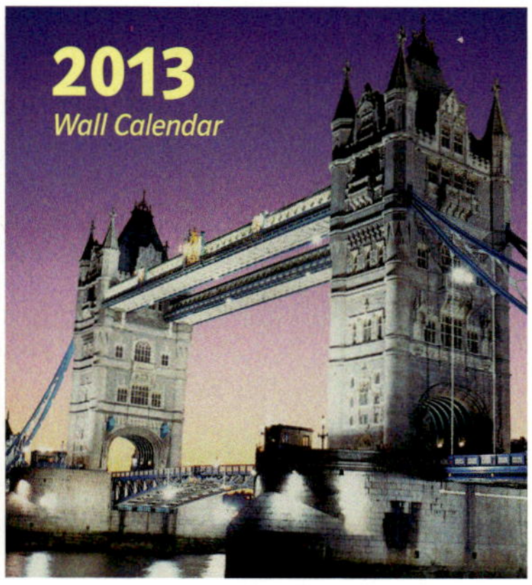

2 I **Work with a partner. Draw up a similar dialogue about a delay in delivery. Then act it out with your partner.**

Phrases

3
R
A1.28

Kirsty Burnham of Global Catering in Manchester asks Kevin Sears to ring an Italian firm about their consignment of Italian speciality convenience foods.

Listen to the dialogue and answer the following questions.

1. Which firm does Kevin Sears work for?
2. What is Chiara Durini's position at Buongusto Italiano?
3. What is the problem with the sell-by date of the Parma ham and the mortadella antipasti?
4. Would it help if Chiara Durini gave Global Catering a discount?
5. By which means of transport is Chiara Durini going to send the replacement delivery?

4
R/P
A1.28

You are Kevin Sears. First copy the form below. Then listen to the conversation again and write a memo in English for your boss, Kirsty Burnham.

TELEPHONE MEMO

For: ______

From: ______

Date: ______

Caller: ______

Subject: ______

5 Nicole Sachse from Getränke König in Halle, Germany, had ordered 3000 sets of long drink glasses from Wexford Crystal in Sanditon, County Cork, Ireland. The consignment arrived punctually, but inspection has revealed that some glasses are broken und some are smaller than the others. Nicole rings Sean O'Sullivan at Wexford Crystal.

Act out their dialogue with your neighbour using the prompts below.

Nicole Sachse		**Sean O'Sullivan**
	←	Wexford Crystal / Exports / Sean O'Sullivan
Nicole Sachse / Getränke König / Halle, Germany / order of 10 September / 3000 sets of long drink glasses	→	on monitor / colours red, blue and green / arrived?
arrived punctually / inspection / disappointed / one box damaged / 50 sets of green glasses broken	←	
	→	sorry to hear / all sets checked before dispatch / must have happened in transit / contact forwarders immediately
terms of delivery DAP Halle / Wexford Crystal deal with forwarder and / or insurance company / need replacements urgently	←	
	→	send replacements / by air / this afternoon
transport free of charge / confirmation by fax	←	
	→	certainly / once more apologies
afraid / must mention / roughly ⅓ of the glasses / slight differences in height / about 1mm shorter	←	
	→	easy to explain / glasses pipe-blown by hand / differences inevitable / sign of hand-made glass / much more valuable / machine-made glasses always identical
sounds plausible / customers may not notice	←	
	→	pleased with the sets?
yes / colours brilliant / crystal glass clear / remind of replacements / good-bye	←	
	→	promise immediate dispatch / again sorry thanks for call / bye

*** 6** **I** **Work with a partner. Sit back to back and act out the telephone conversation using the prompts on the role cards. Then change roles.**

Role card: Partner A (buyer) **Role card partner B ⇨ page 231**

Sie haben über das Internet ein überaus preiswertes Skateboard gekauft und mit Kreditkarte bezahlt. In der Beschreibung des Skateboards auf der Webseite des Verkäufers war als zulässiges Höchstgewicht für den Benutzer 70 kg angegeben. Als das Skateboard wie versprochen nach 3 Tagen ankommt, müssen Sie feststellen, dass auf dem englisch beschrifteten Karton ein zulässiges Höchstgewicht von (nur) 90 lbs (= 40,8 kg) aufgedruckt ist. Sie rufen die Firma an und verlangen Rücknahme des Skateboards.

7 **M** **Communicating across cultures**
Drücken Sie folgende Aussagen in (möglichst höflichem) Englisch aus:

1. Wir teilen Ihnen hiermit mit, dass wir mit Ihrem Kundendienst sehr unzufrieden sind.
2. Die Farbe entspricht nicht dem Muster.
3. Wir bestehen darauf, dass Sie uns den vollen Kaufpreis erstatten.

Communicating across cultures:
Complaining about products or services

In Germany correspondence in connection with complaints tends to be direct, stating the facts bluntly and requiring adjustment in no uncertain tones. This is the accepted usage here and nobody takes offence at the curt and no-nonsense style of German complaints. In the English-speaking world, on the other hand, complaints are formulated in a different way. The style is much more indirect, polite and conciliatory as nothing would be gained by antagonizing the other party; he / she would simply be less cooperative. So remember to express your complaint in a friendly and understanding manner.

Do not say:	Say instead:
I want to complain about …	I'm afraid I have to raise the matter of …
The glasses are broken.	Unfortunately, the glasses are broken.
You have made a mistake.	There must have been an error on your part / There seems to have been a mix-up somewhere.
You are wrong.	I'm afraid I cannot quite agree.
We expect you to send replacements.	We would be grateful if you would send replacements.
Therefore, we request a discount of 20%.	We think a discount of 20% would be appropriate.

8 **Use the Internet to find other examples of cultural differences or problems of intercultural communication. Make notes and compare your findings with the group.**

B Adjusting complaints

It is much easier to hold on to existing customers than to find new ones, so it is essential to manage customer complaints well. Remember, disgruntled customers are twice as likely as satisfied customers to tell others about their experience with your firm. When dealing with customer complaints you should

- thank the customer for making you aware of the problem
- treat the customer with courtesy and patience and tell him that you are sorry
- respond to the complaint quickly, telling the customer what will happen next
- if possible, give an explanation for what has happened
- involve the customer in the process of finding a solution
- suggest a compromise that meets the customer halfway if the complaint is not wholly justified
- ensure that all action promised is executed promptly
- explain the reasons before saying no, if the complaint is unjustified.

1 M **Study the text above and translate the following recommendations taken from a textbook.**

21

Die Erledigung von Reklamationen muss mit großer Sorgfalt geschehen, um den Kunden nicht zu verlieren. Zunächst sollten Sie dem Kunden dafür danken, dass er Sie auf ein Problem aufmerksam gemacht hat, und ihn dann in die Suche nach einer Lösung einbeziehen.

Beschwerden müssen umgehend beantwortet und der Kunde über den Fortgang der Erledigung auf dem Laufenden gehalten werden. Wenn möglich, sollten Sie dem Kunden erklären, wie es zu der für ihn unbefriedigenden Situation kommen konnte. Zudem müssen Sie den Kunden davon überzeugen, dass Sie Maßnahmen treffen werden oder schon eingeleitet haben, die sicherstellen, dass sich solche Vorfälle nicht wiederholen.

Falls die Reklamation nur teilweise begründet ist, sollten Sie versuchen, sich mit dem Kunden auf einen Kompromiss zu einigen. Sind Sie gezwungen, die Reklamation als völlig unbegründet zurückzuweisen, empfiehlt es sich zuerst die Gründe zu erläutern, bevor die Absage erteilt wird.

2 R **Match the complaints on the left with the appropriate explanations on the right.**

1. Although you promised delivery within a week, our order no. 7040 has not yet arrived. Could you please look into this matter?
2. On 18 January we ordered 700 jars of tomato relish by phone but you sent us only 400 jars. Would you please arrange for the missing 300 to be shipped to us immediately?
3. When we signed the contract for the building of the conservatory you promised that the work would be completed in four weeks. That was 2 months ago and the work is still only half finished.
4. The packaging of the DVDs appeared to be in perfect condition. On unpacking the DVDs, however, we discovered a number of scratches. A list of the damaged DVDs is enclosed.

a. 300 jars of tomato relish have already been handed over to our forwarders for transportation to Germany. We are very sorry for this oversight. It seems that the person processing your order must have mistaken the handwritten 7 on the telephone memo for a 4.

b. We are at a loss to understand how this could have happened. Nevertheless we will be sending you replacements for the damaged goods first thing tomorrow morning. A thorough investigation into our quality control procedures has already been initiated.

c. Please accept our apologies for the delay. Your order was dispatched the day before yesterday and should reach you in the next few days. We apologize once more for the delay that was due to the introduction of new software in our dispatch department.

d. I would like to apologize for the delay for which we are, however, not entirely to blame. When work was in progress you asked for a number of alterations that held up work. For example, there was an additional delivery time for the Italian tiles you insisted on instead of the British ones provided for in our offer.

3
R

Kunal Mahajan from India Sports replies to Sarah Brookfield's e-mail concerning the faulty labelling of the polo shirts SPORTS ISLAND had ordered from India Sports.

Complete Kunal's e-mail using the expressions from the box.

prepared to • promise to improve • the inconvenience caused • the trouble you have had • to our attention

From:	mahajan@indiasports.id
To:	sarah.brookfield@sportsisland.co.uk
Cc:	
Sent:	201_-02-01 **Attachments:**
Subject:	Polo shirts, your purchase order No. PH/346/06 of 18 Dec 201_

Dear Ms Brookfield

Thank you for your e-mail drawing a serious problem **1**.

thanks for information

We are very sorry for **2** by the incorrect labelling of the polo shirts and thank you for suggesting a solution. We perfectly agree with you that it would be best to ask a firm in Britain to replace the tags. An ample quantity of new tags have already been dispatched to your address by air.

apologies and suggestion for adjustment

It goes without saying that we are **3** bear the costs for the re-labelling of the polo shirts.

Meanwhile we have started investigations into how this faulty labelling could have happened and **4** our quality control procedures.

promise of improvement

To make up for **5**, we would like to offer you a price reduction of 10% on your next order.

goodwill ending

We look forward to hearing from you again.

Best regards

Kunal Mahajan
Export Manager
India Sports
112 Delhi Road, Meerut-250 001
Uttar Pradesh, India
Tel. +91 121 2512270
Fax +91 121 2512275

4 Restore the correct order of these jumbled elements of a reply to a complaint
R about a delay in delivery.

1 We are, therefore, prepared to release you from the contract.

2 Dear Ms Kirchner

3 We have not contacted you before because we were hoping to locate another manufacturer willing to supply similar tool kits at short notice. So far, however, we have not met with success.

4 Yours sincerely
James Vernon
Export Manager

5 Please accept our sincere apologies. We hope to be of service to you at another time in the future.

6 Re: Your order no. W-549 / 07

7 I'm afraid we are after all unable to execute your order for 1000 household tool kits for the time being as our own supplier, our parent company, has become insolvent.

8 Thank you for your e-mail.

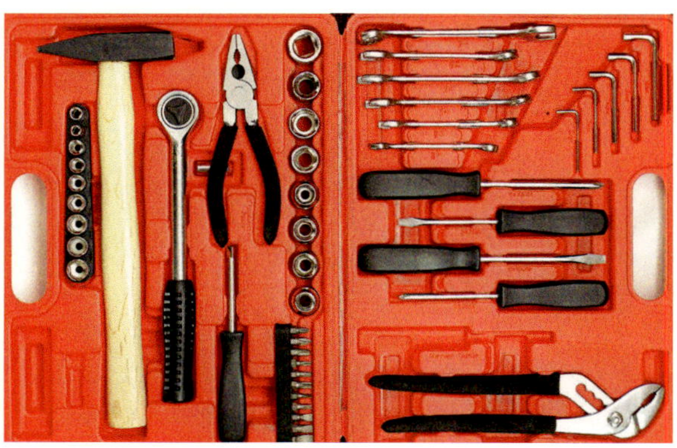

5 P You are Pam Robinson, principal of BUSINESS SPEAK, the language school in Brighton which 2 junior executives from Otto Greiling GmbH, Germany, attended for a week's intensive coaching in business English. Markus Reber from their human resources department has sent you an e-mail complaining about some shortcomings concerning the course from October 14 to 20:

- accommodation at private hotel inadequate – central heating system out of order
- participants' needs (the language of export procedures) not properly taken into account
- one morning teacher did not turn up, took school three hours to organise replacement
- golf course closed for refurbishment

Reply by e-mail, bearing in mind that Markus Reber has been sending staff to your courses for several years.

- spoken with hotel manager, hotel prepared to reduce price by ⅓, cheque under way by post
- export procedures dealt with as always, never any complaint about this before
- apologies for teacher not turning up one morning, had a fall in the bathroom, had to be taken to hospital, you did your best to organise replacement
- participants informed in advance that the golf course would be out of use
- very sorry that participants should be dissatisfied
- sent them each a copy of "Doing Business in the UK" in compensation
- hope that cordial relations will not be affected

6 KMK Sie sind Henry Crawford, der neue Geschäftsführer von East Anglia Stationery Ltd., 6 Malvern Business Park, Ely CB6 4JR, UK. Die deutsche Firma Zuckermann & Sacher, Farinweg 19, 73979 Suessen, bezieht von Ihnen seit Jahren Drucker- und Kopierpapier sowie Umschläge. Christiane Sauer, zuständig für den Einkauf von Büromaterial, ist inzwischen mit Ihrem Service unzufrieden und hat sich bei Ihnen in einem förmlichen Schreiben beschwert (siehe S. 180).

Beantworten Sie ihren Brief in Englisch unter Berücksichtigung folgender Punkte:

- Datum: 5. August
- Vorstellung Ihrer Person
- Ihr Vorgänger, Charles Bingley, nach längerer Krankheit im Ruhestand
- Beanstandete Unzulänglichkeiten verursacht durch Mr. Bingley's Abwesenheit
- Radikale Maßnahmen eingeleitet
- Service in Kürze wieder einwandfrei
- Entschuldigung
- Ersatzlieferung Umschläge bereits unterwegs
- 20 % Rabatt auf diesen Auftrag
- Beanstandete Umschläge werden kommenden Mittwoch abgeholt
- Hoffnung auf weitere gute Beziehungen

Language and grammar
Find the correct form of the verbs in brackets.

1. We will grant you 10% quantity discount if you (order) at least 500 units.
2. We would place a substantial order if you (can promise) delivery within one week.
3. We would not have dispatched the goods if they (not be) in perfect condition.
4. We (be glad) if you looked into the matter without delay.
5. Unless you instruct us to the contrary, shipment (be effected) on receipt of new supplies.
6. It (be) most helpful if the sets could reach us before the end of the month.
7. You would be taking a great risk if you (invest) your money in that project.
8. Should you be uncertain about any aspect of it, please (not hesitate) to give me a call.
9. If we (accept) their order we would have to recruit three additional workers.
10. If she had worked harder she (not fail) the exam.

Language and grammar: Conditional clauses

Bedingungssätze (conditional clauses) werden im Englischen nach einem relativ festen Schema gestaltet. Es gibt drei Grundtypen von Bedingungssätzen:	
Hauptsatz	**Nebensatz der Bedingung**
We will take the goods back (FUTURE) (wir **werden** …)	if you return them at your expense. (PRESENT TENSE)
We would grant you a discount (CONDITIONAL) (wir **würden** …)	if you increased your order. (SIMPLE PAST)
He would have taken part in the meeting (CONDITIONAL PERFECT) (er **hätte** …)	if he had not been away on a business trip. (PAST PERFECT)
Das Schema gilt auch dann, wenn der Nebensatz der Bedingung vor dem Hauptsatz steht:	
If it is fine on Friday	we will have the office party in the park.
If you applied	you would get the job.
If you had applied	you would have got the job.
Ferner gilt das Schema, wenn der Nebensatz durch eine andere Konjunktion eingeleitet wird: wie z. B. unless (wenn nicht, außer wenn), provided (that) (vorausgesetzt, dass), on condition (that) (unter der Bedingung, dass):	
They will not place any further orders	unless you offer a satisfactory solution.
Employees may smoke	provided they go out into the courtyard.
Eine besondere Form stellt der Bedingungssatz ohne Konjunktion dar:	
Should you have any further questions	please do not hesitate to ask.
But for John helping out (If John had not helped out …)	we would never have coped with the sudden demand.
Eine Ausnahme von diesem Schema bildet die höfliche Bitte in der Geschäftskorrespondenz:	
We would be grateful	if you would grant us a respite of 4 weeks.

Phrases: Complaints and adjustments

To start a complaint

We are writing **with** reference to our order no …	Wir nehmen Bezug auf unseren Auftrag Nr. …
We regret to report that we have not yet received the goods ordered **on** 18 May.	Wir bedauern, Ihnen mitteilen zu müssen, dass wir die am 18. Mai bestellten Waren noch nicht erhalten haben.

To give reasons for your complaint

On unpacking the cases our Incoming Goods Control discovered that 15 items are missing.	Beim Auspacken der Kisten stellte unsere Warenannahme fest, dass 15 Positionen fehlen.
We are afraid that several units are – seriously damaged / defective. – broken / badly scratched / stained.	Leider sind mehrere Teile – schwer beschädigt / schadhaft. – zerbrochen / stark zerkratzt / verschmutzt.
The goods should have arrived a week **ago**.	Die Waren hätten schon vor einer Woche eintreffen sollen.
We are sorry to point out that the repair work has been poorly executed.	Wir müssen leider darauf hinweisen, dass die Reparatur schlecht ausgeführt wurde.

To mention likely reasons for the problem

We believe that the damage may be due to rough handling **in** transit.	Wir glauben, dass der Schaden auf unsachgemäße Behandlung beim Transport zurückzuführen ist.
Apparently, our order was **mixed up** with another customer's order.	Unser Auftrag wurde anscheinend mit einem anderen verwechselt.

To inform the seller what you expect him to do and what steps you are taking

Please arrange **for** the immediate dispatch of the missing items.	Bitte sorgen Sie dafür, dass die fehlenden Artikel sofort abgeschickt werden.
We would ask you to – replace the faulty goods **at** your expense. – have the defective articles collected **at** our warehouse – grant us a price reduction **of** 20 %. – cut the price **to** €780.	Wir möchten Sie bitten, – die mangelhafte Ware auf Ihre Kosten zu ersetzen. – die schadhaften Artikel von unserem Lager abholen zu lassen. – uns einen Preisnachlass von 20 % zu gewähren. – den Preis auf €780 zu senken.

To demand prompt adjustment

We expect that you will settle this matter speedily and **to** our entire satisfaction.	Wir erwarten, dass Sie die Sache rasch und zu unserer vollen Zufriedenheit regeln.

To refer to a complaint received

Thank you for your e-mail drawing a serious problem **to** our attention.	Danke für Ihre E-Mail, mit der Sie uns auf ein ernstes Problem aufmerksam gemacht haben.

To apologize

We wish to apologize for this mistake.	Wir bitten für diesen Fehler um Entschuldigung.
We are extremely sorry **for** the poor service you have received.	Es tut uns außerordentlich leid, dass Sie so schlecht bedient wurden.

To explain the problem or promise to investigate it

The damage was caused **by** a software failure.	Der Schaden wurde durch fehlerhafte Software verursacht.
We will investigate the matter thoroughly and inform you of the steps taken.	Wir werden die Angelegenheit gründlich untersuchen und Sie über die Schritte informieren, die wir unternommen haben.

To suggest a solution and inform the buyer what you expect him to do

We are pleased to say that replacements are now **on** their way to you.	Wir freuen uns, Ihnen mitteilen zu können, dass Ersatz bereits unterwegs ist.
Please return the faulty items **at** our expense.	Bitte senden Sie die mangelhaften Artikel auf unsere Kosten zurück.
We are prepared to reduce the price **by** 15 % if you decide to keep the goods.	Wir sind bereit, den Preis um 15 % zu senken, wenn Sie sich entschließen, die Ware zu behalten.

To reject an unfounded claim

After careful examination of the case we must say that the order was carried out in accordance with the contract.	Nach gründlicher Untersuchung des Falles müssen wir festhalten, dass der Auftrag vertragsgemäß ausgeführt wurde.
As we are **in no way** to blame we have no alternative but to reject your claim.	Da uns keinerlei Schuld trifft, bleibt uns nichts anderes übrig, als Ihre Reklamation zurückzuweisen.

To close on a note designed to promote goodwill

We hope that this proposal will find your approval.	Wir hoffen, dieser Vorschlag findet Ihre Zustimmung.
We trust that the solution suggested will help to settle the matter **to** the satisfaction of all parties concerned.	Wir hoffen, dass die vorgeschlagene Lösung dazu beiträgt, die Angelegenheit zur Zufriedenheit aller Beteiligten zu erledigen.

Unit 15
Marketing products and services

WORD BANK

marketing • marketing mix • life cycle • market research • target group • interview • distribution • manufacturer • wholesaler • warehouse • retailer • retail outlets • agent • commission • E-commerce • advertising • slogans • consumer goods • media • mail shots • advertisements • commercials • posters • trade journals • internet advertising • trade fairs • public relations • sponsoring • to conduct research • to aim at • to break bulk • to represent • to advertise • to promote

Marketing includes a wide range of activities. Even when a product or service is still at the idea or design stage, companies set about finding out what sort of a market exists – for instance, what age group they should aim at and how likely people in this age group are to buy this product or service. When a company is planning a new product they need to decide on the "marketing mix" or 4Ps (product, price, place, promotion) – i.e. what kind of product to develop, what price to charge and what channels to sell it through – cheap chain or exclusive boutique, for instance. Finally, they will have to decide how and where to advertise.

1 Life cycle of a product

Products may be thought of as having a life cycle with five phases – introduction, growth, maturity, decline and phasing out. The focus of marketing changes, depending on the phase.

Online-Link
808260-0015

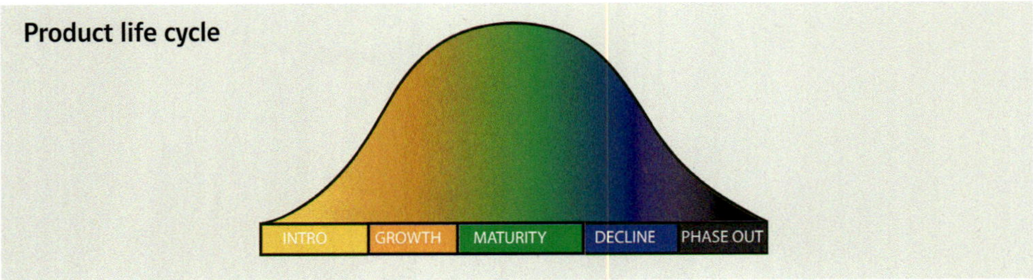

1 R **Study the text on page 193 and the illustration above and decide whether the following statements are TRUE or FALSE.**

1. Marketing is the same as advertising.
2. Marketing includes advertising.
3. Companies first design and produce a product and then see whether there's a market for it or not.
4. It is important for a company to have a clear idea of what group it is targeting.
5. Marketing is the same as selling.
6. It is always best to sell as cheaply as possible.
7. A product has a life cycle of six phases.
8. Sales reach a peak in the last phase.

2 **Use the internet to select what you consider to be the five leading brands in the UK. Make a few notes on what is associated with the brands and discuss your results with the group.**

2 Market research

Companies conduct market research to find out what people think about them and their products. They also try to establish what needs or desires a particular target group may have and how able or willing they will be to pay for a particular product or service. This may involve "desk" research (e.g. statistics) or "field research". The following is an example of field research.

R A1.29 **Listen to the interview. The interviewer is ringing a random sample of people taken from the local telephone book. Complete the following sentences.**

1. Could you possibly spare a few minutes **1**?
2. I am actually in a bit **2**.
3. We are doing a market survey **3**.
4. I tend to book flights and holidays **4**.
5. We are particularly interested in **5**.
6. Do you buy these articles regularly and how much do you **6**?
7. I can do my shopping when I **7**.
8. Prices are often more **8**.
9. I often give up in **9**.
10. Would you visit the website more often if it were **10**?

A Distribution channels

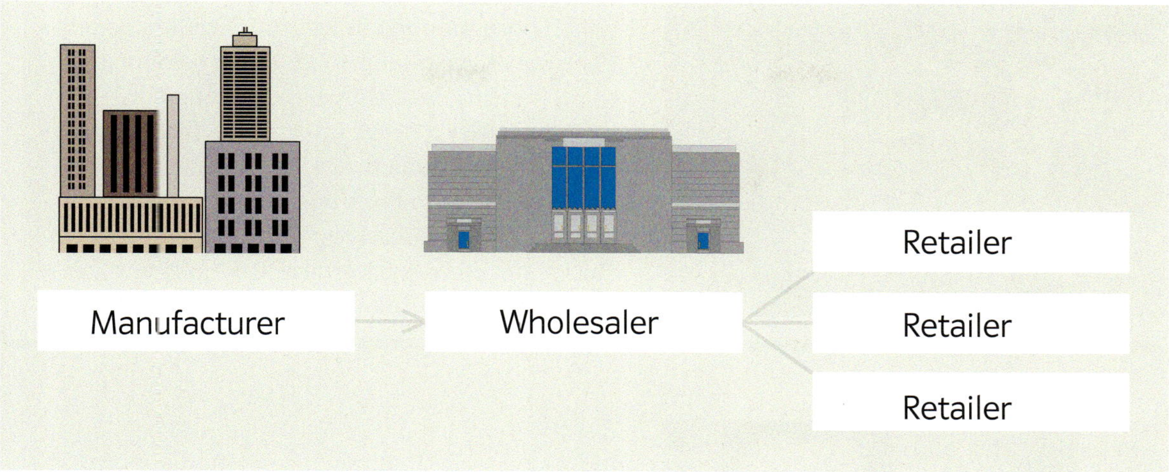

Distribution is also a part of marketing. Traditionally, wholesalers are the link between manufacturers and retailers. Manufacturers generally sell goods in large quantities to wholesalers who sell them on in smaller quantities to retailers (= "breaking bulk"). Retailers sell them to end users.

1 Retailers, wholesalers and agents

Retailers

Retailers ensure a supply of goods to the general public. There is a wide variety of retail outlets, starting with small specialist shops such as independent chemists, beauty consultants, opticians and exclusive fashion boutiques. Most High Street stores are, however, major chains with branches in a large number of towns and often in several countries. Supermarkets generally belong to one of a small number of major chains. Department stores sell many different kinds of goods under one roof. Large retailers, who buy in bulk, may order directly from manufacturers without involving a wholesaler.
Recently, online retailing has become the fastest growing segment.

Wholesalers

Wholesalers provide a range of services from which both manufacturers and retailers benefit. They may have a sales force to keep contact to their customers, they have warehousing facilities, offer a range of products from a number of manufacturers, and may offer credit facilities to their customers. Finally, they provide advisory services. However, wholesalers charge for their services and are, therefore, also a cost factor (putting up the price).

Agents

In foreign trade manufacturers often appoint an agent in the foreign country. This has a number of advantages. The agent speaks the language, he is familiar with the foreign market and will have the necessary contacts. He has an office and possibly warehousing facilities. He is usually paid on a commission basis which means he receives a percentage (say 3%) on sales. He is thus only paid when he succeeds in selling something. His principal has therefore few overheads.

1 Übertragen Sie folgende Sätze ins Deutsche.

KMK

1. Wholesalers are the link between manufacturers and retailers.
2. They may offer credit facilities to their customers.
3. Supermarkets belong to a small number of major chains.
4. Wholesalers charge for their services and are therefore a cost factor.
5. Wholesalers generally have warehousing facilities.

2 Answer the following questions.

1. In what way do wholesalers make life easier for manufacturers?
2. Why does a small retailer (e.g. a 24-hour mini-market or a small fashion boutique) need wholesalers?
3. Why may large retailers try to cut out the wholesaler?
4. Give examples of independent retailers (not part of chains).
5. What is the characteristic feature of a department store?

* 3 Übertragen Sie den obigen Text über „Agents" ins Deutsche.

KMK

4 R

Decide whether the following statements are TRUE or FALSE.

1. Agents are paid a commission whether they sell anything or not.
2. Wholesalers generally have warehousing facilities.
3. Retailers sell to end users.
4. Retailers buy in bulk and sell to wholesalers.
5. Wholesalers perform a useful service both for manufacturers and retailers.

5 P

Describe briefly the activities of retailers, wholesalers and agents.

6 R A1.30

Listen to the following statements in which young people taking part in a training seminar describe their place of employment. Take notes.

7 R/P A1.30

Now listen to the statements again, use your notes and answer the following questions in writing.

1. Does speaker 1 work for a wholesaler?
2. Does speaker 2 work for a retailer?
3. What does speaker 3 mean by "retail customers"?
4. Does speaker 4 work for a retailer or a wholesaler?
5. What sort of a company does speaker 5 work for?
6. What kind of customers help the shop of speaker 6 to survive?
7. Who does the company of speaker 7 sell its products through?
8. What kind of an organisation does speaker 8 work for?

2 E-commerce

1 R

Complete the following text using words from the box.

outlets • major • credit cards • retail • via • online • charges • customers • facilities • wholesalers

An important development at the present time is the rapid growth of e-commerce. This is revolutionising some **1** sectors. Internet retailing operations are growing faster than traditional retail **2**. Shopping and booking flights, hotels and holidays **3** the internet is becoming more and more popular. Some **4** supermarkets have large internet operations. You can do your shopping **5** and have the goods delivered.

Airlines offer online booking **6**, which makes it easy to compare prices and avoid paying travel agents' **7**.

Wholesalers may also offer their **8** internet facilities (Business to Business – B2B – services) to enable them to do their ordering at any time of the day or night. However, internet exchanges are making **9** superfluous in some fields.

E-commerce is at present the fastest growing retail segment paralleled by a rapid increase in the number of **10**.

2 KMK **Beantworten Sie die Fragen zum folgenden Zeitungstext schriftlich in deutscher Sprache.**

1. Warum mussten Online-Einzelhändler ihren Service stark verbessern?
2. Welche Vorteile bietet das Internet beim Preisvergleich?
3. Welche Möglichkeiten gibt es im Internet, sich über Produkte zu informieren?
4. Warum mussten Firmen neue Strategien in der Werbung und im Marketing entwickeln?
5. Welche Altersgruppe soll besonders durch die Internet-Werbung angesprochen werden?

E-Commerce takes off

Consumers love to shop on the internet. After initial problems leading websites now offer an excellent service. Competition on the web is fierce and many sites have had little choice but to raise service levels, often far above those of off-line retailers. Price transparency is the great advantage for the consumer. It is possible to check the price offered by hundreds of merchants with a couple of mouse clicks. Consumers also have access to an unprecedented amount of information, not just from manufacturers' websites but also from online reviews written by other customers.

To reach online customers companies have had to look at new and different advertising and marketing strategies. This is why firms pay for sponsored links to appear on search sites like *Google* and *Yahoo!*. It has become one of the most effective marketing tools, especially for people who spend as much time on the internet as watching television, such as teenagers.

V7 Video Lounge Retailing

BBC Motion Gallery

You are about to see a video on retail marketing. Watch it carefully and then answer the following questions:

1. Describe the marketing expert.
2. The video speaks of "sales consultants" and "professional friends". How is this different from the traditional sales assistant?
3. What method is used to show them how NOT to approach the customer?
4. What is meant by "linked selling"?
5. What are the rewards of successful customer care for the "consultants"?
6. Would you like to be served by this kind of assistant?

B Advertising

There are many different ways of promoting sales and attracting potential clients or customers depending on the product and target group.

1 Advertising consumer goods

Mail shots: One form of advertising we are all confronted with is mail shots. Since a large proportion go straight into the wastepaper basket, companies will try to obtain up to date and selective lists of people who are likely to be really interested. This may be the cheapest and most effective way for local companies to make potential clients aware of their goods and services.

TV advertising is suitable for consumer goods with a very wide appeal. Like **cinema** advertising it can suggest a whole lifestyle associated with the product. TV advertising is very expensive.

Consumer goods can also be advertised on the **radio**, in **newspapers** and **magazines**. In the case of magazines, the manufacturer will be able to appeal to a specific target group (affluent men between the ages of 20 and 30, keen gardeners with sufficient money to buy a glossy magazine, health-conscious young women, retired people with money and time on their hands (grey power!)).

Posters, hoardings / billboards are an effective means of out of home advertising as they reach a large number of people who cannot help noticing them as they pass or drive through the streets.

Internet advertising is also a rapidly growing segment. A website itself is an important part of the way in which a company presents itself. How well-designed and efficient is the website? Does it allow you to do what you want to do with a minimum of complication? We have all experienced frustrating websites which provide a lot of information that one is not interested in, or that do not seem to have a "BACK" button.

1 Match the expressions on the left with the translations on the right.

1. affluent	a. Anziehungskraft
2. appeal	b. ausgewählt
3. glossy	c. hier: auf Hochglanzpapier gedruckt
4. hoardings	d. im Ruhestand/in Rente
5. mail shots	e. Plakatwände
6. retired	f. Postwurfsendungen
7. selective	g. wohlhabend
8. target group	h. Zielgruppe

2 Work in groups. Discuss recent advertisements on TV, in magazines, in the cinema and on posters. Tell your group what you liked or disliked about them. What kind of advertisements are you most influenced by? The following expressions may help to start you off.

I think it's effective because …

I don't like this kind of advertisement because …

It doesn't really appeal to …

Have you seen the most recent ad for … ?

In my opinion the message is …

I'm afraid I don't agree with you because …

I think it is …

I think this commercial is very convincing as …

Internet advertising boom helps Ad.Slot.com to double sales

Ad.Slot.com, one of Europe's biggest independent media buying agencies, says that it will double turnover from placing advertisements on the internet this year as its clients continue to seek alternatives to traditional media.

The company said yesterday that it expects to achieve total sales of more than $450 million this year, up from about $350 million last year. The proportion of sales contributed by the new media rose rapidly to 17 per cent.

In the first few months of the year more money was spent on advertising on the internet and mobile phones and less on advertising in conventional media, like the radio, TV and print media.

A spokesman for the company said that the trend towards advertising in the new media was the result of changing technology and habits. People still watch television and read newspapers, but they use the internet and their mobile phones to socialise and search for information. They have DVD recorders that allow them to skip TV commercials.

3 KMK **Beantworten Sie folgende Fragen zu diesem Zeitungsartikel auf Deutsch.**

1. Wodurch erwartet Ad.Slot.com dieses Jahr seinen Umsatz zu verdoppeln?
2. Welchen Beitrag werden die neuen Medien dabei leisten?
3. Welche Veränderung hat sich in den ersten Monaten dieses Jahres ergeben?
4. Warum nimmt das Interesse an den alternativen Medien zu?
5. In welchen Medien sucht man zunehmend nach Informationen?
6. Warum wird TV-Werbung häufig nicht wahrgenommen?

2 Advertising industrial goods

Where do you advertise if your product is not a consumer good but, say, a specialised machine or precision instrument?

A company can place an advertisement in a trade journal, a specialist periodical devoted to a particular sector.

For these companies the relevant **trade fairs** at which companies in the given sector present their latest products are important. They are attended by many people from the trade, some of them buyers who intend to place orders and competitors who use the trade fair as a means of seeing what the competition is up to. Trade fairs are, therefore, a way of advertising industrial goods.

Companies may write directly to potential customers (direct mail) informing them of their range of products and enclosing sales literature.

* Übertragen Sie den obigen Text ins Deutsche.

M
KMK

3 Public relations (PR)

This is usually distinguished from advertising as the focus is the company rather than specific products. Some companies sponsor sports events, others donate money to universities, schools and cultural events. It may be important for a company to emphasise the amount of money it invests in research, its respect for the environment or multi-ethnic society. They may emphasise their commitment to the local community and try to get positive coverage in the local press. Large companies have PR departments, while in smaller companies there is at least one person responsible for PR. Companies large and small take outside advice from specialist agencies.

Study the above text and say whether the following statements are TRUE or FALSE.

R

1. PR is the same as advertising.
2. Companies sponsor sports events to project a particular image.
3. Small companies are less interested in PR than large companies.
4. All companies use the services of specialist agencies.
5. Some companies are more interested in donating money to universities and schools than sponsoring sports events.

4 Language and techniques of advertising

Advertising is used to establish and remind consumers of a particular brand. Since there are many competing brands (e.g. cars) companies tend to use superlatives such as “the biggest, the best, the latest, the sexiest, the most innovative” etc. For the same reason a company will try to associate its brand with a particular lifestyle and use celebrities to promote this image. Much of modern advertising is persuasive rather than informative and appeals to the emotions and even the subconscious (subliminal advertising). Television commercials often use slogans or jingles which are impossible to forget.

Advertising techniques	
Alliteration:	fabulous faux furs are back in fashion
Exaggeration (hyperbole):	You will love the colossal screen of this superbly designed set; our selection of to die for jewellery.
Dramatisation (imperatives):	Go for rich winter colours like aubergine and rust!
Emotionally charged language:	These driving gloves practically scream sexy and confident.
Jingle:	An old classic jingle is "Don't be vague, ask for Haig" (whisky).
Imagery:	Organic aloe to maintain your mane's gleam; fresh as the morning dew.
Rhymes:	If your man's having stubble trouble get him hooked on this foaming scrub.
Slogan:	You shop we drop (supermarket chain online delivery service playing on the saying "Shop till you drop").
Pun:	Sejuice (seduce + juice = name of a fruit juice bar)

* **1** Study the following advertisements. Say which of the above techniques are used.
R Who are the advertisements aimed at?

VERDANT VERANDAS

Who needs green fingers?

City living is brighter, greener and fresher thanks to the complete planting service for balconies and roof terraces by VERDANT VERANDAS. Theme your own planting, or choose from English Roses (self-explanatory) or Mediterranean Memories (olive trees and Italian herbs).

If you are a **young, high-powered, rushed-off-your-feet executive**, we can transform your life (or at least your balcony!). **You'll be surprised how cheap we are!**

Call today 023 9247 5850 or e-mail us on info@verdantverandas.com

*** 2** P **Design an advertisement for one of the following products or a product of your own choice. Identify the target group and choose the appropriate advertising medium for the products.**

MP3 player • portable phone handset • tablet PC • range of fashion accessories • nail and cosmetics studio • motorbike

Language and grammar

Choose the correct form of the adjective or adverb in brackets.

1. Our elegant sofas are the (good) value ever.
2. We are the market leaders because we have reacted (swiftly) to changing markets.
3. This company has expanded (dramatic) than its competitors over the past year.
4. Last year the winter was (severe) than this year.
5. These are the (late) designer furnishings from Milan.
6. This is the (expensive) holiday I have booked so far.

Language and grammar: Comparatives and superlatives

Adjektive, meist in Form von Komparativen oder Superlativen, spielen in der Werbung eine große Rolle.

Einsilbig gesprochene Adjektive bilden Komparativ und Superlativ durch Anhängen von *-er*, *-est* an das Adjektiv.

bright – brighter – brightest
This car has **smoother** handling than any other car in its class.

Drei- oder mehrsilbige Adjektive bilden Komparativ und Superlativ durch Voranstellen von *more* und *most* vor das Adjektiv.

interesting – more interesting – most interesting
This is the **most sophisticated** MP3 player available today.

Zweisilbige Adjektive werden entweder wie einsilbige oder wie mehrsilbige gesteigert: Adjektive, die auf *-er*, *-ow*, *-y* oder *-le* enden, hängen *-er*, *-est* an. Vor Adjektive, die auf *-ful* oder *-re* enden, wird *more* oder *most* gesetzt.

clever – cleverer – cleverest
pretty – prettier – prettiest
careful – more careful – most careful
narrow – narrower – narrowest
noble – nobler – noblest
obscure – more obscure – most obscure
This is a **most restful** way of spending a weekend abroad.

Einige englische Adjektive besitzen die Wirkung von Superlativen.
Cutting-edge[1] technology goes into this stereo system.
Get this **state of the art** handset at all authorised dealers.
Get the coolest, **up to the minute**, **must-have** accessories at all our boutiques.
This car has **superb** handling.

Auch Adverbien können gesteigert werden. Komparativ und Superlativ von Adverbien wird durch Voranstellen von *more* und *most* gebildet.
quickly – more quickly – most quickly
They dealt with our order **more efficiently** than we had expected.
Technology is changing **more and more rapidly** (= immer schneller).

1 Diese Wendungen können sowohl mit als auch ohne Bindestriche geschrieben werden.

Phrases: Advertising

This state-of-the-art mobile phone is easy to operate with its simple slide-out keyboard.	Dieses Handy, das auf dem neuesten technischen Stand ist, hat eine leicht zu bedienende ausziehbare Tastatur.
It has an easy to use touch screen.	Es hat einen leicht zu bedienenden Touch-Screen.
This must-have versatile gizmo includes all the latest features.	Dieses vielseitige Hi-Tech-Spielzeug, das man unbedingt haben muss, hat all die neuesten Funktionen.
You'll love its slim compact shape.	Die schlanke, kompakte Form wird Sie begeistern.
You'll be bewitched by the dazzling designs of our new collection.	Lassen Sie sich verführen von den bestechenden Designs unserer neuen Kollektion.
The ultimate **in** costume jewellery.	Der ultimative Modeschmuck.
We use a minimum of packaging to minimise the environmental impact.	Wir verwenden ein Minimum an Verpackung, um die Auswirkungen auf die Umwelt so gering wie möglich zu halten.
Your finger-nails will look flawless and perfectly cared **for**.	Ihre Fingernägel sehen makellos und perfekt gepflegt aus.
… subdued autumnal colours …	… dezente Herbstfarben …
This is a portable stereo-system **of** truly diminutive dimensions.	Es handelt sich um eine tragbare Super-Mini-Stereoanlage.
This hand-crafted leather bag combines perfect chic with amazing capacity.	Diese handgearbeitete Ledertasche ist superschick und dabei unglaublich geräumig.
We rely **on** tried and tested craftsmanship.	Wir verlassen uns auf unser erprobtes handwerkliches Können.
Weekends feel simply wonderful in our silky soft-touch tops.	Erleben Sie romantische Wochenenden mit unseren flauschig-kuscheligen Tops.
This downy soft luxury scarf will go with all your winter garments.	Dieser daunenweiche Luxusschal passt zu Ihrer gesamten Wintergarderobe.
… ideal for sensitive skins …	… ideal für die empfindliche Haut …

UNIT 16
Job applications in Germany and the EU

WORD BANK

job application • vacancy • opening • job exchange • job centre • research facilities • recruitment agencies • letter of application • CV • education • training • experience • skills • hobbies • interview • strengths • references • to advertise • to recruit • to apply • to paraphrase • to invite • to shortlist • to employ • European Union • free movement • member countries • European Commission • president • commissioners • Council of Ministers • European Parliament

The first thing is to find a vacancy. Companies advertise openings in newspapers on certain days which differ from place to place and country to country and also from sector to sector. Job exchanges on the Internet have become an important source of information. Often, it is possible to type in your job specification and receive notification by e-mail when anything suitable turns up. Job centres may be able to assist in the search for a suitable position and provide research facilities such as directories and internet access. Finally, there are private sector recruitment agencies which specialise in a particular sector. People often send unsolicited applications to major organisations on the off-chance that they are looking to recruit people.

1 Tell the class how you found your job / apprenticeship. Discuss which of the above are the most effective ways of looking for a job. Give reasons to support your answers.

Online-Link
808260-0016

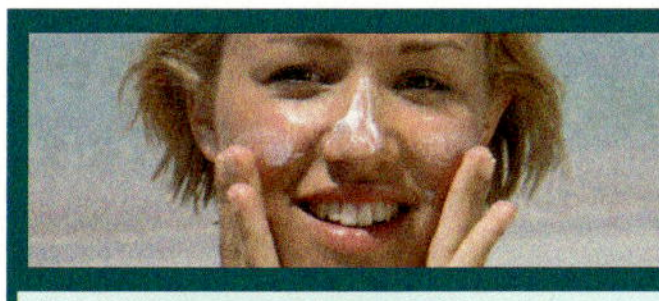

THE CARING COMPANY

NATURAL BEAUTY

first-rate natural products for hair and skin care

We are seeking young persons from the Continent to

assist our Birmingham-based sales team

REF.: NB 605

We offer employment in a challenging, fast-paced environment where enthusiasm is the norm.

Successful applicants will have

- sales experience
- good English language skills
- native speaker competence in Italian, French or German

Successful applicants will be

- PC literate, including Excel
- able to meet deadlines
- self-motivated and hard-working

We offer an attractive salary and will help you with finding accommodation.

If you are interested please send your CV with a covering letter to

Catherine Bennet ▪ Recruitment Officer ▪ NATURAL BEAUTY ▪ 17 Laura Place ▪ Birmingham ▪ BI2 1AC

Automotive Services Ltd

Wholesaler and Importer of Automotive Parts

REF.: JR 673

In view of our rapidly growing business with Continental Europe we are looking to recruit bilingual assistants (German-English or French-English) to work in our import department.

Applicants should be fluent in German or French and have a good command of English. Office skills and familiarity with import procedures are essential. Must enjoy working in a team.

Send application enclosing CV and certificates in English to:

Jennifer O'Rourke (Mrs) | Automotive Services Ltd | 103 Selsdown Drive | London E14 9LA

Small Tour Operator

Requires well-organised full-time travel consultant with admin and accounts background and fluent German and/or French. Hotel or travel experience desirable, but not essential. Must be team worker and have MS Office and typing skills.

Send CV and letter of application by e-mail to jobs@dreamworldholidays.com or by post to:

Dreamworld Holidays

28 Percival St
London
WIT 1DW

Quote ref.: DH 15 Pw

2 R **Read the advertisement on page 208 (Natural Beauty) and formulate the questions to which the following statements are the answers. The elements suggesting the question word are in bold type.**

Example:
Answer: 1. Natural Beauty is based **in Birmingham**.
Question: 1. **Where** is Natural Beauty based?

Answers

1. Natural Beauty is based **in Birmingham**.
2. Natural Beauty is seeking **young persons**.
3. Successful applicants will have **good English language skills**.
4. Successful applicants' mother tongue will be **Italian, French or German**.
5. **The following qualifications** are essential: PC-literacy, ability to work hard and meet deadlines.
6. **Natural Beauty** will help you with finding accommodation.
7. Your CV should be sent **to Catherine Bennet**.

3 I **Discuss with a partner what German qualifications would equip you for the jobs advertised in the three advertisements on page 208.**

4 P **Describe your (future) qualifications (school leaving certificate, e.g. Abitur, apprenticeship, traineeship etc, language certificates) and state briefly what kind of job you would like. For job titles refer back to UNIT 1.**

Example:
"I have just completed my training as a publisher's assistant and would like to work in a publishing house in or around Cologne. I spent a year in the United States and attended High School there, so I'd welcome the opportunity to use my English in my job."

5 KMK **Stellen Sie einem Freund / einer Freundin die Stellenanzeigen auf der Seite 208 auf Deutsch vor. Beachten Sie dabei folgende Punkte:**

- Firma bzw. Branche
- Anforderungen an Bewerber
- Gehalt
- Sonstige Leistungen der Firma
- Standort des Arbeitsplatzes
- Gewünschte Art der Kontaktaufnahme

A Letter of application

Your letter of application should be set out clearly and include the points below:

Thomas Seegers
Georg Weerth Str. 46
40545 Duesseldorf
Tel. +49 211 370 311
thomasseegers@t-online.de

your address and contact details

25 September 201_

date

Mrs Emily Ferguson
Anglo-Hibernian Bank
12 Bishop's Close
London
EC24 3FT
UK

address and name of person to contact, where given

Dear Mrs Ferguson

I saw your advertisement for a bilingual bank clerk for the foreign trade department of your bank on the www.jobsunlimited.co.uk website and should like to apply for this position.

say where you saw the ad

After taking my Abitur (= A-levels), I completed a traineeship at Deutsche Handelsbank in Frankfurt two years ago.

state qualifications

Since then I have been working at the main branch of the same bank in Hamburg. I have specialised in banking services for exporters and have a good knowledge of this segment. For this reason I feel well-qualified for the position advertised.

give details of experience

I have a good command of English. I had eight years of English at school, have visited London several times and spent two months on a placement at Silverstein Merchant Bank in London. I also have a good knowledge of Spanish.

mention other qualifications

I enclose my CV and certified translations of my certificates. I should be pleased to supply names of referees if required.

send CV and copies of certificates

I look forward to hearing from you. I would very much welcome the opportunity of working for a bank in Britain.

closing remarks

Yours sincerely

Thomas Seegers

Enc.

1 Übertragen Sie die folgenden Sätze ins Deutsche.

KMK

1. I have decided to apply on the off-chance.
2. I am interested in applying for this vacancy.
3. I know you are recruiting staff at present.
4. I feel I am suitably qualified for this position.
5. I have completed a traineeship as an export clerk.

2 Complete the following letter of application as the applicant using one of the advertisements on page 208.

P

(Your address etc)

(Company address)

Reference no. (given in advertisement)

Dear Sir/Madam

I saw your **1** in the **2** yesterday and am interested in **3** this position.
I have now completed a **4** as an export clerk. My experience is limited to the **5** of my present firm.
I have a good **6** of English and Spanish and am keen **7** these languages.
I **8** my curriculum vitae and copies of certificates. Please let me know if you **9** the names and addresses of referees.

I look forward to **10** you soon.

With best regards[1]
(Your name and signature)

Enclosures: CV, certificates

[1] "Yours sincerely" is also possible. "Yours faithfully" is very formal and is hardly used nowadays.

B Curriculum Vitae (CV)

A neatly arranged CV is an essential part of any application. The following are two German CVs with paraphrases in English. As indicated in UNIT 1 German job titles often have no direct equivalent in English. It is important that you paraphrase your job title (e.g. Industriekaufmann, Hotelfachfrau etc.) in such a way that a potential employer has a clear and realistic impression of your training and experience. When applying for a job in English - and there is an increasing number of companies in continental Europe whose company language is English - it is important to be aware of differences. In an English CV do not give details of your parents' profession, your religious denomination, or the number of your brothers and sisters. International CVs do not include a photograph. Modern CVs often reverse the chronological order and start with the most recent developments in your career.

1 Study the following CVs of Fatma Gülsuyu and Daniel Paulat with a suggested paraphrase in English.

German CV I

Tabellarischer Lebenslauf

Persönliche Angaben	
Name	Fatma Gülsuyu
Adresse	Dülkener Str. 5, 40235 Düsseldorf Tel.: 0211 571364, E-Mail: fatmaguelsuyu@t-online.de
Staatsangehörigkeit	türkisch
Geburtstag	23.01.89
Geburtsort	Düsseldorf
Familienstand	ledig
Schulbildung	
1995–1999	Grundschule Niederkassel
1999–2007	Schiller-Gymnasium, Düsseldorf
2007	Abitur (Leistungskurse: Englisch, Mathematik, Grundkurse: Sozialwissenschaften, Türkisch Gesamtnote: 2,2)
Tätigkeiten	
August 2005–Juli 2006	Hausaufgabenhilfe im „Lernzentrum", Düsseldorf
August 2006–Juni 2007	Aushilfstätigkeit im Reisebüro „Evren", Düsseldorf
seit September 2007	Ausbildung als Kauffrau für Bürokommunikation im Reisebüro „Evren"
Sprachkenntnisse	Deutsch: wie Muttersprache Türkisch: Muttersprache Englisch: gut in Wort und Schrift Italienisch: Grundkenntnisse
PC-Kenntnisse	Windows, Excel, Powerpoint
Interessen	Musik (Saz spielen, im Chor singen), Volleyball

English paraphrase CV I

Curriculum Vitae

Personal details

Name and address	Fatma Gülsuyu Dülkener Str 5 40235 Düsseldorf, Germany Tel. + 49 (0)211 571364 E-mail: fatmaguelsuyu@t-online.de
Nationality	Turkish
Date of birth	23 January, 1989
Place of birth	Düsseldorf, Germany
Marital status	single

Education

1995–1999	Primary School Niederkassel
1999–2007	Schiller Gymnasium Düsseldorf (grammar school)
2007	Abitur (= A-Levels) (Major subjects: English, Mathematics. Basic courses: Social Sciences, Turkish Overall grade: 2.2 (= good = B)

Job experience and other activities

August 2005 to July 2006	Assisting pupils with homework at the Lernzentrum (Learning Centre) in Düsseldorf
August 2006–June 2007	Temporary employment at the "Evren" travel agency in Düsseldorf
from September 2007	Traineeship as office communications clerk/office management assistant at the "Evren" travel agency

Languages	German: native command Turkish: mother tongue English: good command of both spoken and written English Italian: basic knowledge
Computer skills	Windows, Excel, Powerpoint
Hobbies	Music (playing saz, singing in a choir), volleyball

German CV II

Tabellarischer Lebenslauf

Persönliche Angaben

Name	Daniel Paulat
Adresse	44369 Dortmund Servatiusstr. 37 Tel. 0231 4669834 E-Mail: danielpaulat@aol.com
Staatsangehörigkeit	deutsch
Geburtstag	17.1.1990
Geburtsort	Hagen
Familienstand	ledig

Schulbildung

1996–2000	Grundschule Haspe, Hagen
2000–2004	Albert-Einstein-Realschule, Hagen
2004–2006	Gesamtschule am Teich, Dortmund Abschluss: Fachoberschulreife
2006–2008	Höhere Handelsschule, Kaufmännische Schule II, Dortmund Abschluss: Fachhochschulreife

Ausbildung

2009–2012	Ausbildung zum Industriekaufmann bei Kabel AG, Leverkusen Schwerpunkte: Rechnungswesen, Einkauf
2011	Zertifikatsprüfung Englisch für kaufmännische und verwaltende Berufe, Niveau I
voraussichtlich Mai 2012	Abschlussprüfung

Tätigkeiten

2006–2008	Aushilfstätigkeit als Fahrradkurier
2008–2009	Zivildienst in einer Behindertenwerkstatt

Sonstige Kenntnisse	MS Office, Linux Englisch fließend, Spanisch ausbaufähig
Interessen	Fitness, Fußball, Fantasy-Literatur

English paraphrase CV II

Curriculum Vitae

Personal details

Name	Daniel Paulat
Address	44369 Dortmund, Germany Servatiusstr. 37 Tel.: +49 (0)231 4669834 E-mail: danielpaulat@aol.com
Nationality	German
Date of birth	17 January, 1990
Place of birth	Hagen (North Rhine-Westphalia)
Marital status	single

Education/Training

1996–2000	Primary school Haspe, Hagen
2000–2004	Albert Einstein Realschule (= higher secondary school), Hagen
2004–2006	Gesamtschule am Teich (comprehensive), Dortmund School-leaving certificate: Fachoberschulreife (= certificate enabling student to continue education at higher vocational school)
2006–2008	Höhere Handelschule, Kaufmännische Schule II (higher commercial college), Dortmund Final examination: Fachhochschulreife (examination enabling student to enrol at a polytechnic university)
2009–2012	Traineeship as an industrial clerk/industrial business management assistant at Kabel AG, Leverkusen
2011	Special subjects: accounting, purchasing Zertifikatsprüfung (state examination) English for clerical and administrative professions, Level I
probably May, 2012	Final examination traineeship

Job activities

2006–2008	Temporary employment as cycle courier
2008–2009	Social service (in lieu of military service) in a workshop for handicapped people

Other skills	MS Office, Linux/Fluent English, basic Spanish
Personal interests	Working out, football, fantasy literature

Phrases

2 P Now write your own CV in English using the examples above and referring back to UNIT 1 for job titles. Use a dictionary if necessary.

3 You have applied for a job with GlaxoSmithKline (UK). You feel you have a good chance of being invited to an interview. Research the company and its products and make brief notes in English.

4 I Daniela Zeischegg sent off an application three weeks ago to the British company Tolaron plc in reply to an advertisement in which the company was looking for a German mother-tongue export clerk. Since she has not received a reply she decides to ring the company. Roleplay the dialogue below.

Daniela Zeischegg	David Stedman
put through / human resources department	
	help?
application / three weeks ago / no reply yet / lost in post?	
	spell name / reference
name / reference T027 68P	
	computer / application found / process / send invitation / interview in the next few days
when? how much notice? / book flight	
	1 week / ring immediately / if date inconvenient
look forward / receive reply / thank you	

V8 Video Lounge Travel and Tourism

BBC Motion Gallery

You are about to see a video on the travel and tourist industry. Read through the questions below and listen for the answers as you watch the video:

1. What kind of tour operator does the young man work for?
2. Try and list as many of the qualifications and characteristics that are mentioned as desirable in a tour leader.
3. What kind of person is likely to apply for a job as a tour leader?
4. How did he prepare for his job in Egypt?
5. What sort of disadvantages does life as a tour leader have?

C Interviews

If your application meets with the approval of the company or its personnel department, your name will be put on a shortlist and you will be invited to an interview.

How can you prepare for the interview?

It is important to find out as much as you can about the company, its products and the image it projects so that you make an informed impression and demonstrate that you are interested in the company.

Think beforehand of any questions you would like to ask if they are not covered by the interviewer, e.g. location, type of work, starting salary, opportunities for further training, opportunities to use your language skills, catering arrangements, company pension scheme, how big is the office you will be working in? Will you have contact with customers or is it a back office?

What are your other interests? Think carefully about this. If you say "cinema" expect to be asked about the last film you saw. If you mention an interest in your CV, e.g. working out at a gym, you should think in advance what you would say if asked about it.

Finally, do not underestimate the importance of so-called "soft skills" – a neat, clean appearance, shirt tucked neatly into trousers, polished shoes with laces tied, hair neatly cut and combed, etc. Women should go for a suit or skirt or trousers and jacket. Don't risk wearing jeans and a T-shirt.

1 Answer the following questions on the text above.

R

1. What may happen if the company has a lot of applications and you are one of the fortunate ones?
2. Why is it a good idea to know something about the company?
3. What questions might you want to ask if the interviewer doesn't cover them?
4. What interests or hobbies would you mention?
5. What is meant by the term "soft skills"?

2 R **Choose what you regard as appropriate from this list of do's and don'ts.**

1. Your first question should be about annual holidays.
2. You should dress smartly.
3. You should take some gum with you to chew to help you relax.
4. The interviewer can't expect you to know much about the firm before you even work there.
5. You should feel free to tell the interviewer that you are bored with your present job.
6. You should be prepared (and able) to talk about any interests you mention.
7. You should make eye contact with the interviewer, smile and nod to express agreement or ethusiasm.
8. You should tell the interviewer straight away that you are applying for other jobs at the moment.
9. You should refuse to describe your strengths and weaknesses.

3 P **Send an encouraging e-mail to an anxious friend who has an interview in a couple of days. Make sentences by matching the bubbles with suitable parts from the list below.**

Make sure you …

Wear …

Don't forget to …

Remember to …

Don't wear …

Don't just …

Be sure to …

Be …

Remember…

You mustn't …

… go to bed early the night before.
… go to the hairdresser's beforehand.
… put on a clean set of clothes.
… a sweatshirt or fleece (boy)/see-through top or mini-skirt (girl).
… a smart costume (girl)/jacket (boy).
… wear sneakers.
… have a look at the firm's website before the interview.
… get there on time.
… yourself and act naturally.
… answer "yes" or "no". Take the initiative and volunteer information.
… that there are other fish in the sea.

4 R A1.31 Daniela Zeischegg has been invited to an interview at Tolaron plc's head office in Croydon, South London. She takes an early flight from Cologne-Bonn airport to London Gatwick. She takes the train from Gatwick to South Croydon and presents herself at Tolaron at 11 am. She wears a neatly tailored suit in navy blue and a white blouse.

Listen to the interview and write down the job details mentioned.

5 Listen to the interview again and translate the following sentences into English.

R/M
A1.31

1. Sie haben eine Ausbildung bei einem großen Kölner Unternehmen der verarbeitenden Industrie gemacht.
2. Wir benötigen jemanden, der Deutsch spricht, weil wir eine große Anzahl von Kunden in Deutschland und Österreich haben.
3. Leider können wir Ihnen bei der Suche nach einer Unterkunft nicht behilflich sein.
4. Müsste ich am 1. August anfangen, wie in der Anzeige angegeben?
5. Ich habe mich gefreut, Sie kennen zu lernen. Sie werden von mir hören.

6 Match these 10 questions with the answers given below.

R

1. Why do you wish to leave your present position?
2. What would you say are your strengths and weaknesses?
3. Why would you like to work for this company?
4. Which animal do you most readily identify with?
5. What are your professional aims?
6. What are your expectations as far as salary is concerned?
7. What would you say was your advantage compared with other applicants?
8. What did you find most satisfying in your previous jobs?
9. What three positive things would your previous boss say about you?
10. What reasons would you give why we should employ you?

A. I particularly like lions/monkeys/elephants.
B. I don't know the other applicants. All I know is that I am highly motivated and keen to do this job.
C. Eventually I would like to be an export manager/head of department/set up in business on my own.
D. I am very enthusiastic and have all the necessary qualifications plus good references.
E. I have always enjoyed dealing with people. I liked being in the front office. I had a good rapport with customers.
F. I like my present job and the people I work with but it doesn't give me any opportunity to use my languages/I have no contact with clients.
G. My previous boss would probably say I had a good sense of humour, was good at working to deadlines and that I had a good manner with customers.
H. My strengths are that I'm good at working with clients, deadlines don't faze me. My weaknesses – I need praise and to feel that I'm needed. My motivation level drops if I feel unloved or unappreciated.
I. The company has a very good reputation for well-designed products and a positive approach to the environment. I also know that you have a good reputation as an equal opportunities employer.
J. From advertisements for similar positions I know that the usual starting salary is about Euro 2000. I would be happy with this salary but would hope that the career structure makes promotion possible.

*** 7** **Work with a partner. Prepare and act out the following interview as a role play in English using the prompts on the role cards.**

Phrases

Role card: Partner A (interviewer) **Role card partner B ⇨ page 231**

Sie sind Jennifer O'Rourke von Automotive Services Ltd., London, oder deren Kollege John Middleton. Mittels einer Stellenanzeige haben Sie eine/n zweisprachige/n Mitarbeiter/in für die Importabteilung gesucht. Ein/e Bewerber/in kommt zum Vorstellungsgespräch.

Beginnen Sie das Gespräch mit allgemeinen Fragen z. B. nach:
- Flug
- Heimatstadt des Bewerbers
- Wetter

Fassen Sie die Anforderungen kurz zusammen:
- zweisprachig
- teamfähig
- vertraut mit Einfuhrformalitäten

Fragen Sie nach Berufserfahrung:
- Dauer
- Arbeitsgebiete
- Software-Kenntnisse

Erkundigen Sie sich nach den Gründen für den Wunsch in GB zu arbeiten.

Fragen Sie nach den Gehaltsvorstellungen.

Gehen Sie auf das im CV genannte Interesse an Tennis ein:
- Sie spielen selbst.
- Ihre Firma besorgt für die Mitarbeiter Karten für Wimbledon.

Versprechen Sie in einer Woche Bescheid zu geben.

Verabschieden Sie den Bewerber freundlich.

D Employment in the EU

One of the central principles of the EU is the free movement of labour. This means that in principle any EU citizen can look for a job in any EU member country without having to apply for permits etc. An EU citizen also has the right to take up residence in any EU country.

1
R
A1.32
Jonathan Oxfurt, a 23-year-old German from Quedlinburg who has recently completed an apprenticeship as an export clerk, is thinking of looking for a job in another European country. He is talking on the telephone to an English friend, Daniel Peterson, whom he met while on a work placement in England and who is working in Bracknell at the logistics and warehousing operation of a major supermarket.

Listen to the conversation and decide whether the following statements are TRUE or FALSE.

1. Jonathan has sent off lots of applications.
2. He would need a green card to work in Britain.
3. A lot of companies have their head offices in Bracknell.
4. Jonathan's certificates do not need to be translated into English.
5. Jonathan could stay for a while with Daniel.
6. Daniel suggests he should apply to the export department.

2
R
A1.33
Marcel Krenz has seen that Global Catering are looking for an assistant to the export manager who speaks French and German. Kirsty Burnham has been promoted and the new export manager is Zoe Lovegrove. Marcel is excited about the job and would love to work in Manchester. He decides to ring Kirsty Burnham.

Listen to the dialogue and complete the following sentences.

Would you **1** for a moment, please?
As you know, **2** are now the big thing.
I have seen that your company is advertising for **3** who can speak German.
Of course, it will have to go through **4**.
Tell Herr Diepholz this is **5** for you.
I'll get **6** off right away.

3 **Listen to the dialogue again and translate the following sentences into German.**

R/M
A1.33

1. Kirsty Burnham has been promoted.
2. Global Catering are looking for an assistant to the export manager.
3. We are in the process of acquiring a US chain of organic snack outlets.
4. I would be able to involve you in the US projects.
5. I am dreading telling Herr Diepholz.
6. Keep your fingers crossed!

Communicating across cultures: Job applications

You should NOT include references from previous employers in your application when applying in Britain. You will usually be asked to give the names and addresses of possible referees so that the company can approach them direct. In your covering letter you may indicate that you are prepared to provide names of referees on request.

It is obviously a good idea to ask possible referees beforehand whether they are happy to provide a reference.

You should NOT include a photo in your application when applying in the USA or Britain nor make any reference to your religion or race, unless specifically asked to do so.

E The European Union

1 Basic principles

The free movement of labour was and is one of the central principles in the creation of a unified single market in Europe. The free movement of goods and services is the second and the free movement of capital the third.

The free movement of goods and capital are furthest advanced. Problems of language, cultural differences and tradition make it more difficult for people to move to other countries in the European Union to work than say, to move from New York to San Francisco in the USA. Despite its imperfections as a single market, the EU does offer immense opportunities and the number of people taking advantage of their right to look for employment and take up residence in other EU countries is increasing.

2 Institutions

It has been estimated that sixty per cent of the laws and regulations that affect our lives no longer originate in Berlin, Paris or London, but in Brussels, the seat of the European Commission. This is why it is important to have a basic understanding of EU institutions.

European Commission
At the present time each of the 27 members nominates one commissioner. They are appointed and not elected. Each commissioner has a portfolio, e.g. transport, trade, competition, environment.

The President of the Commission is also nominated by the 27 member countries.

Both the president and the commissioners have to be endorsed by the European Parliament.

What is the role of the Commission?
- It ensures that the various treaties signed by the member states are not violated. It may impose fines.
- It introduces regulations (directives).
- It makes proposals for new legislation.
- It spends the budget agreed upon by the 27 member states which also decide how it is to be spent.

Council of Ministers
Political decisions are taken by the Council of Ministers. This council is made up of 1 minister from each of the 27 member states. When financial or fiscal issues are involved the ministers of finance meet, when agricultural issues are to be dealt with ministers of agriculture meet etc. They have indirect democratic legitimacy as they are elected in their country of origin. The **European Council** consisting of the prime ministers or presidents of the member countries meet up to four times a year to resolve issues which could not be dealt with at a lower level.

European Parliament
Members of the European Parliament are elected in all 27 member states. The prestige of the European Parliament suffers from low participation in the European elections. It does, however, have powers to monitor the work of the commission and even to reject individual commissioners or the commission as a whole.

President
The president is appointed by the 27 member countries for a once-renewable term of 2½ years.

Foreign Affairs
and EU "embassies" abroad are the responisibility of the High Representative of the Union for Foreign Affairs and Security Policy (also appointed by the 27 member countries.)

1 KMK **Beantworten Sie folgende Fragen zum Text über die EU in Deutsch.**

1. Welche Möglichkeiten bietet die EU Menschen, die in ihrem eigenen EU-Mitgliedsstaat keine Arbeit finden?
2. Welchen Einfluss hat die EU auf unser Leben durch Gesetze und Richtlinien?
3. Welche Aufgaben hat die Europäische Kommission?
4. Welche der EU-Institutionen trifft die politischen Entscheidungen?
5. Welche Befugnisse besitzt das Europäische Parlament?

2 **Work in groups. Search the internet and find out more about the EU. What are the latest developments? Present your results to the class.**

3 **Work in groups. Search the internet and find out more about jobs in the EU. What kind of jobs are offered? Present your results to the class.**

Info: EU-Facts and figures

EU member countries (28 at present):

Austria, Belgium, Bulgaria, Croatia, Cyprus, Czech Republic, Denmark, Estonia, Finland, France, Germany, Greece, Hungary, Ireland, Italy, Latvia, Lithuania, Luxemburg, Malta, The Netherlands, Poland, Portugal, Romania, Slovakia, Slovenia, Spain, Sweden, United Kingdom

Total area: 4,423,147 sq. km.

Total population: c. 505.73 million

Total GDP: between $15 and $18 trillion

Languages: There are over 24 official languages. English is spoken by 51% of European citizens – the most widely spoken foreign language.

Phrases: Applications

To refer to the source of address

I saw your advertisement **in** …	Ich habe Ihre Anzeige in … gesehen.
I saw this vacancy advertised **on** the … website.	Ich habe diese Stellenanzeige auf der … Webseite gefunden.
I should like to apply for the position advertised in the …	Ich möchte mich für den in der … ausgeschriebenen Posten bewerben.
I have been given your address **by** … who told me that you have a vacancy **for** …	Ich habe Ihre Anschrift von … bekommen, der mich darauf aufmerksam machte, dass bei Ihnen die Stelle eines … frei geworden ist.
I am applying on the off-chance that you may have a vacancy.	Ich erlaube mir, Ihnen eine Initiativbewerbung zu schicken, für den Fall, dass bei Ihnen eine Stelle frei ist.

To give reasons for applying

I am particularly attracted **to** this position as …	Ich bin an dieser Stelle besonders interessiert, weil …
I have just completed a traineeship **at** …	Ich habe gerade meine Ausbildung bei … abgeschlossen.
I completed an apprenticeship two years ago.	Vor zwei Jahren haben ich meine Ausbildung abgeschlossen.
I have some experience in the export trade.	Ich habe Erfahrungen im Außenhandel.
I am familiar **with** this kind of work.	Mit dieser Tätigkeit bin ich vertraut.
I am used to working with people.	Ich bin es gewohnt mit Menschen zu arbeiten.
I enjoy working with people.	Ich arbeite gern mit anderen Menschen zusammen.
I enjoy working in a team.	Ich arbeite gern im Team.
I would welcome the opportunity to …	Ich würde mich über die Möglichkeit freuen …
I am keen to use my knowledge **of** English and French.	Ich möchte sehr gerne meine Englisch- und Französischkenntnisse anwenden.

To refer to your German school career

From … to … I attended … comparable **to** • primary (UK)/elementary (USA) school • grammar school (UK) • higher secondary school • secondary modern school	Von … bis … besuchte ich • die Grundschule • das Gymnasium • die Realschule • die Hauptschule

• comprehensive (school) • high school (USA) • vocational school • commercial school • business college • polytechnic university, university of applied sciences	• Gesamtschule (Einheitsschule für die Sekundarstufe) • die Berufsschule • die Höhere Handelsschule • das Berufskolleg • die Fachhochschule
In … I obtained the • certificate enabling a student to continue education at higher vocational school • German higher education entrance qualification • German university entrance qualification	Im Jahre … erwarb ich das Zeugnis der • Fachoberschulreife • Fachhochschulreife • allgemeine Hochschulreife (Abitur)
In … I passed the • state examination in English for clerical and administrative professions • Chamber of Commerce examination – "Certified Foreign Language Correspondent" – "English for Commercial Trainees"	Im Jahre … legte ich die … • Zertifikatsprüfung Englisch für kaufmännische und verwaltende Berufe (KMK-Zertifikat) • IHK-Prüfung – „Geprüfte/r Fremdsprachen-korrespondent/in" – „Zusatzqualifikation Englisch für kaufmännische Auszubildende" ab.

To refer to qualifications

I **took** my Abitur two years ago.	Vor zwei Jahren machte ich das Abitur.
My main subjects included English and Maths.	Meine Leistungskurse waren Englisch und Mathematik.
I have trained **as a** …	Ich bin gelernte/r …
I have completed an apprenticeship **in** …	Ich habe eine Ausbildung als … abgeschlossen.
I did my apprenticeship **with** the … company.	Ich habe eine Ausbildung bei der Firma … gemacht.
I spent two months in St. Albans **on** a placement.	Ich war zwei Monate zu einem Praktikum in St. Albans.
I have done a practical **with** a small travel operator.	Ich habe ein Praktikum bei einem kleinen Reiseveranstalter gemacht.
I have good admin and bookkeeping skills.	Ich verfüge über gute Kenntnisse und Fertigkeiten, was Organisation und Buchhaltung angeht.

To refer to certificates and references

I enclose certified copies of my certificates.	Als Anlage übersende ich Ihnen beglaubigte Zeugniskopien.
I enclose certified translations of …	Ich füge beglaubigte Übersetzungen von … bei.
I should be happy to provide the names of referees.	Ich würde Ihnen gerne Referenzen angeben.

To refer to starting date and relocation

I would be able to start **at** short notice.	Ich kann kurzfristig anfangen.
I would have to give the usual notice **at** my present firm.	Ich müsste die übliche Kündungsfrist einhalten.
I could start **on** 1 August.	Ich könnte am 1. August anfangen.
I would be prepared to move **to** …	Ich wäre bereit nach … umzuziehen.

To close the letter

I look forward to hearing from you.	Ich sehe Ihrer Antwort mit Interesse entgegen.
I should be grateful if you would consider my application.	Ich würde mich freuen, wenn Sie meine Bewerbung berücksichtigen.
I hope that you will consider my application suitable and give me the opportunity to present myself **at** an interview.	Ich hoffe, dass Sie meine Bewerbung in Betracht ziehen und mir die Möglichkeit geben, mich Ihnen persönlich vorzustellen.

Role cards Partner B

Unit 5 C 5

Role card: Partner B

Role card partner A ⇨ page 61

1. 0033 (0) 4 92 04 89 20
2. 12 Gansevoort Street New York, NY 10014 USA Tel.: 001-212-2422455 info@usatech.com,
3. www.visitengland.com
4. e-mail: info@shanghai-cd.com, phone: 86-21-5365-8941
5. address: 12J-1 Golden Bell Plaza 18 Huaihai Zhong Lu Shanghai 200021 China

Unit 5 C 8

Role card: Partner A / B

Persons for whom the message is intended:

Mr. Collins

Sales Manager

Miss Otway in Purchasing

Dr. Temme

Frau Sabine Johänntges

Possible contents of message:

Mr. Campbell ill with the flu/ can't take part in the conference

Meeting on Wednesday scheduled from 1:00 pm to 3:30 pm/15 participants

Proposal accepted/further details tomorrow

New deadline for application 16 October, must be kept whatever happens

Flight delayed by one hour/arrival now at 10:15 London Heathrow

Unit 13 C2 3

Role card: Student A (seller) Role card partner B ⇨ page 230

You are the chief-accountant Jane/John Thorpe at Topsweets Ltd. in Edinburgh. At the end of last month but one (use the appropriate month) you supplied 1,500 kgs mint bars to Zuckermann & Sacher in Suessen, Germany, a regular customer of yours.

Ring Zuckermann & Sacher and remind them of your invoice
- invoice No. 34500-2
- invoice amount: €20,450.50
- due date: 14 days ago

Up to now punctual settlements
- invoice overlooked?
- reason for complaint?

Be helpful and polite but insist on payment by the end of next week.
Impossible to grant 3 months' respite for the entire sum.
Insist on down payment of at least half the sum.
Accept one of the solutions offered and close on a friendly note.

Unit 6 B1 1

Role card: Partner B Role card partner A ⇨ page 79

Kirsty Burnham's appointment diary

Monday 9–11 am: meeting to discuss Madrid; 1 pm working lunch with John Markham from PolisMedia; 2.30 pm meeting at office with Barbara Lonsdale from Cosmopolitan Gourmet	**13 June**
Tuesday	**14 June**
Wednesday From 10 am: visiting suppliers in Birmingham	**15 June**
Thursday 5 pm: work-out at Royal Gym with Laurie	**16 June**
Friday 10 am: Leeds/Amanda Rees from Snack Attack/introduction of trial range 4 pm: hairdresser	**17 June**

Unit 9 B 4

Role card: Partner B Role card partner A ⇨ page 121

Jane/James Vernon from Powertools plc, Cardiff, gets a call.
He/she offers to send brochures, price lists and detailed technical descriptions by e-mail and asks for Hammer Werkzeughandel's e-mail address.
Details about delivery times, quantity discounts etc. are dealt with in the brochure.
Jane/James thanks the caller for his/her interest in Powertool's products.

Unit 6 A 8

Role card: Partner B Role card partner A ⇨ page 78

Sie sind James Critchley von der Firma SmartMart Ltd. und wollen für eine Geschäftsreise in den USA ein Auto mieten. Jennifer Ainsworth von Saskatchewan Airlines hat Ihnen die Mietwagenfirma Excelsior Limos Inc. in Chicago empfohlen. **Rufen Sie dort an.**

- Auto vom 25. bis 30. Juni benötigt
- Abholung und Rückgabe am Flughafen O'Hare in Chicago
- Kleinwagen genügt/Preis für fünf Tage?/Versicherung inbegriffen?
- Zusatzversicherung für Selbstbeteiligung (excess coverage) erwünscht
- Rabatt für Kunden der Saskatchewan Airlines?
- Gesamtpreis für eine Woche?
- Zahlung per Kreditkarte?
- Visa Nr. 4731 5026 7100 5314, gültig bis 07/14
- Adresse: Brunswick Avenue, Brighton BN3 1NA, UK

Unit 13 C2 3

Role card: Student B (buyer) Role card partner A ⇨ page 229

Sie (eigener Name) bearbeiten die Rechnungen der Firma Zuckermann & Sacher in Suessen. Ende vorletzten Monats hatten Sie von der Firma Topsweets Ltd aus Edinburgh, Schottland, 1500 kg Pfefferminzriegel bezogen. Die Rechnung war vor 14 Tagen fällig. Nun ruft Sie Jane/John Thorpe deswegen an.

Fragen Sie nach Rechnungsnummer, -datum und -betrag.
Kein Versehen, kein Grund zur Beanstandung
Entschuldigung für Zahlungsverzug
Grund: Insolvenz eines wichtigen Kunden, einer Kette von Süßwarengeschäften
Bitte um 3 Monate Zahlungsaufschub
Falls abgelehnt: Ihr Verhandlungsspielraum für Anzahlung: €7,000–10,000
Ihr Verhandlungsspielraum für Restzahlung:

- in 3 Raten im Abstand von 6 Wochen oder
- gesamter Rest in 10 Wochen.

Bei Entgegenkommen weitere Aufträge

Unit 14 A2 6

Role card: Partner B (seller) **Role card partner A ⇨ page 184**

You receive a call from a customer who had expected to be supplied with a skateboard for a maximum weight of 70 kg. On checking the package the customer has found that the maximum admissible weight is only 90 lbs. The price the customer paid is the price for this smaller model. However, on your website you had quoted this lower price for the bigger model by mistake. Apologize. Try to persuade the customer to keep the smaller skateboard – as a present for a kid? – and promise to let him have the bigger one half price. Should the customer refuse this generous offer you will have to agree to take back the small skateboard at your expense and refund the purchase price.

Unit 16 C 7

Role card: Partner B (interviewee) **Role card partner A ⇨ page 220**

Sie (eigener Name) haben sich bei Automotive Services Ltd., London, als zweisprachige/r Importsachbearbeiter/in beworben und sind zu einem Vorstellungsgespräch eingeladen worden. Sie sind 23 Jahre alt und haben vor einem Jahr Ihre Ausbildung als Kaufmann/-frau im Groß- und Außenhandel beendet.

Beantworten Sie die allgemeinen Fragen zu Beginn ganz nach Wunsch
- Flug angenehm/unruhig
- Wetter heiter/wolkig
- einige Sätze zu ihrer Heimatstadt

Sie kennen die Anforderungen und glauben sie vollständig zu erfüllen
- Deutsch Muttersprache, Englisch gut: Insgesamt 9 Jahre in der Schule, 1 Jahr in USA
- arbeiten gern im Team
- mit allen Export- und Importverfahren vertraut

Berufserfahrung
- Ausbildung in verschiedenen Abteilungen eines Stuttgarter Automobilherstellers (Verkauf, Einkauf, Lagerhaltung, Rechnungs- und Personalwesen)
- nach Abschluss der Lehre ein volles Jahr bis jetzt in einer Importabteilung für elektronische Bauelemente
- vertraut mit SAP Office

Begründen Sie Ihre Absicht in GB zu arbeiten ganz nach Ihrer Wahl
Gehaltsvorstellung noch nicht konkret, in Deutschland ca. €2000 pro Monat

Tennis
- Sie spielen für Ihren Klub in der Regionalliga
- Sie versuchen immer möglichst viel von Wimbledon im Fernsehen zu sehen

Bitten Sie um baldige Nachricht, weil Sie rechtzeitig kündigen müssen.

Videotraining: Englische Aussprache

Perfekte englische Aussprache leicht gemacht: Mit dem Lernprogramm zur englischen Lautschrift können Sie alle Laute einüben. Wählen Sie einfach in der Navigation rechts den entsprechenden Reiter (Vowels oder Consonants) aus und dann klicken Sie auf das gewünschte phonetische Symbol. Sprechen Sie die Wörter laut nach.
Unter www.klett.de geben Sie einfach den Online-Link 808201-1000 ein. Von dort aus können Sie die Webanwendung online starten

(AE) = American English
(BE) = British English
LG = Language and grammar

Unit 1

	to include [ɪn'klu:d]	einschließen, beinhalten, umfassen
	for instance [fər‿'ɪnstəns]	zum Beispiel
	professional [prə'feʃənl]	beruflich, professionell
	formal ['fɔ:ml]	förmlich
	casual ['kæʒjʊəl]	zwanglos

A Talking about yourself

	vocational school [vəʊ'keɪʃənl ˌsku:l]	Berufsschule
1	**brief(ly)** [bri:f(lɪ)]	kurz
	to do a traineeship [du:‿ə ˌtreɪ'ni:ʃɪp]	eine Ausbildung machen
	office administration clerk [ˌɒfɪs‿ədˌmɪnɪ'streɪʃn ˌklɑ:k]	Bürokaufmann/-frau
	to design [dɪ'zaɪn]	entwerfen
	export clerk ['ekspɔ:t ˌklɑ:k]	Exportkaufmann/-frau
	to support [sə'pɔ:t]	unterstützen, helfen
	to work out [wɜ:k 'aʊt]	sich körperlich fit halten, trainieren
	gym [dʒɪm]	Turnhalle, Fitnessraum
	industrial business management assistant [ɪnˌdʌstrɪəl ˌbɪznɪs 'mænɪdʒmənt əˌsɪstənt]	Industriekaufmann/ -frau
	industrial clerk [ɪn'dʌstrɪəl ˌklɑ:k]	Industriekaufmann/ -frau
	original(ly) [ə'rɪdʒənl(ɪ)]	ursprünglich
	Sicily ['sɪsəlɪ]	Sizilien
	cooking ['kʊkɪŋ]	Art zu kochen, Küche
	first name [ˌfɜ:st 'neɪm]	Vorname
2	**statement** ['steɪtmənt]	Aussage, Äußerung
	dish [dɪʃ]	Speise, Gericht, Schüssel
	Bavaria [bə'veərɪə]	Bayern
3	**advertising agency** ['ædvətaɪzɪŋ ˌeɪdʒənsɪ]	Werbeagentur
	advertising assistant ['ædvətaɪzɪŋ əˌsɪstənt]	Kaufmann/-frau für Marketingkommunikation
	work-out ['wɜ:kaʊt]	Fitnesstraining
4	**surname** ['sɜ:neɪm]	Familienname
	long-distance running [ˌlɒŋdɪstəns 'rʌnɪŋ]	Langstreckenlauf
	wholesale and export clerk [ˌhəʊlseɪl ənd 'ekspɔ:t ˌklɑ:k]	Kaufmann/-frau im Groß- und Außenhandel
	ballet ['bæleɪ]	(klassisches) Ballett
	travel agency ['trævl ˌeɪdʒənsɪ]	Reisebüro
	travel consultant ['trævl kənˌsʌltənt]	Reiseverkehrskaufmann/-frau
	Mediterranean countries [medɪtəˌreɪnɪən 'kʌntrɪz]	Länder am Mittelmeer
	diving ['daɪvɪŋ]	Tauchen, Tauchsport
	to go window-shopping [gəʊ‿'wɪndəʊ ˌʃɒpɪŋ]	einen Schaufensterbummel machen
	hint [hɪnt]	Hinweis, Andeutung
	bank clerk ['bæŋk‿ˌklɑ:k]	Bankkaufmann/-frau
5	**office management assistant** [ˌɒfɪs 'mænɪdʒmənt əˌsɪstənt]	Bürokaufmann/-frau
	management assistant in wholesale and foreign trade ['mænɪdʒmənt əˌsɪstənt ɪn ˌhəʊlseɪl ənd ˌfɒrən 'treɪd]	Kaufmann/-frau im Groß- und Außenhandel
	bank business management assistant [ˌbæŋk ˌbɪznɪs 'mænɪdʒmənt əˌsɪstənt]	Bankkaufmann/-frau
	management assistant in advertising ['mænɪdʒmənt əˌsɪstənt ɪn 'ædvətaɪzɪŋ]	Werbekaufmann/-frau
	management assistant in freight forwarding ['mænɪdʒmənt əˌsɪstənt ɪn ˌfreɪt 'fɔ:wədɪŋ]	Speditionskaufmann/ -frau
	management assistant in retail business ['mænɪdʒmənt əˌsɪstənt ɪn ˌri:teɪl 'bɪznɪs]	Kaufmann/-frau im Einzelhandel
	management assistant in publishing ['mænɪdʒmənt əˌsɪstənt ɪn 'pʌblɪʃɪŋ]	Verlagskaufmann/-frau
	insurance business management assistant [ˌɪnʃɔ:rəns ˌbɪznɪs 'mænɪdʒmənt əˌsɪstənt]	Versicherungskaufmann/-frau

freight forwarding and logistics services clerk [ˌfreɪt ˈfɔːwədɪŋ ənd ləˌdʒɪstɪks ˈsɜːvɪsɪz ˌklɑːk] – Kaufmann/-frau für Spedition und Logistikdienstleistung
IT specialist [ˌaɪˈtiː ˌspeʃəlɪst] – Fachinformatiker/in
retail management assistant [ˌriːteɪl ˈmænɪdʒmənt əˌsɪstənt] – Kaufmann/-frau im Einzelhandel
publisher's assistant [ˈpʌblɪʃəz əˌsɪstənt] – Verlagskaufmann/-frau
insurance clerk [ɪnˈʃɔːrəns ˌklɑːk] – Kaufmann/-frau für Versicherungen und Finanzen
novel [ˈnɒvl] – Roman
cycling [ˈsaɪklɪŋ] – Radfahren
Sci-Fi film [ˈsaɪfaɪ ˌfɪlm] – Science-Fiction-Film
to go clubbing [gəʊ ˈklʌbɪŋ] – in die Disko gehen

B Young people talk about their (future) professions

vocational college [vəʊˈkeɪʃənl ˌkɒlɪdʒ] – Berufskolleg, Berufsfachschule
trainee [ˌtreɪˈniː] – Auszubildende/r
high street bank [ˌhaɪstriːt ˈbæŋk] – Bank mit zahlreichen Zweigstellen
foreign language correspondent / secretary with modern languages [ˌfɒrən ˈlæŋgwɪdʒ kɒrɪˌspɒndənt / ˌsekrətrɪ wɪð ˌfɒrən ˈlæŋgwɪdʒɪz] – Fremdsprachenkorrespondent/in
event management assistant [ɪˌvent ˈmænɪdʒmənt əˌsɪstənt] – Veranstaltungskaufmann/-frau
wholesaler [ˈhəʊlˌseɪlə] – Großhändler
electrical goods industry [ɪˌlektrɪkl ˈgʊdz ˌɪndəstrɪ] – Elektroartikelbranche
to take part in [ˌteɪk ˈpɑːt ɪn] – teilnehmen an
1 **automobile sales management assistant** [ˌɔːtəməʊbiːl ˌseɪlz ˈmænɪdʒmənt əˌsɪstənt] – Automobilkaufmann/-frau
management assistant in event organisation [mænɪdʒmənt əˌsɪstənt ɪn ɪˌvent ˌɔːgənaɪˈzeɪʃn] – Veranstaltungskaufmann/-frau
management assistant in informatics [ˈmænɪdʒmənt əˌsɪstənt ɪn ˌɪnfəˈmætɪks] – Informatikkaufmann/-frau
management assistant in office communication [ˈmænɪdʒmənt əˌsɪstənt ɪn ˌɒfɪs kəˌmjuːnɪˈkeɪʃn] – Kaufmann/-frau für Bürokommunikation
management assistant for tourism and leisure [ˈmænɪdʒmənt əˌsɪstənt fə ˌtʊərɪzm ən ˈleʒə] – Kaufmann/-frau für Tourismus und Freizeit
3 **to insert** [ɪnˈsɜːt] – einfügen
training course [ˈtreɪnɪŋ ˌkɔːs] – Ausbildungslehrgang
5 **prospects** [ˈprɒspekts] – Aussichten
promotion [prəˈməʊʃn] – Aufstieg, Beförderung
opportunity [ˌɒpəˈtjuːnətɪ] – Gelegenheit
building materials [ˈbɪldɪŋ məˌtɪərɪəlz] – Baustoffe, -material

to advise [ədˈvaɪz] – beraten, benachrichtigen
to work on one's own [ˌwɜːk ɒn wʌnz ˈəʊn] – selbständig arbeiten
7 **to paraphrase** [ˈpærəfreɪz] – umschreiben

Unit 2

to make someone feel welcome [meɪk ˌsʌmwʌn fiːl ˈwelkəm] – dafür sorgen, dass sich jemand wohl fühlt
helpful [ˈhelpfəl] – hilfsbereit
impression [ɪmˈpreʃn] – Eindruck
to entertain [ˌentəˈteɪn] – sich um jemanden kümmern, unterhalten
lingua franca [ˌlɪŋgwə ˈfræŋkə] – Verkehrssprache
1 **to meet someone** [ˈmiːt ˌsʌmwʌn] – jemanden kennenlernen, treffen
corridor [ˈkɒrɪdɔː] – Gang

A Greeting visitors

food processing company [ˈfuːd ˌprəʊsesɪŋ ˌkʌmpənɪ] – Lebensmittel verarbeitendes Unternehmen
major [ˈmeɪdʒə] – wichtig, groß
range [reɪndʒ] – Sortiment
1 **refreshments** [rɪˈfreʃmənts] – Erfrischung(en)
in charge of [ɪn ˈtʃɑːdʒ əv] – verantwortlich für
2 **assortment** [əˈsɔːtmənt] – Sortiment, Kollektion
to let someone know [let ˌsʌmwʌn ˈnəʊ] – jemandem Bescheid sagen
bubbles [ˈbʌblz] – Blasen, Bläschen
sparkling mineral water [ˌspɑːklɪŋ ˈmɪnərəl ˌwɔːtə] – Mineralwasser mit Kohlensäure
staff [stɑːf] – Personal, Belegschaft
branch [brɑːntʃ] – Zweig; Zweigstelle, Filiale
we've already met [wiːv ˌɔːlredɪ ˈmet] – wir kennen uns schon

B Making conversation

1 **straightforward** [ˌstreɪtˈfɔːwəd] – einfach, unkompliziert
to take [teɪk] – *(hier:)* in Anspruch nehmen, dauern
as a result of [əz ə rɪˈzʌlt əv] – auf Grund
surprisingly [səˈpraɪzɪŋlɪ] – überraschenderweise
lately [ˈleɪtlɪ] – in letzter Zeit
among [əˈmʌŋ] – unter
quarter finals [ˌkwɔːtə ˈfaɪnlz] – Viertelfinale
vibrant [ˈvaɪbrənt] – lebendig
gig [gɪg] – Musikevent
club [klʌb] – Disko
definitely [ˈdefɪnətlɪ] – auf jeden Fall
2 **bumpy** [ˈbʌmpɪ] – unruhig, holprig
overcast [ˈəʊvəkɑːst] – bedeckt, bezogen (Himmel)
to support [səˈpɔːt] – unterstützen
train ride [ˈtreɪn ˌraɪd] – Zugfahrt
punctual [ˈpʌŋktʃʊəl] – pünktlich
3 **I'm on a diet** [aɪm ˌɒn ə ˈdaɪət] – ich mache eine Diät
What is the weather like? [ˌwɒt ɪz ðə ˈweðə ˌlaɪk] – Wie ist das Wetter?
apple juice [ˈæpl ˌdʒuːs] – Apfelsaft
4 **jumbled** [ˈdʒʌmbld] – durcheinander geworfen

	awful ['ɔ:fəl]	scheußlich
	drizzle ['drɪzl]	Nieselregen
	to improve [ɪm'pru:v]	besser werden, sich verbessern
	dreadful ['dredfəl]	entsetzlich
	changeable ['tʃeɪndʒəbl]	wechselhaft
	topic of conversation [ˌtɒpɪk əv ˌkɒnvə'seɪʃn]	Gesprächsthema
	superb [su:'pɜ:b]	hervorragend
	ghastly ['gɑ:stlɪ]	entsetzlich
	terrible ['terɪbl]	furchtbar
	newsagent ['nju:zˌeɪdʒənt]	Zeitungshändler/in
	weather forecast ['weðə ˌfɔ:kɑ:st]	Wettervorhersage
5	**prompt** [prɒmpt]	Hinweis, Stichwort
	tedious ['ti:dɪəs]	langweilig, lästig
	tailback ['teɪlbæk]	Stau
	slight drizzle [ˌslaɪt‿'drɪzl]	leichter Nieselregen
	fog [fɒg]	Nebel
	gale-force winds [ˌgeɪlfɔ:s 'wɪndz]	stürmische Winde
	exhibition [ˌeksɪ'bɪʃn]	Ausstellung
	noisy ['nɔɪzɪ]	laut
	tournament ['tɔ:nəmənt]	Turnier

C Giving directions

	to lose one's way [ˌlu:z wʌnz 'weɪ]	sich verirren, sich verlaufen
	receptionist [rɪ'sepʃənɪst]	Rezeptionist/in, Mitarbeiter/in am Empfang
	to direct someone [daɪ'rekt ˌsʌmwʌn, dɪ'rekt ˌsʌmwʌn]	jemandem den Weg sagen/zeigen
1	**floor plan** ['flɔ: ˌplæn]	Grundriss
	ladies' room (AE) ['leɪdɪz ˌru:m]	Damentoilette
	restroom (AE) ['restˌru:m]	Toilette
	on the left / left-hand side [ɒn ðə 'left / ˌlefthænd 'saɪd]	links
	second floor [ˌsekənd 'flɔ:]	zweite Etage
	advertising ['ædvətaɪzɪŋ]	Werbung
	storage ['stɔ:rɪdʒ]	Abstellraum
	open-plan office [ˌəʊpnplæn 'ɒfɪs]	Großraumbüro
	lift [lɪft]	Aufzug
	first floor [ˌfɜ:st 'flɔ:]	erste Etage
	data processing, EDP ['deɪtə ˌprəʊsesɪŋ, ˌi:di:'pi:]	Datenverarbeitung, EDV
	research ['ri:sɜ:tʃ]	Forschung
	Gents / Ladies [dʒents / 'leɪdɪz]	Herren-/Damen-WC
	ground floor [ˌgraʊnd 'flɔ:]	Parterre, Erdgeschoss
	chief accountant [ˌtʃi:f ə'kaʊntənt]	Leiter/in des Rechnungswesens
	canteen [kæn'ti:n]	Kantine
	stationery ['steɪʃənrɪ]	Schreibwaren, Büromaterial
	main entrance [ˌmeɪn 'entrəns]	Haupteingang
	on/to the right [ɒn/tʊ ðə 'raɪt]	rechts
2	**Could you tell me the way to ...?** [kʊd‿jʊ ˌtel mɪ ðə 'weɪ tʊ]	Können Sie mir sagen, wie ich zu/nach ... komme?
	I need to freshen up a bit [aɪ ˌni:d‿tə ˌfreʃn 'ʌp ə ˌbɪt]	ich muss mich ein bisschen frisch machen
3	**sights** [saɪts]	Sehenswürdigkeiten
	destination [ˌdestɪ'neɪʃn]	(Reise-)Ziel
	main road [ˌmeɪn 'rəʊd]	Hauptstraße
	up the hill [ˌʌp ðə 'hɪl]	den Berg hinauf
	sharp [ʃɑ:p]	scharf
	bend [bend]	Kurve
	junction ['dʒʌŋkʃn]	Kreuzung
	opposite ['ɒpəzɪt]	gegenüber
	roundabout ['raʊndəbaʊt]	Kreisverkehr
	town hall [ˌtaʊn 'hɔ:l]	Rathaus
4	**square** [skweə]	Platz
	ancient ['eɪnʃnt]	alt
	unique [ju:'ni:k]	einzigartig
	towering ['taʊərɪŋ]	turmhoch, überragend
	gothic ['gɒθɪk]	gotisch
	conspicuous [kən'spɪkjʊəs]	auffällig
	patron saint [ˌpeɪtrən 'seɪnt]	Schutzheilige/r
	to end up [end 'ʌp]	*(hier:)* landen
	dominated ['dɒmɪneɪtɪd]	beherrscht, dominiert
	striking ['straɪkɪŋ]	auffallend
	bright yellow [ˌbraɪt 'jeləʊ]	leuchtend gelb
	to house [haʊz]	beherbergen
	magnificent [mæg'nɪfɪsənt]	großartig, prächtig
	state rooms ['steɪt ˌru:mz]	Empfangssäle
	formal park [ˌfɔ:ml 'pɑ:k]	Parkanlage
	upmarket [ˌʌp'mɑ:kɪt]	anspruchsvoll
	brewery ['bru:ərɪ]	Brauerei
	pretzel ['pretsl]	Brezel

D Describing the layout of the premises and carrying out a tour of the firm for visitors

	premises ['premɪsɪz]	Firmengelände, -gebäude
1	**to surround** [sə'raʊnd]	umgeben
	countryside ['kʌntrɪsaɪd]	Landschaft, Gegend
	kitchen facilities ['kɪtʃɪn fəˌsɪlətɪz]	Küchenanlagen
	consideration [kənˌsɪdə'reɪʃn]	Erwägung, Überlegung
	market research [ˌmɑ:kɪt 'ri:sɜ:tʃ]	Marktforschung
	air-conditioning ['eəkənˌdɪʃənɪŋ]	Klimaanlage
	senior ['si:njə]	höherrangig
	sociable ['səʊʃəbl]	gesellig, umgänglich
	nutritional science [nju:ˌtrɪʃənl 'saɪəns]	Ernährungswissenschaft
	balanced ['bælənst]	ausgewogen
	cost price ['kɒst ˌpraɪs]	Selbstkostenpreis
	nutritionally conscious [nju:ˌtrɪʃənlɪ 'kɒnʃəs]	ernährungsbewusst
	airy ['eərɪ]	luftig
	produce ['prɒdju:s]	(landwirtschaftliche) Erzeugnisse
	paramount ['pærəmaʊnt]	vorrangig
	to guarantee [ˌgærən'ti:]	garantieren
	organic [ɔ:'gænɪk]	biologisch, Bio-
	label ['leɪbl]	Etikett, Aufkleber
	to modify ['mɒdɪfaɪ]	ab-, verändern
	to redesign [ˌri:dɪ'zaɪn]	neu-, umgestalten
	to finalise ['faɪnəlaɪz]	abschließen
	trial order [ˌtraɪəl 'ɔ:də]	Probeauftrag
2	**memo** ['meməʊ]	Aktennotiz
	brief [bri:f]	kurz

E Taking foreign visitors to a restaurant

	to join [dʒɔɪn]	*(hier:)* sich jemandem anschließen, mitkommen
1	**starter** ['stɑ:tə]	Vorspeise
	main course [ˌmeɪn 'kɔ:s]	Hauptgericht, -gang
	dessert [dɪ'zɜ:t]	Nachspeise
	spicy ['spaɪsɪ]	würzig
	onion ['ʌnjən]	Zwiebel
	mushrooms ['mʌʃru:mz]	Champignons, Pilze
	garlic ['gɑ:lɪk]	Knoblauch
	breadcrumbs ['bredkrʌmz]	Brotkrümel, Paniermehl
	disgusting [dɪs'gʌstɪŋ]	abscheulich
	carnivorous [kɑ:'nɪvərəs]	fleischfressend
	deer [dɪə]	Rotwild
	dumpling ['dʌmplɪŋ]	Kloß, Knödel
	venison ['venɪsən]	Hirsch, Rotwild (als Fleisch)
	to wait one's turn [ˌweɪt wʌnz 'tɜ:n]	warten bis man an die Reihe kommt
	to marinate ['mærɪneɪt]	marinieren, einlegen
	cabbage ['kæbɪdʒ]	Kohl
	to tempt [tempt]	in Versuchung führen
	leeks [li:ks]	Lauch
	vegan ['vi:gən]	Veganer/in
	chilled [tʃɪld]	eisgekühlt
	veggieburger ['vedʒɪˌbɜ:gə]	Gemüsebratling
	joint [dʒɔɪnt]	gemeinsam
	business venture ['bɪznɪs ˌventʃə]	geschäftliches Unternehmen
2	**beef broth** [ˌbi:f 'brɒθ]	Fleischbrühe
	cucumber ['kju:kʌmbə]	Gurke
	French fries [ˌfrentʃ 'fraɪz]	Pommes frites
	fried potatoes [ˌfraɪd pə'teɪtəʊz]	Bratkartoffeln
	sausage ['sɒsɪdʒ]	Wurst
	mashed potatoes [ˌmæʃt pə'teɪtəʊz]	Kartoffelpüree
	meatballs ['mi:tbɔ:lz]	Frikadellen
	pea soup [ˌpi: 'su:p]	Erbsensuppe
	roast pork [ˌrəʊst 'pɔ:k]	Schweinebraten
	ground beef [ˌgraʊnd 'bi:f]	Rindergehacktes
	ground (coffee beans) [graʊnd]	gemahlen (Kaffeebohnen)
	mince(d) meat ['mɪns(t) ˌmi:t]	Gehacktes
	to chop [tʃɒp]	klein schneiden, hacken
	stuffed [stʌft]	gefüllt
	rice [raɪs]	Reis
	meat [mi:t]	Fleisch
	veal [vi:l]	Kalbfleisch
	lamb [læm]	Lamm
	to boil [bɔɪl]	kochen, sieden
	to bake [beɪk]	backen, im Ofen braten
	to stew [stju:]	kochen, dünsten, schmoren
	poultry ['pəʊltrɪ]	Geflügel
	chicken ['tʃɪkɪn]	Hähnchen, Hühnerfleisch
	turkey ['tɜ:kɪ]	Pute, Truthahn
	smoked [sməʊkt]	geräuchert
	salmon ['sæmən]	Lachs
	trout [traʊt]	Forelle
	plaice [pleɪs]	Scholle
	haddock ['hædək]	Schellfisch
	to taste [teɪst]	schmecken
	game [geɪm]	Wild
	rabbit ['ræbɪt]	Kaninchen
	hot [hɒt]	heiß, scharf
	sour [saʊə]	sauer
	vegetable(s) ['vedʒtəbl(z)]	Gemüse
	bean [bi:n]	Bohne
	carrots ['kærəts]	Möhren, Karotten
	tart [tɑ:t]	herb, säuerlich
	peppers ['pepəz]	Paprikaschoten
	cauliflower ['kɒlɪˌflaʊə]	Blumenkohl
	Brussels sprouts [ˌbrʌslz 'spraʊts]	Rosenkohl
	savoury ['seɪvərɪ]	herzhaft, pikant
	asparagus [ə'spærəgəs]	Spargel
	it tastes like … [ɪt ˌteɪsts laɪk '…]	es schmeckt wie …
3	**jelly** ['dʒelɪ]	Götterspeise, Gelee, Aspik
	berry ['berɪ]	Beere
	to thicken ['θɪkn]	eindicken
	corn starch ['kɔ:n ˌstɑ:tʃ]	Stärkemehl
	parsley ['pɑ:slɪ]	Petersilie
	pork escalope [ˌpɔ:k 'eskəlɒp]	Schweineschnitzel
	lettuce ['letɪs]	Kopfsalat
	vinegar ['vɪnɪgə]	Essig
	dressing ['dresɪŋ]	Salatsoße
4	**amateur chefs** [ˌæmətjʊə 'ʃefs]	Hobbyköche
	fermented white cabbage [fəˌmentɪd ˌwaɪt 'kæbɪdʒ]	Sauerkraut
	mixed [mɪkst]	gemischt
	lentils ['lentəlz]	Linsen
	stew, soup [stju:, su:p]	Eintopf
5	**menu** ['menju:]	Speisekarte
6	**favourite (dish)** [ˌfeɪvərɪt 'dɪʃ]	Lieblings(-gericht)
LG	**to give someone a ring** [gɪv ˌsʌmwʌn ə 'rɪŋ]	jemanden anrufen
	to let someone know [let ˌsʌmwʌn 'nəʊ]	Bescheid sagen
	to dry [draɪ]	abtrocknen
	to pass a message on [ˌpɑ:s ə 'mesɪdʒ ɒn]	eine Nachricht weitergeben
	to pick someone up [pɪk ˌsʌmwʌn 'ʌp]	jemanden abholen
	move [mu:v]	*(hier:)* Umzug
	to give someone a lift [gɪv ˌsʌmwʌn ə 'lɪft]	jemanden mitnehmen (im Wagen)
	to stand in for someone [stænd 'ɪn fə ˌsʌmwʌn]	jemanden vertreten
	to keep an eye on [ˌki:p ən 'aɪ ɒn]	aufpassen auf

Unit 3

sales literature ['seɪlz ˌlɪtrətʃə]	Prospektmaterial
to attempt [ə'tempt]	versuchen, sich bemühen
to create [krɪ'eɪt]	(er)schaffen, erzeugen, erstellen
particular [pə'tɪkjələ]	besonders, speziell
image ['ɪmɪdʒ]	Bild, Vorstellung

	to refer to [rɪ'fɜː tuː]	ver-, hinweisen auf, sich beziehen auf
	to emphasise ['emfəsaɪz]	betonen, hervorheben
1	**old-established** [ˌəʊldɪ'stæblɪʃt]	alteingesessen
	reliable [rɪ'laɪəbl]	zuverlässig
	to take advantage of [ˌteɪk əd'vɑːntɪdʒ ɒv]	sich zunutze machen, ausnutzen
	state-of-the-art [ˌsteɪtəvðɪ'ɑːt]	auf dem neuesten Stand (der Technik)

A Introducing a firm and giving a brief history

	interview ['ɪntəvjuː]	Vorstellungsgespräch, Interview
	brochure ['brəʊʃə]	Broschüre, Prospekt
	shoemaker ['ʃuːˌmeɪkə]	Schuhmacher/in, Schuster/in
	local ['ləʊkl]	örtlich, ortsansässig, hiesig
	neighbouring ['neɪbərɪŋ]	benachbart
	to order ['ɔːdə]	bestellen; anordnen
	to employ [ɪm'plɔɪ]	beschäftigen, einstellen
	staff [stɑːf]	Belegschaft, Personal
	to rent [rent]	mieten
	machinery [mə'ʃiːnərɪ]	Maschinen
	to require [rɪ'kwaɪə]	benötigen, erfordern, verlangen
	manufacturing [ˌmænjə'fæktʃərɪŋ]	Fertigung, Fabrikation
	to prosper ['prɒspə]	gedeihen, florieren
	to take over [ˌteɪk 'əʊvə]	(eine Firma) übernehmen
	athlete ['æθliːt]	Sportler/in, Athlet/in
	to compete [kəm'piːt]	an einem Wettkampf teilnehmen, konkurrieren
	workforce ['wɜːkfɔːs]	Belegschaft, Gesamtheit der Mitarbeiter
	range of products [ˌreɪndʒ əv 'prɒdʌkts]	Produktpalette
	market leader [ˌmɑːkɪt 'liːdə]	Marktführer
	to take up [teɪk 'ʌp]	aufnehmen, sich verlegen auf; hochheben
	production site [prə'dʌkʃn ˌsaɪt]	Fertigungsstätte, Produktionsbetrieb
	to feature ['fiːtʃə]	eine Rolle spielen, sich auszeichnen, kennzeichnen
	world championship [ˌwɜːld 'tʃæmpɪənʃɪp]	Weltmeisterschaft
1	**to found** [faʊnd]	gründen
	apart from [ə'pɑːt frəm]	abgesehen von
3	**on a large scale** [ɒn ə ˌlɑːdʒ 'skeɪl]	in großem Stil/Umfang
	assortment [ə'sɔːtmənt]	Sortiment, Kollektion, Auswahl
	dominant ['dɒmɪnənt]	beherrschend, dominierend
5	**abroad** [ə'brɔːd]	im/ins/aus dem Ausland
	fair [feə]	Messe
	managing director [ˌmænɪdʒɪŋ dɪ'rektə]	Geschäftsführer/in
	to provide [prə'vaɪd]	(be)liefern, zur Verfügung stellen, bieten
	private individual [ˌpraɪvət ˌɪndɪ'vɪdʒʊəl]	Privatperson
	time-consuming ['taɪmkənˌsjuːmɪŋ]	zeitraubend
	sufficient(ly) [sə'fɪʃənt(lɪ)]	genug, genügend, ausreichend
	secure [sɪ'kjʊə, sɪ'kjɔː]	sicher
	amazing [ə'meɪzɪŋ]	erstaunlich
	feasibility study [ˌfiːzə'bɪlətɪ ˌstʌdɪ]	Machbarkeitsstudie
	to establish [ɪ'stæblɪʃ]	ein-, errichten, gründen
	start-up (business) ['stɑːtʌp (ˌbɪznɪs)]	Neugründung, junges Unternehmen
	expenditure [ɪk'spendɪtʃə]	Ausgaben, Auslagen
	efficient [ɪ'fɪʃnt]	leistungsfähig, wirksam, tüchtig
	capable ['keɪpəbl]	in der Lage, fähig, tüchtig
	hit [hɪt]	Schlag, Stoß; Treffer; *(hier:)* Zugriff
	inadequate [ɪ'nædɪkwət]	unzureichend, unzulänglich
	overwhelmed [ˌəʊvə'welmd]	überwältigt
	in line with [ɪn 'laɪn wɪð]	in Übereinstimmung mit, parallel zu
	mart [mɑːt]	Markt
	to charge [tʃɑːdʒ]	verlangen, berechnen; vorwerfen; beauftragen
	commission [kə'mɪʃn]	Provision
	to go public [gəʊ 'pʌblɪk]	sich in eine Aktiengesellschaft umwandeln, an die Börse gehen
7	**to earn one's living** [ˌɜːn wʌnz 'lɪvɪŋ]	seinen Lebensunterhalt verdienen

B Describing products and services

	brand [brænd]	(Handels-)Marke, Güte-, Kennzeichen
	minute [maɪ'njuːt]	peinlich genau; winzig
	to fuse [fjuːz]	verschmelzen
	fashion ['fæʃn]	Mode
	effort ['efət]	Anstrengung, Bemühung
	athletics [æθ'letɪks]	(Leicht-)Athletik
	decade ['dekeɪd]	Jahrzehnt
	prestigious [pres'tɪdʒəs]	angesehen, renommiert
	shopping cart ['ʃɒpɪŋ‿kɑːt]	Einkaufswagen
	to track [træk]	verfolgen
	imprint ['ɪmprɪnt]	Impressum
	disclaimer [dɪ'skleɪmə]	Haftungsausschluss, Widerruf
1	**frequent(ly)** ['friːkwənt(lɪ)]	häufig, oft
	to place an order [ˌpleɪs ən 'ɔːdə]	einen Auftrag erteilen
	repairs [rɪ'peəz]	Reparatur
3	**leisure** ['leʒə]	Freizeit, Muße
	convincing [kən'vɪnsɪŋ]	überzeugend

Unit 4

	spacious ['speɪʃəs]	geräumig
	purpose-built [ˌpɜ:pəs'bɪlt]	für bestimmten Zweck gebaut
	major ['meɪdʒə]	groß, wichtig, Haupt-
	to accommodate [ə'kɒmədeɪt]	unterbringen, Platz bieten
	prestigious [pres'tɪdʒəs]	repräsentativ
	converted [kən'vɜ:tɪd]	umgebaut
	back office [ˌbæk 'ɒfɪs]	Büro ohne Publikumsverkehr
	front office [frʌnt 'ɒfɪs]	Büro mit Publikumsverkehr
	access ['ækses]	Zugang

A The office environment

	calculator ['kælkjəleɪtə]	Taschenrechner
	memory stick ['memrɪ ˌstɪk]	USB-Speicher
	pot plant ['pɒt ˌplɑ:nt]	Topfpflanze
	scotch tape [ˌskɒtʃ 'teɪp]	Klebeband
	desk lamp ['desk ˌlæmp]	Schreibtischlampe
	biro ['baɪrəʊ]	Kugelschreiber
	desk tidy ['desk ˌtaɪdɪ]	Stifteköcher
	desk [desk]	Schreibtisch
	pair of scissors [ˌpeər‿əv 'sɪzəz]	Schere
	stapling machine / stapler ['steɪplɪŋ məˌʃi:n / 'steɪplə]	Tacker
	note pad ['nəʊtpæd]	Notizblock
	wastepaper bin [weɪst'peɪpə ˌbɪn]	Papierkorb
	swivel chair [ˌswɪvl 'tʃeə]	Drehstuhl
	tray [treɪ]	Ablagekorb
	ruler ['ru:lə]	Lineal
	filing cabinet ['faɪlɪŋ ˌkæbɪnət]	Aktenschrank, Ablage
	punch [pʌntʃ]	Locher
	rubber, eraser ['rʌbə, ɪ'reɪzə]	Radiergummi
	keyboard ['ki:bɔ:d]	Tastatur
1	**equipment** [ɪ'kwɪpmənt]	Geräte
3	**electrical equipment** [ɪˌlektrɪkl ɪ'kwɪpmənt]	Elektrogeräte
7	**grid** [grɪd]	Raster
	computer projector [kəmˌpju:tə prə'dʒektə]	Beamer
	view [vju:]	*(hier:)* Ausblick
	privacy ['prɪvəsɪ]	private Atmosphäre
	to get on well [get ˌɒn 'wel]	gut miteinander auskommen

B Catering in the office

1	**attached** [ə'tætʃt]	angeschlossen
	fridge [frɪdʒ]	Kühlschrank
	coffee break ['kɒfɪ ˌbreɪk]	Kaffeepause
	to watch [wɒtʃ]	aufpassen auf
	calorie count ['kælərɪ ˌkaʊnt]	Kalorienangabe
	a set break [ə ˌset 'breɪk]	eine Pause zu festgesetzter Zeit
	convenience food [kən'vi:nɪəns ˌfu:d]	Fertiggerichte
	upmarket [ˌʌp'mɑ:kɪt]	im oberen Marktsegment
	appetising ['æpətaɪzɪŋ]	schmackhaft
	filled rolls [ˌfɪld 'rəʊlz]	belegte Brötchen
	deadline ['dedlaɪn]	(letzte) Frist, (letzter) Termin
2	**energy content** ['enədʒɪ ˌkɒntent]	Brennwert (Energiegehalt)

C The company's organization chart

1	**owner** ['əʊnə]	Eigentümer/in
	personal assistant [ˌpɜ:sənl ə'sɪstent]	Sekretär/in
	elderly person [ˌeldəlɪ 'pɜ:sn]	ältere Person
	superior [su:'pɪərɪə]	Vorgesetzte/r
	accountant [ə'kaʊntənt]	Bilanzprüfer/in, Buchprüfer/in
	head of department [ˌhed‿əv dɪ'pɑ:tmənt]	Abteilungsleiter/in
	motor-car mechanic [ˌməʊtəkɑ: mə'kænɪk]	Kfz-Mechaniker/in
	in charge of [ɪn 'tʃɑ:dʒ‿əv]	verantwortlich für, betraut mit
	managing director [ˌmænɪdʒɪŋ dɪ'rektə]	Geschäftsführer/in
	sister-in-law ['sɪstərɪnlɔ:]	Schwägerin
	to report to [rɪ'pɔ:t‿tu:]	unterstehen
	administration [ədˌmɪnɪ'streɪʃn]	Verwaltung
	purchasing (department) ['pɜ:tʃəsɪŋ (dɪˌpɑ:tmənt)]	Einkauf(sabteilung)
	sales (department) ['seɪlz (dɪˌpɑ:tmənt)]	Verkauf(sabteilung)
	customer service [ˌkʌstəmə 'sɜ:vɪs]	Kundendienst
	to tend to be ['tend‿tʊ bi:]	dazu neigen
	chief executive officer (CEO) [ˌtʃi:f ɪgˌzekjətɪv 'ɒfɪsə]	Firmenchef/in, Vorstandsvorsitzende/r
	chairman of the board [ˌtʃeəmən əv‿ðə 'bɔ:d]	Vorstandsvorsitzender
	personnel [ˌpɜ:sən'el]	Personal
	legal ['li:gl]	juristisch, rechtlich, gesetzlich
	scope [skəʊp]	Umfang, Bereich
	duties ['dju:tɪz]	*(hier:)* Aufgaben
3	**current** ['kʌrənt]	laufend, gegenwärtig, derzeitig
	responsible for [rɪ'spɒnsəbl fɔ:]	verantwortlich für
	general manager [ˌdʒenərəl 'mænɪdʒə]	Hauptgeschäftsführer/in
LG	**to persuade** [pə'sweɪd]	überreden
	pronounced [prə'naʊnst]	ausgeprägt

Unit 5

	essential [ɪ'senʃl]	wichtig, wesentlich
	tool [tu:l]	Werkzeug
	advent ['ædvent]	Ankunft
	telephony [tə'lefənɪ]	Telefonverkehr
1	**enterprise** ['entəpraɪz]	Unternehmen
	public ['pʌblɪk]	Öffentlichkeit

A Appliances and components

	appliances [ə'plaɪənsɪz]	Geräte
	components [kəm'pəʊnənts]	Bestandteile, Bauelemente

1	**fixed line set** [ˌfɪkstlaɪn 'set]	Festnetzanlage
	answering machine ['ɑ:nsərɪŋ məˌʃi:n]	Anrufbeantworter
	to replace [rɪ'pleɪs]	auflegen; *(auch:)* ersetzen
	receiver [rɪ'si:və]	Hörer
	engaged [ɪn'geɪdʒd]	besetzt
	dialling tone ['daɪəlɪŋ ˌtəʊn]	Freizeichen
	landline ['lændlaɪn]	Festnetz(leitung)
	to receive [rɪ'si:v]	erhalten, empfangen
	old-fashioned [ˌəʊld'fæʃnd]	altmodisch
	telephone directory ['teləfəʊn daɪˌrektərɪ, 'teləfəʊn dɪˌrektərɪ]	Telefonbuch
	business section ['bɪznɪs‿sekʃn]	Gewerbeteil
	Directory Enquiries [daɪˌrektərɪ‿ɪn'kwaɪərɪz, dɪˌrektərɪ‿ɪn'kwaɪərɪz]	Telefonauskunft
	applications [ˌæplɪ'keɪʃnz]	Anwendungen, Funktionen

B Receiving and redirecting calls

	to redirect [ˌri:daɪ'rekt, ˌri:dɪ'rekt]	umleiten
1	**to put someone through** [pʊt ˌsʌmwʌn 'θru:]	durchstellen, verbinden
	extension [ɪk'stenʃn]	Durchwahl, Nebenstelle
	to hold [həʊld]	*(hier:)* warten
	accounts [ə'kaʊnts]	Rechnungsabteilung
	dreadful ['dredfəl]	schrecklich
	to ache [eɪk]	schmerzen, wehtun
	customer relations [ˌkʌstəmə rɪ'leɪʃnz]	Kundendienst
2	**to bear with someone** [beə 'wɪð ˌsʌmwʌn]	*(hier:)* etwas Geduld haben
4	**immediate** [ɪ'mi:dɪət]	sofortig
	comeback ['kʌmbæk]	*(hier:)* Reaktion
	unavoidable [ˌʌnə'vɔɪdəbl]	unvermeidlich
	to wonder ['wʌndə]	sich fragen
	embarrassment [ɪm'bærəsmənt]	Verlegenheit
	to express [ɪk'spres]	ausdrücken
	awful ['ɔ:fəl]	schrecklich
	abroad [ə'brɔ:d]	im Ausland
	to some extent [tə ˌsʌm ɪk'stent]	in gewissem Maße
	justified ['dʒʌstɪfaɪd]	gerechtfertigt
	gestures ['dʒestʃəz]	Gesten, Gestik
	despair [dɪ'speə]	Verzweiflung
	calm [kɑ:m]	ruhig
5	**precisely then** [prɪˌsaɪslɪ 'ðen]	gerade dann
	at short notice [ət ˌʃɔ:t‿'nəʊtɪs]	kurzfristig
	line [laɪn]	Verbindung
	get [get]	*(hier:)* mitbekommen, hören
	patience ['peɪʃəns]	Geduld
6	**to cut off** [kʌt 'ɒf]	*(hier:)* unterbrechen
	to catch [kætʃ]	*(hier:)* mitbekommen

C Taking messages

	to take a message [ˌteɪk ə 'mesɪdʒ]	eine Nachricht entgegennehmen
1	**to take down** [teɪk‿'daʊn]	notieren
	relevant ['reləvənt]	wichtig, sachdienlich
	postcode ['pəʊstkəʊd]	Postleitzahl
	accurate(ly) ['ækjərət(lɪ)]	genau, präzise, akkurat
	precisely [prɪ'saɪslɪ]	*(hier:)* genau, präzise
	form [fɔ:m]	Formular
	to record [rɪ'kɔ:d]	aufzeichnen
2	**to make up** [meɪk 'ʌp]	*(hier:)* erfinden
5	**to postpone** [pəs'pəʊn]	verschieben
	paper ['peɪpə]	*(hier:)* Vortrag
	relieved [rɪ'li:vd]	erleichtert
	venue ['venju:]	Veranstaltungsort
	suburb ['sʌbɜ:b]	Vorort, Stadtteil im Außenbezirk
	query ['kwɪərɪ]	Frage
	to emphasise ['emfəsaɪz]	betonen
	joint venture [ˌdʒɔɪnt 'ventʃə]	Joint Venture (Gemeinschaftsunternehmen)
7	**purchasing manager** ['pɜ:tʃəsɪŋ ˌmænɪdʒə]	Leiter/in des Einkaufs
	in stock [ɪn 'stɒk]	vorrätig
	to ship [ʃɪp]	versenden, verschiffen

D Making telephone calls

	suitable ['su:təbl]	geeignet
	polite [pə'laɪt]	höflich
	I'm afraid ... [aɪm ə'freɪd]	Leider ...
	request [rɪ'kwest]	Bitte
	impolite [ˌɪmpə'laɪt]	unhöflich
	to come across [ˌkʌm ə'krɒs]	*(hier:)* wirken
1	**packaging material** ['pækɪdʒɪŋ məˌtɪərɪəl]	Verpackungsmaterial
	sales literature ['seɪlz ˌlɪtrətʃə]	Prospektmaterial, Kataloge etc.
	cottage ['kɒtɪdʒ]	*(hier:)* Ferienhäuschen
	to sleep [sli:p]	*(hier:)* Schlafmöglichkeit bieten
	adult ['ædʌlt]	Erwachsene/r
	peak season [ˌpi:k 'si:zn]	Hochsaison
	booking charge ['bʊkɪŋ ˌtʃɑ:dʒ]	Buchungsgebühr
	rent [rent]	Miete
	balance ['bæləns]	*(hier:)* Rest(betrag)
	debit card ['debɪt‿kɑ:d]	Scheckkarte, Bankkarte
	payable to ['peɪəbl tu:]	zahlbar an
2	**size** [saɪz]	Größe
	location [ləʊ'keɪʃn]	Standort
	charge [tʃɑ:dʒ]	Kosten, Gebühr
	additional [ə'dɪʃənl]	zusätzlich

E Formulating messages for the answering machine and the mailbox

1	**to pronounce** [prə'naʊns]	aussprechen
	concise [kən'saɪs]	kurz und bündig
	to pause [pɔ:z]	eine Pause einlegen
2	**appointment** [ə'pɔɪntmənt]	*(hier:)* Treffen, Termin
	advantage [əd'vɑ:ntɪdʒ]	Vorteil
	to avoid [ə'vɔɪd]	vermeiden
	necessity [nə'sesətɪ]	Notwendigkeit
	virtually ['vɜ:tʃʊəlɪ]	fast, so gut wie
	slight [slaɪt]	geringfügig
	delay [dɪ'leɪ]	Verzögerung
LG	**facilities** [fə'sɪlətɪz]	Anlagen, Einrichtungen
	independent [ˌɪndɪ'pendənt]	unabhängig
	import licence ['ɪmpɔ:t ˌlaɪsəns]	Importlizenz, Einfuhrgenehmigung

to refer to [rɪ'fɜ: tu:] – sich beziehen auf
complaint [kəm'pleɪnt] – Beschwerde, Mängelrüge
author ['ɔ:θə] – Verfasser/in, Autor/in, *(hier:)* Urheber/in
study group ['stʌdɪ ˌgru:p] – Arbeitsgruppe

Unit 6

clerical staff ['klerɪkl ˌstɑ:f] – Büropersonal, Sachbearbeiter
on behalf of [ɒn bɪ'hɑ:f‿əv] – im Auftrag von, für
to keep a record [ˌki:p ə 'rekɔ:d] – aufzeichnen
to facilitate [fə'sɪlɪteɪt] – ermöglichen
proceedings [prə'si:dɪŋz] – *(hier:)* Ablauf der Konferenz

A Flights and accommodation

accommodation [əˌkɒmə'deɪʃn] – Unterbringung
1 **executives** [ɪg'zekjətɪvz] – leitende Angestellte
to attend a fair [əˌtend ə 'feə] – an einer Messe teilnehmen
premises ['premɪsɪz] – Geschäftsräume
opposite number [ˌɒpəzɪt 'nʌmbə] – Gegenüber, Kollege/Kollegin
headquarters [ˌhed'kwɔ:təz] – Hauptverwaltung
to oversee [ˌəʊvə'si:] – beaufsichtigen, leiten
single room [ˌsɪŋgl 'ru:m] – Einzelzimmer
Bavarian cuisine [bəˌveərɪən kwɪz'i:n] – bayerische Küche
agenda [ə'dʒendə] – Tagesordnung; Termine
modification [ˌmɒdɪfɪ'keɪʃn] – Änderung
to cater for ['keɪtə fɔ:] – *(hier:)* etwas bieten für
2 **query** ['kwɪərɪ] – Anfrage
to pick up [pɪk 'ʌp] – abholen
to require [rɪ'kwaɪə] – benötigen
3 **rush** [rʌʃ] – Ansturm
ensuite bathroom [ˌɒnswi:t‿'bɑ:θru:m] – eigenes Bad (Hotelzimmer)
shuttle service ['ʃʌtl ˌsɜ:vɪs] – Pendelbus
special features [ˌspeʃl 'fi:tʃəz] – besondere Eigenschaften
exhibition grounds [ˌeksɪ'bɪʃn ˌgraʊndz] – Ausstellungsgelände
6 **monitor** ['mɒnɪtə] – PC-Bildschirm
booking reference ['bʊkɪŋ ˌrefrəns] – Buchungsnummer
confirmation [ˌkɒnfə'meɪʃn] – Bestätigung
aisle [aɪl] – Gang (Flugzeug/Kirche/Supermarkt)
to choose [tʃu:z] – wählen
8 **car hire/rental company** ['kɑ:ˌhaɪə/ˌrentl ˌkʌmpənɪ] – Mietwagenfirma
to take a call [ˌteɪk ə 'kɔ:l] – einen Anruf entgegennehmen
limit ['lɪmɪt] – Beschränkung
included in the price [ɪnˌklu:dɪd ɪn ðə 'praɪs] – im Preis enthalten
accident ['æksɪdənt] – Unfall

additional/supplementary insurance [əˌdɪʃənl/ˌsʌplɪmentərɪ‿ɪn'ʃɔ:rəns] – Zusatzversicherung
discount ['dɪskaʊnt] – Rabatt
expiry date [ɪk'spaɪərɪ ˌdeɪt] – Verfallsdatum (bei Kreditkarten)

B Meetings, conferences and fairs

1 **appointment** [ə'pɔɪntmənt] – Termin
integration [ˌɪntɪ'greɪʃn] – Eingliederung, Integration
product range ['prɒdʌkt ˌreɪndʒ] – Produktpalette
to fit in with [ˌfɪt 'ɪn wɪð] – sich richten nach
diary ['daɪərɪ] – Terminkalender, Tagebuch
likewise ['laɪkwaɪz] – ebenfalls
to cover ['kʌvə] – *(hier:)* berücksichtigen
greater Munich area [ˌgreɪtə 'mju:nɪk ˌeərɪə] – Großraum München
supplementary charge [ˌsʌplɪmentərɪ 'tʃɑ:dʒ] – Zuschlag
indicator ['ɪndɪkeɪtə] – Anzeiger, Anzeigetafel
timetable ['taɪmˌteɪbl] – Fahrplan
to assume [ə'sju:m] – annehmen
selection [sə'lekʃn] – Auswahl
venue ['venju:] – *(hier:)* Treffpunkt
as a rule [əz‿ə 'ru:l] – in der Regel
waiter service ['weɪtə ˌsɜ:vɪs] – Bedienung
turn-taking ['tɜ:nˌteɪkɪŋ] – sich anstellen, warten bis man dran ist
to observe [əb'zɜ:v] – beachten
visible ['vɪzəbl] – sichtbar
crowded ['kraʊdɪd] – überfüllt
barman/barmaid ['bɑ:mən/'bɑ:meɪd] – Bedienung hinter der Theke
in principle [ɪn 'prɪnsəpl] – im Prinzip
embarrassed [ɪm'bærəst] – peinlich, verlegen
straight away [ˌstreɪtə'weɪ] – sofort
to round up [raʊnd 'ʌp] – aufrunden
bill [bɪl] – Rechnung
fare [feə] – Fahrpreis
change [tʃeɪndʒ] – Wechselgeld
tray [treɪ] – Tablett
tip [tɪp] – *(hier:)* Trinkgeld

2
1 **draft** [drɑ:ft] – Entwurf
minutes ['mɪnɪts] – Protokoll
consumer [kən'sju:mə] – Verbraucher/in
health [helθ] – Gesundheit
concerns [kən'sɜ:nz] – *(hier:)* Sorgen, Fragen
obesity [əʊ'bi:sətɪ] – Fettleibigkeit, klinisches Übergewicht
organic foods [ɔ:'gænɪk ˌfu:dz] – Bio-Lebensmittel
market research [ˌmɑ:kɪt 'ri:sɜ:tʃ] – Marktforschung
other business [ˌʌðə 'bɪznɪs] – Verschiedenes
2 **to enclose** [ɪn'kləʊz] – beifügen
to request [rɪ'kwest] – bitten um
notification [ˌnəʊtɪfɪ'keɪʃn] – Mitteilung, Benachrichtigung
additions [ə'dɪʃnz] – Hinzufügungen

	in the course of [ɪn ðə 'kɔːs‿əv]	im Laufe
3	**to assist** [ə'sɪst]	helfen
	to supervise ['suːpəvaɪz]	beaufsichtigen
	soft drinks [ˌsɒft‿'drɪŋks]	alkoholfreie Getränke
	sparkling mineral water [ˌspɑːklɪŋ 'mɪnərəl ˌwɔːtə]	Sprudel
	available [ə'veɪləbl]	vorhanden, verfügbar
	equipment [ɪ'kwɪpmənt]	Geräte, Ausrüstung
	in working order [ɪn ˌwɜːkɪŋ‿'ɔːdə]	funktionstüchtig
	to be on hand [bɪ‿ɒn 'hænd]	zugegen sein, da sein
	assistance [ə'sɪstəns]	Hilfe
	to leave much to be desired [liːv ˌmʌtʃ tʊ bɪ dɪ'zaɪəd]	viel zu wünschen übrig lassen
	to interpret [ɪn'tɜːprɪt]	dolmetschen
4	**to take the minutes** [ˌteɪk ðə 'mɪnɪts]	Protokoll führen
	record ['rekɔːd]	Aufzeichnung
	those involved [ˌðəʊz ɪn'vɒlvd]	die Beteiligten
	evidence ['evɪdəns]	Beweismittel
	in law [ɪn 'lɔː]	rechtlich, vor Gericht
	those present [ˌðəʊz 'preznt]	die Anwesenden
	apology [ə'pɒlədʒɪ]	Entschuldigung
	non-attendance [ˌnɒnə'tendəns]	Fehlen, Abwesenheit
	chairman ['tʃeəmən]	Vorsitzender
	chair, chairperson [tʃeə, 'tʃeəˌpɜːsn]	Vorsitzende/r
	account [ə'kaʊnt]	*(hier:)* Bericht, Aufzeichnung
	figures ['fɪgəz]	Zahlen
	for approval [fər‿ə'pruːvl]	zur Genehmigung
	topics ['tɒpɪks]	*(hier:)* Punkte, Themen
	largely ['lɑːdʒlɪ]	weitgehend
	restricted [rɪ'strɪktɪd]	beschränkt
5	**to return** [rɪ'tɜːn]	*(hier:)* zurückschicken
	application [ˌæplɪ'keɪʃn]	*(hier:)* Antrag
	kitchenette [ˌkɪtʃɪ'net]	Kochgelegenheit; Teeküche
	interpreter [ɪn'tɜːprɪtə]	Dolmetscher/in
	to recommend [ˌrekə'mend]	empfehlen
	suitable ['suːtəbl]	geeignet
1	**corner stand** ['kɔːnə ˌstænd]	Eckstand
LG	**attachment (email)** [ə'tætʃmənt]	Anhang
	payment, money transfer, remittance ['peɪmənt, 'mʌnɪ ˌtrænsfɜː, rɪ'mɪtəns]	Überweisung
	competitor [kəm'petɪtə]	Mitbewerber/in
	to undercut [ˌʌndə'kʌt]	unterbieten
	raw materials [ˌrɔː mə'tɪərɪəlz]	Rohstoffe
	supplier [sə'plaɪə]	Lieferant, Zulieferer

Unit 7

	to require [rɪ'kwaɪə]	*(hier:)* verlangen, auffordern
	to range from … to ['reɪndʒ frəm … tʊ]	reichen von … bis
	as a whole [əz‿ə 'həʊl]	insgesamt
	scared [skeəd]	ängstlich
	audience ['ɔːdɪəns]	Publikum
	ability [ə'bɪlətɪ]	Fähigkeit
	oral ['ɔːrəl]	mündlich
	key [kiː]	Schlüssel
	skill [skɪl]	Fertigkeit
	to acquire [ə'kwaɪə]	sich aneignen
	delivery [dɪ'lɪvərɪ]	*(hier:)* das Halten (eines Vortrags)
	content ['kɒntent]	Inhalt

A Preparing a presentation

	brief [briːf]	kurz
	at your disposal [ət‿jɔː dɪ'spəʊzl]	zur Verfügung
	hints [hɪnts]	Hinweise
	objective [əb'dʒektɪv]	Ziel
	to absorb [əb'zɔːb]	aufnehmen
	prompt cards ['prɒmpt‿kɑːdz]	Stichwortkarten
	to avoid [ə'vɔɪd]	vermeiden
	conclusion [kən'kluːʒn]	Schluss
	overview ['əʊvəvjuː]	Überblick
	to cover ['kʌvə]	decken, abdecken
	to divide up [dɪˌvaɪd 'ʌp]	einteilen, aufteilen
	according to [ə'kɔːdɪŋ‿tʊ]	entsprechend, gemäß
	to reinforce [ˌriːɪn'fɔːs]	verstärken
	visual aids [ˌvɪʒʊəl 'eɪdz]	visuelle Hilfsmittel
	slide [slaɪd]	Folie
	to arouse [ə'raʊz]	wecken (Interesse, Gefühle)
	to double ['dʌbl]	*(hier:)* eine doppelte Funktion erfüllen
	transparencies [træn'spærənsɪz]	Folien
	graph [grɑːf]	Grafik
	flowcharts ['fləʊˌtʃɑːts]	Flussdiagramme
	cues [kjuːz]	Stichworte
	upper and lower case letters [ˌʌpər‿ən ˌləʊə keɪs 'letəz]	Groß- und Kleinbuchstaben
2	**old-established** [ˌəʊldɪ'stæblɪʃt]	alteingeführt
	convenience foods [kən'viːnɪəns ˌfuːdz]	Fertiggerichte
	range [reɪndʒ]	Sortiment
	dish [dɪʃ]	*(hier:)* Speise, Gericht
	board meetings ['bɔːd ˌmiːtɪŋz]	Vorstandssitzungen
	leisure ['leʒə]	Freizeit, freie Zeit
	imaginative [ɪ'mædʒɪnətɪv]	phantasievoll
	to pop into [ˌpɒp 'ɪntʊ]	eben schnell hineintun
	briefcase ['briːfkeɪs]	Aktentasche
	to bore [bɔː]	langweilen
	via ['vaɪə, 'viːə]	über
	to underestimate [ˌʌndər'estɪmeɪt]	unterschätzen
3	**corporate (e.g. culture)** ['kɔːpərət]	Unternehmens- (z. B. -kultur), bezogen auf Firmen/Unternehmen
4	**location** [ləʊ'keɪʃn]	Standort
	selection [sə'lekʃn]	Auswahl
	domestic market [dəˌmestɪk 'mɑːkɪt]	Inlandsmarkt
	feature ['fiːtʃə]	Eigenschaft
	environmentally friendly [ɪnˌvaɪərənˌmentəlɪ 'frendlɪ]	umweltfreundlich

5	**venue** ['venju:]	Veranstaltungsort, Gerichtsstand

B Delivering a presentation

	to remind [rɪ'maɪnd]	erinnern
	to ensure [ɪn'ʃɔ:]	sicherstellen, gewährleisten
	body language ['bɒdɪ ˌlæŋgwɪdʒ]	Körpersprache
	computer projector [kəmˌpju:tə prə'dʒektə]	Beamer
	to operate ['ɒpəreɪt]	bedienen
	to rehearse [rɪ'hɜ:s]	proben, einüben
	preferably ['prefrəblɪ]	vorzugsweise
	to get something over [ˌget ˌsʌmθɪŋ 'əʊvə]	etwas hinter sich bringen
	to make sure [meɪk 'ʃɔ:]	sich vergewissern
	monotonous(ly) [mə'nɒtənəs(lɪ)]	eintönig
	to wave your arms around [ˌweɪv jɔ:r ˌɑ:mz əˌraʊnd]	mit den Armen herumfuchteln
	appropriate [ə'prəʊprɪət]	angemessen
	confident ['kɒnfɪdənt]	selbstbewusst
	feedback ['fi:dbæk]	Rückmeldungen, Feedback
	to become aware [bɪˌkʌm ə'weə]	bewusst werden
	how you come across [ˌhaʊ jʊ ˌkʌm ə'krɒs]	welchen Eindruck man macht
	prerequisite [ˌpri:'rekwɪzɪt]	Voraussetzung, Bedingung
2	**to assess** [ə'ses]	*(hier:)* bewerten, einschätzen
	evaluation scheme [ɪˌvæljʊ'eɪʃn ˌski:m]	Bewertungsschema
	to award points [əˌwɔ:d 'pɔɪnts]	Punkte vergeben (z. B. Wettbewerb)
	heading ['hedɪŋ]	Rubrik
	evidence ['evɪdəns]	*(hier:)* Anzeichen
	well-substantiated [ˌwelsʌb'stænʃieɪtɪd]	gut belegt
	humorous ['hju:mərəs]	humorvoll
3	**ambitious** [æm'bɪʃəs]	ehrgeizig, anspruchsvoll
	rising demand for [ˌraɪzɪŋ dɪ'mɑ:nd fə]	steigende Nachfrage nach
	copper ['kɒpə]	Kupfer
	site [saɪt]	Standort, Abbaustelle
	rapid ['ræpɪd]	schnell
	to soar [sɔ:]	emporschnellen
	construction work [kən'strʌkʃn wɜ:k]	Bauarbeiten
	to jump [dʒʌmp]	springen, sprunghaft ansteigen
	slice [slaɪs]	Scheibe, Anteil
	exploration [ˌeksplə'reɪʃn]	Erkundung neuer Lagerstätten, Probegrabungen/-bohrungen
	pie chart ['paɪ ˌtʃɑ:t]	Tortendiagramm
	proportion [prə'pɔ:ʃn]	Anteil
	expenditure [ɪk'spendɪtʃə]	Ausgaben
	to emphasise ['emfəsaɪz]	betonen
	in the foreseeable future [ɪn ðə fɔ:ˌsi:əbl 'fju:tʃə]	in absehbarer Zukunft
	excitement [ɪk'saɪtmənt]	*(hier:)* Interesse
	investment portfolio [ɪn'vestmənt ˌpɔ:tˌfəʊlɪəʊ]	Bestand an Wertpapieren
	bar chart ['bɑ: ˌtʃɑ:t]	Balkendiagramm
	line graph ['laɪn ˌgrɑ:f]	Liniendiagramm
1	**to rise, rose, risen** [raɪz, rəʊz, rɪzn]	steigen
	to increase [ɪn'kri:s]	zunehmen
	to jump by ... from ... to ... ['dʒʌmp ˌbaɪ ... frəm ... tʊ ...]	sprunghaft ansteigen um ... von ... auf ...
	peak [pi:k]	Gipfel, Höchststand
	to remain unchanged [rɪˌmeɪn ʌn'tʃeɪndʒd]	unverändert bleiben
	flat [flæt]	flach
	to fluctuate ['flʌktʃʊeɪt]	schwanken
	to decline [dɪ'klaɪn]	sinken, zurückgehen
	to drop [drɒp]	fallen
	to slump [slʌmp]	stark fallen
	average price [ˌævrɪdʒ 'praɪs]	Durchschnittspreis
	low [ləʊ]	Tief(punkt)
	gathering ['gæðərɪŋ]	Versammlung
	description [dɪ'skrɪpʃn]	Beschreibung
	decline [dɪ'klaɪn]	Rückgang
	steady, steadily ['stedɪ(lɪ)]	stetig
	moderate(ly) ['mɒdərət(lɪ)]	mäßig, maßvoll
	gradual(ly) ['grædʒʊəl(ɪ)]	allmählich
	slight(ly) [slaɪt(lɪ)]	geringfügig
	significant(ly) [sɪg'nɪfɪkənt(lɪ)]	bedeutend
	in fourth place [ɪn ˌfɔ:θ 'pleɪs]	an vierter Stelle
	at the bottom [ət ðə 'bɒtm]	unten
	at the top [ət ðə 'tɒp]	oben, an der Spitze
2	**customer base** ['kʌstəmə ˌbeɪs]	Kundenstamm
	approx(imately) [ə'prɒks(ɪmətlɪ)]	ungefähr, ca.
	closely followed by [ˌkləʊslɪ 'fɒləʊd ˌbaɪ]	*(hier:)* dicht gefolgt von
	8000 and 6000 customers, respectively ['eɪt ˌθaʊsənd ənd 'sɪks ˌθaʊsənd ˌkʌstəməz rɪ'spektɪvlɪ]	8000 bzw. 6000 Kunden
	percentage [pə'sentɪdʒ]	Prozentsatz
	to account for [ə'kaʊnt fɔ:]	ausmachen
	nail varnish ['neɪl ˌvɑ:nɪʃ]	Nagellack
	lipstick ['lɪpstɪk]	Lippenstift

Unit 8

essential [ɪ'senʃl]	wesentlich
documentation [ˌdɒkjəmen'teɪʃn]	Nachweis, Dokumentierung
to ensure [ɪn'ʃɔ:]	sicherstellen, dafür sorgen
misunderstanding [ˌmɪsʌndə'stændɪŋ]	Missverständnis
to arise, arose, arisen [ə'raɪz, ə'rəʊz, ə'rɪzn]	entstehen, auftreten
however [haʊ'evə]	jedoch
recent ['ri:sənt]	nicht lange zurückliegend, vor kurzem geschehen
increasing(ly) [ɪn'kri:sɪŋ(lɪ)]	zunehmend
formal ['fɔ:ml]	förmlich, formell

largely ['lɑːdʒlɪ]	weitgehend
degree [dɪ'griː]	Grad, Ausmaß; akademischer Grad
1 **grid** [grɪd]	Raster
attachment [ə'tætʃmənt]	Anhang (E-Mail)
unauthorised [ʌn'ɔːθəraɪzd]	unbefugt
authenticity [ɔːθen'tɪsɪtɪ]	Echtheit
signature ['sɪgnətʃə]	Unterschrift
unsatisfactory [ʌnˌsætɪs'fæktərɪ]	unbefriedigend, ungenügend, unzureichend
unreliable [ˌʌnrɪ'laɪəbl]	unzuverlässig
whenever [wen'evə]	immer dann, wenn
evidence ['evɪdəns]	Beweis, Nachweis
to recognize ['rekəgnaɪz]	erkennen, anerkennen
court [kɔːt]	Gericht(shof), Hof
legal ['liːgl]	rechtlich, gesetzlich, legal, juristisch
context ['kɒntekst]	Zusammenhang, Kontext
contract ['kɒntrækt]	Vertrag
complaint [kəm'pleɪnt]	Beschwerde, Mängelrüge
covering letter ['kʌvərɪŋ ˌletə]	Begleitschreiben
enclosure [ɪn'kləʊʒə]	Anlage (Brief)
2 **protective software** [prəˌtektɪv 'sɒftweə]	Software zum Schutz
to be likely [bɪ 'laɪklɪ]	wahrscheinlich sein, wahrscheinlich geschehen

A Layout and components of business correspondence

layout ['leɪaʊt]	Anordnung, Gestaltung
components [kəm'pəʊnənts]	Bestandteile
1 **subject** ['sʌbdʒɪkt]	Gegenstand, *(hier:)* Betreff
package tour ['pækɪdʒ‿tʊə]	Pauschalreise
salutation [ˌsæljə'teɪʃn]	Begrüßung, *(hier:)* Anrede
incentive [ɪn'sentɪv]	Anreiz
sales representative ['seɪlz reprɪˌzentətɪv]	Handelsvertreter/in
preliminary [prɪ'lɪmɪnərɪ]	vorläufig
complimentary close [ˌkɒmplɪmentərɪ 'kləʊz]	Grußformel
signature footer ['sɪgnətʃə ˌfʊtə]	Unterschriftsfußzeilen
slight [slaɪt]	leicht, gering(fügig), kaum merklich
to enter ['entə]	eintreten; eintragen, eingeben
recipient [rɪ'sɪpɪənt]	Empfänger
or else [ɔːr‿'els]	andernfalls, sonst
abbreviation [əˌbriːvɪ'eɪʃn]	Abkürzung
to insert [ɪn'sɜːt]	einfügen, einlegen
carbon paper ['kɑːbn ˌpeɪpə]	Kohlepapier
blank [blæŋk]	unbeschrieben, leer
message ['mesɪdʒ]	Nachricht, Botschaft
to forward ['fɔːwəd]	weiterleiten, befördern, transportieren
file [faɪl]	Akte, Datei
to attach [ə'tætʃ]	anhängen (Datei), befestigen, anbringen
precise [prɪ'saɪs]	genau, exakt, präzise
subject matter ['sʌbdʒɪkt ˌmætə]	Gegenstand, Thema
to prevent [prɪ'vent]	hindern, verhindern, vermeiden
to delete [dɪ'liːt]	löschen, tilgen, streichen
brackets ['brækɪts]	Klammern
characters ['kærəktəz]	*(hier:)* Buchstaben, Zeichen
1 **appropriate** [ə'prəʊprɪət]	geeignet, passend, angebracht
germ [dʒɜːm]	Bazillus, Keim
suspicious [sə'spɪʃəs]	verdächtig
to pass on [pɑːs 'ɒn]	weiterreichen, -geben
addressee [ˌædres'iː]	Adressat, Empfänger
2 **to restore** [rɪ'stɔː]	wiederherstellen, restaurieren
to jumble ['dʒʌmbl]	durcheinander werfen/bringen
picnic hamper ['pɪknɪk ˌhæmpə]	Picknickkorb
delivery [dɪ'lɪvərɪ]	Lieferung, Auslieferung
3 **to focus** ['fəʊkəs]	(sich) konzentrieren, in den Mittelpunkt stellen
to capitalize ['kæpɪtəlaɪz]	in Großbuchstaben schreiben
sparing(ly) ['speərɪŋ(lɪ)]	sparsam, mäßig
exclamation mark [ˌekskləˈmeɪʃn ˌmɑːk]	Ausrufungszeichen
to assume [ə'sjuːm]	annehmen, von etwas ausgehen
to be on a familiar footing [bɪ‿ɒn ə fəˌmɪlɪə 'fʊtɪŋ]	auf vertrautem Fuße stehen
2 **established** [ɪ'stæblɪʃt]	eingeführt, feststehend
covering page ['kʌvərɪŋ ˌpeɪdʒ]	Deckblatt
plain [pleɪn]	schlicht, unscheinbar; *(hier:)* ungemustert, einfarbig
navy ['neɪvɪ]	Marine; *(hier:)* marineblau
by return [baɪ rɪ'tɜːn]	umgehend
to advise [əd'vaɪz]	(be)raten; benachrichtigen
both ... and ... [bəʊθ ... ənd ...]	sowohl ... als auch ...
to record [rɪ'kɔːd]	aufzeichnen, eintragen
to interrupt [ˌɪntə'rʌpt]	unterbrechen, stören
to refer to [rɪ'fɜː tuː]	ver-/hinweisen auf, sich beziehen auf
1 **spacing** ['speɪsɪŋ]	Abstände, Abstandseinteilung
to bring forward [ˌbrɪŋ 'fɔːwəd]	vorziehen, vorverlegen
co-operation [kəʊˌɒpə'reɪʃn]	Mit-, Zusammenarbeit; *(hier:)* Hilfe
3	
1 **rules** [ruːlz]	Regeln, Vorschriften
regulations [ˌregjə'leɪʃnz]	Vorschriften, Verordnungen
occasion [ə'keɪʒn]	Anlass, Gelegenheit
food processing ['fuːd ˌprəʊsesɪŋ]	Verarbeitung von Lebensmitteln

	initials [ɪ'nɪʃlz]	Initialen, Anfangsbuchstaben des Namens
	signatory ['sɪgnətərɪ]	Unterzeichner/in
	letterhead ['letəhed]	Briefkopf
	usage ['ju:sɪdʒ]	Gepflogenheit, Gewohnheit, Praxis
	to omit [əʊ'mɪt]	aus-, weglassen
	partnership ['pɑ:tnəʃɪp]	Personengesellschaft
	marital status [ˌmærɪtl 'steɪtəs]	Familienstand
	postal code ['pəʊstl ˌkəʊd]	Postleitzahl
	whereas [weə'ræz]	wohingegen, dagegen
	to be in line with [bi‿ɪn 'laɪn wɪð]	übereinstimmen, im Einklang stehen mit
	to precede [pri:'si:d]	vor(an)gehen, -stehen
	bold type [ˌbəʊld‿'taɪp]	Fettdruck
	on behalf of [ɒn bɪ'hɑ:f‿əv]	im Namen von, im Auftrag von
3	**imagination** [ɪˌmædʒɪ'neɪʃn]	Phantasie, Vorstellungskraft
	fabulous ['fæbjələs]	fabelhaft, sagenhaft, toll
	to appeal [ə'pi:l]	ansprechen, gefallen; appellieren
	early order discount [ˌɜ:lɪ‿ɔ:də 'dɪskaʊnt]	Frühbuchungsrabatt

B Structure and style of business correspondence

1	**paragraph** ['pærəgrɑ:f]	Absatz
	to contain [kən'teɪn]	enthalten
	to provide [prə'vaɪd]	liefern, beschaffen, versorgen, bieten
	convenient [kən'vi:nɪənt]	passend, bequem
	to sum up [ˌsʌm 'ʌp]	zusammenfassen, -rechnen
	schedule ['ʃedju:l, 'skedju:l]	Schema, Aufstellung, (Termin-)Plan
	familiarity [fəˌmɪlɪ'ærətɪ]	(plumpe) Vertraulichkeit, Vertrautheit
2	**linking words** ['lɪŋkɪŋ ˌwɜ:dz]	verbindende Wörter
	smooth(ly) ['smu:ð(lɪ)]	glatt, reibungslos
	text-building block ['tekstbɪldɪŋ blɒk]	Textbaustein
	moreover [mɔ:r'əʊvə]	überdies, außerdem
	to imply [ɪm'plaɪ]	beinhalten, besagen, stillschweigend voraussetzen
	this is why [ˌðɪs ɪz 'waɪ]	daher, deshalb, deswegen
	thus [ðʌs]	folglich, somit
	retail sales [ˌri:teɪl 'seɪlz]	Umsatz im Einzelhandel
	to stagnate [stæg'neɪt]	stagnieren
	substantial [səb'stænʃl]	beträchtlich, erheblich
	severe(ly) [sə'vɪə(lɪ)]	schwer, ernstlich, streng, hart
	flooding ['flʌdɪŋ]	Überschwemmung
	prolonged [prəʊ'lɒŋd]	langanhaltend
	electricity cut [elɪk'trɪsətɪ ˌkʌt]	Stromsperre
	entire(ly) [ɪn'taɪə(lɪ)]	ganz, gänzlich
	execution [ˌeksɪ'kju:ʃn]	Aus-, Durchführung
	concession [kən'seʃn]	Zugeständnis
LG	**outcome** ['aʊtkʌm]	Ergebnis
	inconvenience [ˌɪnkən'vi:nɪəns]	Unannehmlichkeiten
	incident ['ɪnsɪdənt]	Zwischenfall, Ereignis
	to entrust [ɪn'trʌst]	anvertrauen
	oversight ['əʊvəsaɪt]	Versehen
	air freight ['eə ˌfreɪt]	Luftfracht
	management ['mænɪdʒmənt]	Geschäftsleitung
	detailed ['di:teɪld]	ausführlich
	delay [dɪ'leɪ]	Verzögerung
	to consider [kən'sɪdə]	erwägen, überlegen; ansehen als
	impolite [ˌɪmpə'laɪt]	unhöflich
	to be inclined [bɪ‿ɪn'klaɪnd]	dazu neigen, geneigt sein
	to tend to be ['tend‿tʊ bi:]	dazu neigen
	factual ['fæktʃʊəl]	sachlich, den Tatsachen entsprechend
	superfluous [su:'pɜ:flʊəs]	überflüssig
	rude [ru:d]	grob, ungehobelt, unverschämt

Unit 9

	enquiry, inquiry [ɪn'kwaɪərɪ]	Anfrage, Nachfrage
	business terms ['bɪznɪs ˌtɜ:mz]	Geschäftsbedingungen
	quotation [kwəʊ'teɪʃn]	Preisangebot
	convenient [kən'vi:nɪənt]	bequem, praktisch
	to locate [ləʊ'keɪt]	ausfindig machen, lokalisieren
	supplier [sə'plaɪə]	Lieferant, Anbieter
	search engine ['sɜ:tʃ ˌendʒɪn]	Suchmaschine
	source [sɔ:s]	Quelle, Ursprung
	trade association ['treɪd əsəʊʃɪˌeɪʃn]	Branchenverband
	trade fair ['treɪd ˌfeə]	(Fach-)Messe
	exhibition [ˌeksɪ'bɪʃn]	Ausstellung
	agent ['eɪdʒənt]	(Handels-)Vertreter/in
	advertising campaign ['ædvətaɪzɪŋ‿kæmˌpeɪn]	Werbekampagne, -feldzug

A Enquiries in writing

1	**purchasing manager** ['pɜ:tʃəsɪŋ ˌmænɪdʒə]	Einkaufsleiter/in
	retailer ['ri:teɪlə]	Einzelhändler/in
	outlet ['aʊtlet]	Verkaufsstelle, Laden(geschäft)
	discount ['dɪskaʊnt]	Rabatt, Nachlass
	terms of payment and delivery [ˌtɜ:mz‿əv ˌpeɪmənt ənd‿dɪ'lɪvərɪ]	Zahlungs- und Lieferbedingungen
	to place an order [ˌpleɪs ən 'ɔ:də]	einen Auftrag erteilen
	stock [stɒk]	Vorrat, Lager(bestand)
	in conclusion [ɪn‿kən'klu:ʒn]	zum Abschluss, abschließend
	sample ['sɑ:mpl]	Muster, Probe(exemplar)
2	**to comprise** [kəm'praɪz]	umfassen
3	**quantity discount** [ˌkwɒntətɪ 'dɪskaʊnt]	Mengenrabatt
	trial order [ˌtraɪəl 'ɔ:də]	Probeauftrag
	mint bar ['mɪnt‿bɑ:]	Pfefferminzriegel
	confectionery [kən'fekʃənrɪ]	Süßwaren
	sweets [swi:ts]	Süßwaren, Süßigkeiten
	advertisement [əd'vɜ:tɪsmənt, 'ædvətaɪzmənt]	Anzeige
	issue ['ɪʃu:]	*(hier:)* Ausgabe, Heft

reception [rɪ'sepʃn] Empfang
embassy ['embəsɪ] Botschaft(sgebäude)
4 **imagination** [ɪˌmædʒɪ'neɪʃn] Phantasie, Vorstellungskraft

5 **crystal glass** [ˌkrɪstl 'glɑ:s] Kristallglas
gift box ['gɪft ˌbɒks] Geschenkkarton
leading ['li:dɪŋ] führend
beverage wholesaler [ˌbevərɪdʒ 'həʊlˌseɪlə] Getränkegroßhandlung

B Enquiries by phone

1 **generous** ['dʒenərəs] großzügig
volume order [ˌvɒlju:m 'ɔ:də] Großauftrag
3 **crash course** ['kræʃ ˌkɔ:s] Kompaktkurs
4 **household tool kit** [ˌhaʊshəʊld‿'tu:l ˌkɪt] Haushaltswerkzeugsatz
to grant [grɑ:nt] gewähren
to retain [rɪ'teɪn] halten, beibehalten
trade discount [ˌtreɪd‿'dɪskaʊnt] Händler-, Wiederverkaufsrabatt
introductory discount [ˌɪntrədʌktərɪ 'dɪskaʊnt] Einführungsrabatt
cash discount [ˌkæʃ 'dɪskaʊnt] Skonto
5 **to launch** [lɔ:ntʃ] einführen, starten, in die Wege leiten
to register ['redʒɪstə] eintragen, registrieren
to qualify for ['kwɒlɪfaɪ fɔ:] Voraussetzungen erfüllen für, Anspruch haben auf
6 **incentive** [ɪn'sentɪv] Anreiz
smoked salmon [ˌsməʊkt 'sæmən] Räucherlachs
LG **deadline** ['dedlaɪn] letzte Frist, letzter Termin
in confidence [ɪn‿'kɒnfɪdəns] vertraulich
minor ['maɪnə] gering(fügig)
representative [ˌreprɪ'zentətɪv] Vertreter/in
comparative(ly) [kəm'pærətɪv(lɪ)] vergleichsweise
to execute ['eksɪkju:t] aus-, durchführen

Unit 10

offer ['ɒfə] Angebot
solicited offer [səˌlɪsɪtɪd 'ɒfə] verlangtes Angebot
unsolicited offer [ˌʌnsəlɪsɪtɪd 'ɒfə] unverlangtes Angebot
quotation [kwəʊ'teɪʃn] Angebot mit Preisangabe
cost estimate ['kɒst ˌestɪmət] Kostenvoranschlag
expressly [ɪk'spreslɪ] ausdrücklich
to be subject to [bɪ 'sʌbdʒɪkt‿tu:] unterliegen, abhängen von, unterworfen sein
prices are subject to change without notice ['praɪsɪz‿ə ˌsʌbdʒɪkt‿tʊ ˌtʃeɪndʒ wɪðˌaʊt 'nəʊtɪs] Preisänderungen vorbehalten
without engagement [wɪˌðaʊt ɪŋ'geɪdʒmənt] freibleibend
valid ['vælɪd] gültig, bindend, rechtskräftig
stock [stɒk] Vorrat, Lager(bestand)
as long as stocks last [əz ˌlɒŋ əz‿ˌstɒks 'lɑ:st] solange Vorrat reicht
2 **to make an offer** [ˌmeɪk ən 'ɒfə] ein Angebot abgeben
potential customer [pəˌtenʃl 'kʌstəmə] Interessent/in
to carry out work [ˌkærɪ‿aʊt 'wɜ:k] Arbeit ausführen
prospective [prəs'pektɪv] zukünftig, voraussichtlich, potentiell
to process ['prəʊses] be-, verarbeiten

A Offers in writing

1 **sample** ['sɑ:mpl] Muster, Probestück
to exceed [ɪk'si:d] übersteigen, überschreiten
quantity discount [ˌkwɒntətɪ 'dɪskaʊnt] Mengenrabatt
to quote [kwəʊt] Preis angeben; zitieren
terms of delivery [ˌtɜ:mz‿əv dɪ'lɪvərɪ] Lieferbedingungen
cash with order [ˌkæʃ wɪð 'ɔ:də] Bezahlung bei Auftragserteilung
account [ə'kaʊnt] Konto; Rechnung
open account terms [ˌəʊpn əˌkaʊnt‿'tɜ:mz] offenes Zahlungsziel
quarterly ['kwɔ:təlɪ] vierteljährlich
settlement ['setlmənt] Abrechnung, Bezahlung, Ausgleich, Erledigung
terms of payment [ˌtɜ:mz‿əv 'peɪmənt] Zahlungsbedingungen
consumer [kən'sju:mə] Verbraucher/in
association [əˌsəʊʃɪ'eɪʃn] Vereinigung, Verband
comfort ['kʌmfət] Behaglichkeit, Komfort; Trost
durability [ˌdjʊərə'bɪlətɪ] Haltbarkeit
to despatch, dispatch [dɪ'spætʃ] (ab-/ver-)senden, (ab-/ver-)schicken
business relations ['bɪznɪs rɪˌleɪʃnz] Geschäftsbeziehungen
2 **mint bar** ['mɪnt‿bɑ:] Pfefferminzriegel
net [net] netto
premises ['premɪsɪz] Geschäftsräume, Firmengebäude, -gelände
receipt of order [rɪˌsi:t əv 'ɔ:də] Auftragseingang
to depend on [dɪ'pend ɒn] abhängen von
to convince [kən'vɪns] überzeugen
assortment [ə'sɔ:tmənt] Sortiment, Auswahl
delighted [dɪ'laɪtɪd] entzückt, begeistert
discerning [dɪ'sɜ:nɪŋ] anspruchsvoll, guten Geschmack besitzend
folder ['fəʊldə] Falt-, Prospektblatt
3 **to take into account** [teɪk ˌɪntʊ‿ə'kaʊnt] berücksichtigen
backlit ['bæklɪt] von hinten/innen beleuchtet
substitute ['sʌbstɪtju:t] Ersatz (durch Ähnliches)
life [laɪf] Lebensdauer
battery ['bætərɪ] Batterie
to grant a discount [ˌgrɑ:nt ə 'dɪskaʊnt] Rabatt einräumen
to indicate ['ɪndɪkeɪt] angeben, nennen

4 **reference** ['refrəns]	Bezug
less [les]	abzüglich

B Offers by phone

1 **overseas** [ˌəʊvə'si:z]	aus dem / ins Ausland, ausländisch
to run out of sth. [rʌn 'aʊt əv ˌsʌmθɪŋ]	ausgehen, zur Neige gehen
colour printer ['kʌlə ˌprɪntə]	Farbdrucker
to stock up on [stɒk 'ʌp ɒn]	Lager(bestand) auffüllen
steel [sti:l]	Stahl
to soar [sɔ:]	sprunghaft steigen, in die Höhe schnellen
to adjust [ə'dʒʌst]	anpassen, sich anpassen
competition [ˌkɒmpə'tɪʃn]	Konkurrenz, Wettbewerb
to face [feɪs]	sich gegenübersehen, konfrontiert sein mit
trade discount ['treɪd ˌdɪskaʊnt]	Wiederverkaufsrabatt, Händlerrabatt
generous ['dʒenərəs]	großzügig
one-off [ˌwʌn'ɒf]	Einmal-

C Comparing options

1 **charge** [tʃɑ:dʒ]	Belastung, Gebühr
free of charge [ˌfri: əv 'tʃɑ:dʒ]	kostenlos, unentgeltlich
tailor-made [ˌteɪlə'meɪd]	maßgeschneidert
staff [stɑ:f]	Personal, Belegschaft
fossils ['fɒsəlz]	Fossilien, Versteinerungen
special treat [ˌspeʃl 'tri:t]	besonderes Vergnügen, spezielles Extra
tuition [tjʊ'ɪʃn]	Unterricht, Unterweisung
at short notice [ət ˌʃɔ:t 'nəʊtɪs]	kurzfristig, ohne lange Voranmeldung
fee [fi:]	Gebühr, Honorar
participant [pɑ:'tɪsɪpənt]	Teilnehmer/in
pearl [pɜ:l]	Perle
resort [rɪ'zɔ:t]	Urlaubs-, Badeort
full board [ˌfʊl 'bɔ:d]	Vollpension
celebrated ['seləbreɪtɪd]	gefeiert
novelist ['nɒvəlɪst]	Romanschriftsteller/in
host family ['həʊst ˌfæməlɪ]	Gastfamilie
professional [prə'feʃənl]	freiberuflich; Freiberufler/in
native ['neɪtɪv]	einheimisch, inländisch, Landes-
vibrant ['vaɪbrənt]	lebendig, pulsierend
half board [ˌhɑ:f 'bɔ:d]	Halbpension
to accompany [ə'kʌmpənɪ]	begleiten
admirable ['ædmərəbl]	bewundernswert, ausgezeichnet
balance ['bæləns]	Rest, Saldo; Gleichgewicht
commencement [kə'mensmənt]	Anfang, Beginn
2 **parent company** [ˌpeərənt 'kʌmpənɪ]	Muttergesellschaft

D INCOTERMS (Terms of delivery)

obligation [ˌɒblɪ'geɪʃn]	Verpflichtung, Verbindlichkeit
to draw up [drɔ:ˌ'ʌp]	zusammenstellen, verfassen
to update [ʌp'deɪt]	aktualisieren
quay [ki:]	Kai, Dock, Anlegestelle
passing of risk [ˌpɑ:sɪŋ əv 'rɪsk]	Gefahrenübergang
carrier ['kærɪə]	Frachtführer
carriage ['kærɪdʒ]	Transport(kosten), Fracht(kosten)
insurance [ɪn'ʃɔ:rəns]	Versicherung
place of destination [ˌpleɪs əv ˌdestɪ'neɪʃn]	Bestimmungsort
duty ['dju:tɪ]	*(hier:)* Zoll(gebühr)
customs formalities ['kʌstəmz fɔ:ˌmælətɪz]	Zollformalitäten
port of shipment [ˌpɔ:t əv 'ʃɪpmənt]	Verschiffungshafen
port of destination [ˌpɔ:t əv ˌdestɪ'neɪʃn]	Bestimmungshafen
1 **plant** [plɑ:nt]	Werk, Anlage; Pflanze
dock [dɒk]	Dock, Kai, Hafenbecken
2 **import licence** ['ɪmpɔ:t ˌlaɪsəns]	Einfuhrgenehmigung, Importlizenz
parcel post ['pɑ:sl ˌpəʊst]	Paketpost
ginger cookies [ˌdʒɪndʒə 'kʊkɪz]	Ingwerkekse
scarce(ly) ['skeəs(lɪ)]	knapp; kaum

Unit 11

order ['ɔ:də]	Auftrag, Bestellung
to place an order [ˌpleɪs ən 'ɔ:də]	einen Auftrag erteilen
initial order [ɪˌnɪʃl 'ɔ:də]	Erstauftrag
trial order [ˌtraɪəl 'ɔ:də]	Probeauftrag
merchandise ['mɜ:tʃəndaɪs]	Ware, Gut, Handelsartikel
repeat order [rɪˌpi:t 'ɔ:də]	Folgeauftrag
standing order [ˌstændɪŋ 'ɔ:də]	Dauerauftrag
interval ['ɪntəvl]	Abstand
order on call [ˌɔ:dər ɒn 'kɔ:l]	Abrufauftrag
concept ['kɒnsept]	Konzept, Begriff, Auffassung

A Orders in writing

to impress [ɪm'pres]	beeindrucken
durability [ˌdjʊərə'bɪlətɪ]	Haltbarkeit
to conduct a test [kənˌdʌkt ə 'test]	einen Test durchführen
1 **to confirm** [kən'fɜ:m]	bestätigen
to transfer [træns'fɜ:]	überweisen, übertragen
to remit [rɪ'mɪt]	überweisen
invoice ['ɪnvɔɪs]	Rechnung
to collect [kə'lekt]	abholen, (ein)sammeln
shortly ['ʃɔ:tlɪ]	in Kürze, bald
consignment [kən'saɪnmənt]	(Waren-)Sendung, Lieferung
approval [ə'pru:vl]	Billigung, Zustimmung, Beifall
description [dɪ'skrɪpʃn]	Beschreibung

2	**to stress** [stres]	betonen
	shirt [ʃɜ:t]	(Herren-)Hemd
	to point out [pɔɪnt 'aʊt]	hinweisen auf
	to qualify for ['kwɒlɪfaɪ fɔ:]	Voraussetzungen erfüllen für, Anspruch haben auf
	bank transfer ['bæŋk ˌtrænsfɜ:]	Banküberweisung
3	**stationery** ['steɪʃənrɪ]	Büro-, Papierwaren
	proud(ly) [praʊd(lɪ)]	stolz
	multilingual [ˌmʌltɪ'lɪŋgwəl]	vielsprachig, mehrsprachig
	range [reɪndʒ]	Sortiment, Kollektion, Auswahl
	kitten ['kɪtn]	Kätzchen
	smitten ['smɪtn]	hingerissen
	to sell well [ˌsel 'wel]	sich gut verkaufen, gut gehen
	puppy ['pʌpɪ]	Hündchen, Welpe
	bright [braɪt]	hell, glänzend
	to capture ['kæptʃə]	(ein)fangen
	to romp [rɒmp]	herumtollen
	nobility [nəʊ'bɪlətɪ]	Adel, Vornehmheit
	available [ə'veɪləbl]	erhältlich
	order confirmation ['ɔ:də kɒnfəˌmeɪʃn]	Auftragsbestätigung
4	**gift box** ['gɪft ˌbɒks]	Geschenkkarton
	to observe the delivery period [əbˌzɜ:v ðə dɪ'lɪvərɪ ˌpɪərɪəd]	Lieferfrist einhalten
	general terms and conditions [ˌdʒenərəl ˌtɜ:mz ənd kən'dɪʃnz]	allgemeine Geschäftsbedingungen

B Orders by phone

	delicatessens [ˌdelɪkə'tesənz]	Feinkostgeschäfte
1	**urgent** ['ɜ:dʒənt]	dringend, eilig
	to stage [steɪdʒ]	veranstalten
	meatball ['mi:tbɔ:l]	Frikadelle
	dressing ['dresɪŋ]	*(hier:)* Salatsoße/Dressing
	platter ['plætə]	Servierplatte, (Holz-)Teller
	mustard ['mʌstəd]	Senf
	salmon ['sæmən]	Lachs
	horseradish ['hɔ:sˌrædɪʃ]	Meerrettich
	to be in demand [bɪ‿ɪn dɪ'mɑ:nd]	gefragt sein, nachgefragt werden
	stuffed [stʌft]	*(hier:)* gefüllt
	airfreight ['eəfreɪt]	Luftfracht
	suggestion [sə'dʒestʃn]	Vorschlag
	to share the costs [ˌʃeə ðə 'kɒsts]	sich die Kosten teilen
	basically ['beɪsɪklɪ]	im Grunde
	advertising ['ædvətaɪzɪŋ]	Werbung
	obvious(ly) ['ɒbvɪəs(lɪ)]	offensichtlich
	retail trade ['ri:teɪl ˌtreɪd]	Einzelhandel
	straight away [ˌstreɪtə'weɪ]	sofort, unverzüglich
	follow-up order [ˌfɒləʊ‿ʌp 'ɔ:də]	Folgeauftrag
3	**at the latest** *(nachgestellt)* [ət‿ðə 'leɪtɪst]	spätestens
	reception [rɪ'sepʃn]	Empfang
	sunset ['sʌnset]	Sonnenuntergang
	to contain [kən'teɪn]	enthalten
	artificial [ˌɑ:tɪ'fɪʃl]	künstlich
	flavouring ['fleɪvərɪŋ]	Geschmackszusatz, Aroma
	to accommodate [ə'kɒmədeɪt]	unterbringen, *(hier:)* entgegenkommen
LG	**forwarders** ['fɔ:wədəz]	Spedition, Transportgesellschaft
	member ['membə]	Mitglied
	to join [dʒɔɪn]	beitreten, mitmachen
	crude oil [ˌkru:d 'ɔɪl]	Rohöl
	to set [set]	festsetzen, ansetzen, einrichten
	quota ['kwəʊtə]	Quote, Rate, Kontingent, Anteil
	subsidiary [səb'sɪdɪərɪ]	Tochtergesellschaft
	proposal [prə'pəʊzl]	Vorschlag
	to rule [ru:l]	entscheiden, verfügen, anordnen

Unit 12

shipping ['ʃɪpɪŋ]	Seetransport, Verschiffung, Versand
to forecast ['fɔ:kɑ:st]	vorhersagen
decade ['dekeɪd]	Jahrzehnt
cargo ['kɑ:gəʊ]	(See-)Fracht, Ladung
bulk cargo [ˌbʌlk‿'kɑ:gəʊ]	Massengutfracht, Schüttgutladung
non-bulk cargo [ˌnɒnbʌlk‿'kɑ:gəʊ]	Stückgutfracht
to stack [stæk]	aufstapeln, aufschichten
ferry ['ferɪ]	Fähre
to load [ləʊd]	beladen, einladen
to unload [ʌn'ləʊd]	entladen, löschen
car carrier ['kɑ: ˌkærɪə]	Autotransporter, -transportschiff
vehicle ['vɪəkl]	Fahrzeug
port [pɔ:t]	Hafen
to deepen ['di:pn]	vertiefen, tiefer machen
to accommodate [ə'kɒmədeɪt]	aufnehmen, unterbringen, entgegenkommen
average consumer [ˌævrɪdʒ kən'sju:mə]	Durchschnittsverbraucher
irritation [ɪrɪ'teɪʃn]	Verärgerung
global economy [ˌgləʊbl ɪ'kɒnəmɪ]	Weltwirtschaft
industry analyst ['ɪndəstrɪ‿ænəlɪst]	Branchenexperte/-expertin
to facilitate [fə'sɪlɪteɪt]	ermöglichen, erleichtern
economic growth [ˌi:kənɒmɪk‿'grəʊθ]	Wirtschaftswachstum
trade flows ['treɪd ˌfləʊz]	Handelsströme
in terms of [ɪn 'tɜ:mz‿əv]	in Bezug auf, was … betrifft
raw materials [ˌrɔ: mə'tɪərɪəlz]	Rohstoffe
stagnation [stæg'neɪʃn]	Stillstand
carrier ['kærɪə]	Frachtführer
terminal operator ['tɜ:mɪnl ˌɒpəreɪtə]	Betreiber eines Terminals
facilities [fə'sɪlətɪz]	Einrichtungen, Anlagen

	supply/demand ratio [səˌplaɪ dɪ'mɑ:nd ˌreɪʃɪəʊ]	Verhältnis zwischen Angebot und Nachfrage
	inadequate [ɪ'nædɪkwət]	unzureichend

A Modes of transport

	mode of transport [ˌməʊd əv 'trænspɔ:t]	Transportart
	freight forwarding company [ˌfreɪt 'fɔ:wədɪŋ‿kʌmpənɪ]	Spedition, Transportunternehmen
	to handle ['hændl]	handhaben, erledigen, bearbeiten
1	**consignment** [kən'saɪnmənt]	(Waren-)Sendung, Lieferung
	destination [ˌdestɪ'neɪʃn]	Bestimmung(sort)
	rail transport ['reɪl ˌtrænspɔ:t]	Schienentransport
	bulk goods [ˌbʌlk'gʊdz]	Massen-, Schüttgüter
	crude oil [ˌkru:d 'ɔɪl]	Rohöl
	iron ore ['aɪən‿ɔ:]	Eisenerz
	market share [ˌmɑ:kɪt 'ʃeə]	Marktanteil
	harmful ['hɑ:mfəl]	schädlich
	environment [ɪn'vaɪərənmənt]	Umwelt, Umfeld
	rail siding ['reɪl ˌsaɪdɪŋ]	Gleisanschluss
	van [væn]	Kleintransporter
	virtually ['vɜ:tʃʊəlɪ]	nahezu, so gut wie, praktisch
	pollution [pə'lu:ʃn]	(Umwelt-)Verschmutzung
	theft [θeft]	Diebstahl
	highway robbery [ˌhaɪweɪ 'rɒbərɪ]	Raubüberfälle auf Fernstraßen
	to involve [ɪn'vɒlv]	mit sich bringen, nach sich ziehen
	carriage by sea [ˌkærɪdʒ baɪ 'si:]	Seetransport
	bulky ['bʌlkɪ]	sperrig, unhandlich, übergroß
	perishable ['perɪʃəbl]	(leicht) verderblich
	spare parts [ˌspeə 'pɑ:ts]	Ersatzteile
	seaworthy packing [ˌsi:wɜ:ðɪ 'pækɪŋ]	seemäßige Verpackung
2	**medical supplies** [ˌmedɪkl sə'plaɪz]	Artikel zur medizinischen Versorgung
	printing press ['prɪntɪŋ ˌpres]	Druckerpresse

B Packing

	regardless of [rɪ'gɑ:dləs əv]	ungeachtet, trotz
1	**bale** [beɪl]	Ballen
	bundle with steel strapping [ˌbʌndl wɪð ˌsti:l 'stræpɪŋ]	Bündel mit Stahlbandumreifung
	coil on euro-pallet [ˌkɔɪl ɒn 'ju:rəʊˌpælɪt]	Rolle, Coil auf Europalette
	crate [kreɪt]	Lattenkiste
	drum [drʌm]	Fass, Barrel
	foil-wrapped cardboard box [ˌfɔɪlræpt‿kɑ:dbɔ:d‿'bɒks]	folienumwickelter Karton
	plastic box with mouldings [ˌplæstɪk 'bɒks wɪð 'məʊldɪŋz]	Kunststoffbox mit Formeinlagen
	pallet [pælɪt]	Palette
	wooden case [ˌwʊdn 'keɪs]	Holzkiste
2	**pure new wool** [ˌpjʊə nju: 'wʊl]	reine Schurwolle
	steel rods [sti:l 'rɒdz]	Stahlstäbe
	replacement Mp3 player [rɪˌpleɪsmənt ˌempi:'θri: ˌpleɪə]	Ersatz-Mp3-Spieler

C Dispatch advice

	dispatch advice [dɪ'spætʃ ədˌvaɪs]	Versandanzeige
1		
1	**to accompany** [ə'kʌmpənɪ]	begleiten
	warehouse ['weəhaʊs]	Lager(haus)
	assurance [ə'ʃɔ:rəns]	Zusicherung, Versicherung
	triple-walled cardboard box [ˌtrɪplwɔ:ld‿kɑ:dbɔ:d‿'bɒks]	3-wandiger Karton
	consignment note [kən'saɪnmənt ˌnəʊt]	Frachtbrief
	packing list ['pækɪŋ ˌlɪst]	Packliste
	commercial invoice [kəˌmɜ:ʃl 'ɪnvɔɪs]	Handelsrechnung
2	**to process** ['prəʊsəs]	bearbeiten, verarbeiten
	markings ['mɑ:kɪŋz]	Markierung
2		
1	**to confirm** [kən'fɜ:m]	bestätigen
	standard lamp ['stændəd ˌlæmp]	Stehlampe
	uplighter ['ʌplaɪtə]	Deckenfluter
	coffee table ['kɒfɪ ˌteɪbl]	Couchtisch
	to debit to s.o.'s account [ˌdebɪt‿tʊ ˌsʌmwʌnz ə'kaʊnt]	das Konto von jemandem belasten
	amount [ə'maʊnt]	Betrag, Summe
2	**confident** ['kɒnfɪdənt]	zuversichtlich

D Documents in foreign trade

	waybill ['weɪbɪl]	Frachtbrief
	bill of lading (B/L) [ˌbɪl‿əv 'leɪdɪŋ]	Konnossement, Seefrachtbrief
	document of title [ˌdɒkjəmənt əv 'taɪtl]	Eigentumsurkunde
	lawful holder [ˌlɔ:fəl 'həʊldə]	rechtmäßige(r) Inhaber(in)/Besitzer(in)
	damage ['dæmɪdʒ]	Beschädigung, Schaden
	certificate of origin [səˌtɪfɪkət‿əv 'ɒrɪdʒɪn]	Ursprungszeugnis
	to legalize ['li:gəlaɪz]	beglaubigen, legalisieren
	insurance policy [ɪn'ʃɔ:rəns ˌpɒləsɪ]	Versicherungspolice
	insurance certificate [ɪn'ʃɔ:rəns‿səˌtɪfɪkət]	Versicherungsschein, -zertifikat
	form [fɔ:m]	*(hier:)* Formular
2	**shipper** ['ʃɪpə]	*(hier:)* Versender/in, Verfrachter/in
	liner ['laɪnə]	Linienschiff
	consignee [ˌkɒnsaɪ'ni:]	Empfänger/in
	to notify ['nəʊtɪfaɪ]	benachrichtigen
	vessel ['vesl]	Schiff
	port of discharge [ˌpɔ:t əv 'dɪstʃɑ:dʒ]	Entladehafen
	gross weight [ˌgrəʊs 'weɪt]	Bruttogewicht
	measurement ['meʒəmənt]	*(hier:)* Abmessungen
	lump sum [ˌlʌmp 'sʌm]	Pauschalsumme
	premium ['pri:mɪəm]	Prämie
	insured [ɪn'ʃɔ:d]	*(hier:)* Versicherungsnehmer/in, Versicherte/r
3	**staff member** ['stɑ:f ˌmembə]	Mitarbeiter/in

Unit 13

reminder [rɪ'maɪndə]	(Zahlungs-)Erinnerung, Mahnung
currency ['kʌrənsɪ]	Währung
inhabitants [ɪn'hæbɪtənts]	Einwohner/innen
scale [skeɪl]	Maß, Maßstab
Middle Ages [ˌmɪdl 'eɪdʒɪz]	Mittelalter
coin [kɔɪn]	Münze, Geldstück
banknote ['bæŋknəʊt]	Geldschein

A The Invoice

tax [tæks]	Steuer
VAT (value-added tax) [ˌviːeɪ'tiː (ˌvæljuː‿ædɪd‿'tæks)]	Mehrwertsteuer
IBAN (international bank account number) ['aɪbæn, ˌaɪbiːeɪ'en (ˌɪntənæʃənl 'bæŋk əˌkaʊnt ˌnʌmbə)]	Internationale Kontonummer
BIC (bank identifier code) [ˌbiːaɪ'siː (ˌbæŋk aɪ'dentɪfaɪə ˌkəʊd)]	Internationaler Bank-Code
proforma invoice [prəʊˌfɔːmər‿'ɪnvɔɪs]	Proformarechnung
eventual(ly) [ɪ'ventʃʊəl(ɪ)]	letztendlich, letztlich, schließlich
import licence ['ɪmpɔːt ˌlaɪsəns]	Einfuhrgenehmigung, Importlizenz
2 **trial order** [ˌtraɪəl 'ɔːdə]	Probeauftrag
to confirm [kən'fɜːm]	bestätigen
to pick up [pɪk 'ʌp]	abholen
to instruct [ɪn'strʌkt]	anweisen, unterweisen
at your earliest convenience [ət‿jɔːr‿ɜːlɪəst kən'viːnɪəns]	so bald wie möglich
to remit [rɪ'mɪt]	überweisen
account [ə'kaʊnt]	Konto
comfortable ['kʌmftəbl]	bequem
serviceable ['sɜːvɪsəbl]	zweckdienlich, praktisch, strapazierfähig
durable ['djʊərəbl]	haltbar
stylish ['staɪlɪʃ]	schick, modisch
tax-exempt intra-Community delivery [ˌtæksɪg'zemt ˌɪntrəkə'mjuːnətɪ dɪ'lɪvərɪ]	steuerfreie Innergemeinschaftslieferung (innerhalb der EU)

B Means and terms of payment

1 **means of payment** ['miːnz‿əv 'peɪmənt]	Zahlungsmittel
to issue ['ɪʃuː]	ausstellen, (her)ausgeben
to advance [əd'vɑːns]	vorschießen, auslegen
to debit to an account [ˌdebɪt‿tʊ‿ən ə'kaʊnt]	von einem Konto abbuchen
cardholder ['kɑːdˌhəʊldə]	Karteninhaber/in
debit card ['debɪt‿kɑːd]	Bankkarte
account-holder [ə'kaʊntˌhəʊldə]	Kontoinhaber/in
to withdraw money from an account [wɪð'drɔː ˌmʌnɪ frəm ən ə'kaʊnt]	Geld von einem Konto abheben
cash point ['kæʃpɔɪnt]	Geldautomat
ATM (automated teller machine) [ˌeɪtiː'em, ˌɔːtəmeɪtɪd‿'telə məˌʃiːn]	Geldautomat
cheque (BE), check (AE) [tʃek]	Scheck
written order [ˌrɪtn 'ɔːdə]	schriftliche Anweisung
named [neɪmd]	namentlich genannt
bearer ['beərə]	*(hier:)* Überbringer
crossed cheque [ˌkrɒst‿'tʃek]	Verrechnungsscheck
to pay into a bank account [peɪ‿ˌɪntʊ‿ə 'bæŋk əˌkaʊnt]	auf ein Konto einzahlen
bill of exchange [bɪl‿əv ɪks'tʃeɪndʒ]	Wechsel
on demand [ɒn dɪ'mɑːnd]	auf Verlangen
nowadays ['naʊədeɪz]	heutzutage
at sight [ət 'saɪt]	bei Sicht
on presentation [ɒn ˌprezən'teɪʃn]	bei Vorlage
to grant credit [ˌgrɑːnt‿'kredɪt]	Kredit gewähren
2 **by means of** [ˌbaɪ 'miːnz‿əv]	mittels
to order ['ɔːdə]	auffordern
to stipulate, to specify ['stɪpjəleɪt, 'spesɪfaɪ]	vorschreiben
wording ['wɜːdɪŋ]	Formulierung
3 **overindebted** [ˌəʊvərɪn'detɪd]	überschuldet
to turn down [tɜːn 'daʊn]	ablehnen
check-out ['tʃekaʊt]	(Supermarkt-)Kasse
to overtake [ˌəʊvə'teɪk]	überholen
cash payment [ˌkæʃ 'peɪmənt]	Barzahlung
retail outlet [ˌriːteɪl 'aʊtlet]	Einzelhandelsverkaufsstelle
adult ['ædʌlt]	Erwachsene/r
average ['ævrɪdʒ]	Durchschnitt
provider [prə'vaɪdə]	Versorger, Anbieter, Lieferant
spokesman ['spəʊksmən]	Sprecher
debt level ['det ˌlevl]	Schuldenstand
e-commerce ['iːˌkɒmɜːs]	Internet-Handel
fashion chain ['fæʃn ˌtʃeɪn]	Kette von Modegeschäften
2 **creditworthiness** ['kredɪtˌwɜːðɪnəs]	Kreditwürdigkeit
payment in advance [ˌpeɪmənt ɪn əd'vɑːns]	Vorauszahlung
to manufacture to specification [ˌmænjə'fæktʃə tʊ ˌspesɪfɪ'keɪʃn]	als Sonderanfertigung herstellen
staggered payment [ˌstægəd 'peɪmənt]	gestaffelte Zahlungsweise
with order [wɪð 'ɔːdə]	bei Auftragserteilung
on delivery [ɒn dɪ'lɪvərɪ]	bei Lieferung
cash on delivery [ˌkæʃ‿ɒn dɪ'lɪvərɪ]	Zahlung durch Nachnahme / bei Lieferung
carrier ['kærɪə]	Frachtführer
proof [pruːf]	Beweis, Nachweis
open credit [ˌəʊpn 'kredɪt]	Zahlung gegen einfache Rechnung
to be entitled [bɪ‿ɪn'taɪtld]	berechtigt sein, Anspruch haben
to deduct [dɪ'dʌkt]	abziehen
cash discount [ˌkæʃ 'dɪskaʊnt]	Skonto, Barzahlungsrabatt

comparative(ly) [kəm'pærətɪv(lɪ)] – verhältnismäßig
to trust [trʌst] – vertrauen
customary ['kʌstəmərɪ] – üblich
open account [ˌəʊpn ə'kaʊnt] – offenes Zahlungsziel
statement of account [ˌsteɪtmənt ɒv ə'kaʊnt] – Kontoauszug
letter of credit [ˌletər‿əv 'kredɪt] – Akkreditiv
clean bill of lading ['kli:n ˌbɪl‿əv 'leɪdɪŋ] – reines Konnossement
irrevocable [ˌɪrɪ'vəʊkəbl] – unwiderruflich
to revoke [rɪ'vəʊk] – widerrufen, annullieren, stornieren
consent [kən'sent] – Zustimmung, Einwilligung
opening bank [ˌəʊpnɪŋ 'bæŋk] – ausstellende Bank
to prove [pru:v] – beweisen, nachweisen
1 **in our favour** [ɪn‿ˌaʊə 'feɪvə] – zu unseren Gunsten
payable at ['peɪəbl ət] – zahlbar bei
valid until [ˌvælɪd ʌnˌtɪl] – gültig bis
2 **to disclose** [dɪs'kləʊz] – offenlegen, preisgeben
due [dju:] – fällig
drill head ['drɪl ˌhed] – Bohrkopf
to insist on [ɪn'sɪst ɒn] – bestehen auf
substantial [səb'stænʃl] – erheblich, beträchtlich

C Reminders

to collect the invoice amount [kəˌlekt‿ðɪ‿'ɪnvɔɪs əˌmaʊnt] – den Rechnungsbetrag eintreiben
insistent [ɪn'sɪstənt] – nachdrücklich
to suggest [sə'dʒest] – *(hier:)* andeuten, zu verstehen geben
to overlook [ˌəʊvə'lʊk] – übersehen
to threaten ['θretn] – drohen
interest ['ɪntrəst] – Zinsen
interest on arrears [ˌɪntrəst ɒn ə'rɪəz] – Verzugszinsen
legal steps [ˌli:gl 'steps] – juristische Schritte
1 **department store** [dɪ'pɑ:tmənt ˌstɔ:] – Waren-, Kaufhaus
urgent ['ɜ:dʒənt] – dringend, eilig
communication [kəˌmju:nɪ'keɪʃn] – Nachricht, Mitteilung, Information
accounts [ə'kaʊnts] – Buchhaltung, Rechnungswesen
1 **to be aware of a problem** [bɪ‿əˌweər‿əv ə 'prɒbləm] – sich eines Problems bewusst sein
records ['rekɔ:dz] – Unterlagen, Verzeichnisse
to settle an invoice [ˌsetl ən 'ɪnvɔɪs] – eine Rechnung begleichen
settlement ['setlmənt] – (Rechnungs-)Ausgleich, Zahlung
2 **faulty** ['fɒltɪ, 'fɔ:ltɪ] – fehlerhaft
operations [ˌɒpə'reɪʃnz] – *(hier:)* Betrieb
3 **in full** [ɪn 'fʊl] – in voller Höhe
state of affairs [ˌsteɪt‿əv ə'feəz] – Zustand, Stand der Dinge
previous ['pri:vɪəs] – vorherig, vorangegangen, früher
4 **to transfer** [træns'fɜ:] – überweisen
to grant a respite [ˌgrɑ:nt ə 'respaɪt] – einen Zahlungsaufschub gewähren
remittance [rɪ'mɪtəns] – Überweisung
severe(ly) [sə'vɪə(lɪ)] – hart, streng, strikt, scharf
gale [geɪl] – Orkan, Sturm
to devastate ['devəsteɪt] – verwüsten
to take off the roof [ˌteɪk ɒf ðə 'ru:f] – das Dach abdecken
to soak [səʊk] – durchnässen, einweichen
to assess [ə'ses] – abschätzen, bewerten
to compensate ['kɒmpənseɪt] – entschädigen
replacement [rɪ'pleɪsmənt] – Ersatz
extension [ɪk'stenʃn] – Zahlungsaufschub
to grant a concession [ˌgrɑ:nt ə kən'seʃn] – ein Zugeständnis machen
remainder, balance [rɪ'meɪndə, 'bæləns] – Restbetrag
5 **overdue** [ˌəʊvə'dju:] – überfällig
oversight ['əʊvəsaɪt] – Versehen
delay in payment [dɪˌleɪ‿ɪn 'peɪmənt] – Zahlungsverzug
LG **business unit, division** ['bɪznɪs ˌju:nɪt, dɪ'vɪʒn] – Geschäftseinheit
to cancel an invoice [ˌkænsl ən 'ɪnvɔɪs] – Rechnung stornieren
to notify ['nəʊtɪfaɪ] – benachrichtigen
administrator [əd'mɪnɪstreɪtə] – Vergleichs-, Vermögensverwalter
emphasis ['emfəsɪs] – Nachdruck
to return [rɪ'tɜ:n] – zurückschicken
components [kəm'pəʊnənts] – (Bestand-)Teile
negotiation [nɪˌgəʊʃɪ'eɪʃn] – Verhandlung
to balance ['bæləns] – ausgleichen, ins Gleichgewicht bringen
budget ['bʌdʒɪt] – (Staats-)Haushalt, Etat

Unit 14

complaint [kəm'pleɪnt] – Beschwerde, Beanstandung, Reklamation, Mängelrüge
adjustment [ə'dʒʌstmənt] – Ausgleich, Bereinigung, Erledigung

A Making complaints

even though [ˌi:vn 'ðəʊ] – obgleich
faulty ['fɒltɪ, 'fɔ:ltɪ] – fehlerhaft, mangelhaft
anger ['æŋgə] – Zorn
calm [kɑ:m] – ruhig, gelassen
mug [mʌg] – Becher
replacement [rɪ'pleɪsmənt] – Ersatz(lieferung)
2 **price reduction** ['praɪs rɪˌdʌkʃn] – Preisnachlass
to improve [ɪm'pru:v] – verbessern
to render a service [ˌrendər‿ə 'sɜ:vɪs] – einen Dienst leisten, eine Dienstleistung erbringen
surplus ['sɜ:pləs] – überschüssig
credit note ['kredɪt‿ˌnəʊt] – Gutschrift
3 **building site** ['bɪldɪŋ ˌsaɪt] – Baustelle
beetle ['bi:tl] – Käfer
to refund [ˌri:'fʌnd] – erstatten

	detective novel [dɪ'tektɪv ˌnɒvl]	Kriminalroman
	sole [səʊl]	Sohle
1	**incoming goods control** [ˌɪnkʌmɪŋ‿'gʊdz kənˌtrəʊl]	Wareneingangskontrolle
	to label ['leɪbl]	etikettieren, kennzeichnen, beschriften
	purchase order ['pɜ:tʃɪs ˌɔ:də]	Bestellung, Lieferungsauftrag
	in due course [ɪn ˌdju: 'kɔ:s]	fristgemäß
	merchandise ['mɜ:tʃəndaɪs]	Ware
	dismayed [dɪ'smeɪd]	entsetzt
	tag [tæg]	Etikett, Schildchen
	to sew, sewed, sewn [səʊ, səʊd, səʊn]	nähen
	garment ['gɑ:mənt]	Kleidungsstück
	to commission [kə'mɪʃn]	beauftragen
	to remove [rɪ'mu:v]	entfernen
	reworking [ˌri:'wɜ:kɪŋ]	Um-, Nacharbeitung
2	**tool kit** ['tu:l ˌkɪt]	Werkzeugsatz
	impatient [ɪm'peɪʃnt]	ungeduldig
	to cancel an order [ˌkænsl ən 'ɔ:də]	einen Auftrag annullieren
3	**personnel department** [ˌpɜ:sən'el dɪˌpɑ:tmənt]	Personalabteilung
	junior executive [ˌdʒu:nɪər‿ɪg'zekjətɪv]	Nachwuchsführungskraft
	coaching ['kəʊtʃɪŋ]	Training
	participant [pɑ:'tɪsɪpənt]	Teilnehmer/in
	to satisfy ['sætɪsfaɪ]	zufrieden stellen
	to attend a course [əˌtend ə 'kɔ:s]	an einem Kurs teilnehmen
	principal ['prɪnsəpl]	*(hier:)* Schulleiter/in
	shortcomings ['ʃɔ:tˌkʌmɪŋz]	Unzulänglichkeiten
	inadequate [ɪ'nædɪkwət]	unzureichend
	out of order [ˌaʊt‿əv 'ɔ:də]	kaputt, außer Betrieb
	to take into account [teɪk ˌɪntʊ‿ə'kaʊnt]	berücksichtigen
	to turn up [tɜ:n 'ʌp]	erscheinen, auftauchen
	refurbishment [ˌri:'fɜ:bɪʃmənt]	Renovierung
	refund ['ri:fʌnd]	Erstattung
4	**stationery** ['steɪʃənrɪ]	Büromaterial
	envelope ['envələʊp]	(Brief-)Umschlag
	contact person ['kɒntækt ˌpɜ:sn]	Ansprechpartner/in
	to renew a contract [rɪˌnju:‿ə 'kɒntrækt]	einen Vertrag verlängern
2 / 1	**multilingual** [ˌmʌltɪ'lɪŋgwəl]	mehr-, vielsprachig
	wall calendar ['wɔ:l ˌkæləndə]	Wandkalender
	to get around to it [get ə'raʊnd‿tʊ‿ɪt]	dazu kommen, Zeit dazu haben
3	**convenience food** [kən'vi:nɪəns ˌfu:d]	Fertiggericht(e)
	sell-by date ['selbaɪˌdeɪt]	Verfallsdatum (Lebensmittel)
	smudged [smʌdʒd]	verwischt, verschmiert
	illegible [ɪ'ledʒəbl]	unleserlich
	to affect [ə'fekt]	betreffen, beeinflussen
	ham [hæm]	Schinken
	whatever the price [wɒtˌevə ðə 'praɪs]	ganz unabhängig vom Preis
	to comply with regulations [kəmˌplaɪ wɪð ˌregjə'leɪʃnz]	Vorschriften einhalten
	defective [dɪ'fektɪv]	schadhaft, beschädigt
	to destroy [dɪ'strɔɪ]	vernichten, zerstören
	empty ['emptɪ]	leer
	to settle the matter ['setl ðə ˌmætə]	die Angelegenheit erledigen
	satisfaction [ˌsætɪs'fækʃn]	Zufriedenheit
5	**to reveal** [rɪ'vi:l]	enthüllen, aufzeigen
	in transit [ɪn 'trænzɪt]	beim Transport
	forwarders ['fɔ:wədəz]	Spedition
	roughly one third [ˌrʌflɪ ˌwʌn 'θɜ:d]	rund ein Drittel
	height [haɪt]	Höhe
	pipe-blown by hand [ˌpaɪpbləʊn baɪ 'hænd]	mundgeblasen
	plausible ['plɔ:zɪbl]	plausibel, einleuchtend, glaubhaft
	valuable ['væljʊəbl]	wertvoll
6	**maximum admissible weight** [ˌmæksɪməm ədˌmɪsəbl 'weɪt]	zulässiges Höchstgewicht
	to label, to provide with an inscription ['leɪbl, prəˌvaɪd wɪð ən ɪn'skrɪpʃn]	beschriften
	lbs (pounds) [paʊndz]	(englische) Pfund (453,59 g)
7	**service centre/center** ['sɜ:vɪs‿sentə]	Kundendienst(zentrum)
	blunt(ly) [blʌnt(lɪ)]	*(hier:)* unverblümt
	usage ['ju:sɪdʒ]	übliche Praxis
	to take offence at sth. [teɪk ə'fens ət ˌsʌmθɪŋ]	etwas übel nehmen
	curt [kɜ:t]	knapp, schroff
	conciliatory [kən'sɪlɪətrɪ]	versöhnlich
	to antagonize [æn'tægənaɪz]	vor den Kopf stoßen
	to be cooperative [bɪ kəʊ'ɒprətɪv]	zur Zusammenarbeit bereit sein
	understanding [ˌʌndə'stændɪŋ]	verständnisvoll
	to raise a matter ['reɪz ə ˌmætə]	eine Sache ansprechen
	error ['erə]	Irrtum
	mix-up ['mɪksʌp]	Verwechslung

B Adjusting complaints

	to manage complaints [ˌmænɪdʒ kəm'pleɪnts]	Beschwerden bearbeiten
	disgruntled [dɪs'grʌntld]	verärgert, verstimmt
	courtesy ['kɜ:təsɪ]	Höflichkeit
	to respond [rɪ'spɒnd]	antworten, reagieren
	to meet halfway [mi:t ˌhɑ:f'weɪ]	auf halbem Weg entgegenkommen
	justified ['dʒʌstɪfaɪd]	gerechtfertigt, berechtigt
1	**care** [keə]	Sorgfalt
	to involve [ɪn'vɒlv]	einbeziehen
	progress ['prəʊgres]	Fortgang
	to keep informed [ˌki:p ɪn'fɔ:md]	auf dem Laufenden halten
	justified complaint [ˌdʒʌstɪfaɪd‿kəm'pleɪnt]	begründete Reklamation
	to reject [rɪ'dʒekt]	zurückweisen
	to give a refusal, to refuse a request [ˌgɪv ə rɪ'fju:zl, rɪˌfju:z ə rɪ'kwest]	Absage erteilen

2	**jar** [dʒɑ:]	Glas (z. B. Marmelade), Topf (z. B. Senf)
	tomato relish [tə,mɑ:təʊ 'relɪʃ]	Tomatenrelish
	conservatory [kən'sɜ:vətrɪ]	Wintergarten
	to initiate [ɪ'nɪʃieɪt]	in die Wege leiten, einleiten
	scratch [skrætʃ]	Kratzer
	to be to blame [bɪ tʊ 'bleɪm]	schuld sein
	to be in progress [bɪ‿ɪn 'prəʊɡres]	im Gang sein
	alteration [,ɒltə'reɪʃn, ,ɔ:ltə'reɪʃn]	Änderung
	tiles [taɪlz]	Fliesen, Kacheln
3	**serious** ['sɪərɪəs]	ernst, schwerwiegend
	ample ['æmpl]	reichlich, üppig
	to go without saying [ɡəʊ wɪð,aʊt‿'seɪɪŋ]	selbstverständlich sein
	investigation [ɪn,vestɪ'ɡeɪʃn]	Untersuchung
4	**to release from a contract** [rɪ,li:s frəm ə 'kɒntrækt]	von einem Vertrag entbinden
	to locate [ləʊ'keɪt]	ausfindig machen
	at short notice [ət ,ʃɔ:t‿'nəʊtɪs]	kurzfristig
	re [ri:]	bezüglich, wegen
	for the time being [fə ðə ,taɪm 'bi:ɪŋ]	zurzeit, vorläufig
	parent company [,peərənt 'kʌmpənɪ]	Muttergesellschaft
	insolvent [ɪn'sɒlvənt]	zahlungsunfähig
5	**human resources department** [,hju:mən 'ri:sɔ:sɪz dɪ,pɑ:tmənt]	Personalabteilung
	cordial ['kɔ:dɪəl]	herzlich, freundlich
6	**retirement** [rɪ'taɪəmənt]	Ruhestand
	to initiate measures [ɪ,nɪʃieɪt 'meʒəz]	Maßnahmen einleiten
LG	**faultless, perfect, unobjectionable** ['fɒltləs / 'fɔ:ltləs, 'pɜ:fɪkt, ,ʌnəb'dʒekʃənəbl]	einwandfrei
	to instruct to the contrary [ɪn,strʌkt‿tʊ ðə 'kɒntrərɪ]	gegenteilige Anweisungen erteilen
	to recruit [rɪ'kru:t]	anwerben, einstellen
	courtyard ['kɔ:tjɑ:d]	Hof
	to cope with sth. ['kəʊp wɪð ,sʌmθɪŋ]	fertig werden mit etwas, etwas schaffen
	respite ['respaɪt]	Zahlungsaufschub

Unit 15

	wide range [,waɪd 'reɪndʒ]	breite Palette
	stage [steɪdʒ]	*(hier:)* Stadium
	to set about [set ə'baʊt]	sich daran machen
	age group [eɪdʒ ,ɡru:p]	Altersgruppe
	to charge [tʃɑ:dʒ]	*(hier:)* berechnen
	channel ['tʃænl]	*(hier:)* Vertriebsweg
	cheap chain ['tʃi:p ,tʃeɪn]	Billigladenkette
1	**introduction** [,ɪntrə'dʌkʃn]	Einführung
	growth [ɡrəʊθ]	Wachstum
	maturity [mə'tjʊərətɪ]	Reife
	decline [dɪ'klaɪn]	Rückgang
	to phase out [feɪz 'aʊt]	allmählich vom Markt zurückziehen
	focus ['fəʊkəs]	Schwerpunkt
	depending on [dɪ'pendɪŋ ɒn]	je nach, abhängig von
1	**to target** ['tɑ:ɡɪt]	ansprechen, anpeilen
2	**market research** [,mɑ:kɪt 'ri:sɜ:tʃ]	Marktforschung
	to conduct [kən'dʌkt]	durchführen
	to establish [ɪ'stæblɪʃ]	*(hier:)* feststellen
	needs [ni:dz]	Bedarf, Bedürfnisse
	desires [dɪ'zaɪəz]	Wünsche
	to be able [bɪ‿'eɪbl]	in der Lage sein
	willing ['wɪlɪŋ]	bereit
	to involve [ɪn'vɒlv]	*(hier:)* beinhalten
	desk research ['desk ,ri:sɜ:tʃ]	(Markt-)Forschung am Schreibtisch
	field research ['fi:ld ,ri:sɜ:tʃ]	Feldforschung
	random sample [,rændəm 'sɑ:mpl]	Zufallsprobe
	to spare [speə]	übrig haben
	actually ['æktʃʊəlɪ]	eigentlich
	to be in a hurry [bɪ‿ɪn ə 'hʌrɪ]	es eilig haben
	market survey [,mɑ:kɪt 'sɜ:veɪ]	Marktstudie, -untersuchung
	to tend to book flights [,tend‿tʊ ,bʊk 'flaɪts]	Flüge häufig buchen
	regularly ['reɡjələlɪ]	regelmäßig
	to spend [spend]	ausgeben
	to suppose [sə'pəʊz]	vermuten
	conventional [kən'venʃənl]	herkömmlich, traditionell
	outlets ['aʊtlets]	Verkaufsstellen
	to simplify ['sɪmplɪfaɪ]	vereinfachen
	competitive prices [kəm,petətɪv 'praɪsɪz]	günstige, konkurrenzfähige Preise

A Distribution channels

	distribution channels [dɪstrɪ'bju:ʃn ,tʃænlz]	Vertriebskanäle
	manufacturer [,mænjə'fæktʃərə]	Hersteller/in, Produzent/in
	wholesaler ['həʊl,seɪlə]	Großhändler
	retailer ['ri:teɪlə]	Einzelhändler
	link [lɪŋk]	Verbindung, Bindeglied
	generally ['dʒenrəlɪ]	im Allgemeinen
	to sell on [sel 'ɒn]	weiterverkaufen
	to break bulk [,breɪk 'bʌlk]	große Gebinde aufbrechen
	end user ['end‿ju:zə]	Endverbraucher
1	**agent** ['eɪdʒənt]	Handelsvertreter/in, Vertretung
	to ensure [ɪn'ʃɔ:]	sichern, gewährleisten
	supply [sə'plaɪ]	Angebot
	variety [və'raɪətɪ]	Vielfalt
	retail outlets [,ri:teɪl 'aʊtlets]	Einzelhandelsgeschäfte
	specialist shops [,speʃəlɪst 'ʃɒps]	Fachgeschäfte
	chemist ['kemɪst]	Apotheker/in
	beauty consultant ['bju:tɪ kən,sʌltənt]	Kosmetiker/in
	optician [ɒp'tɪʃnz]	Optiker/in
	high street stores [,haɪstri:t 'stɔ:z]	Geschäfte in der Innenstadt
	major ['meɪdʒə]	groß, wichtig
	branch [brɑ:ntʃ]	Filiale

	department store [dɪ'pɑ:tmənt ˌstɔ:]	Warenhaus, Kaufhaus
	roof [ru:f]	Dach
	in bulk [ɪn 'bʌlk]	in großen Mengen
	to involve [ɪn'vɒlv]	*(hier:)* einbeziehen
	segment ['segmənt]	Marktsegment
	to provide [prə'vaɪd]	zur Verfügung stellen
	to benefit ['benəfɪt]	profitieren
	sales force ['seɪlz ˌfɔ:s]	Vertreterstab
	warehouse ['weəhaʊs]	Lager
	to offer credit facilities [ˌɒfə 'kredɪt fəˌsɪlətɪz]	Kredite anbieten
	advisory services [əd'vaɪzərɪ ˌsɜ:vɪsɪz]	Beratungsdienst
	to charge for ['tʃɑ:dʒ fɔ:]	bezahlen lassen
	foreign trade [ˌfɒrən 'treɪd]	Außenhandel
	to appoint [ə'pɔɪnt]	ernennen, bestellen
	advantage [əd'vɑ:ntɪdʒ]	Vorteil
	familiar with [fə'mɪlɪə wɪð]	vertraut mit
	commission [kə'mɪʃn]	Provision
	percentage [pə'sentɪdʒ]	Prozentsatz
	thus [ðʌs]	daher
	to succeed in [sək'si:d ɪn]	gelingen
	principal ['prɪnsɪpl]	*(hier:)* Auftraggeber/in
	overheads ['əʊvəhedz]	fixe Kosten
2	**to cut out** [kʌt 'aʊt]	umgehen
	characteristic feature [ˌkærəktərɪstɪk 'fi:tʃə]	typisches Merkmal
6	**to take part in** [ˌteɪk 'pɑ:t ɪn]	teilnehmen an
	place of employment [ˌpleɪs əv ɪm'plɔɪmənt]	Arbeitsstätte
	brand [brænd]	Marke, Markenartikel
	spirits ['spɪrɪts]	Spirituosen
7	**retail customers** [ˌri:teɪl 'kʌstəməz]	Privatkunden (bei einer Bank)
	to survive [sə'vaɪv]	überleben
	organisation [ˌɔ:gənaɪ'zeɪʃn]	Firma, Unternehmen, Organisation
2		
1	**development** [dɪ'veləpmənt]	Entwicklung
	sector ['sektə]	Branche
	retailing operations ['ri:teɪlɪŋ‿ɒpəˌreɪʃnz]	Einzelhandelsgeschäftstätigkeit
	to have the goods delivered [ˌhæv ðə ˌgʊdz dɪ'lɪvəd]	sich die Ware liefern lassen
	to compare [kəm'peə]	vergleichen
	to avoid [ə'vɔɪd]	vermeiden
	travel agent ['trævl ˌeɪdʒənt]	Reisebüro
	to enable [ɪ'neɪbl]	in die Lage versetzen
	internet exchanges ['ɪntənet ɪksˌtʃeɪndʒɪz]	Online-Börsen
	superfluous [su:'pɜ:flʊəs]	überflüssig
	is paralleled by [ɪz 'pærəleld‿baɪ]	geht einher mit
2	**to improve** [ɪm'pru:v]	verbessern
	advantage [əd'vɑ:ntɪdʒ]	Vorteil
	comparing prices [kəmˌpeərɪŋ 'praɪsɪz]	Preisvergleich
	to develop [dɪ'veləp]	entwickeln
	to appeal to [ə'pi:l tu:]	ansprechen
	consumer [kən'sju:mə]	Verbraucher/in
	initial [ɪ'nɪʃl]	anfänglich
	reviews [rɪ'vju:z]	Berichte, Besprechungen
	fierce [fɪəs]	*(hier:)* scharf
	to have little choice but [hæv ˌlɪtl 'tʃɔɪs bət]	keine andere Wahl haben als
	to raise [reɪz]	erhöhen
	to check [tʃek]	(über)prüfen
	effective [ɪ'fektɪv]	wirksam
	marketing tools ['mɑ:kɪtɪŋ ˌtu:lz]	Marketinginstrumente
	merchants ['mɜ:tʃənts]	Händler
	to have access to [hæv 'ækses tu:]	Zugang haben zu
	unprecedented [ʌn'presɪdəntɪd]	noch nie dagewesen
	sales consultant ['seɪlz kənˌsʌltənt]	Verkaufsberater/in
	sales assistant ['seɪlz‿əˌsɪstənt]	Verkäufer/in
	to approach [ə'prəʊtʃ]	sich nähern, herangehen an, ansprechen
	to link [lɪŋk]	verbinden, verknüpfen

B Advertising

	to promote sales [prəˌməʊt 'seɪlz]	den Absatz fördern
	potential customers [pəˌtenʃl 'kʌstəməz]	mögliche Kunden
1	**consumer goods** [kən'sju:mə ˌgʊdz]	Konsumgüter
	mail shots ['meɪl ˌʃɒts]	Postwurfsendungen
	proportion [prə'pɔ:ʃn]	Anteil
	straight [streɪt]	*(hier:)* geradewegs, direkt
	wastepaper basket [weɪst'peɪpə ˌbɑ:skɪt]	Papierkorb
	to obtain [əb'teɪn]	erhalten
	selective [sə'lektɪv]	ausgewählt
	to make someone aware of [ˌmeɪk ˌsʌmwʌn ə'weər‿əv]	jemanden aufmerksam machen auf
	TV advertising, TV commercials [ˌti:vi: 'ædvətaɪzɪŋ, ˌti:vi: kə'mɜ:ʃlz]	TV-Werbung
	appeal [ə'pi:l]	Anziehung(skraft)
	to suggest [sə'dʒest]	*(hier:)* hinweisen auf, suggerieren
	to associate with [ə'səʊʃɪeɪt wɪð]	in Verbindung bringen mit
	to appeal to someone [ə'pi:l tʊ ˌsʌmwʌn]	jemanden ansprechen
	affluent ['æflʊənt]	wohlhabend
	keen [ki:n]	eifrig
	sufficient [sə'fɪʃənt]	genügend
	glossy ['glɒsɪ]	Hochglanz-
	health-conscious [ˌhelθ'kɒnʃəs]	gesundheitsbewusst
	retired [rɪ'taɪəd]	im Ruhestand, pensioniert
	to have time on their hands [hæv ˌtaɪm ɒn ðeə 'hændz]	Zeit (übrig) haben
	hoardings (BE) ['hɔ:dɪŋz]	Plakatwände
	billboards (AE) ['bɪlbɔ:dz]	Plakatwände
	to present [prɪ'zent]	vorstellen
	to experience [ɪk'spɪərɪəns]	erleben
2	**to dislike** [dɪ'slaɪk]	nicht mögen
	to influence ['ɪnflʊəns]	beeinflussen

	it doesn't appeal to me [ɪt‿dʌznt əˌpiː l tʊ 'miː]	es gefällt mir nicht
	message ['mesɪdʒ]	*(hier:)* Botschaft
	to double ['dʌbl]	verdoppeln
	turnover ['tɜːnˌəʊvə]	Umsatz, Absatz
	to achieve [ə'tʃiːv]	erreichen, erzielen
	to contribute [kən'trɪbjuːt]	beitragen
	spokesman ['spəʊksmən]	Sprecher
	to skip [skɪp]	überspringen
	habits ['hæbɪts]	Gewohnheiten
3	**turnover, sales** ['tɜːnˌəʊvə, seɪlz]	Umsatz
	contribution [ˌkɒntrɪ'bjuːʃn]	Beitrag
	change(s) [tʃeɪndʒ, 'tʃeɪndʒɪz]	Veränderung
	to occur, to result [ə'kɜː, rɪ'zʌlt]	sich ergeben
	increasing(ly) [ɪn'kriːsɪŋ(lɪ)]	zunehmend
2	**industrial goods** [ɪnˌdʌstrɪəl 'gʊdz]	Industrieerzeugnisse
	precision instruments [prɪˌsɪʒn 'ɪnstrəmənts]	Präzisionsinstrumente
	trade journal ['treɪd‿dʒɜːnl]	Fachzeitschrift
	periodical [ˌpɪərɪ'ɒdɪkl]	Zeitschrift
	devoted [dɪ'vəʊtɪd]	gewidmet
	trade fair ['treɪd ˌfeə]	Fachmesse
	to attend [ə'tend]	besuchen (Messe, Schule)
	buyer ['baɪə]	Einkäufer/in
	to intend [ɪn'tend]	beabsichtigen
	competitors [kəm'petɪtəz]	Wettbewerber
	to be up to [bɪ‿'ʌp tuː]	im Schilde führen, anstellen
3	**public relations** [ˌpʌblɪk rɪ'leɪʃnz]	Öffentlichkeitsarbeit
	to donate [dəʊ'neɪt]	spenden
	to emphasise ['emfəsaɪz]	betonen
	environment [ɪn'vaɪərənmənt]	Umwelt
	commitment to [kə'mɪtmənt‿tuː]	Engagement für
	community [kə'mjuːnətɪ]	Gemeinschaft
	press coverage ['pres ˌkʌvərɪdʒ]	Berichterstattung in der Presse
	outside advice [ˌaʊtsaɪd əd'vaɪs]	Beratung von außen
	specialist agency [ˌspeʃəlɪst 'eɪdʒənsɪ]	Fachagentur
	to project an image [prəˌdʒekt ən 'ɪmɪdʒ]	ein Image pflegen
4	**to remind someone** [rɪ'maɪnd ˌsʌmwʌn]	jemanden erinnern
	celebrity [sə'lebrətɪ]	Berühmtheit
	persuasive [pə'sweɪsɪv]	überredend
	subconscious [sʌb'kɒnʃəs]	Unterbewusstsein
	subliminal [sʌb'lɪmɪnl]	unterhalb der Schwelle des Bewusstseins
	jingles ['dʒɪŋglz]	Reime
	fabulous ['fæbjələs]	fantastisch
	faux fur [ˌfəʊ 'fɜː]	Kunstpelz
	exaggeration [ɪgˌzædʒə'reɪʃn]	Übertreibung
	hyperbole [haɪ'pɜːbəlɪ]	Übertreibung
	screen [skriːn]	Bildschirm
	superb(ly) [suː'pɜːb(lɪ)]	ausgezeichnet
	set [set]	(Fernseh-)Apparat
	to die for [tə 'daɪ fɔː]	zum Sterben schön
	imperative [ɪm'perətɪv]	Befehlsform
	rust [rʌst]	rostfarben
	emotionally charged [ɪˌməʊʃənlɪ 'tʃɑːdʒd]	emotional aufgeladen
	driving gloves ['draɪvɪŋ‿ˌglʌvz]	Autohandschuhe
	to scream [skriːm]	schreien
	confident ['kɒnfɪdənt]	selbstbewusst
	imagery ['ɪmɪdʒrɪ]	sprachliche Bilder
	organic [ɔː'gænɪk]	Bio-
	mane [meɪn]	Mähne
	gleam [gliːm]	Schimmer, Glanz
	dew [djuː]	Tau
	stubble trouble ['stʌbl ˌtrʌbl]	Probleme mit Bartstoppeln
	hooked on ['hʊkt ɒn]	süchtig nach
	foaming scrub [ˌfəʊmɪŋ 'skrʌb]	Peelingschaum
1	**verdant** ['vɜːdənt]	üppig grün
	to have green fingers [hæv ˌgriːn 'fɪŋgəz]	einen grünen Daumen haben
	bright [braɪt]	hell, leuchtend
	to theme [θiːm]	nach einem Motto/ Thema gestalten
	self-explanatory [ˌselfɪk'splænətrɪ]	selbsterklärend
	Mediterranean [ˌmedɪtər'eɪnɪən]	Mittelmeer
	memories ['memərɪz]	Erinnerungen
	olive trees ['ɒlɪv ˌtriːz]	Olivenbäume
	herbs [hɜːbz]	Kräuter
	high-powered [ˌhaɪ'paʊəd]	dynamisch
	rushed-off-your-feet [ˌrʌʃtɒfjɔː'fiːt]	vielbeschäftigt
	executive [ɪg'zekjətɪv]	leitende/r Angestellte/r
	to transform [træns'fɔːm]	verwandeln
	invigorating [ɪn'vɪgəreɪtɪŋ]	belebend, erfrischend
	ultimate ['ʌltɪmət]	(aller)höchst, äußerst, maximal
	sensation [sen'seɪʃn]	Gefühl
	fragrance ['freɪgrəns]	Duft
	splash [splæʃ]	Spritzer, Schuss
2	**appropriate** [ə'prəʊprɪət]	angemessen
	accessories [ək'sesərɪz]	Accessoires, Zubehör
	nail [neɪl]	Nagel
LG	**good value** [ˌgʊd 'væljuː]	preisgünstig
	swift(ly) ['swɪft(lɪ)]	schnell
	furnishings ['fɜːnɪʃɪŋz]	Einrichtungsgegenstände
	handling ['hændlɪŋ]	*(hier:)* Fahreigenschaften
	sophisticated [sə'fɪstɪkeɪtɪd]	(technisch) hoch entwickelt
	obscure [əb'skjʊə]	unbekannt
	cutting-edge [ˌkʌtɪŋ 'edʒ]	auf dem neuesten Stand
	state-of-the-art [ˌsteɪtəvðɪ'ɑːt]	auf dem neuesten Stand der Technik

Unit 16

	application [ˌæplɪ'keɪʃn]	Bewerbung
	vacancy ['veɪkənsɪ]	offene Stelle
	openings ['əʊpnɪŋz]	offene Stellen
	to differ ['dɪfə]	unterschiedlich sein
	job exchanges ['dʒɒb ɪksˌtʃeɪndʒɪz]	Job-, Stellenbörsen

source [sɔ:s] — Quelle
job specification [ˌdʒɒb ˌspesɪfɪ'keɪʃn] — Stellenbeschreibung
notification [ˌnəʊtɪfɪ'keɪʃn] — Benachrichtigung
suitable ['su:təbl] — geeignet
to turn up [tɜ:n 'ʌp] — auftauchen
directory [daɪ'rektərɪ, dɪ'rektərɪ] — Nachschlagewerk
recruitment agencies [rɪ'kru:tmənt ˌeɪdʒənsɪz] — Stellenvermittlungsagenturen
unsolicited [ˌʌnsə'lɪsɪtɪd] — unverlangt
on the off-chance [ɒn ðɪ‿'ɒftʃɑ:ns] — auf Verdacht
to recruit [rɪ'kru:t] — einstellen
1 **first-rate** [ˌfɜ:st'reɪt] — erstklassig
skin care ['skɪn ˌkeə] — Hautpflege
to seek, sought, sought [si:k, sɔ:t, sɔ:t] — suchen
employment [ɪm'plɔɪmənt] — Beschäftigung
challenging ['tʃælɪndʒɪŋ] — herausfordernd
fast-paced [ˌfɑ:st'peɪst] — tempogeladen
enthusiasm [ɪn'θju:zɪæzm] — Begeisterung
applicant ['æplɪkənt] — Bewerber/in
experience [ɪk'spɪərɪəns] — Erfahrung
PC literate [ˌpi:si:'lɪtrət] — PC-erfahren
to meet deadlines [mi:t‿'dedlaɪnz] — Termine/Fristen einhalten
salary ['sælərɪ] — Gehalt
accommodation [əˌkɒmə'deɪʃn] — Unterkunft, Wohnung
CV (curriculum vitae) [ˌsi:'vi: (kəˌrɪkjələm 'vi:taɪ)] — tabellarischer Lebenslauf
covering letter ['kʌvərɪŋ ˌletə] — Begleitschreiben
bilingual [baɪ'lɪŋgwəl] — zweisprachig
fluent ['flu:ənt] — fließend
a good command of English [ə ˌgʊd kəˌmɑ:nd əv 'ɪŋglɪʃ] — gute Englischkenntnisse
familiarity [fəˌmɪlɪ'ærətɪ] — Vertrautheit
procedures [prə'si:dʒəz] — Verfahren
to enclose [ɪn'kləʊz] — beifügen
tour operator ['tʊər‿ˌɒpəreɪtə] — Reiseveranstalter
admin and accounts [ˌædmɪn ən‿ə'kaʊnts] — Verwaltung und Rechnungswesen
background ['bækgraʊnd] — *(hier:)* Ausbildung/Erfahrung
desirable [dɪ'zaɪərəbl] — wünschenswert
2 **based in** ['beɪst ɪn] — mit Sitz in
mother tongue [ˌmʌðə 'tʌŋ] — Muttersprache
essential [ɪ'senʃl] — wichtig, wesentlich
PC-literacy [ˌpi:si:'lɪtrəsɪ] — PC-Kenntnisse
3 **to equip** [ɪ'kwɪp] — *(hier:)* befähigen, *(sonst:)* ausstatten, ausrüsten
4 **school-leaving certificate** [ˌsku:l‿li:vɪŋ sə'tɪfɪkət] — Schulabschlusszeugnis
brief(ly) [bri:f(lɪ)] — kurz
to complete [kəm'pli:t] — abschließen
publisher's assistant ['pʌblɪʃəz əˌsɪstənt] — Verlagskaufmann/-frau
publishing house ['pʌblɪʃɪŋ ˌhaʊs] — Verlag

A Letter of application

person to contact [ˌpɜ:sn tə 'kɒntækt] — Kontaktperson
main branch [ˌmeɪn 'brɑ:ntʃ] — Hauptfiliale
details ['di:teɪlz] — Einzelheiten
placement ['pleɪsmənt] — Praktikum
certified ['sɜ:tɪfaɪd] — beglaubigt
referee [ˌrefər'i:] — *(hier:)* jemand, der eine Empfehlung / ein Zeugnis schreibt
2 **keen** [ki:n] — sehr interessiert, eifrig
enclosure [ɪn'kləʊʒə] — Anlage

B Curriculum Vitae (CV)

neat(ly) [ni:t(lɪ)] — ordentlich, adrett
equivalent [ɪ'kwɪvələnt] — Entsprechung
to paraphrase ['pærəfreɪz] — umschreiben
impression [ɪm'preʃn] — Eindruck
aware [ə'weə] — bewusst
denomination [dɪˌnɒmɪ'neɪʃn] — Konfession (Religion)
to reverse [rɪ'vɜ:s] — umkehren
temporary ['tempərərɪ] — vorübergehend, befristet
travel agency ['trævl ˌeɪdʒənsɪ] — Reisebüro
command [kə'mɑ:nd] — *(hier:)* Beherrschung
to enrol [ɪn'rəʊl] — sich einschreiben
accounting [ə'kaʊntɪŋ] — Rechnungswesen
social service [ˌsəʊʃl 'sɜ:vɪs] — Ersatzdienst
in lieu of [ɪn 'lju:‿əv] — an Stelle von
handicapped ['hændɪkæpt] — behindert
3 **to put through** [pʊt‿'θru:] — verbinden
human resources (department) [ˌhju:mən 'ri:sɔ:sɪz (dɪˌpɑ:tmənt)] — Personalabteilung
to give notice [ˌgɪv 'nəʊtɪs] — *(hier:)* im Voraus Bescheid sagen
inconvenient [ˌɪnkən'vi:nɪənt] — ungünstig

C Interviews

to meet with approval [ˌmi:t wɪð ə'pru:vl] — auf Zustimmung stoßen
to be put on a shortlist [bɪ ˌpʊt ɒn‿ə 'ʃɔ:tlɪst] — in die engere Auswahl kommen
to project an image [prəˌdʒekt ən 'ɪmɪdʒ] — ein Image projizieren
beforehand [bɪ'fɔ:hænd] — vorher
further training [ˌfɜ:ðə 'treɪnɪŋ] — Weiterbildung
gym [dʒɪm] — Turnhalle, Fitness-Center
in advance [ɪn əd'vɑ:ns] — im Voraus
to underestimate [ˌʌndər'estɪmeɪt] — unterschätzen
to tuck into [ˌtʌk 'ɪntu:] — hineinstecken in
polished ['pɒlɪʃt] — mit Schuhcreme geputzt, poliert
laces ['leɪsɪz] — Schnürsenkel
to tie [taɪ] — binden
to comb [kəʊm] — kämmen
to go for ['gəʊ fə] — wählen
suit [su:t] — Kostüm (Damen), Anzug
2 **annual holidays** [ˌænjʊəl 'hɒlɪdeɪz] — Jahresurlaub
smart [smɑ:t] — ordentlich, gepflegt, schick
bored [bɔ:d] — gelangweilt
strengths [streŋkθs] — Stärken

4	**electronic components** [elekˌtrɒnɪk‿kəm'pəʊnənts]	elektronische Bauelemente
	tailored suit [ˌteɪləd 'su:t]	Kostüm
	navy blue [ˌneɪvɪ 'blu:]	dunkelblau
	letting agent ['letɪŋ ˌeɪdʒənt]	Makler/in für Mietimmobilien, -wohnungen
	to give notice [ˌgɪv 'nəʊtɪs]	*(hier:)* kündigen
5	**to do an apprenticeship / a traineeship** [ˌdu:‿ən ə'prentɪʃɪp / ə ˌtreɪ'ni:ʃɪp]	eine Ausbildung machen
	manufacturing (industry) [ˌmænjə'fæktʃərɪŋ (ˌɪndəstrɪ)]	verarbeitende Industrie
	to need, to require [ni:d, rɪ'kwaɪə]	benötigen
	Austria ['ɒstrɪə]	Österreich
	advertisement ['ædvətaɪzmənt, əd'vɜ:tɪsmənt]	Anzeige
6	**previous** ['pri:vɪəs]	früher, vorhergehend
	eventually [ɪ'ventʃʊəlɪ]	mit der Zeit, schließlich
	to set up in business on one's own [set ˌʌp ɪn 'bɪznɪs ɒn wʌnz‿əʊn]	eine eigene Firma gründen
	reference ['refrəns]	Arbeitszeugnis
	rapport [ræ'pɔ:, rə'pɔ:]	Verhältnis
	manner ['mænə]	Umgangsstil
	to faze [feɪz]	aus der Fassung bringen
	praise [preɪz]	Lob
	to drop [drɒp]	sinken, fallen (lassen)
	unappreciated [ˌʌnə'pri:ʃieɪtɪd]	nicht genügend geschätzt
	reputation [ˌrepjə'teɪʃn]	Ruf
	approach [ə'prəʊtʃ]	Haltung, Herangehensweise, Ansatz
	equal opportunities employer [ˌi:kwəl ɒpə'tju:nətɪz ɪmˌplɔɪə]	Firma, der Chancengleichheit ein Anliegen ist
	promotion [prə'məʊʃn]	Beförderung
7	**able to work in a team** [ˌeɪbl tʊ ˌwɜ:k ɪn‿ə 'ti:m]	teamfähig
	field (of work) [fi:ld (əv‿wɜ:k)]	Arbeitsgebiet

D Employment in the EU

	free movement of labour [ˌfri: ˌmu:vmənt əv 'leɪbə]	Freizügigkeit der Arbeitnehmer, freie Wahl des Arbeitsplatzes
	permit ['pɜ:mɪt]	Genehmigung, Erlaubnis
	to take up residence [ˌteɪk ʌp 'rezɪdəns]	wohnhaft werden
1	**work placement** ['wɜ:k ˌpleɪsmənt]	Praktikum
	logistics and warehousing operation [ləˌdʒɪstɪks ənd 'weəhaʊzɪŋ‿ɒpəˌreɪʃn]	Logistik- und Lagerungsunternehmen
	residence permit ['rezɪdəns ˌpɜ:mɪt]	Aufenthaltsgenehmigung
	green card [ˌgri:n‿'kɑ:d]	Arbeitserlaubnis für die USA
	unemployment [ˌʌnɪm'plɔɪmənt]	Arbeitslosigkeit
	landlady ['lændˌleɪdɪ]	Vermieterin
2	**to promote** [prə'məʊt]	befördern
	right away [ˌraɪtə'weɪ]	sofort
3	**to acquire** [ə'kwaɪə]	kaufen, übernehmen
	to dread sth. [dred]	Angst vor etwas haben
	to keep one's fingers crossed [ˌki:p wʌnz 'fɪŋgəz ˌkrɒst]	den Daumen halten
	to bear with s.o. [beə 'wɪð ˌsʌmwʌn]	*(hier:)* so lange warten (am Telefon)
	to go through the usual channels [ˌgəʊ θru: ðə 'ju:ʒʊəl ˌtʃænlz]	die üblichen Instanzen durchlaufen
	to appeal [ə'pi:l]	*(hier:)* appellieren
	to approach [ə'prəʊtʃ]	*(hier:)* ansprechen, anschreiben
	on request [ɒn rɪ'kwest]	wenn gewünscht, *(sonst:)* auf Anfrage
	obvious(ly) ['ɒbvɪəs(lɪ)]	offensichtlich

E The European Union

1	**unified** ['ju:nɪfaɪd]	einheitlich
	single market [ˌsɪŋgl 'mɑ:kɪt]	Binnenmarkt
	free movement of goods [ˌfri: ˌmu:vmənt əv 'gʊdz]	freier Warenverkehr
	furthest ['fɜ:ðɪst]	am weitesten
	advanced [əd'vɑ:nst]	fortgeschritten
	imperfections [ˌɪmpə'fekʃnz]	Mängel
	to take advantage of [ˌteɪk əd'vɑ:ntɪdʒ ɒv]	ausnutzen, in Anspruch nehmen
2	**to estimate** ['estɪmeɪt]	schätzen
	regulation [ˌregjə'leɪʃn]	Vorschrift, Regelung
	to affect [ə'fekt]	sich auswirken auf
	to originate [ə'rɪdʒəneɪt]	den Ursprung haben
	to nominate ['nɒmɪneɪt]	ernennen
	to appoint [ə'pɔɪnt]	bestellen, ernennen
	to elect [ɪ'lekt]	wählen
	portfolio [pɔ:t'fəʊlɪəʊ]	*(hier:)* Ressort (Tätigkeitsbereich)
	to endorse [ɪn'dɔ:s]	*(hier:)* im Amt bestätigen
	treaty ['tri:tɪ]	Vertrag (zwischen Staaten)
	to violate ['vaɪəleɪt]	verstoßen gegen
	to impose [ɪm'pəʊz]	verhängen (Strafe)
	fine [faɪn]	Geldstrafe
	directives [daɪ'rektɪvz, dɪ'rektɪvz]	Richtlinien
	proposals [prə'pəʊzlz]	Vorschläge
	legislation [ˌledʒɪ'sleɪʃn]	Gesetze
	budget ['bʌdʒɪt]	Haushalt
	fiscal ['fɪskl]	steuerpolitisch
	issues ['ɪʃu:z]	Fragen
	to deal with ['di:l wɪð]	behandeln
	legitimacy [lɪ'dʒɪtɪməsɪ]	Legitimität
	country of origin [ˌkʌntrɪ‿əv 'ɒrɪdʒɪn]	Herkunftsland
	to suffer ['sʌfə]	leiden
	participation [pɑ:ˌtɪsɪ'peɪʃn]	*(hier:)* Wahlbeteiligung
	powers ['paʊəz]	Befugnisse
	to monitor ['mɒnɪtə]	kontrollieren
	to reject [rɪ'dʒekt]	ablehnen
1	**member country** ['membə ˌkʌntrɪ]	Mitgliedsstaat
	to make/take decisions [ˌmeɪk/ˌteɪk dɪ'sɪʒnz]	Entscheidungen treffen

(AE) = American English
(BE) = British English

A

abbreviation [əˌbriːvɪ'eɪʃn] Abkürzung 101
ability [ə'bɪlətɪ] Fähigkeit 88
able to work in a team [ˌeɪbl tʊ ˌwɜːk ɪn‿ə 'tiːm] teamfähig 220
abroad [ə'brɔːd] im/ins/aus dem Ausland 35
to absorb [əb'zɔːb] aufnehmen 89
access ['ækses] Zugang 43
accessories [ək'sesərɪz] Accessoires, Zubehör 204
accident ['æksɪdənt] Unfall 78
to accommodate [ə'kɒmədeɪt] aufnehmen, unterbringen, entgegenkommen 151
accommodation [əˌkɒmə'deɪʃn] Unterkunft, Wohnung 208
to accompany [ə'kʌmpənɪ] begleiten 155
according to [ə'kɔːdɪŋ‿tʊ] entsprechend, gemäß 89
account [ə'kaʊnt] Konto 163
accountant [ə'kaʊntənt] Bilanzprüfer/in, Buchprüfer/in 48
to account for [ə'kaʊnt fɔː] ausmachen 96
account-holder [ə'kaʊntˌhəʊldə] Kontoinhaber/in 165
accounting [ə'kaʊntɪŋ] Rechnungswesen 215
accounts [ə'kaʊnts] Rechnungsabteilung, Buchhaltung, Rechnungswesen 55
accurate(ly) ['ækjərət(lɪ)] genau, präzise, akkurat 59
to ache [eɪk] schmerzen, wehtun 55
to achieve [ə'tʃiːv] erreichen, erzielen 201
a couple of [ə 'kʌpl əv] ein paar 198
to acquire [ə'kwaɪə] sich aneignen 88
actually ['æktʃʊəlɪ] eigentlich 194
additions [ə'dɪʃnz] Hinzufügungen 80
additional [ə'dɪʃənl] zusätzlich 64
addressee [ˌædres'iː] Adressat, Empfänger 102
to adjust [ə'dʒʌst] anpassen, sich anpassen 132
adjustment [ə'dʒʌstmənt] Ausgleich, Bereinigung, Erledigung 176
admin and accounts [ˌædmɪn ən‿ə'kaʊnts] Verwaltung und Rechnungswesen 208
administration [ədˌmɪnɪ'streɪʃn] Verwaltung 48
administrator [əd'mɪnɪstreɪtə] Vergleichs-, Vermögensverwalter 173
admirable ['ædmərəbl] bewundernswert, ausgezeichnet 134
adult ['ædʌlt] Erwachsene/r 166
to advance [əd'vɑːns] vorschießen, auslegen 165
advanced [əd'vɑːnst] fortgeschritten 222
advantage [əd'vɑːntɪdʒ] Vorteil 66
advent ['ædvent] Ankunft 53
advertisement [əd'vɜːtɪsmənt, 'ædvətaɪz‿mənt] Anzeige 118
advertising ['ædvətaɪzɪŋ] Werbung 147
advertising agency ['ædvətaɪzɪŋ ˌeɪd‿ʒənsɪ] Werbeagentur 8
advertising assistant ['ædvətaɪzɪŋ əˌsɪstənt] Kaufmann/-frau für Marketingkommunikation 8
advertising campaign ['ædvətaɪzɪŋ‿kæmˌpeɪn] Werbekampagne, -feldzug 116
to advise [əd'vaɪz] (be)raten; benachrichtigen 104
advisory services [əd'vaɪzərɪ ˌsɜːvɪsɪz] Beratungsdienst 196
to affect [ə'fekt] sich auswirken auf 223
affluent ['æflʊənt] wohlhabend 199
age group ['eɪdʒ ˌgruːp] Altersgruppe 193
agenda [ə'dʒendə] Tagesordnung; Termine 75
agent ['eɪdʒənt] (Handels-)Vertreter/in 116
air-conditioning ['eəkənˌdɪʃənɪŋ] Klimaanlage 24
air freight ['eə ˌfreɪt] Luftfracht 112
airline ['eəlaɪn] Fluggesellschaft 197
airy ['eərɪ] luftig 24
aisle [aɪl] Gang (Flugzeug/Kirche/Supermarkt) 77
alteration [ˌɒltə'reɪʃn, ˌɔːltə'reɪʃn] Änderung 186
amateur chefs [ˌæmətjʊə 'ʃefs] Hobbyköche 27
amazing [ə'meɪzɪŋ] erstaunlich 35
ambitious [æm'bɪʃəs] ehrgeizig, anspruchsvoll 92
among [ə'mʌŋ] unter 18
amount [ə'maʊnt] Betrag, Summe 157
ample ['æmpl] reichlich, üppig 187
ancient ['eɪnʃnt] alt 23
anger ['æŋgə] Zorn 176
annual holidays [ˌænjʊəl 'hɒlɪdeɪz] Jahresurlaub 218
answering machine ['ɑːnsərɪŋ məˌʃiːn] Anrufbeantworter 54
to antagonize [æn'tægənaɪz] vor den Kopf stoßen 184
apart from [ə'pɑːt frəm] abgesehen von 34
apology [ə'pɒlədʒɪ] Entschuldigung 82
appeal [ə'piːl] Anziehung(skraft) 199
to appeal to [ə'piːl tuː] ansprechen, gefallen; appellieren 109
appetising ['æpətaɪzɪŋ] schmackhaft 47
apple juice ['æpl ˌdʒuːs] Apfelsaft 19
appliances [ə'plaɪənsɪz] Geräte 54
applicant ['æplɪkənt] Bewerber/in 208
application [ˌæplɪ'keɪʃn] Bewerbung 207
applications [ˌæplɪ'keɪʃnz] Anwendungen, Funktionen 54
to appoint [ə'pɔɪnt] bestellen, ernennen 223
appointment [ə'pɔɪntmənt] *(hier:)* Treffen, Termin 66
approach [ə'prəʊtʃ] Haltung, Herangehensweise, Ansatz 219
to approach [ə'prəʊtʃ] sich nähern, herangehen an, ansprechen 198
appropriate [ə'prəʊprɪət] geeignet, passend, angebracht 102
approval [ə'pruːvl] Billigung, Zustimmung, Beifall 142
approx(imately) [ə'prɒks(ɪmətlɪ)] ungefähr, ca. 95
to arise, arose, arisen [ə'raɪz, ə'rəʊz, ə'rɪzn] entstehen, auftreten 98
to arouse [ə'raʊz] wecken (Interesse, Gefühle) 89
artificial [ˌɑːtɪ'fɪʃl] künstlich 148
as a result of [əz‿ə rɪ'zʌlt əv] auf Grund 18
as a rule [əz‿ə 'ruːl] in der Regel 79
as a whole [əz‿ə 'həʊl] insgesamt 88
a set break [ə ˌset 'breɪk] eine Pause zu festgesetzter Zeit 47
as long as stocks last [əz ˌlɒŋ əz‿ˌstɒks 'lɑːst] solange Vorrat reicht 126
asparagus [ə'spærəgəs] Spargel 26
to assess [ə'ses] *(hier:)* bewerten, einschätzen 92
to assist [ə'sɪst] helfen 207
assistance [ə'sɪstəns] Hilfe 81
to associate with [ə'səʊʃɪeɪt wɪð] in Verbindung bringen mit 199
association [əˌsəʊʃɪ'eɪʃn] Vereinigung, Verband 128
assortment [ə'sɔːtmənt] Sortiment, Auswahl 129
to assume [ə'sjuːm] annehmen, von etwas ausgehen 103
assurance [ə'ʃɔːrəns] Zusicherung, Versicherung 155
athlete ['æθliːt] Sportler/in, Athlet/in 33
athletics [æθ'letɪks] (Leicht-)Athletik 37
ATM (automated teller machine) [ˌeɪtiː'em, ˌɔːtəmeɪtɪd‿'telə məˌʃiːn] Geldautomat 165
at short notice [ət ˌʃɔːt‿'nəʊtɪs] kurzfristig, ohne lange Voranmeldung 57
at sight [ət 'saɪt] bei Sicht 165

to attach [ə'tætʃ] anhängen (Datei), befestigen, anbringen 101
attached [ə'tætʃt] angeschlossen 47
attachment (email) [ə'tætʃmənt] Anhang 84
to attempt [ə'tempt] versuchen, sich bemühen 32
to attend [ə'tend] besuchen (Messe, Schule) 202
to attend a course [əˌtend ə 'kɔ:s] an einem Kurs teilnehmen 180
to attend a fair [əˌtend ə 'feə] an einer Messe teilnehmen 75
at the bottom [ət‿ðə 'bɒtm] unten 95
at the latest *(nachgestellt)* [ət‿ðə 'leɪtɪst] spätestens 148
at the top [ət‿ðə 'tɒp] oben, an der Spitze 95
at your disposal [ət‿jɔ: dɪ'spəʊzl] zur Verfügung 89
at your earliest convenience [ət‿jɔ:r‿ˌɜ:lɪəst kən'vi:nɪəns] so bald wie möglich 163
audience ['ɔ:dɪəns] Publikum 88
authenticity [ɔ:θen'tɪsɪtɪ] Echtheit 99
author ['ɔ:θə] Verfasser/in, Autor/in, *(hier:)* Urheber/in 68
automobile sales management assistant [ˌɔ:təməʊbi:l ˌseɪlz 'mænɪdʒmənt əˌsɪstənt] Automobilkaufmann/-frau 11
available [ə'veɪləbl] erhältlich 145
average ['ævrɪdʒ] Durchschnitt 166
average consumer [ˌævrɪdʒ kən'sju:mə] Durchschnittsverbraucher 151
average price [ˌævrɪdʒ 'praɪs] Durchschnittspreis 94
to avoid [ə'vɔɪd] vermeiden 66
to award points [əˌwɔ:d‿'pɔɪnts] Punkte vergeben (z. B. Wettbewerb) 92
aware [ə'weə] bewusst 212
awful ['ɔ:fəl] scheußlich, schrecklich 19

B

background ['bækgraʊnd] *(hier:)* Ausbildung/Erfahrung 208
backlit ['bæklɪt] von hinten/innen beleuchtet 130
back office [ˌbæk 'ɒfɪs] Büro ohne Publikumsverkehr 43
to bake [beɪk] backen, im Ofen braten 26
balance ['bæləns] Rest, Saldo; Gleichgewicht 134
to balance ['bæləns] ausgleichen, ins Gleichgewicht bringen 173
balanced ['bælənst] ausgewogen 24
bale [beɪl] Ballen 154
ballet ['bæleɪ] (klassisches) Ballett 8
bank business management assistant [ˌbæŋk ˌbɪznɪs 'mænɪdʒmənt əˌsɪstənt] Bankkaufmann/-frau 9
bank clerk ['bæŋk‿klɑ:k] Bankkaufmann/-frau 8
banknote ['bæŋknəʊt] Geldschein 162
bank transfer ['bæŋk ˌtrænsfɜ:] Banküberweisung 144
bar chart ['bɑ: ˌtʃɑ:t] Balkendiagramm 93
barman/barmaid ['bɑ:mən/'bɑ:meɪd] Bedienung hinter der Theke 79
based in ['beɪst ɪn] mit Sitz in 209
basically ['beɪsɪklɪ] im Grunde 147
battery ['bætərɪ] Batterie 130
Bavarian cuisine [bəˌveərɪən kwɪz'i:n] bayerische Küche 75
to be able [bɪ‿'eɪbl] in der Lage sein 194
bean [bi:n] Bohne 26
bearer ['beərə] *(hier:)* Überbringer 165
to bear with someone [beə 'wɪð ˌsʌmwʌn] *(hier:)* etwas Geduld haben 55
beauty consultant ['bju:tɪ kənˌsʌltənt] Kosmetiker/in 195
to be aware of a problem [bɪ‿əˌweər‿əv ə 'prɒbləm] sich eines Problems bewusst sein 169
to become aware [bɪˌkʌm ə'weə] bewusst werden 91
to be cooperative [bɪ kəʊ'ɒprətɪv] zur Zusammenarbeit bereit sein 184
beef broth [ˌbi:f 'brɒθ] Fleischbrühe 26
to be entitled [bɪ‿ɪn'taɪtld] berechtigt sein, Anspruch haben 167
beetle ['bi:tl] Käfer 177
beforehand [bɪ'fɔ:hænd] vorher 217
to be in a hurry [bɪ‿ɪn ə 'hʌrɪ] es eilig haben 194
to be inclined [bɪ‿ɪn'klaɪnd] dazu neigen, geneigt sein 113
to be in demand [bɪ‿ɪn dɪ'mɑ:nd] gefragt sein, nachgefragt werden 147
to be in line with [bɪ‿ɪn 'laɪn wɪð] übereinstimmen, im Einklang stehen mit 108
to be in progress [bɪ‿ɪn 'prəʊgres] im Gang sein 186
to be likely [bɪ 'laɪklɪ] wahrscheinlich sein, wahrscheinlich geschehen 99
bend [bend] Kurve 22
to benefit ['benəfɪt] profitieren 196
to be on a familiar footing [bɪ‿ɒn ə fəˌmɪlɪə 'fʊtɪŋ] auf vertrautem Fuße stehen 103
to be on hand [bɪ‿ɒn 'hænd] zugegen sein, da sein 81
to be put on a shortlist [bɪ ˌpʊt ɒn‿ə 'ʃɔ:tlɪst] in die engere Auswahl kommen 217
berry ['berɪ] Beere 27
to be subject to [bɪ 'sʌbdʒɪkt‿tu:] unterliegen, abhängen von, unterworfen sein 126
to be to blame [bɪ tʊ 'bleɪm] schuld sein 186
to be up to [bɪ‿'ʌp tu:] im Schilde führen, anstellen 202
beverage wholesaler [ˌbevərɪdʒ 'həʊlˌseɪlə] Getränkegroßhandlung 119
BIC (bank identifier code) [ˌbi:aɪ'si: (ˌbæŋk aɪ'dentɪfaɪə ˌkəʊd)] Internationaler Bank-Code 163
bilingual [baɪ'lɪŋgwəl] zweisprachig 208
bill [bɪl] Rechnung 80
billboards *(AE)* ['bɪlbɔ:dz] Plakatwände 199
bill of exchange [bɪl‿əv ɪks'tʃeɪndʒ] Wechsel 165
bill of lading (B/L) [ˌbɪl‿əv 'leɪdɪŋ] Konnossement, Seefrachtbrief 158
biro ['baɪrəʊ] Kugelschreiber 44
blank [blæŋk] unbeschrieben, leer 101
blunt(ly) [blʌnt(lɪ)] *(hier:)* unverblümt 184
board meetings ['bɔ:d ˌmi:tɪŋz] Vorstandssitzungen 90
body language ['bɒdɪ ˌlæŋgwɪdʒ] Körpersprache 91
to boil [bɔɪl] kochen, sieden 26
bold type [ˌbəʊld‿'taɪp] Fettdruck 108
booking charge ['bʊkɪŋ ˌtʃɑ:dʒ] Buchungsgebühr 63
booking reference ['bʊkɪŋ ˌrefrəns] Buchungsnummer 77
to bore [bɔ:] langweilen 90
bored [bɔ:d] gelangweilt 218
both ... and ... [bəʊθ ... ənd ...] sowohl ... als auch ... 105
brackets ['brækɪts] Klammern 101
branch [brɑ:ntʃ] Filiale 195
brand [brænd] Marke, Markenartikel 197
breadcrumbs ['bredkrʌmz] Brotkrümel, Paniermehl 25
to break bulk [ˌbreɪk 'bʌlk] große Gebinde aufbrechen 195
brewery ['bru:ərɪ] Brauerei 23
brief(ly) [bri:f(lɪ)] kurz 7
briefcase ['bri:fkeɪs] Aktentasche 90
bright [braɪt] hell, glänzend 145
bright yellow [ˌbraɪt 'jeləʊ] leuchtend gelb 23
to bring forward [ˌbrɪŋ 'fɔ:wəd] vorziehen, vorverlegen 105
brochure ['brəʊʃə] Broschüre, Prospekt 33
Brussels sprouts [ˌbrʌslz‿'spraʊts] Rosenkohl 26
bubbles ['bʌblz] Blasen, Bläschen 17
budget ['bʌdʒɪt] Haushalt 223
building materials ['bɪldɪŋ məˌtɪərɪəlz] Baustoffe, -material 12
building site ['bɪldɪŋ ˌsaɪt] Baustelle 177
bulk goods [ˌbʌlk‿'gʊdz] Massen-, Schüttgüter 152

bulky ['bʌlkɪ] sperrig, unhandlich, übergroß 152
bumpy ['bʌmpɪ] unruhig, holprig 18
bundle with steel strapping [ˌbʌndl wɪð ˌsti:l 'stræpɪŋ] Bündel mit Stahlbandumreifung 154
business relations ['bɪznɪs rɪˌleɪʃnz] Geschäftsbeziehungen 128
business section ['bɪznɪs‿ˌsekʃn] Gewerbeteil 54
business terms ['bɪznɪs ˌtɜ:mz] Geschäftsbedingungen 116
business unit, division ['bɪznɪs ˌju:nɪt, dɪ'vɪʒn] Geschäftseinheit 173
business venture ['bɪznɪs ˌventʃə] geschäftliches Unternehmen 25
buyer ['baɪə] Einkäufer/in 202
by means of [ˌbaɪ 'mi:nz‿əv] mittels 166
by return [baɪ rɪ'tɜ:n] umgehend 104

C

cabbage ['kæbɪdʒ] Kohl 25
calculator ['kælkjəleɪtə] Taschenrechner 44
calm [kɑ:m] ruhig, gelassen 176
calorie count ['kælərɪ ˌkaʊnt] Kalorienangabe 47
to cancel an invoice [ˌkænsl ən 'ɪnvɔɪs] eine Rechnung stornieren 173
to cancel an order [ˌkænsl ən 'ɔ:də] einen Auftrag annullieren 179
canteen [kæn'ti:n] Kantine 21
capable ['keɪpəbl] in der Lage, fähig, tüchtig 35
to capitalize ['kæpɪtəlaɪz] in Großbuchstaben schreiben 103
to capture ['kæptʃə] (ein)fangen 145
carbon paper ['kɑ:bn ˌpeɪpə] Kohlepapier 101
car carrier ['kɑ: ˌkærɪə] Autotransporter, -transportschiff 151
cardholder ['kɑ:dˌhəʊldə] Karteninhaber/in 165
care [keə] Sorgfalt 185
cargo ['kɑ:gəʊ] (See-)Fracht, Ladung 151
car hire/rental company ['kɑ:ˌhaɪə/ˌrentl ˌkʌmpənɪ] Mietwagenfirma 78
carnivorous [kɑ:'nɪvərəs] fleischfressend 25
carriage ['kærɪdʒ] Transport(kosten), Fracht(kosten) 136
carriage by sea [ˌkærɪdʒ baɪ 'si:] Seetransport 152
carrier ['kærɪə] Frachtführer 151
carrots ['kærəts] Möhren, Karotten 26
to carry out work [ˌkærɪ‿aʊt 'wɜ:k] Arbeit ausführen 127
cash discount [ˌkæʃ 'dɪskaʊnt] Skonto, Barzahlungsrabatt 167
cash on delivery [ˌkæʃ‿ɒn dɪ'lɪvərɪ] Zahlung durch Nachnahme / bei Lieferung 167
cash payment [ˌkæʃ 'peɪmənt] Barzahlung 166
cash point ['kæʃpɔɪnt] Geldautomat 165
cash with order [ˌkæʃ wɪð 'ɔ:də] Bezahlung bei Auftragserteilung 128
casual ['kæʒjʊəl] zwanglos 6
to catch [kætʃ] *(hier:)* mitbekommen 57
to cater for ['keɪtə fɔ:] *(hier:)* etwas bieten für 75
cauliflower ['kɒlɪˌflaʊə] Blumenkohl 26
celebrated ['seləbreɪtɪd] gefeiert 133
celebrity [sə'lebrətɪ] Berühmtheit 202
certificate of origin [səˌtɪfɪkət‿əv 'ɒrɪd‿ʒɪn] Ursprungszeugnis 158
certified ['sɜ:tɪfaɪd] beglaubigt 210
chair, chairperson [tʃeə, 'tʃeəˌpɜ:sn] Vorsitzende/r 82
chairman ['tʃeəmən] Vorsitzender 82
chairman of the board [ˌtʃeəmən əv‿ðə 'bɔ:d] Vorstandsvorsitzender 48
challenging ['tʃælɪndʒɪŋ] herausfordernd 208
change(s) [tʃeɪndʒ, 'tʃeɪndʒɪz] Veränderung 201
change [tʃeɪndʒ] Wechselgeld 80
changeable ['tʃeɪndʒəbl] wechselhaft 19
channel ['tʃænl] *(hier:)* Vertriebsweg 193
characters ['kærəktəz] *(hier:)* Buchstaben, Zeichen 101
characteristic feature [ˌkærəktərɪstɪk 'fi:tʃə] typisches Merkmal 196
charge [tʃɑ:dʒ] Belastung, Gebühr 133
to charge [tʃɑ:dʒ] *(hier:)* berechnen 193
cheap chain ['tʃi:p ˌtʃeɪn] Billigladenkette 193
to check [tʃek] (über)prüfen 198
check-out ['tʃekaʊt] (Supermarkt-)Kasse 166
chemist ['kemɪst] Apotheker/in 195
cheque *(BE)*, **check** *(AE)* [tʃek] Scheck 165
chief accountant [ˌtʃi:f ə'kaʊntənt] Leiter/in des Rechnungswesens 21
chief executive officer (CEO) [ˌtʃi:f ɪgˌzekjətɪv 'ɒfɪsə] Firmenchef/in, Vorstandsvorsitzende/r 48
chilled [tʃɪld] eisgekühlt 25
to choose [tʃu:z] wählen 77
to chop [tʃɒp] klein schneiden, hacken 26
clean bill of lading ['kli:n ˌbɪl‿əv 'leɪdɪŋ] reines Konnossement 167
clerical staff ['klerɪkl ˌstɑ:f] Büropersonal, Sachbearbeiter 74
closely followed by [ˌkləʊslɪ 'fɒləʊd‿baɪ] *(hier:)* dicht gefolgt von 95
club [klʌb] Disko 18
coaching ['kəʊtʃɪŋ] Training 180
coffee table ['kɒfɪ ˌteɪbl] Couchtisch 157
coil on euro-pallet [ˌkɔɪl ɒn 'ju:rəʊˌpælɪt] Rolle, Coil auf Europalette 154
coin [kɔɪn] Münze, Geldstück 162
to collect [kə'lekt] abholen, (ein)sammeln 142
to collect the invoice amount [kəˌlekt‿ðɪ‿'ɪnvɔɪs əˌmaʊnt] den Rechnungsbetrag eintreiben 169
colour printer ['kʌlə ˌprɪntə] Farbdrucker 132
to comb [kəʊm] kämmen 217
to come across [ˌkʌm ə'krɒs] *(hier:)* wirken 63
comeback ['kʌmbæk] *(hier:)* Reaktion 55
comfort ['kʌmfət] Behaglichkeit, Komfort; Trost 128
comfortable ['kʌmftəbl] bequem 163
command [kə'mɑ:nd] *(hier:)* Beherrschung 213
commencement [kə'mensmənt] Anfang, Beginn 134
commercial invoice [kəˌmɜ:ʃl 'ɪnvɔɪs] Handelsrechnung 155
to commission [kə'mɪʃn] beauftragen 178
commission [kə'mɪʃn] Provision 35
commitment to [kə'mɪtmənt‿tu:] Engagement für 202
communication [kəˌmju:nɪ'keɪʃn] Nachricht, Mitteilung, Information 169
community [kə'mju:nətɪ] Gemeinschaft 202
comparative(ly) [kəm'pærətɪv(lɪ)] verhältnismäßig 167
to compare [kəm'peə] vergleichen 197
comparing prices [kəmˌpeərɪŋ 'praɪsɪz] Preisvergleich 198
to compensate ['kɒmpənseɪt] entschädigen 171
to compete [kəm'pi:t] an einem Wettkampf teilnehmen, konkurrieren 33
competition [ˌkɒmpə'tɪʃn] Konkurrenz, Wettbewerb 132
competitive prices [kəmˌpetətɪv 'praɪsɪz] günstige, konkurrenzfähige Preise 194
competitor [kəm'petɪtə] Mitbewerber/in 84
complaint [kəm'pleɪnt] Beschwerde, Beanstandung, Reklamation, Mängelrüge 176
to complete [kəm'pli:t] abschließen 209
complimentary close [ˌkɒmplɪmentərɪ 'kləʊz] Grußformel 100

to comply with regulations [kəm,plaɪ wɪð ˌregjə'leɪʃnz] Vorschriften einhalten 182
components [kəm'pəʊnənts] Bestandteile 100
to comprise [kəm'praɪz] umfassen 118
computer projector [kəm,pju:tə prə'dʒektə] Beamer 91
concept ['kɒnsept] Konzept, Begriff, Auffassung 141
concerns [kən'sɜ:nz] *(hier:)* Sorgen, Fragen 80
concession [kən'seʃn] Zugeständnis 111
conciliatory [kən'sɪlɪətrɪ] versöhnlich 184
concise [kən'saɪs] kurz und bündig 65
conclusion [kən'klu:ʒn] Schluss 89
to conduct a test [kən,dʌkt ə 'test] einen Test durchführen 142
confectionery [kən'fekʃənrɪ] Süßwaren 118
confident ['kɒnfɪdənt] selbstbewusst 203
to confirm [kən'fɜ:m] bestätigen 163
confirmation [ˌkɒnfə'meɪʃn] Bestätigung 77
consent [kən'sent] Zustimmung, Einwilligung 167
conservatory [kən'sɜ:vətrɪ] Wintergarten 186
to consider [kən'sɪdə] erwägen, überlegen; ansehen als 113
consideration [kən,sɪdə'reɪʃn] Erwägung, Überlegung 24
consignee [ˌkɒnsaɪ'ni:] Empfänger/in 159
consignment [kən'saɪnmənt] (Waren-) Sendung, Lieferung 152
consignment note [kən'saɪnmənt ˌnəʊt] Frachtbrief 155
conspicuous [kən'spɪkjʊəs] auffällig 23
construction work [kən'strʌkʃn ˌwɜ:k] Bauarbeiten 92
consumer [kən'sju:mə] Verbraucher/in 198
consumer goods [kən'sju:mə ˌgʊdz] Konsumgüter 199
contact person ['kɒntækt ˌpɜ:sn] Ansprechpartner/in 180
to contain [kən'teɪn] enthalten 148
content ['kɒntent] Inhalt 88
context ['kɒntekst] Zusammenhang, Kontext 99
contract ['kɒntrækt] Vertrag 99
to contribute [kən'trɪbju:t] beitragen 201
contribution [ˌkɒntrɪ'bju:ʃn] Beitrag 201
convenience food [kən'vi:nɪəns ˌfu:d] Fertiggerichte 47
convenient [kən'vi:nɪənt] bequem, praktisch 116
conventional [kən'venʃənl] herkömmlich, traditionell 194
converted [kən'vɜ:tɪd] umgebaut 43
to convince [kən'vɪns] überzeugen 129
convincing [kən'vɪnsɪŋ] überzeugend 38
cooking ['kʊkɪŋ] Art zu kochen, Küche 7
co-operation [kəʊˌɒpə'reɪʃn] Mit-, Zusammenarbeit; *(hier:)* Hilfe 105
to cope with sth. ['kəʊp wɪð ˌsʌmθɪŋ] fertig werden mit etwas, etwas schaffen 190
copper ['kɒpə] Kupfer 92
cordial ['kɔ:dɪəl] herzlich, freundlich 189
corner stand ['kɔ:nə ˌstænd] Eckstand 83
corn starch ['kɔ:n ˌstɑ:tʃ] Stärkemehl 27
corporate (e.g. culture) ['kɔ:pərət] Unternehmens- (z. B. -kultur) 90
corridor ['kɒrɪdɔ:] Gang 16
cost estimate ['kɒst ˌestɪmət] Kostenvoranschlag 126
cost price ['kɒst ˌpraɪs] Selbstkostenpreis 24
cottage ['kɒtɪdʒ] *(hier:)* Ferienhäuschen 63
country of origin [ˌkʌntrɪ‿əv 'ɒrɪdʒɪn] Herkunftsland 223
countryside ['kʌntrɪsaɪd] Landschaft, Gegend 24
court [kɔ:t] Gericht(shof), Hof 99
courtesy ['kɜ:təsɪ] Höflichkeit 185
courtyard ['kɔ:tjɑ:d] Hof 190
to cover ['kʌvə] decken, abdecken 89
covering letter ['kʌvərɪŋ ˌletə] Begleitschreiben 208
covering page ['kʌvərɪŋ ˌpeɪdʒ] Deckblatt 104
crash course ['kræʃ ˌkɔ:s] Kompaktkurs 121
crate [kreɪt] Lattenkiste 154
to create [krɪ'eɪt] (er)schaffen, erzeugen, erstellen 32
credit note ['kredɪt‿ˌnəʊt] Gutschrift 177
creditworthiness ['kredɪt,wɜ:ðɪnəs] Kreditwürdigkeit 167
crossed cheque [ˌkrɒst‿'tʃek] Verrechnungsscheck 165
crowded ['kraʊdɪd] überfüllt 79
crude oil [ˌkru:d 'ɔɪl] Rohöl 152
crystal glass [ˌkrɪstl 'glɑ:s] Kristallglas 119
cucumber ['kju:kʌmbə] Gurke 26
cues [kju:z] Stichworte 89
currency ['kʌrənsɪ] Währung 162
current ['kʌrənt] laufend, gegenwärtig, derzeitig 49
curt [kɜ:t] knapp, schroff 184
customary ['kʌstəmərɪ] üblich 167
customer base ['kʌstəmə ˌbeɪs] Kundenstamm 95
customer relations [ˌkʌstəmə rɪ'leɪʃnz] Kundendienst 55
customer service [ˌkʌstəmə 'sɜ:vɪs] Kundendienst 48
customs formalities ['kʌstəmz fɔ:ˌmælətɪz] Zollformalitäten 136
to cut off [kʌt 'ɒf] unterbrechen 57
to cut out [kʌt 'aʊt] umgehen 196
cutting-edge [ˌkʌtɪŋ 'edʒ] auf dem neuesten Stand 205
CV (curriculum vitae) [ˌsi:'vi: (kəˌrɪkjələm 'vi:taɪ)] tabellarischer Lebenslauf 208
cycling ['saɪklɪŋ] Radfahren 9

D

damage ['dæmɪdʒ] Beschädigung, Schaden 158
data processing, EDP ['deɪtə ˌprəʊsesɪŋ, ˌi:di:'pi:] Datenverarbeitung, EDV 21
deadline ['dedlaɪn] letzte Frist 123
to deal with ['di:l wɪð] behandeln 223
debit card ['debɪt‿ˌkɑ:d] Bankkarte 165
to debit to s.o.'s account [ˌdebɪt‿tʊ ˌsʌmwʌnz ə'kaʊnt] das Konto von jemandem belasten 157
debt level ['det ˌlevl] Schuldenstand 166
decade ['dekeɪd] Jahrzehnt 37
(to) decline [dɪ'klaɪn] sinken, zurückgehen; Rückgang 94
to deduct [dɪ'dʌkt] abziehen 167
to deepen ['di:pn] vertiefen 151
deer [dɪə] Rotwild 25
defective [dɪ'fektɪv] schadhaft 182
definitely ['defɪnətlɪ] auf jeden Fall 18
degree [dɪ'gri:] Grad, Ausmaß; akademischer Grad 98
delay [dɪ'leɪ] Verzögerung 66
delay in payment [dɪˌleɪ‿ɪn 'peɪmənt] Zahlungsverzug 172
to delete [dɪ'li:t] löschen, tilgen 101
delicatessens [ˌdelɪkə'tesənz] Feinkostgeschäfte 147
delighted [dɪ'laɪtɪd] entzückt, begeistert 129
delivery [dɪ'lɪvərɪ] *(hier:)* das Halten (eines Vortrags) 88; Lieferung, Auslieferung 102
denomination [dɪˌnɒmɪ'neɪʃn] Konfession (Religion) 212
department store [dɪ'pɑ:tmənt ˌstɔ:] Warenhaus, Kaufhaus 195
depending on [dɪ'pendɪŋ ɒn] je nach, abhängig von 193
to depend on [dɪ'pend ɒn] abhängen von 129
description [dɪ'skrɪpʃn] Beschreibung 143
to design [dɪ'zaɪn] entwerfen 7
desirable [dɪ'zaɪərəbl] wünschenswert 208
desires [dɪ'zaɪəz] Wünsche 194

desk [desk] Schreibtisch 44
desk research ['desk ˌri:sɜ:tʃ] (Markt-) Forschung am Schreibtisch 194
desk tidy ['desk ˌtaɪdɪ] Stifteköcher 44
despair [dɪ'speə] Verzweiflung 55
to despatch, dispatch [dɪ'spætʃ] (ab-/ver-)senden, (ab-/ver-)schicken 128
despite [dɪ'spaɪt] trotz 222
dessert [dɪ'zɜ:t] Nachspeise 25
destination [ˌdestɪ'neɪʃn] Bestimmungsort 152
to destroy [dɪ'strɔɪ] vernichten, zerstören 182
details ['di:teɪlz] Einzelheiten 210
detailed ['di:teɪld] ausführlich 112
detective novel [dɪ'tektɪv ˌnɒvl] Kriminalroman 177
to devastate ['devəsteɪt] verwüsten 171
to develop [dɪ'veləp] entwickeln 198
development [dɪ'veləpmənt] Entwicklung 197
devoted [dɪ'vəʊtɪd] gewidmet 201
dew [dju:] Tau 203
dialling tone ['daɪəlɪŋ ˌtəʊn] Freizeichen 54
diary ['daɪərɪ] Terminkalender 78
to die for [tə 'daɪ fɔ:] zum Sterben schön 203
to differ ['dɪfə] unterschiedlich sein 207
directives [daɪ'rektɪvz, dɪ'rektɪvz] Richtlinien 223
directory [daɪ'rektərɪ, dɪ'rektərɪ] Nachschlagewerk 207
Directory Enquiries [daɪˌrektərɪ‿ɪn'kwaɪərɪz, dɪˌrektərɪ‿ɪn'kwaɪərɪz] Telefonauskunft 54
to direct someone [daɪ'rekt ˌsʌmwʌn, dɪ'rekt ˌsʌmwʌn] jemandem den Weg sagen/zeigen 21
discerning [dɪ'sɜ:nɪŋ] anspruchsvoll, guten Geschmack besitzend 129
disclaimer [dɪ'skleɪmə] Haftungsausschluss, Widerruf 37
to disclose [dɪs'kləʊz] offenlegen, preisgeben 168
discount ['dɪskaʊnt] Rabatt 117
disgruntled [dɪs'grʌntld] verärgert, verstimmt 185
disgusting [dɪs'gʌstɪŋ] abscheulich 25
dish [dɪʃ] *(hier:)* Speise, Gericht 90
to dislike [dɪ'slaɪk] nicht mögen 200
dismayed [dɪ'smeɪd] entsetzt 178
dispatch advice [dɪ'spætʃ ədˌvaɪs] Versandanzeige 155
distribution channels [dɪstrɪ'bju:ʃn ˌtʃænlz] Vertriebskanäle 195
to divide up [dɪˌvaɪd 'ʌp] einteilen, aufteilen 89
diving ['daɪvɪŋ] Tauchen, Tauchsport 8
to do an apprenticeship [ˌdu:‿ən ə'prentɪʃɪp] eine Ausbildung machen 219
to do a traineeship [du:‿ə ˌtreɪ'ni:ʃɪp] eine Ausbildung machen 7
dock [dɒk] Dock, Hafenbecken 137
documentation [ˌdɒkjəmen'teɪʃn] Nachweis, Dokumentierung 98
document of title [ˌdɒkjəmənt əv 'taɪtl] Eigentumsurkunde 158
domestic market [dəˌmestɪk 'mɑ:kɪt] Inlandsmarkt 91
dominant ['dɒmɪnənt] beherrschend, dominierend 34
dominated ['dɒmɪneɪtɪd] beherrscht, dominiert 23
to donate [dəʊ'neɪt] spenden 202
to double ['dʌbl] *(hier:)* eine doppelte Funktion erfüllen 89
draft [drɑ:ft] Entwurf 80
to draw up [drɔ:‿'ʌp] zusammenstellen, verfassen 135
dreadful ['dredfəl] schrecklich 55
to dread sth. [dred] Angst vor etwas haben 222
dressing ['dresɪŋ] Salatsoße 27
drill head ['drɪl ˌhed] Bohrkopf 168
driving gloves ['draɪvɪŋ‿ˌglʌvz] Autohandschuhe 203
drizzle ['drɪzl] Nieselregen 19
to drop [drɒp] fallen 94
drum [drʌm] Fass, Barrel 154
to dry [draɪ] abtrocknen 28
due [dju:] fällig 168
dumpling ['dʌmplɪŋ] Kloß, Knödel 25
durability [ˌdjʊərə'bɪlətɪ] Haltbarkeit 142
durable ['djʊərəbl] haltbar 163
duties ['dju:tɪz] *(hier:)* Aufgaben 48
duty ['dju:tɪ] *(hier:)* Zoll(gebühr) 136

E

early order discount [ˌɜ:lɪ‿ɔ:də 'dɪs‿kaʊnt] Frühbuchungsrabatt 109
to earn one's living [ˌɜ:n wʌnz 'lɪvɪŋ] seinen Lebensunterhalt verdienen 36
e-commerce ['i:ˌkɒmɜ:s] Internet-Handel 166
economic growth [ˌi:kənɒmɪk‿'grəʊθ] Wirtschaftswachstum 151
effective [ɪ'fektɪv] wirksam 198
efficient [ɪ'fɪʃnt] leistungsfähig, wirksam, tüchtig 35
effort ['efət] Anstrengung, Bemühung 37
elderly person [ˌeldəlɪ 'pɜ:sn] ältere Person 48
to elect [ɪ'lekt] wählen 223
electrical equipment [ɪˌlektrɪkl ɪ'kwɪpmənt] Elektrogeräte 45
electrical goods industry [ɪˌlektrɪkl 'gʊdz ˌɪndəstrɪ] Elektroartikelbranche 10
electricity cut [elɪk'trɪsətɪ ˌkʌt] Stromsperre 111
electronic components [elekˌtrɒnɪk‿kəm'pəʊnənts] elektronische Bauelemente 218
embarrassed [ɪm'bærəst] peinlich, verlegen 80
embarrassment [ɪm'bærəsmənt] Verlegenheit 55
embassy ['embəsɪ] Botschaft(sgebäude) 118
emotionally charged [ɪˌməʊʃənlɪ 'tʃɑ:dʒd] emotional aufgeladen 203
emphasis ['emfəsɪs] Nachdruck 173
to emphasise ['emfəsaɪz] betonen, hervorheben 32
to employ [ɪm'plɔɪ] beschäftigen, einstellen 33
employment [ɪm'plɔɪmənt] Beschäftigung 208
empty ['emptɪ] leer 182
to enable [ɪ'neɪbl] in die Lage versetzen 197
to enclose [ɪn'kləʊz] beifügen 208
enclosure [ɪn'kləʊʒə] Anlage (Brief) 99
to endorse [ɪn'dɔ:s] *(hier:)* im Amt bestätigen 223
to end up [end 'ʌp] *(hier:)* landen 23
end user ['end‿ju:zə] Endverbraucher 195
energy content ['enədʒɪ ˌkɒntent] Brennwert (Energiegehalt) 47
engaged [ɪn'geɪdʒd] besetzt 54
engine ['endʒɪn] Motor 154
enquiry, inquiry [ɪn'kwaɪərɪ] Anfrage, Nachfrage 116
to enrol [ɪn'rəʊl] sich einschreiben 215
ensuite bathroom [ˌɒnswi:t‿'bɑ:θru:m] eigenes Bad (Hotelzimmer) 76
to ensure [ɪn'ʃɔ:] sicherstellen, dafür sorgen 98
to enter ['entə] eintreten; eintragen, eingeben 101
enterprise ['entəpraɪz] Unternehmen 53
to entertain [ˌentə'teɪn] sich um jemanden kümmern, unterhalten 16
enthusiasm [ɪn'θju:zɪæzm] Begeisterung 208
entire(ly) [ɪn'taɪə(lɪ)] ganz, gänzlich 111
to entrust [ɪn'trʌst] anvertrauen 112
envelope ['envələʊp] (Brief-)Umschlag 180
environment [ɪn'vaɪərənmənt] Umwelt, Umfeld 152
environmentally friendly [ɪnˌvaɪərənˌmentəlɪ 'frendlɪ] umweltfreundlich 91
equal opportunities employer [ˌi:kwəl ɒpə'tju:nətɪz ɪmˌplɔɪə] Firma, der Chancengleichheit ein Anliegen ist 219
to equip [ɪ'kwɪp] *(hier:)* befähigen, *(sonst:)* ausstatten, ausrüsten 209

equipment [ɪ'kwɪpmənt] Geräte 44
equivalent [ɪ'kwɪvələnt] Entsprechung 212
error ['erə] Irrtum 184
essential [ɪ'senʃl] wesentlich 209
to establish [ɪ'stæblɪʃ] *(hier:)* feststellen 194
established [ɪ'stæblɪʃt] eingeführt, feststehend 104
to estimate ['estɪmeɪt] schätzen 223
evaluation scheme [ɪˌvæljʊ'eɪʃn ˌski:m] Bewertungsschema 92
even though [ˌi:vn 'ðəʊ] obgleich 176
event management assistant [ɪˌvent 'mænɪdʒmənt əˌsɪstənt] Veranstaltungskaufmann/-frau 10
eventual(ly) [ɪ'ventʃʊəl(ɪ)] letztendlich, letztlich, schließlich 163
evidence ['evɪdəns] Beweis, Nachweis 99
exaggeration [ɪgˌzædʒə'reɪʃn] Übertreibung 203
to exceed [ɪk'si:d] übersteigen, überschreiten 128
excitement [ɪk'saɪtmənt] *(hier:)* Interesse 92
exclamation mark [ˌeksklə'meɪʃn ˌmɑ:k] Ausrufungszeichen 103
to execute ['eksɪkju:t] aus-, durchführen 123
execution [ˌeksɪ'kju:ʃn] Aus-, Durchführung 111
executives [ɪg'zekjətɪvz] leitende Angestellte 75
exhibition [ˌeksɪ'bɪʃn] Ausstellung 116
exhibition grounds [ˌeksɪ'bɪʃn ˌgraʊndz] Ausstellungsgelände 76
expenditure [ɪk'spendɪtʃə] Ausgaben, Auslagen 35
experience [ɪk'spɪərɪəns] Erfahrung 208
to experience [ɪk'spɪərɪəns] erleben 200
expiry date [ɪk'spaɪərɪ ˌdeɪt] Verfallsdatum (bei Kreditkarten) 78
exploration [ˌeksplə'reɪʃn] Erkundung neuer Lagerstätten, Probegrabungen/-bohrungen 92
export clerk ['ekspɔ:t ˌklɑ:k] Exportkaufmann/-frau 7
to express [ɪk'spres] ausdrücken 55
expressly [ɪk'spreslɪ] ausdrücklich 126
extension [ɪk'stenʃn] Durchwahl, Nebenstelle 55

F

fabulous ['fæbjələs] fabelhaft, sagenhaft, toll 109
to face [feɪs] sich gegenübersehen, konfrontiert sein mit 132
to facilitate [fə'sɪlɪteɪt] ermöglichen, erleichtern 74
facilities [fə'sɪlətɪz] Einrichtungen, Anlagen 68
factual ['fæktʃʊəl] sachlich, den Tatsachen entsprechend 113
fair [feə] Messe 35
familiarity [fəˌmɪlɪ'ærətɪ] Vertrautheit 208
familiar with [fə'mɪlɪə wɪð] vertraut mit 196
fare [feə] Fahrpreis 80
fashion ['fæʃn] Mode 37
fashion chain ['fæʃn ˌtʃeɪn] Kette von Modegeschäften 166
fast-paced [ˌfɑ:st'peɪst] tempogeladen 208
faultless, perfect, unobjectionable ['fɒltləs / 'fɔ:ltləs, 'pɜ:fɪkt, ˌʌnəb'dʒekʃənəbl] einwandfrei 189
faulty ['fɒltɪ, 'fɔ:ltɪ] fehlerhaft 176
faux fur [ˌfəʊ 'fɜ:] Kunstpelz 203
favourite (dish) [ˌfeɪvərɪt 'dɪʃ] Lieblings(-gericht) 27
to faze [feɪz] aus der Fassung bringen 219
feasibility study [ˌfi:zə'bɪlətɪ ˌstʌdɪ] Machbarkeitsstudie 35
feature ['fi:tʃə] Eigenschaft 91
to feature ['fi:tʃə] eine Rolle spielen, sich auszeichnen, kennzeichnen 33
fee [fi:] Gebühr, Honorar 133
feedback ['fi:dbæk] Rückmeldungen, Feedback 91
fermented white cabbage [fəˌmentɪd ˌwaɪt 'kæbɪdʒ] Sauerkraut 27
ferry ['ferɪ] Fähre 151
field (of work) [fi:ld (əv‿wɜ:k)] Arbeitsgebiet 220
field research ['fi:ld ˌri:sɜ:tʃ] Feldforschung 194
fierce [fɪəs] *(hier:)* scharf 198
figures ['fɪgəz] Zahlen 82
file [faɪl] Akte, Datei 101
filing cabinet ['faɪlɪŋ ˌkæbɪnət] Aktenschrank, Ablage 44
filled rolls [ˌfɪld 'rəʊlz] belegte Brötchen 47
to finalise ['faɪnəlaɪz] abschließen 24
fine [faɪn] Geldstrafe 223B
first floor [ˌfɜ:st 'flɔ:] erste Etage (BE); Erdgeschoss (AE) 21
first name [ˌfɜ:st 'neɪm] Vorname 7
first-rate [ˌfɜ:st'reɪt] erstklassig 208
fiscal ['fɪskl] steuerpolitisch 223
to fit in with [ˌfɪt 'ɪn wɪð] sich richten nach 78
fixed line set [ˌfɪkstlaɪn 'set] Festnetzanlage 54
flat [flæt] flach 94
flavouring ['fleɪvərɪŋ] Geschmackszusatz, Aroma 148
flooding ['flʌdɪŋ] Überschwemmung 111
floor plan ['flɔ: ˌplæn] Grundriss 21
flowcharts ['fləʊˌtʃɑ:ts] Flussdiagramme 89
to fluctuate ['flʌktʃʊeɪt] schwanken 94
fluent ['flu:ənt] fließend 208
foaming scrub [ˌfəʊmɪŋ 'skrʌb] Peelingschaum 203
focus ['fəʊkəs] Schwerpunkt 193
to focus ['fəʊkəs] (sich) konzentrieren, in den Mittelpunkt stellen 103
fog [fɒg] Nebel 20
foil-wrapped cardboard box [ˌfɔɪl‿ræpt‿kɑ:dbɔ:d‿'bɒks] folienumwickelter Karton 154
folder ['fəʊldə] Falt-, Prospektblatt 129
follow-up order [ˌfɒləʊ‿ʌp 'ɔ:də] Folgeauftrag 147
food processing ['fu:d ˌprəʊsesɪŋ] Verarbeitung von Lebensmitteln 106
food processing company ['fu:d ˌprəʊsesɪŋ ˌkʌmpənɪ] Lebensmittel verarbeitendes Unternehmen 17
for approval [fər‿ə'pru:vl] zur Genehmigung 82
to forecast ['fɔ:kɑ:st] vorhersagen 151
foreign language correspondent/ secretary with modern languages [ˌfɒrən 'læŋgwɪdʒ kɒrɪˌspɒndənt / ˌsekrətrɪ wɪð ˌfɒrən 'læŋgwɪdʒɪz] Fremdsprachenkorrespondent/in 10
foreign trade [ˌfɒrən 'treɪd] Außenhandel 196
for instance [fər‿'ɪnstəns] zum Beispiel 6
form [fɔ:m] Formular 59
formal ['fɔ:ml] förmlich, formell 98
formal park [ˌfɔ:ml 'pɑ:k] Parkanlage 23
for the time being [fə ðə ˌtaɪm 'bi:ɪŋ] zurzeit, vorläufig 188
to forward ['fɔ:wəd] weiterleiten, befördern, transportieren 101
forwarders ['fɔ:wədəz] Spedition 183
fossils ['fɒsəlz] Fossilien, Versteinerungen 133
to found [faʊnd] gründen 34
fragrance ['freɪgrəns] Duft 204
free movement of goods [ˌfri: ˌmu:vmənt əv 'gʊdz] freier Warenverkehr 222
free movement of labour [ˌfri: ˌmu:vmənt əv 'leɪbə] Freizügigkeit der Arbeitnehmer, freie Wahl des Arbeitsplatzes 221
free of charge [ˌfri:‿əv 'tʃɑ:dʒ] kostenlos, unentgeltlich 133
freight forwarding and logistics services clerk [ˌfreɪt 'fɔ:wədɪŋ ənd ləˌdʒɪstɪks‿'sɜ:vɪsɪz ˌklɑ:k] Kaufmann/-frau für Spedition und Logistikdienstleistung 9
freight forwarding company [ˌfreɪt 'fɔ:wədɪŋ‿ˌkʌmpənɪ] Spedition, Transportunternehmen 152
French fries [ˌfrentʃ 'fraɪz] Pommes frites 26

frequent(ly) ['fri:kwənt(lɪ)] häufig, oft 37
fridge [frɪdʒ] Kühlschrank 47
fried potatoes [ˌfraɪd̮pəˈteɪtəʊz] Bratkartoffeln 26
front office [ˌfrʌnt ˈɒfɪs] Büro mit Publikumsverkehr 43
full board [ˌfʊl ˈbɔ:d] Vollpension 133
furnishings [ˈfɜ:nɪʃɪŋz] Einrichtungsgegenstände 205
further training [ˌfɜ:ðə ˈtreɪnɪŋ] Weiterbildung 217
furthest [ˈfɜ:ðɪst] am weitesten 222
to fuse [fju:z] verschmelzen 37

G

gale [geɪl] Orkan, Sturm 171
gale-force winds [ˌgeɪlfɔ:s ˈwɪndz] stürmische Winde 20
game [geɪm] Wild 26
garlic [ˈgɑ:lɪk] Knoblauch 25
garment [ˈgɑ:mənt] Kleidungsstück 178
gathering [ˈgæðərɪŋ] Versammlung 94
generally [ˈdʒenrəlɪ] im Allgemeinen 195
general manager [ˌdʒenərəl ˈmænɪdʒə] Hauptgeschäftsführer/in 49
general terms and conditions [ˌdʒe̮nərəl ˌtɜ:mz ənd kənˈdɪʃnz] allgemeine Geschäftsbedingungen 146
generous [ˈdʒenərəs] großzügig 132
Gents/Ladies [dʒents/ˈleɪdɪz] Herren-/Damen-WC (BE) 21
germ [dʒɜ:m] Bazillus, Keim 102
gestures [ˈdʒestʃəz] Gesten, Gestik 55
to get [get] *(hier:)* mitbekommen, hören 57
to get around to it [get əˈraʊnd̮tʊ̮ɪt] dazu kommen, Zeit dazu haben 181
to get on well [get ˌɒn ˈwel] gut miteinander auskommen 46
to get something over [ˌget ˌsʌmθɪŋ ˈəʊvə] etwas hinter sich bringen 91
ghastly [ˈgɑ:stlɪ] entsetzlich 19
gift box [ˈgɪft ˌbɒks] Geschenkkarton 146
gig [gɪg] Musikevent 18
ginger cookies [ˌdʒɪndʒə ˈkʊkɪz] Ingwerkekse 138
to give a refusal, to refuse a request [ˌgɪv ə rɪˈfju:zl, rɪˌfju:z ə rɪˈkwest] Absage erteilen 185
to give notice [ˌgɪv ˈnəʊtɪs] *(hier:)* im Voraus Bescheid sagen 216
to give someone a lift [gɪv ˌsʌmwʌn ə ˈlɪft] jemanden mitnehmen (im Wagen) 28
to give someone a ring [gɪv ˌsʌmwʌn ə ˈrɪŋ] jemanden anrufen 28
gleam [gli:m] Schimmer, Glanz 203
global economy [ˌgləʊbl ɪˈkɒnəmɪ] Weltwirtschaft 151
glossy [ˈglɒsɪ] Hochglanz- 199
to go clubbing [gəʊ ˈklʌbɪŋ] in die Disko gehen 9
to go for [ˈgəʊ fə] wählen 217
good value [ˌgʊd ˈvælju:] preisgünstig 205
to go public [gəʊ ˈpʌblɪk] sich in eine Aktiengesellschaft umwandeln, an die Börse gehen 35
to go through the usual channels [ˌgəʊ θru: ðə ˈju:ʒʊəl ˌtʃænlz] die üblichen Instanzen durchlaufen 222
to go window-shopping [gəʊ̮ˈwɪndəʊ ˌʃɒpɪŋ] einen Schaufensterbummel machen 8
to go without saying [gəʊ wɪðˌaʊt̮ ˈseɪɪŋ] selbstverständlich sein 187
gradual(ly) [ˈgrædʒʊəl(ɪ)] allmählich 94
to grant [grɑ:nt] gewähren 121
to grant a concession [ˌgrɑ:nt ə kənˈseʃn] ein Zugeständnis machen 171
to grant a discount [ˌgrɑ:nt ə ˈdɪskaʊnt] Rabatt einräumen 130
to grant a respite [ˌgrɑ:nt ə ˈrespaɪt] einen Zahlungsaufschub gewähren 171
to grant credit [ˌgrɑ:nt̮ˈkredɪt] Kredit gewähren 165
graph [grɑ:f] Grafik 89
green card [ˌgri:n̮ˈkɑ:d] Arbeitserlaubnis für die USA 221
to have green fingers [hæv ˌgri:n ˈfɪŋgəz] einen grünen Daumen haben 203
grid [grɪd] Raster 98
gross weight [ˌgrəʊs ˈweɪt] Bruttogewicht 159
ground (coffee beans) [graʊnd] gemahlen 26
ground beef [ˌgraʊnd̮ˈbi:f] Rindergehacktes 26
ground floor [ˌgraʊnd ˈflɔ:] Parterre, Erdgeschoss (BE) 21
growth [grəʊθ] Wachstum 193
to guarantee [ˌgærənˈti:] garantieren 24
gym [dʒɪm] Turnhalle, Fitnessraum 7

H

habits [ˈhæbɪts] Gewohnheiten 201
haddock [ˈhædək] Schellfisch 26
half board [ˌhɑ:f ˈbɔ:d] Halbpension 134
ham [hæm] Schinken 182
handicapped [ˈhændɪkæpt] behindert 215
to handle [ˈhændl] handhaben, erledigen, bearbeiten 152
handling [ˈhændlɪŋ] *(hier:)* Fahreigenschaften 205
harmful [ˈhɑ:mfəl] schädlich 152
to have access to [hæv ˈækses tu:] Zugang haben zu 198
to have little choice but [hæv ˌlɪtl ˈtʃɔɪs bət] keine andere Wahl haben als 198
to have the goods delivered [ˌhæv ðə ˌgʊdz dɪˈlɪvəd] sich die Ware liefern lassen 197
heading [ˈhedɪŋ] Rubrik 92
head of department [ˌhed̮əv dɪˈpɑ:tmənt] Abteilungsleiter/in 48
headquarters [ˌhedˈkwɔ:təz] Hauptverwaltung 75
health [helθ] Gesundheit 80
health-conscious [ˌhelθˈkɒnʃəs] gesundheitsbewusst 199
height [haɪt] Höhe 183
to help [help] behilflich sein 219
helpful [ˈhelpfəl] hilfsbereit 16
herbs [hɜ:bz] Kräuter 203
high-powered [ˌhaɪˈpaʊəd] dynamisch 203
high street bank [ˌhaɪstri:t̮ˈbæŋk] Bank mit zahlreichen Zweigstellen 10
high street stores [ˌhaɪstri:t ˈstɔ:z] Geschäfte in der Innenstadt 195
highway robbery [ˌhaɪweɪ ˈrɒbərɪ] Raubüberfälle auf Fernstraßen (AE) 152
hint [hɪnt] Hinweis, Andeutung 8
hit [hɪt] Schlag, Stoß; Treffer; *(hier:)* Zugriff 35
hoardings *(BE)* [ˈhɔ:dɪŋz] Plakatwände 199
to hold [həʊld] *(hier:)* warten 55
hooked on [ˈhʊkt ɒn] süchtig nach 203
horseradish [ˈhɔ:sˌrædɪʃ] Meerrettich 147
host family [ˈhəʊst ˌfæməlɪ] Gastfamilie 133
hot [hɒt] heiß, scharf 26
to house [haʊz] beherbergen 23
household tool kit [ˌhaʊshəʊld̮ˈtu:l ˌkɪt] Haushaltswerkzeugsatz 121
however [haʊˈevə] jedoch 98
how you come across [ˌhaʊ jʊ ˌkʌm əˈkrɒs] welchen Eindruck man macht 91
human resources department [ˌhju:mən ˈri:sɔ:sɪz dɪˌpɑ:tmənt] Personalabteilung 189
humorous [ˈhju:mərəs] humorvoll 92
hyperbole [haɪˈpɜ:bəlɪ] Übertreibung 203

I

IBAN (international bank account number) [ˈaɪbæn, ˌaɪbi:eɪˈen (ˌɪntənæʃənl ˈbæŋk əˌkaʊnt ˌnʌmbə)] Internationale Kontonummer 163
illegible [ɪˈledʒəbl] unleserlich 182
I'm afraid ... [aɪm əˈfreɪd] leider ... 63
image [ˈɪmɪdʒ] Bild, Vorstellung 32

imagery ['ɪmɪdʒri] sprachliche Bilder 203
imagination [ɪˌmædʒɪ'neɪʃn] Phantasie, Vorstellungskraft 118
imaginative [ɪ'mædʒɪnətɪv] phantasievoll 90
immediate [ɪ'mi:diət] sofortig 55
I'm on a diet [aɪm ˌɒn ə 'daɪət] ich mache eine Diät 19
impatient [ɪm'peɪʃnt] ungeduldig 179
imperative [ɪm'perətɪv] Befehlsform 203
imperfections [ˌɪmpə'fekʃnz] Mängel 222
to imply [ɪm'plaɪ] beinhalten, besagen, stillschweigend voraussetzen 111
impolite [ˌɪmpə'laɪt] unhöflich 113
import licence ['ɪmpɔ:t ˌlaɪsəns] Importlizenz, Einfuhrgenehmigung 68
to impose [ɪm'pəʊz] verhängen (Strafe) 223
to impress [ɪm'pres] beeindrucken 142
impression [ɪm'preʃn] Eindruck 16
imprint ['ɪmprɪnt] Impressum 37
to improve [ɪm'pru:v] verbessern 198
inadequate [ɪ'nædɪkwət] unzureichend 151
in advance [ɪn əd'vɑ:ns] im Voraus 217
in bulk [ɪn 'bʌlk] in großen Mengen 195
incentive [ɪn'sentɪv] Anreiz 100
in charge of [ɪn 'tʃɑ:dʒ‿əv] verantwortlich für 17
incident ['ɪnsɪdənt] Zwischenfall, Ereignis 112
to include [ɪn'klu:d] einschließen, beinhalten, umfassen 6
incoming goods control [ˌɪnkʌmɪŋ‿'gʊdz kənˌtrəʊl] Wareneingangskontrolle 178
in conclusion [ɪn‿kən'klu:ʒn] zum Abschluss, abschließend 117
in confidence [ɪn‿'kɒnfɪdəns] vertraulich 123
inconvenience [ˌɪnkən'vi:nɪəns] Unannehmlichkeiten 112
inconvenient [ˌɪnkən'vi:nɪənt] ungünstig 216
to increase [ɪn'kri:s] zunehmen 94
increasing(ly) [ɪn'kri:sɪŋ(lɪ)] zunehmend 98
independent [ˌɪndɪ'pendənt] unabhängig 68
to indicate ['ɪndɪkeɪt] angeben, nennen 130
indicator ['ɪndɪkeɪtə] Anzeiger, Anzeigetafel 79
in due course [ɪn ˌdju: 'kɔ:s] fristgemäß 178
industrial business management assistant [ɪnˌdʌstrɪəl ˌbɪznɪs 'mænɪdʒmənt əˌsɪstənt] Industriekaufmann/-frau 7
industrial clerk [ɪn'dʌstrɪəl ˌklɑ:k] Industriekaufmann/-frau 7
industrial goods [ɪnˌdʌstrɪəl 'gʊdz] Industrieerzeugnisse 201
industry analyst ['ɪndəstri‿ˌænəlɪst] Branchenexperte/-expertin 151
to influence ['ɪnflʊəns] beeinflussen 200
in fourth place [ɪn ˌfɔ:θ 'pleɪs] an vierter Stelle 95
in full [ɪn 'fʊl] in voller Höhe 170
inhabitants [ɪn'hæbɪtənts] Einwohner/innen 162
initials [ɪ'nɪʃlz] Initialen, Anfangsbuchstaben des Namens 107
initial [ɪ'nɪʃl] anfänglich 198
initial order [ɪˌnɪʃl 'ɔ:də] Erstauftrag 141
to initiate [ɪ'nɪʃieɪt] in die Wege leiten, einleiten 186
to initiate measures [ɪˌnɪʃieɪt 'meʒəz] Maßnahmen einleiten 189
in law [ɪn 'lɔ:] rechtlich, vor Gericht 82
in lieu of [ɪn 'lju:‿əv] an Stelle von 215
in line with [ɪn 'laɪn wɪð] in Übereinstimmung mit, parallel zu 35
in our favour [ɪn‿aʊə 'feɪvə] zu unseren Gunsten 168
in principle [ɪn 'prɪnsəpl] im Prinzip 80
to insert [ɪn'sɜ:t] einfügen, einlegen 101
to insist on [ɪn'sɪst ɒn] bestehen auf 168
insistent [ɪn'sɪstənt] nachdrücklich 169
insolvent [ɪn'sɒlvənt] zahlungsunfähig 188
in stock [ɪn 'stɒk] vorrätig 62
to instruct [ɪn'strʌkt] anweisen, unterweisen 163
to instruct to the contrary [ɪnˌstrʌkt‿tʊ ðə 'kɒntrəri] gegenteilige Anweisungen erteilen 190
insurance [ɪn'ʃɔ:rəns] Versicherung 136
insurance business management assistant [ˌɪnʃɔ:rəns ˌbɪznɪs 'mænɪdʒmənt əˌsɪstənt] Versicherungskaufmann/-frau 9
insurance certificate [ɪn'ʃɔ:rəns‿səˌtɪfɪkət] Versicherungsschein, -zertifikat 158
insurance clerk [ɪn'ʃɔ:rəns ˌklɑ:k] Kaufmann/-frau für Versicherungen und Finanzen 9
insurance policy [ɪn'ʃɔ:rəns ˌpɒləsi] Versicherungspolice 158
insured [ɪn'ʃɔ:d] *(hier:)* Versicherungsnehmer/in, Versicherte/r 159
integration [ˌɪntɪ'greɪʃn] Eingliederung, Integration 78
to intend [ɪn'tend] beabsichtigen 202
interest ['ɪntrəst] Zinsen 169
interest in ['ɪntrəst ɪn] Interesse an 201
interest on arrears [ˌɪntrəst ɒn ə'rɪəz] Verzugszinsen 169
in terms of [ɪn 'tɜ:mz‿əv] in Bezug auf, was … betrifft 151
internet exchanges ['ɪntənet ɪksˌtʃeɪndʒɪz] Online-Börsen 197
to interpret [ɪn'tɜ:prɪt] dolmetschen 81
interpreter [ɪn'tɜ:prɪtə] Dolmetscher/in 83
to interrupt [ˌɪntə'rʌpt] unterbrechen, stören 105
interval ['ɪntəvl] Abstand 141
interview ['ɪntəvju:] Vorstellungsgespräch, Interview 33
in the course of [ɪn ðə 'kɔ:s‿əv] im Laufe 80
in the foreseeable future [ɪn ðə fɔ:ˌsi:əbl 'fju:tʃə] in absehbarer Zukunft 93
in transit [ɪn 'trænzɪt] beim Transport 183
introduction [ˌɪntrə'dʌkʃn] Einführung 193
introductory discount [ˌɪntrədʌktəri 'dɪskaʊnt] Einführungsrabatt 121
investigation [ɪnˌvestɪ'geɪʃn] Untersuchung 187
investment portfolio [ɪn'vestmənt‿pɔ:tˌfəʊliəʊ] Bestand an Wertpapieren 92
invigorating [ɪn'vɪgəreɪtɪŋ] belebend, erfrischend 204
invoice ['ɪnvɔɪs] Rechnung 142
to involve [ɪn'vɒlv] *(hier:)* beinhalten 194
in working order [ɪn ˌwɜ:kɪŋ‿'ɔ:də] funktionstüchtig 81
iron ore ['aɪən‿ɔ:] Eisenerz 152
irrevocable [ˌɪrɪ'vəʊkəbl] unwiderruflich 167
irritation [ɪrɪ'teɪʃn] Verärgerung 151
is paralleled by [ɪz 'pærəleld‿baɪ] geht einher mit 197
issue ['ɪʃu:] *(hier:)* Ausgabe, Heft 118
issues ['ɪʃu:z] Fragen 223
to issue ['ɪʃu:] ausstellen, (her)ausgeben 165
it doesn't appeal to me [ɪt‿dʌznt əˌpi:l tʊ 'mi:] es gefällt mir nicht 200
IT specialist [ˌaɪ'ti: ˌspeʃəlɪst] Fachinformatiker/in 9
it tastes like … [ɪt‿teɪsts laɪk '…] es schmeckt wie … 26

J

jar [dʒɑ:] Glas (z. B. Marmelade), Topf (z. B. Senf) 186
jelly ['dʒeli] Götterspeise, Gelee 27
jingles ['dʒɪŋglz] Reime 202
job exchanges ['dʒɒb ɪksˌtʃeɪndʒɪz] Job-, Stellenbörsen 207
job specification [ˌdʒɒb ˌspesɪfɪ'keɪʃn] Stellenbeschreibung 207

to join [dʒɔɪn] *(hier:)* sich jemandem anschließen, mitkommen 25
joint [dʒɔɪnt] gemeinsam 25
joint venture [ˌdʒɔɪnt 'ventʃə] Joint Venture (Gemeinschaftsunternehmen) 61
to jumble ['dʒʌmbl] durcheinander werfen/bringen 102
jumbled ['dʒʌmbld] durcheinander geworfen 19
to jump [dʒʌmp] springen, sprunghaft ansteigen 92
to jump by ... from ... to ... ['dʒʌmp‿baɪ ... frəm ... tʊ ...] sprunghaft ansteigen um ... von ... auf ... 94
junction ['dʒʌŋkʃn] Kreuzung 22
junior executive [ˌdʒu:nɪər‿ɪg'zekjətɪv] Nachwuchsführungskraft 180
justified ['dʒʌstɪfaɪd] gerechtfertigt 55
justified complaint [ˌdʒʌstɪfaɪd‿kəm'pleɪnt] begründete Reklamation 185

K

keen [ki:n] sehr interessiert, eifrig 211
to keep an eye on [ˌki:p ən 'aɪ‿ɒn] aufpassen auf 28
to keep a record [ˌki:p ə 'rekɔ:d] aufzeichnen 74
to keep informed [ˌki:p ɪn'fɔ:md] auf dem Laufenden halten 185
to keep one's fingers crossed [ˌki:p wʌnz 'fɪŋgəz ˌkrɒst] den Daumen halten 222
key [ki:] Schlüssel 88
keyboard ['ki:bɔ:d] Tastatur 44
kitchenette [ˌkɪtʃɪ'net] Kochgelegenheit; Teeküche 83
kitchen facilities ['kɪtʃɪn fəˌsɪlətɪz] Küchenanlagen 24
kitten ['kɪtn] Kätzchen 145

L

label ['leɪbl] Etikett, Aufkleber 24
to label ['leɪbl] etikettieren, kennzeichnen, beschriften 178
laces ['leɪsɪz] Schnürsenkel 217
ladies' room ['leɪdɪz ˌru:m] Damentoilette (AE) 21
lamb [læm] Lamm 26
landlady ['lændˌleɪdɪ] Vermieterin 221
landline ['lændlaɪn] Festnetz(leitung) 54
largely ['lɑ:dʒlɪ] weitgehend 98
lately ['leɪtlɪ] in letzter Zeit 18
to launch [lɔ:ntʃ] einführen, starten, in die Wege leiten 122
lawful holder [ˌlɔ:fəl 'həʊldə] rechtmäßige(r) Inhaber(in)/Besitzer(in) 158
layout ['leɪaʊt] Anordnung, Gestaltung 100
lbs (pounds) [paʊndz] (englische) Pfund (453,59 g) 184
leading ['li:dɪŋ] führend 119
to leave much to be desired [li:v ˌmʌtʃ tʊ bɪ dɪ'zaɪəd] viel zu wünschen übrig lassen 81
leeks [li:ks] Lauch 25
legal ['li:gl] rechtlich, gesetzlich, legal, juristisch 99
to legalize ['li:gəlaɪz] beglaubigen, legalisieren 158
legal steps [ˌli:gl 'steps] juristische Schritte 169
legislation [ˌledʒɪ'sleɪʃn] Gesetze 223
legitimacy [lɪ'dʒɪtɪməsɪ] Legitimität 223
leisure ['leʒə] Freizeit, freie Zeit 90
lentils ['lentəlz] Linsen 27
less [les] abzüglich 131
to let someone know [let ˌsʌmwʌn 'nəʊ] Bescheid sagen 28
letterhead ['letəhed] Briefkopf 107
letter of credit [ˌletər‿əv 'kredɪt] Akkreditiv 167
letting agent ['letɪŋ ˌeɪdʒənt] Makler/in für Mietimmobilien, -wohnungen 218
lettuce ['letɪs] Kopfsalat 27
life [laɪf] Lebensdauer 130
lift [lɪft] Aufzug 21
likewise ['laɪkwaɪz] ebenfalls 78
limit ['lɪmɪt] Beschränkung 78
line [laɪn] Verbindung 57
line graph ['laɪn ˌgrɑ:f] Liniendiagramm 93
liner ['laɪnə] Linienschiff 159
lingua franca [ˌlɪŋgwə 'fræŋkə] Verkehrssprache 16
link [lɪŋk] Verbindung, Bindeglied 195
to link [lɪŋk] verbinden, verknüpfen 198
linking words ['lɪŋkɪŋ ˌwɜ:dz] verbindende Wörter 111
lipstick ['lɪpstɪk] Lippenstift 96
to load [ləʊd] beladen, einladen 151
local ['ləʊkl] örtlich, ortsansässig 33
to locate [ləʊ'keɪt] ausfindig machen, lokalisieren 116
location [ləʊ'keɪʃn] Standort 91
logistics and warehousing operation [ləˌdʒɪstɪks ənd 'weəhaʊzɪŋ‿ɒpəˌreɪʃn] Logistik- und Lagerungsunternehmen 221
long-distance running [ˌlɒŋdɪstəns 'rʌnɪŋ] Langstreckenlauf 8
to lose one's way [ˌlu:z wʌnz 'weɪ] sich verirren, sich verlaufen 21
low [ləʊ] Tief(punkt) 94
lump sum [ˌlʌmp 'sʌm] Pauschalsumme 159

M

machinery [mə'fi:nərɪ] Maschinen 33
magnificent [mæg'nɪfɪsənt] großartig, prächtig 23
mail shots ['meɪl ˌʃɒts] Postwurfsendungen 199
main branch [ˌmeɪn 'brɑ:ntʃ] Hauptfiliale 210
main course [ˌmeɪn 'kɔ:s] Hauptgericht, -gang 25
main entrance [ˌmeɪn 'entrəns] Haupteingang 21
main road [ˌmeɪn 'rəʊd] Hauptstraße 22
major ['meɪdʒə] groß, wichtig, Haupt- 43
to make an offer [ˌmeɪk ən 'ɒfə] ein Angebot abgeben 127
to make someone aware of [ˌmeɪk ˌsʌmwʌn ə'weər‿əv] jemanden aufmerksam machen auf 199
to make someone feel welcome [meɪk ˌsʌmwʌn fi:l 'welkəm] dafür sorgen, dass sich jemand wohl fühlt 16
to make sure [meɪk 'ʃɔ:] sich vergewissern 91
to make/take decisions [ˌmeɪk/ˌteɪk dɪ'sɪʒnz] Entscheidungen treffen 224
to make up [meɪk 'ʌp] *(hier:)* erfinden 59
to manage complaints [ˌmænɪdʒ kəm'pleɪnts] Beschwerden bearbeiten 185
management ['mænɪdʒmənt] Geschäftsleitung 112
management assistant for tourism and leisure ['mænɪdʒmənt əˌsɪstənt fə ˌtʊərɪzm ən 'leʒə] Kaufmann/-frau für Tourismus und Freizeit 11
management assistant in advertising ['mænɪdʒmənt əˌsɪstənt ɪn 'ædvətaɪzɪŋ] Werbekaufmann/-frau 11
management assistant in event organisation ['mænɪdʒmənt əˌsɪstənt ɪn ɪˌvent ˌɔ:gənaɪ'zeɪʃn] Veranstaltungskaufmann/-frau 11
management assistant in freight forwarding ['mænɪdʒmənt əˌsɪstənt ɪn ˌfreɪt 'fɔ:wədɪŋ] Speditionskaufmann/-frau 9
management assistant in informatics ['mænɪdʒmənt əˌsɪstənt ɪn ˌɪnfə'mætɪks] Informatikkaufmann/-frau 11
management assistant in office communication ['mænɪdʒmənt əˌsɪstənt ɪn ˌɒfɪs kəˌmju:nɪ'keɪʃn] Kaufmann/-frau für Bürokommunikation 11
management assistant in publishing ['mænɪdʒmənt əˌsɪstənt ɪn 'pʌblɪʃɪŋ] Verlagskaufmann/-frau 9
management assistant in retail business ['mænɪdʒmənt əˌsɪstənt ɪn ˌri:teɪl 'bɪznɪs] Kaufmann/-frau im Einzelhandel 9
management assistant in wholesale and foreign trade ['mænɪdʒmənt əˌsɪstənt ɪn ˌhəʊlseɪl ənd ˌfɒrən 'treɪd]

Kaufmann/-frau im Groß- und Außenhandel **9**
managing director [ˌmænɪdʒɪŋ dɪ'rektə] Geschäftsführer/in **48**
mane [meɪn] Mähne **203**
manner ['mænə] Umgangsstil **219**
manufacturer [ˌmænjə'fæktʃərə] Hersteller/in, Produzent/in **195**
to manufacture to specification [ˌmænjə'fæktʃə tʊ ˌspesɪfɪ'keɪʃn] als Sonderanfertigung herstellen **167**
manufacturing [ˌmænjə'fæktʃərɪŋ] Fertigung, Fabrikation **33**
manufacturing (industry) [ˌmænjə'fæktʃərɪŋ (ˌɪndəstrɪ)] verarbeitende Industrie **219**
to marinate ['mærɪneɪt] marinieren, einlegen **25**
marital status [ˌmærɪtl 'steɪtəs] Familienstand **107**
marketing tools ['mɑːkɪtɪŋ ˌtuːlz] Marketinginstrumente **198**
market leader [ˌmɑːkɪt 'liːdə] Marktführer **33**
market research [ˌmɑːkɪt 'riːsɜːtʃ] Marktforschung **194**
market share [ˌmɑːkɪt 'ʃeə] Marktanteil **152**
market survey [ˌmɑːkɪt 'sɜːveɪ] Marktstudie, -untersuchung **194**
markings ['mɑːkɪŋz] Markierung **156**
mart [mɑːt] Markt **35**
mashed potatoes [ˌmæʃt‿pə'teɪtəʊz] Kartoffelpüree **26**
maturity [mə'tjʊərətɪ] Reife **193**
maximum admissible weight [ˌmæk‿sɪməm ədˌmɪsəbl 'weɪt] zulässiges Höchstgewicht **184**
means of payment ['miːnz‿əv 'peɪmənt] Zahlungsmittel **165**
measurement ['meʒəmənt] *(hier:)* Abmessungen **159**
meat [miːt] Fleisch **26**
meatballs ['miːtbɔːlz] Frikadellen **26**
medical supplies [ˌmedɪkl sə'plaɪz] Artikel zur medizinischen Versorgung **153**
Mediterranean countries [medɪtərˌeɪnɪən 'kʌntrɪz] Länder am Mittelmeer **8**
to meet deadlines [miːt‿'dedlaɪnz] Termine/Fristen einhalten **208**
to meet halfway [miːt ˌhɑːf'weɪ] auf halbem Weg entgegenkommen **185**
to meet someone ['miːt ˌsʌmwʌn] jemanden kennenlernen, treffen **16**
to meet with approval [ˌmiːt wɪð ə'pruːvl] auf Zustimmung stoßen **217**
member ['membə] Mitglied **149**
member country ['membə ˌkʌntrɪ] Mitgliedsstaat **224**
memo ['meməʊ] Aktennotiz **24**
memories ['memərɪz] Erinnerungen **203**
memory stick ['memrɪ ˌstɪk] USB-Speicher **44**
menu ['menjuː] Speisekarte **27**
merchandise ['mɜːtʃəndaɪs] Ware, Gut, Handelsartikel **141**
merchants ['mɜːtʃənts] Händler **198**
message ['mesɪdʒ] Nachricht **101**
Middle Ages [ˌmɪdl 'eɪdʒɪz] Mittelalter **162**
mince(d) meat ['mɪns(t) ˌmiːt] Gehacktes **26**
minor ['maɪnə] gering(fügig) **123**
mint bar ['mɪnt‿bɑː] Pfefferminzriegel **129**
minute [maɪ'njuːt] peinlich genau; winzig **37**
minutes ['mɪnɪts] Protokoll **80**
misunderstanding [ˌmɪsʌndə'stændɪŋ] Missverständnis **98**
mixed [mɪkst] gemischt **27**
mix-up ['mɪksʌp] Verwechslung **184**
mode of transport [ˌməʊd əv 'trænspɔːt] Transportart **152**
moderate(ly) ['mɒdərət(lɪ)] mäßig, maßvoll **94**
modification [ˌmɒdɪfɪ'keɪʃn] Änderung **75**
to modify ['mɒdɪfaɪ] ab-, verändern **24**
monitor ['mɒnɪtə] PC-Bildschirm **77**
to monitor ['mɒnɪtə] kontrollieren **223**
monotonous(ly) [mə'nɒtənəs(lɪ)] eintönig **91**
moreover [mɔːr'əʊvə] überdies, außerdem **111**
mother tongue [ˌmʌðə 'tʌŋ] Muttersprache **209**
motor-car mechanic [ˌməʊtəkɑː mə'kænɪk] Kfz-Mechaniker/in **48**
move [muːv] *(hier:)* Umzug **28**
mug [mʌg] Becher **176**
multilingual [ˌmʌltɪ'lɪŋgwəl] mehr-, vielsprachig **181**
mushrooms ['mʌʃruːmz] Champignons, Pilze **25**
mustard ['mʌstəd] Senf **147**

N

nail [neɪl] Nagel **204**
nail varnish ['neɪl ˌvɑːnɪʃ] Nagellack **96**
named [neɪmd] namentlich genannt **165**
native ['neɪtɪv] einheimisch, inländisch, Landes- **133**
navy ['neɪvɪ] Marine; *(hier:)* marineblau **104**
navy blue [ˌneɪvɪ 'bluː] dunkelblau **218**
neat(ly) [niːt(lɪ)] ordentlich, adrett **212**
necessity [nə'sesətɪ] Notwendigkeit **66**
needs [niːdz] Bedarf, Bedürfnisse **194**
to need, to require [niːd, rɪ'kwaɪə] benötigen **219**
negotiation [nɪˌgəʊʃɪ'eɪʃn] Verhandlung **173**
neighbouring ['neɪbərɪŋ] benachbart **33**
net [net] netto **129**
newsagent ['njuːzˌeɪdʒənt] Zeitungshändler/in **19**
nobility [nəʊ'bɪlətɪ] Adel **145**
noisy ['nɔɪzɪ] laut **20**
to nominate ['nɒmɪneɪt] ernennen **223**
non-attendance [ˌnɒnə'tendəns] Fehlen, Abwesenheit **82**
non-bulk cargo [ˌnɒnbʌlk‿'kɑːgəʊ] Stückgutfracht **151**
note pad ['nəʊtpæd] Notizblock **44**
notification [ˌnəʊtɪfɪ'keɪʃn] Benachrichtigung **207**
to notify ['nəʊtɪfaɪ] benachrichtigen **173**
novel ['nɒvl] Roman **9**
novelist ['nɒvəlɪst] Romanschriftsteller/in **133**
nowadays ['naʊədeɪz] heutzutage **165**
nutritionally conscious [njuːˌtrɪʃənlɪ 'kɒnʃəs] ernährungsbewusst **24**
nutritional science [njuːˌtrɪʃənl 'saɪəns] Ernährungswissenschaft **24**

O

obesity [əʊ'biːsətɪ] Fettleibigkeit, klinisches Übergewicht **80**
objective [əb'dʒektɪv] Ziel **89**
obligation [ˌɒblɪ'geɪʃn] Verpflichtung, Verbindlichkeit **135**
obscure [əb'skjʊə] unbekannt **205**
to observe [əb'zɜːv] beachten **79**
to observe the delivery period [əbˌzɜːv ðə dɪ'lɪvərɪ ˌpɪərɪəd] Lieferfrist einhalten **146**
to obtain [əb'teɪn] erhalten **199**
obvious(ly) ['ɒbvɪəs(lɪ)] offensichtlich **147**
occasion [ə'keɪʒn] Anlass, Gelegenheit **106**
to occur, to result [ə'kɜː, rɪ'zʌlt] sich ergeben **201**
offer ['ɒfə] Angebot **126**
to offer credit facilities [ˌɒfə 'kredɪt fəˌsɪlətɪz] Kredite anbieten **196**
office administration clerk [ˌɒfɪs‿ədˌmɪnɪ'streɪʃn ˌklɑːk] Bürokaufmann/-frau **7**
office management assistant [ˌɒfɪs 'mænɪdʒmənt əˌsɪstənt] Bürokaufmann/-frau **9**
old-established [ˌəʊldɪ'stæblɪʃt] alteingesessen **32**
old-fashioned [ˌəʊld'fæʃnd] altmodisch **54**
olive trees ['ɒlɪv ˌtriːz] Olivenbäume **203**
to omit [əʊ'mɪt] aus-, weglassen **107**

on a large scale [ɒn ə ˌlɑːdʒ 'skeɪl] in großem Stil/Umfang 34
on behalf of [ɒn bɪ'hɑːf‿əv] im Auftrag von, für 74
on delivery [ɒn dɪ'lɪvərɪ] bei Lieferung 167
on demand [ɒn dɪ'mɑːnd] auf Verlangen 165
one-off [ˌwʌn'ɒf] Einmal- 132
onion ['ʌnjən] Zwiebel 25
on presentation [ɒn ˌprezən'teɪʃn] bei Vorlage 165
on request [ɒn rɪ'kwest] wenn gewünscht, *(sonst:)* auf Anfrage 222
on the left/left-hand side [ɒn ðə 'left / ˌlefthænd 'saɪd] links 21
on the off-chance [ɒn ðɪ‿'ɒftʃɑːns] auf Verdacht 207
on/to the right [ɒn/tʊ ðə 'raɪt] rechts 21
open account terms [ˌəʊpn əˌkaʊnt‿'tɜːmz] offenes Zahlungsziel 128
open credit [ˌəʊpn 'kredɪt] Zahlung gegen einfache Rechnung 167
openings ['əʊpnɪŋz] offene Stellen 207
opening bank [ˌəʊpnɪŋ 'bæŋk] ausstellende Bank 167
open-plan office [ˌəʊpnplæn 'ɒfɪs] Großraumbüro 21
to operate ['ɒpəreɪt] bedienen 91
operations [ˌɒpə'reɪʃnz] *(hier:)* Betrieb 170
opportunity [ˌɒpə'tjuːnətɪ] Gelegenheit 12
opposite ['ɒpəzɪt] gegenüber 22
opposite number [ˌɒpəzɪt 'nʌmbə] Gegenüber, Kollege/Kollegin 75
optician [ɒp'tɪʃn] Optiker/in 195
oral ['ɔːrəl] mündlich 88
order ['ɔːdə] Auftrag, Bestellung 141
to order ['ɔːdə] bestellen; anordnen 33
order confirmation ['ɔːdə kɒnfəˌmeɪʃn] Auftragsbestätigung 145
order on call [ˌɔːdər‿ɒn 'kɔːl] Abrufauftrag 141
or else [ɔːr‿'els] andernfalls, sonst 101
organic [ɔː'gænɪk] biologisch, Bio- 24
organic foods [ɔː'gænɪk ˌfuːdz] Bio-Lebensmittel 80
organisation [ˌɔːgənaɪ'zeɪʃn] Firma, Unternehmen, Organisation 197
original(ly) [ə'rɪdʒənl(ɪ)] ursprünglich 7
to originate [ə'rɪdʒəneɪt] den Ursprung haben 223
other business [ˌʌðə 'bɪznɪs] Verschiedenes 80
outcome ['aʊtkʌm] Ergebnis 112
outlet ['aʊtlet] Verkaufsstelle, Laden(geschäft) 117
out of order [ˌaʊt‿əv 'ɔːdə] kaputt, außer Betrieb 180
outside advice [ˌaʊtsaɪd əd'vaɪs] Beratung von außen 202
overcast ['əʊvəkɑːst] bedeckt, bezogen (Himmel) 18
overdue [ˌəʊvə'djuː] überfällig 172
overheads ['əʊvəhedz] fixe Kosten 196
overindebted [ˌəʊvərɪn'detɪd] überschuldet 166
to overlook [ˌəʊvə'lʊk] übersehen 169
overseas [ˌəʊvə'siːz] aus dem/ins Ausland, ausländisch 132
to oversee [ˌəʊvə'siː] beaufsichtigen, leiten 75
oversight ['əʊvəsaɪt] Versehen 112
to overtake [ˌəʊvə'teɪk] überholen 166
overview ['əʊvəvjuː] Überblick 89
overwhelmed [ˌəʊvə'welmd] überwältigt 35
owner ['əʊnə] Eigentümer/in 48

P

package tour ['pækɪdʒ‿ˌtʊə] Pauschalreise 100
packaging material ['pækɪdʒɪŋ məˌtɪərɪəl] Verpackungsmaterial 63
packing list ['pækɪŋ ˌlɪst] Packliste 155
pair of scissors [ˌpeər‿əv 'sɪzəz] Schere 44
pallet [pælɪt] Palette 154
paper ['peɪpə] *(hier:)* Vortrag 61
paragraph ['pærəgrɑːf] Absatz 110
paramount ['pærəmaʊnt] vorrangig 24
to paraphrase ['pærəfreɪz] umschreiben 212
parcel post ['pɑːsl ˌpəʊst] Paketpost 138
parent company [ˌpeərənt 'kʌmpənɪ] Muttergesellschaft 188
parsley ['pɑːslɪ] Petersilie 27
participant [pɑː'tɪsɪpənt] Teilnehmer/in 180
participation [pɑːˌtɪsɪ'peɪʃn] *(hier:)* Wahlbeteiligung 223
particular [pə'tɪkjələ] besonders, speziell 32
partnership ['pɑːtnəʃɪp] Personengesellschaft 107
to pass a message on [ˌpɑːs ə 'mesɪdʒ ɒn] eine Nachricht weitergeben 28
passing of risk [ˌpɑːsɪŋ əv 'rɪsk] Gefahrenübergang 136
to pass on [pɑːs 'ɒn] weiterreichen, -geben 102
patience ['peɪʃəns] Geduld 57
patron saint [ˌpeɪtrən 'seɪnt] Schutzheilige/r 23
to pause [pɔːz] eine Pause einlegen 65
payable at ['peɪəbl ət] zahlbar bei 168
payable to ['peɪəbl tuː] zahlbar an 63
to pay into a bank account [peɪ‿ˌɪntʊ‿ə 'bæŋk əˌkaʊnt] auf ein Konto einzahlen 165
payment in advance [ˌpeɪmənt ɪn əd'vɑːns] Vorauszahlung 167
payment, money transfer, remittance ['peɪmənt, 'mʌnɪ ˌtrænsfɜː, rɪ'mɪtəns] Überweisung 84
PC-literacy [ˌpiːsiː'lɪtrəsɪ] PC-Kenntnisse 209
PC literate [ˌpiːsiː'lɪtrət] PC-erfahren 208
peak [piːk] Gipfel, Höchststand 94
peak season [ˌpiːk 'siːzn] Hochsaison 63
pearl [pɜːl] Perle 133
pea soup [ˌpiː 'suːp] Erbsensuppe 26
peppers ['pepəz] Paprikaschoten 26
percentage [pə'sentɪdʒ] Prozentsatz 196
periodical [ˌpɪərɪ'ɒdɪkl] Zeitschrift 201
perishable ['perɪʃəbl] (leicht) verderblich 152
permit ['pɜːmɪt] Genehmigung, Erlaubnis 221
personal assistant [ˌpɜːsənl ə'sɪstent] Sekretär/in 48
personnel [ˌpɜːsən'el] Personal 48
personnel department [ˌpɜːsən'el dɪˌpɑːtmənt] Personalabteilung 180
person to contact [ˌpɜːsn tə 'kɒntækt] Kontaktperson 210
to persuade [pə'sweɪd] überreden 50
persuasive [pə'sweɪsɪv] überredend 202
to phase out [feɪz 'aʊt] allmählich vom Markt zurückziehen 193
to pick someone up [pɪk ˌsʌmwʌn 'ʌp] jemanden abholen 28
to pick up [pɪk 'ʌp] abholen 163
picnic hamper ['pɪknɪk ˌhæmpə] Picknickkorb 102
pie chart ['paɪ ˌtʃɑːt] Tortendiagramm 92
pipe-blown by hand [ˌpaɪpbləʊn baɪ 'hænd] mundgeblasen 183
to place an order [ˌpleɪs ən 'ɔːdə] einen Auftrag erteilen 117
placement ['pleɪsmənt] Praktikum 210
place of destination [ˌpleɪs əv ˌdestɪ'neɪʃn] Bestimmungsort 136
place of employment [ˌpleɪs əv ɪm'plɔɪmənt] Arbeitsstätte 197
plaice [pleɪs] Scholle 26
plain [pleɪn] schlicht, unscheinbar; *(hier:)* ungemustert, einfarbig 104
plant [plɑːnt] Werk, Anlage; Pflanze 137
plastic box with mouldings [ˌplæstɪk 'bɒks wɪð 'məʊldɪŋz] Kunststoffbox mit Formeinlagen 154
platter ['plætə] Servierplatte, (Holz-)Teller 147
plausible ['plɔːzɪbl] plausibel, einleuchtend, glaubhaft 183
to point out [pɔɪnt 'aʊt] hinweisen auf 144
polished ['pɒlɪʃt] mit Schuhcreme geputzt, poliert 217

polite [pə'laɪt] höflich 63
pollution [pə'lu:ʃn] (Umwelt-)Verschmutzung 152
to pop into [,pɒp 'ɪntʊ] eben schnell hineintun 90
pork escalope [,pɔ:k 'eskəlɒp] Schweineschnitzel 27
port [pɔ:t] Hafen 151
portfolio [pɔ:t'fəʊlɪəʊ] *(hier:)* Ressort (Tätigkeitsbereich) 223
port of destination [,pɔ:t əv ,destɪ'neɪʃn] Bestimmungshafen 136
port of discharge [,pɔ:t əv 'dɪstʃɑ:dʒ] Entladehafen 159
port of shipment [,pɔ:t əv 'ʃɪpmənt] Verschiffungshafen 136
postal code ['pəʊstl ,kəʊd] Postleitzahl 107
postcode ['pəʊstkəʊd] Postleitzahl 59
poster ['pəʊstə] Plakat 199
to postpone [pəs'pəʊn] verschieben 61
potential customer [pə,tenʃl 'kʌstəmə] Interessent/in 127
pot plant ['pɒt ,plɑ:nt] Topfpflanze 44
poultry ['pəʊltrɪ] Geflügel 26
powers ['paʊəz] Befugnisse 223
praise [preɪz] Lob 219
to precede [pri:'si:d] vor(an)gehen, -stehen 108
precise(ly) [prɪ'saɪs(lɪ)] genau, exakt, präzise 59
precisely then [prɪ,saɪslɪ 'ðen] gerade dann 57
precision instruments [prɪ,sɪʒn 'ɪnstrə‿mənts] Präzisionsinstrumente 201
preferably ['prefrəblɪ] vorzugsweise 91
preliminary [prɪ'lɪmɪnərɪ] vorläufig 100
premises ['premɪsɪz] Geschäftsräume, Firmengebäude, -gelände 24
premium ['pri:mɪəm] Prämie 159
prerequisite [,pri:'rekwɪzɪt] Voraussetzung, Bedingung 91
to present [prɪ'zent] vorstellen 200
press coverage ['pres ,kʌvərɪdʒ] Berichterstattung in der Presse 202
prestigious [pres'tɪdʒəs] repräsentativ 43
pretzel ['pretsl] Brezel 23
to prevent [prɪ'vent] hindern, verhindern, vermeiden 101
previous ['pri:vɪəs] früher, vorhergehend 219
price reduction ['praɪs rɪ,dʌkʃn] Preisnachlass 177
prices are subject to change without notice ['praɪsɪz‿ə ,sʌbdʒɪkt‿tʊ ,tʃeɪndʒ wɪð,aʊt 'nəʊtɪs] Preisänderungen vorbehalten 126
principal ['prɪnsəpl] Schulleiter/in, Auftraggeber/in 180
printing press ['prɪntɪŋ ,pres] Druckerpresse 153
privacy ['praɪvəsɪ] private Atmosphäre, Privatleben 46
private individual [,praɪvət ,ɪndɪ'vɪdʒʊəl] Privatperson 35
procedures [prə'si:dʒəz] Verfahren 208
proceedings [prə'si:dɪŋz] *(hier:)* Ablauf der Konferenz 74
to process ['prəʊsəs] bearbeiten, verarbeiten 127
produce ['prɒdju:s] (landwirtschaftliche) Erzeugnisse 24
production site [prə'dʌkʃn ,saɪt] Fertigungsstätte, Produktionsbetrieb 33
product range ['prɒdʌkt ,reɪndʒ] Produktpalette 78
professional [prə'feʃənl] beruflich, professionell 6
proforma invoice [prəʊ,fɔ:mər‿'ɪnvɔɪs] Proformarechnung 163
progress ['prəʊgres] Fortgang 185
to project an image [prə,dʒekt ən 'ɪmɪdʒ] ein Image pflegen 202
prolonged [prəʊ'lɒŋd] langanhaltend 111
to promote [prə'məʊt] befördern 221
to promote sales [prə,məʊt 'seɪlz] den Absatz fördern 199
promotion [prə'məʊʃn] Aufstieg, Beförderung 12
prompt [prɒmpt] Hinweis, Stichwort 20
prompt cards ['prɒmpt‿kɑ:dz] Stichwortkarten 89
to pronounce [prə'naʊns] aussprechen 65
pronounced [prə'naʊnst] ausgeprägt 50
proof [pru:f] Beweis, Nachweis 167
proportion [prə'pɔ:ʃn] Anteil 92
proposal [prə'pəʊzl] Vorschlag 149
prospects ['prɒspekts] Aussichten 12
prospective [prəs'pektɪv] zukünftig, voraussichtlich, potentiell 127
to prosper ['prɒspə] gedeihen, florieren 33
protective software [prə,tektɪv 'sɒft‿weə] Software zum Schutz 99
proud(ly) [praʊd(lɪ)] stolz 145
to prove [pru:v] beweisen, nachweisen 167
to provide [prə'vaɪd] zur Verfügung stellen 196
provider [prə'vaɪdə] Versorger, Anbieter, Lieferant 166
public ['pʌblɪk] Öffentlichkeit 53
public relations [,pʌblɪk rɪ'leɪʃnz] Öffentlichkeitsarbeit 202
publisher's assistant ['pʌblɪʃəz ə,sɪstənt] Verlagskaufmann/-frau 9
publishing house ['pʌblɪʃɪŋ ,haʊs] Verlag 209
punch [pʌntʃ] Locher 44
punctual ['pʌŋktʃʊəl] pünktlich 19
puppy ['pʌpɪ] Hündchen, Welpe 145
purchase order ['pɜ:tʃɪs ,ɔ:də] Bestellung, Lieferungsauftrag 178
purchasing (department) ['pɜ:tʃəsɪŋ (dɪ,pɑ:tmənt)] Einkauf(sabteilung) 48
purchasing manager ['pɜ:tʃəsɪŋ ,mæ‿nɪdʒə] Einkaufsleiter/in 117
pure new wool [,pjʊə nju: 'wʊl] reine Schurwolle 154
purpose-built [,pɜ:pəs'bɪlt] für bestimmten Zweck gebaut 43
to put someone through [pʊt ,sʌmwʌn 'θru:] durchstellen, verbinden 55

Q

to qualify for ['kwɒlɪfaɪ fɔ:] Voraussetzungen erfüllen für, Anspruch haben auf 144
quantity discount [,kwɒntətɪ 'dɪskaʊnt] Mengenrabatt 128
quarter finals [,kwɔ:tə 'faɪnlz] Viertelfinale 18
quarterly ['kwɔ:təlɪ] vierteljährlich 128
quay [ki:] Kai, Dock, Anlegestelle 135
query ['kwɪərɪ] Anfrage 75
quota ['kwəʊtə] Quote, Rate, Kontingent, Anteil 149
quotation [kwəʊ'teɪʃn] Preisangebot 116
to quote [kwəʊt] Preis angeben; zitieren 128

R

rabbit ['ræbɪt] Kaninchen 26
rail siding ['reɪl ,saɪdɪŋ] Gleisanschluss 152
rail transport ['reɪl ,trænspɔ:t] Schienentransport 152
to raise [reɪz] erhöhen 198
to raise a matter ['reɪz ə ,mætə] eine Sache ansprechen 184
random sample [,rændəm 'sɑ:mpl] Zufallsprobe 194
to range from ... to ['reɪndʒ frəm ... tʊ] reichen von ... bis 88
range of products [,reɪndʒ əv 'prɒdʌkts] Produktpalette 33
rapid ['ræpɪd] schnell 92
rapport [ræ'pɔ:, rə'pɔ:] Verhältnis 219
raw materials [,rɔ: mə'tɪərɪəlz] Rohstoffe 151
re [ri:] bezüglich, wegen 188
receipt of order [rɪ,si:t əv 'ɔ:də] Auftragseingang 129
to receive [rɪ'si:v] erhalten, empfangen 54
receiver [rɪ'si:və] Hörer 54
recent ['ri:sənt] nicht lange zurückliegend, vor kurzem geschehen 98
reception [rɪ'sepʃn] Empfang 118
receptionist [rɪ'sepʃənɪst] Rezeptionist/in, Mitarbeiter/in am Empfang 21
recipient [rɪ'sɪpɪənt] Empfänger 101

to recognize ['rekəgnaɪz] erkennen, anerkennen 99
to recommend [ˌrekə'mend] empfehlen 83
record ['rekɔ:d] Aufzeichnung 82
to record [rɪ'kɔ:d] aufzeichnen, eintragen 105
to recruit [rɪ'kru:t] einstellen 207
recruitment agencies [rɪ'kru:tmənt ˌeɪdʒənsɪz] Stellenvermittlungsagenturen 207
to redesign [ˌri:dɪ'zaɪn] neu-, umgestalten 24
to redirect [ˌri:daɪ'rekt, ˌri:dɪ'rekt] umleiten 55
referee [ˌrefər'i:] *(hier:)* jemand, der eine Empfehlung / ein Zeugnis schreibt 210
reference ['refrəns] Bezug 131
to refer to [rɪ'fɜ: tu:] sich beziehen auf 68
refreshments [rɪ'freʃmənts] Erfrischung(en) 17
refund ['ri:fʌnd] Erstattung 180
to refund [ˌri:'fʌnd] erstatten 177
refurbishment [ˌri:'fɜ:bɪʃmənt] Renovierung 180
regardless of [rɪ'gɑ:dləs əv] ungeachtet, trotz 154
to register ['redʒɪstə] eintragen, registrieren 122
regularly ['regjələlɪ] regelmäßig 194
regulations [ˌregjə'leɪʃnz] Vorschriften, Verordnungen 106
to rehearse [rɪ'hɜ:s] proben, einüben 91
to reinforce [ˌri:ɪn'fɔ:s] verstärken 89
to reject [rɪ'dʒekt] ablehnen 223
to release from a contract [rɪˌli:s frəm ə 'kɒntrækt] von einem Vertrag entbinden 188
relevant ['reləvənt] wichtig, sachdienlich 59
reliable [rɪ'laɪəbl] zuverlässig 32
relieved [rɪ'li:vd] erleichtert 61
remainder, balance [rɪ'meɪndə, 'bæ‿ləns] Restbetrag 171
to remain unchanged [rɪˌmeɪn ʌn'tʃeɪndʒd] unverändert bleiben 94
to remind [rɪ'maɪnd] erinnern 91
reminder [rɪ'maɪndə] (Zahlungs-)Erinnerung, Mahnung 162
to remind someone [rɪ'maɪnd ˌsʌmwʌn] jemanden erinnern 202
to remit [rɪ'mɪt] überweisen 163
remittance [rɪ'mɪtəns] Überweisung 171
to remove [rɪ'mu:v] entfernen 178
to render a service [ˌrendər‿ə 'sɜ:vɪs] einen Dienst leisten, eine Dienstleistung erbringen 177
to renew a contract [rɪˌnju:‿ə 'kɒntrækt] einen Vertrag verlängern 180
rent [rent] Miete 63
to rent [rent] mieten 33
repairs [rɪ'peəz] Reparatur 37
repeat order [rɪˌpi:t 'ɔ:də] Folgeauftrag 141
to replace [rɪ'pleɪs] auflegen; *(auch:)* ersetzen 54
replacement Mp3 player [rɪˌpleɪsmənt ˌempi:'θri: ˌpleɪə] Ersatz-Mp3-Spieler 154
to report to [rɪ'pɔ:t‿tu:] unterstehen 48
representative [ˌreprɪ'zentətɪv] Vertreter/in 123
reputation [ˌrepjə'teɪʃn] Ruf 219
request [rɪ'kwest] Bitte 63
to request [rɪ'kwest] bitten um 80
to require [rɪ'kwaɪə] *(hier:)* verlangen, auffordern 88
research ['ri:sɜ:tʃ] Forschung 21
residence permit ['rezɪdəns ˌpɜ:mɪt] Aufenthaltsgenehmigung 221
resort [rɪ'zɔ:t] Urlaubs-, Badeort 133
8000 and 6000 customers, respectively ['eɪt‿θaʊsənd ənd 'sɪks ˌθaʊsənd ˌkʌstəməz rɪ'spektɪvlɪ] 8000 bzw. 6000 Kunden 95
respite ['respaɪt] Zahlungsaufschub 190
to respond [rɪ'spɒnd] antworten, reagieren 185
responsible for [rɪ'spɒnsəbl fɔ:] verantwortlich für 49
to restore [rɪ'stɔ:] wiederherstellen, restaurieren 102
restricted [rɪ'strɪktɪd] beschränkt 82
restroom ['rest,ru:m] Toilette (AE) 21
retail customers [ˌri:teɪl 'kʌstəməz] Privatkunden (bei einer Bank) 197
retailer ['ri:teɪlə] Einzelhändler 117
retailing operations ['ri:teɪlɪŋ‿ ɒpəˌreɪʃnz] Einzelhandelsgeschäftstätigkeit 197
retail management assistant [ˌri:teɪl 'mænɪdʒmənt əˌsɪstənt] Kaufmann/-frau im Einzelhandel 9
retail outlet [ˌri:teɪl 'aʊtlet] Einzelhandelsverkaufsstelle 166
retail sales [ˌri:teɪl 'seɪlz] Umsatz im Einzelhandel 111
retail trade ['ri:teɪl ˌtreɪd] Einzelhandel 147
to retain [rɪ'teɪn] halten, beibehalten 121
retired [rɪ'taɪəd] im Ruhestand, pensioniert 199
retirement [rɪ'taɪəmənt] Ruhestand 189
to return [rɪ'tɜ:n] *(hier:)* zurückschicken 83
to reveal [rɪ'vi:l] enthüllen, aufzeigen 183
to reverse [rɪ'vɜ:s] umkehren 212
reviews [rɪ'vju:z] Berichte, Besprechungen 198
to revoke [rɪ'vəʊk] widerrufen, annullieren, stornieren 167
reworking [ˌri:'wɜ:kɪŋ] Um-, Nacharbeitung 178
rice [raɪs] Reis 26
right away [ˌraɪtə'weɪ] sofort 221
to rise, rose, risen [raɪz, rəʊz, rɪzn] steigen 94
rising demand for [ˌraɪzɪŋ dɪ'mɑ:nd fə] steigende Nachfrage nach 92
roast pork [ˌrəʊst‿'pɔ:k] Schweinebraten 26
to romp [rɒmp] herumtollen 145
roof [ru:f] Dach 195
roughly one third [ˌrʌflɪ ˌwʌn 'θɜ:d] rund ein Drittel 183
roundabout ['raʊndəbaʊt] Kreisverkehr 22
to round up [raʊnd 'ʌp] aufrunden 80
rubber, eraser ['rʌbə, ɪ'reɪzə] Radiergummi 44
rude [ru:d] grob, ungehobelt, unverschämt 113
to rule [ru:l] entscheiden, verfügen, anordnen 149
rules [ru:lz] Regeln, Vorschriften 106
ruler ['ru:lə] Lineal 44
to run out of sth. [rʌn 'aʊt əv ˌsʌmθɪŋ] ausgehen, zur Neige gehen 132
rush [rʌʃ] Ansturm 76
rushed-off-your-feet [ˌrʌʃtɒfjɔ:'fi:t] vielbeschäftigt 203
rust [rʌst] rostfarben 203

S

salary ['sælərɪ] Gehalt 208
sales (department) ['seɪlz (dɪˌpɑ:tmənt)] Verkauf(sabteilung) 48
sales assistant ['seɪlz‿əˌsɪstənt] Verkäufer/in 198
sales consultant ['seɪlz kənˌsʌltənt] Verkaufsberater/in 198
sales force ['seɪlz ˌfɔ:s] Vertreterstab 196
sales literature ['seɪlz ˌlɪtrətʃə] Prospektmaterial 32
sales representative ['seɪlz reprɪˌzentətɪv] Handelsvertreter/in 100
salmon ['sæmən] Lachs 26
salutation [ˌsæljə'teɪʃn] Begrüßung, *(hier:)* Anrede 100
sample ['sɑ:mpl] Muster, Probestück 128
satisfaction [ˌsætɪs'fækʃn] Zufriedenheit 182
to satisfy ['sætɪsfaɪ] zufrieden stellen 180
sausage ['sɒsɪdʒ] Wurst 26
savoury ['seɪvərɪ] herzhaft, pikant 26
scale [skeɪl] Maß, Maßstab 162
scarce(ly) ['skeəs(lɪ)] knapp; kaum 138
scared [skeəd] ängstlich 88

schedule ['ʃedju:l, 'skedju:l] Schema, Aufstellung, (Termin-)Plan 110
school-leaving certificate [ˌsku:l‿li:vɪŋ sə'tɪfɪkət] Schulabschlusszeugnis 209
Sci-Fi film ['saɪfaɪ ˌfɪlm] Science-Fiction-Film 9
scope [skəʊp] Umfang, Bereich 48
scotch tape [ˌskɒtʃ 'teɪp] Klebeband 44
scratch [skrætʃ] Kratzer 186
to scream [skri:m] schreien 203
screen [skri:n] Bildschirm 203
search engine ['sɜ:tʃ ˌendʒɪn] Suchmaschine 116
seat [si:t] Sitz 223
seaworthy packing [ˌsi:wɜ:ðɪ 'pækɪŋ] seemäßige Verpackung 152
second floor [ˌsekənd 'flɔ:] zweite Etage (BE); erste Etage (AE) 21
sector ['sektə] Branche 197
secure [sɪ'kjʊə, sɪ'kjɔ:] sicher 35
to seek, sought, sought [si:k, sɔ:t, sɔ:t] suchen 208
segment ['segmənt] Marktsegment 195
selection [sə'lekʃn] Auswahl 91
selective [sə'lektɪv] ausgewählt 199
self-explanatory [ˌselfɪk'splænətrɪ] selbsterklärend 203
sell-by date ['selbaɪˌdeɪt] Verfallsdatum (Lebensmittel) 182
to sell on [sel 'ɒn] weiterverkaufen 195
to sell well [ˌsel 'wel] sich gut verkaufen, gut gehen 145
senior ['si:njə] höherrangig 24
sensation [sen'seɪʃn] Gefühl 204
serious ['sɪərɪəs] ernst, schwerwiegend 187
serviceable ['sɜ:vɪsəbl] zweckdienlich, praktisch, strapazierfähig 163
service centre/center ['sɜ:vɪs‿sentə] Kundendienst(zentrum) 184
set [set] (Fernseh-)Apparat 203
to set [set] festsetzen, ansetzen, einrichten 149
to set about [set ə'baʊt] sich daran machen 193
to settle an invoice [ˌsetl ən 'ɪnvɔɪs] eine Rechnung begleichen 169
settlement ['setlmənt] Abrechnung, Bezahlung, Ausgleich, Erledigung 128
to settle the matter ['setl ðə ˌmætə] die Angelegenheit erledigen 182
to set up in business on one's own [set ˌʌp ɪn 'bɪznɪs ɒn wʌnz‿əʊn] eine eigene Firma gründen 219
severe(ly) [sə'vɪə(lɪ)] schwer, ernstlich, streng, hart 111
to sew, sewed, sewn [səʊ, səʊd, səʊn] nähen 178
to share the costs [ˌʃeə ðə 'kɒsts] sich die Kosten teilen 147
sharp [ʃɑ:p] scharf 22
to ship [ʃɪp] versenden, verschiffen 62
shipper ['ʃɪpə] *(hier:)* Versender/in, Verfrachter/in 159
shipping ['ʃɪpɪŋ] Seetransport, Verschiffung, Versand 151
shirt [ʃɜ:t] (Herren-)Hemd 144
shoemaker ['ʃu:ˌmeɪkə] Schuhmacher/in, Schuster/in 33
shopping cart ['ʃɒpɪŋ‿kɑ:t] Einkaufswagen 37
shortcomings ['ʃɔ:tˌkʌmɪŋz] Unzulänglichkeiten 180
shortly ['ʃɔ:tlɪ] in Kürze, bald 142
shuttle service ['ʃʌtl ˌsɜ:vɪs] Pendelbus 76
sights [saɪts] Sehenswürdigkeiten 22
signatory ['sɪgnətərɪ] Unterzeichner/in 107
signature ['sɪgnətʃə] Unterschrift 99
signature footer ['sɪgnətʃə ˌfʊtə] Unterschriftsfußzeilen 100
significant(ly) [sɪg'nɪfɪkənt(lɪ)] bedeutend 94
to simplify ['sɪmplɪfaɪ] vereinfachen 194
single ['sɪŋgl] ledig 213
single market [ˌsɪŋgl 'mɑ:kɪt] Binnenmarkt 222
single room [ˌsɪŋgl 'ru:m] Einzelzimmer 75
sister-in-law ['sɪstərɪnlɔ:] Schwägerin 48
site [saɪt] Standort, Abbaustelle 92
size [saɪz] Größe 64
skill [skɪl] Fertigkeit 88
skin care ['skɪn ˌkeə] Hautpflege 208
to skip [skɪp] überspringen 201
to sleep [sli:p] *(hier:)* Schlafmöglichkeit bieten 63
slice [slaɪs] Scheibe, Anteil 92
slide [slaɪd] Folie 89
slight(ly) [slaɪt(lɪ)] geringfügig 66
slight drizzle [ˌslaɪt‿'drɪzl] leichter Nieselregen 20
to slump [slʌmp] stark fallen 94
smart [smɑ:t] ordentlich, gepflegt, schick 218
smitten ['smɪtn] hingerissen 145
smoked [sməʊkt] geräuchert 26
smoked salmon [ˌsməʊkt 'sæmən] Räucherlachs 122
smooth(ly) [smu:ð(lɪ)] glatt, reibungslos 111
smudged [smʌdʒd] verwischt, verschmiert 182
to soak [səʊk] durchnässen, einweichen 171
to soar [sɔ:] sprunghaft steigen, in die Höhe schnellen 92
sociable ['səʊʃəbl] gesellig, umgänglich 24
social service [ˌsəʊʃl 'sɜ:vɪs] Ersatzdienst 215
soft drinks [ˌsɒft‿'drɪŋks] alkoholfreie Getränke 81
sole [səʊl] Sohle 177
solicited offer [səˌlɪsɪtɪd 'ɒfə] verlangtes Angebot 126
to some extent [tə ˌsʌm ɪk'stent] in gewissem Maße 55
sophisticated [sə'fɪstɪkeɪtɪd] hoch entwickelt, technisch ausgefeilt 205
sour [saʊə] sauer 26
source [sɔ:s] Quelle 207
spacing ['speɪsɪŋ] Abstände, Abstandseinteilung 105
spacious ['speɪʃəs] geräumig 43
to spare [speə] übrig haben 194
spare parts [ˌspeə 'pɑ:ts] Ersatzteile 152
sparing(ly) ['speərɪŋ(lɪ)] sparsam, mäßig 103
sparkling mineral water [ˌspɑ:klɪŋ 'mɪnərəl ˌwɔ:tə] Sprudel, Mineralwasser mit Kohlensäure 17
special features [ˌspeʃl 'fi:tʃəz] besondere Eigenschaften 76
specialist agency [ˌspeʃəlɪst 'eɪdʒənsɪ] Fachagentur 202
specialist shops [ˌspeʃəlɪst 'ʃɒps] Fachgeschäfte 195
special treat [ˌspeʃl 'tri:t] besonderes Vergnügen, spezielles Extra 133
to spend [spend] ausgeben 194
spicy ['spaɪsɪ] würzig 25
spirits ['spɪrɪts] Spirituosen 197
splash [splæʃ] Spritzer, Schuss 204
spokesman ['spəʊksmən] Sprecher 201
square [skweə] Platz 23
to stack [stæk] aufstapeln, aufschichten 151
staff [stɑ:f] Belegschaft, Personal 33
staff member ['stɑ:f ˌmembə] Mitarbeiter/in 160
stage [steɪdʒ] *(hier:)* Stadium 193
to stage [steɪdʒ] veranstalten 147
staggered payment [ˌstægəd 'peɪmənt] gestaffelte Zahlungsweise 167
to stagnate [stæg'neɪt] stagnieren 111
stagnation [stæg'neɪʃn] Stillstand 151
standard lamp ['stændəd ˌlæmp] Stehlampe 157
to stand in for someone [stænd 'ɪn fə ˌsʌmwʌn] jemanden vertreten 28
standing order [ˌstændɪŋ 'ɔ:də] Dauerauftrag 141
stapling machine/stapler ['steɪplɪŋ məˌʃi:n / 'steɪplə] Tacker 44
starter ['stɑ:tə] Vorspeise 25
start-up (business) ['stɑ:tʌp (ˌbɪznɪs)] Neugründung, junges Unternehmen 35
statement ['steɪtmənt] Aussage, Äußerung 8
statement of account [ˌsteɪtmənt əv ə'kaʊnt] Kontoauszug 167

state of affairs [ˌsteɪt‿əv ə'feəz] Zustand, Stand der Dinge 170
state-of-the-art [ˌsteɪtəvðɪ'ɑ:t] auf dem neuesten Stand (der Technik) 32
state rooms ['steɪt ˌru:mz] Empfangssäle 23
stationery ['steɪʃənrɪ] Büromaterial 180
steady, steadily ['stedɪ(lɪ)] stetig 94
steel [sti:l] Stahl 132
steel rods [ˌsti:l 'rɒdz] Stahlstäbe 154
stew, soup [stju:, su:p] Eintopf 27
to stew [stju:] kochen, dünsten, schmoren 26
to stipulate, to specify ['stɪpjəleɪt, 'spesɪfaɪ] vorschreiben 166
stock [stɒk] Vorrat, Lager(bestand) 126
to stock up on [stɒk 'ʌp ɒn] Lager(bestand) auffüllen 132
storage ['stɔ:rɪdʒ] Abstellraum 21
straight [streɪt] *(hier:)* geradewegs, direkt 199
straight away [ˌstreɪtə'weɪ] sofort, unverzüglich 147
straightforward [ˌstreɪt'fɔ:wəd] einfach, unkompliziert 18
strengths [streŋkθs] Stärken 218
to stress [stres] betonen 144
striking ['straɪkɪŋ] auffallend 23
stubble trouble ['stʌbl ˌtrʌbl] Probleme mit Bartstoppeln 203
study group ['stʌdɪ ˌgru:p] Arbeitsgruppe 68
stuffed [stʌft] gefüllt 26
stylish ['staɪlɪʃ] schick, modisch 163
subconscious [sʌb'kɒnʃəs] Unterbewusstsein 202
subject ['sʌbdʒɪkt] Gegenstand, *(hier:)* Betreff 100
subject matter ['sʌbdʒɪkt ˌmætə] Gegenstand, Thema 101
subliminal [sʌb'lɪmɪnl] unterhalb der Schwelle des Bewusstseins 202
subsidiary [səb'sɪdɪərɪ] Tochtergesellschaft 149
substantial [səb'stænʃl] erheblich, beträchtlich 168
substitute ['sʌbstɪtju:t] Ersatz (durch Ähnliches) 130
suburb ['sʌbɜ:b] Vorort, Stadtteil im Außenbezirk 61
to succeed in [sək'si:d ɪn] gelingen 196
to suffer ['sʌfə] leiden 223
sufficient(ly) [sə'fɪʃənt(lɪ)] genug, genügend, ausreichend 35
to suggest [sə'dʒest] *(hier:)* hinweisen auf, suggerieren 199
suggestion [sə'dʒestʃn] Vorschlag 147
suit [su:t] Kostüm (Damen), Anzug 217
suitable ['su:təbl] geeignet 207
to sum up [sʌm 'ʌp] zusammenfassen, -rechnen 110
sunset ['sʌnset] Sonnenuntergang 148
superb(ly) [su:'pɜ:b(lɪ)] hervorragend, ausgezeichnet 19
superfluous [su:'pɜ:flʊəs] überflüssig 197
superior [su:'pɪərɪə] Vorgesetzte/r 48
to supervise ['su:pəvaɪz] beaufsichtigen 81
supplementary charge [ˌsʌplɪmentərɪ 'tʃɑ:dʒ] Zuschlag 79
supplier [sə'plaɪə] Lieferant, Anbieter 116
supply [sə'plaɪ] Angebot 195
supply/demand ratio [səˌplaɪ dɪ'mɑ:nd ˌreɪʃɪəʊ] Verhältnis zwischen Angebot und Nachfrage 151
to support [sə'pɔ:t] unterstützen, helfen 7
to suppose [sə'pəʊz] vermuten 194
surname ['sɜ:neɪm] Familienname 8
surplus ['sɜ:pləs] überschüssig 177
surprisingly [sə'praɪzɪŋlɪ] überraschenderweise 18
to surround [sə'raʊnd] umgeben 24
to survive [sə'vaɪv] überleben 197
suspicious [sə'spɪʃəs] verdächtig 102
sweets [swi:ts] Süßwaren, Süßigkeiten 118
swift(ly) ['swɪft(lɪ)] schnell 205
swivel chair [ˌswɪvl 'tʃeə] Drehstuhl 44

T

tag [tæg] Etikett, Anhängeschildchen 178
tailback ['teɪlbæk] Stau 20
tailored suit [ˌteɪləd 'su:t] Kostüm 218
tailor-made [ˌteɪlə'meɪd] maßgeschneidert 133
to take [teɪk] *(hier:)* in Anspruch nehmen, dauern 18
to take a call [ˌteɪk ə 'kɔ:l] einen Anruf entgegennehmen 78
to take advantage of [ˌteɪk əd'vɑ:ntɪdʒ ɒv] ausnutzen, in Anspruch nehmen 222
to take a message [ˌteɪk ə 'mesɪdʒ] eine Nachricht entgegennehmen 59
to take down [teɪk‿'daʊn] notieren 59
to take into account [teɪk ˌɪntʊ‿ə'kaʊnt] berücksichtigen 180
to take offence at sth. [teɪk ə'fens ət ˌsʌmθɪŋ] etwas übel nehmen 184
to take off the roof [ˌteɪk ɒf ðə 'ru:f] das Dach abdecken 171
to take over [ˌteɪk 'əʊvə] (eine Firma) übernehmen 33
to take part in [ˌteɪk 'pɑ:t ɪn] teilnehmen an 10
to take the minutes [ˌteɪk ðə 'mɪnɪts] Protokoll führen 82
to take up [teɪk 'ʌp] aufnehmen, sich verlegen auf; hochheben 33
to take up residence [ˌteɪk ʌp 'rezɪdəns] wohnhaft werden 221
to target ['tɑ:gɪt] ansprechen, anpeilen 194
tart [tɑ:t] herb, säuerlich 26
to taste [teɪst] schmecken 26
tax [tæks] Steuer 163
tax-exempt intra-Community delivery [ˌtæksɪg'zemt ˌɪntrəkə'mju:nətɪ dɪ'lɪvərɪ] steuerfreie Innergemeinschaftslieferung (innerhalb der EU) 164
tedious ['ti:dɪəs] langweilig, lästig 20
telephone directory ['teləfəʊn daɪˌrektərɪ, 'teləfəʊn dɪˌrektərɪ] Telefonbuch 54
telephony [tə'lefənɪ] Telefonverkehr 53
temporary ['tempərərɪ] vorübergehend, befristet 213
to tempt [tempt] in Versuchung führen 25
to tend to be ['tend‿tʊ bi:] dazu neigen 113
to tend to book flights [ˌtend‿tʊ ˌbʊk 'flaɪts] Flüge häufig buchen 194
terminal operator ['tɜ:mɪnl ˌɒpəreɪtə] Betreiber/in eines Terminals 151
terms of delivery [ˌtɜ:mz‿əv dɪ'lɪvərɪ] Lieferbedingungen 128
terms of payment [ˌtɜ:mz‿əv 'peɪmənt] Zahlungsbedingungen 128
terms of payment and delivery [ˌtɜ:mz‿əv ˌpeɪmənt ənd‿dɪ'lɪvərɪ] Zahlungs- und Lieferbedingungen 117
terrible ['terɪbl] furchtbar 19
text-building block ['tekstbɪldɪŋ ˌblɒk] Textbaustein 111
theft [θeft] Diebstahl 152
to theme [θi:m] nach einem Motto/Thema gestalten 203
to thicken ['θɪkn] eindicken 27
this is why [ˌðɪs ɪz 'waɪ] daher, deshalb, deswegen 111
those involved [ˌðəʊz ɪn'vɒlvd] die Beteiligten 82
those present [ˌðəʊz 'preznt] die Anwesenden 82
to threaten ['θretn] drohen 169
thus [ðʌs] daher 196
to tie [taɪ] binden 217
tiles [taɪlz] Fliesen, Kacheln 186
time-consuming ['taɪmkənˌsju:mɪŋ] zeitraubend 35
to have time on their hands [hæv ˌtaɪm ɒn ðeə 'hændz] Zeit (übrig) haben 199
timetable ['taɪmˌteɪbl] Fahrplan 79
tip [tɪp] *(hier:)* Trinkgeld 80
tomato relish [təˌmɑ:təʊ 'relɪʃ] Tomatenrelish 186
tool [tu:l] Werkzeug 53
tool kit ['tu:l ˌkɪt] Werkzeugsatz 179
topics ['tɒpɪks] *(hier:)* Punkte, Themen 82

topic of conversation [ˌtɒpɪk əv ˌkɒnvəˈseɪʃn] Gesprächsthema 19
tournament [ˈtɔːnəmənt] Turnier 20
tour operator [ˈtʊər‿ɒpəreɪtə] Reiseveranstalter 208
towering [ˈtaʊərɪŋ] turmhoch, überragend 23
town hall [ˌtaʊn ˈhɔːl] Rathaus 22
to track [træk] verfolgen 37
trade association [ˈtreɪd əsəʊʃiˌeɪʃn] Branchenverband 116
trade discount [ˈtreɪd‿dɪskaʊnt] Wiederverkaufsrabatt, Händlerrabatt 121
trade fair [ˈtreɪd ˌfeə] (Fach-)Messe 116
trade flows [ˈtreɪd ˌfləʊz] Handelsströme 151
trade journal [ˈtreɪd‿dʒɜːnl] Fachzeitschrift 201
trainee [ˌtreɪˈniː] Auszubildende/r 10
training course [ˈtreɪnɪŋ ˌkɔːs] Ausbildungslehrgang 12
train ride [ˈtreɪn ˌraɪd] Zugfahrt 19
to transfer [trænsˈfɜː] überweisen, übertragen 142
to transform [trænsˈfɔːm] verwandeln 203
transparencies [trænˈspærənsɪz] Folien 89
travel agency [ˈtrævl ˌeɪdʒənsɪ] Reisebüro 8
travel agent [ˈtrævl ˌeɪdʒənt] Reisebüro 197
travel consultant [ˈtrævl kənˌsʌltənt] Reiseverkehrskaufmann/-frau 8
tray [treɪ] Ablagekorb 44
treaty [ˈtriːtɪ] Vertrag (zwischen Staaten) 223
trial order [ˌtraɪəl ˈɔːdə] Probeauftrag 141
triple-walled cardboard box [ˌtrɪplwɔːld‿kɑːdbɔːd‿ˈbɒks] 3-wandiger Karton 155
trousers [ˈtraʊzəz] Hose 217
trout [traʊt] Forelle 26
to trust [trʌst] vertrauen 167
to tuck into [ˌtʌk ˈɪntuː] hineinstecken in 217
tuition [tjʊˈɪʃn] Unterricht, Unterweisung 133
turkey [ˈtɜːkɪ] Pute, Truthahn 26
to turn down [tɜːn ˈdaʊn] ablehnen 166
turnover [ˈtɜːnˌəʊvə] Umsatz, Absatz 201
turn-taking [ˈtɜːnˌteɪkɪŋ] sich anstellen, warten bis man dran ist 79
to turn up [tɜːn ˈʌp] auftauchen 207
TV advertising, TV commercials [ˌtiːviː ˈædvətaɪzɪŋ, ˌtiːviː kəˈmɜːʃlz] TV-Werbung 199

U

ultimate [ˈʌltɪmət] (aller)höchst, äußerst, maximal 204
unappreciated [ˌʌnəˈpriːʃieɪtɪd] nicht genügend geschätzt 219
unauthorised [ʌnˈɔːθəraɪzd] unbefugt 99
unavoidable [ˌʌnəˈvɔɪdəbl] unvermeidlich 55
to undercut [ˌʌndəˈkʌt] unterbieten 84
to underestimate [ˌʌndərˈestɪmeɪt] unterschätzen 90
understanding [ˌʌndəˈstændɪŋ] verständnisvoll 184
unemployment [ˌʌnɪmˈplɔɪmənt] Arbeitslosigkeit 221
unified [ˈjuːnɪfaɪd] einheitlich 222
unique [juːˈniːk] einzigartig 23
to unload [ʌnˈləʊd] entladen, löschen 151
unprecedented [ʌnˈpresɪdəntɪd] noch nie dagewesen 198
unreliable [ˌʌnrɪˈlaɪəbl] unzuverlässig 99
unsatisfactory [ʌnˌsætɪsˈfæktərɪ] unbefriedigend, ungenügend, unzureichend 99
unsolicited offer [ˌʌnsəlɪsɪtɪd ˈɒfə] unverlangtes Angebot 126
to update [ʌpˈdeɪt] aktualisieren 135
uplighter [ˈʌplaɪtə] Deckenfluter 157
upmarket [ʌpˈmɑːkɪt] im oberen Marktsegment 47
upper and lower case letters [ˌʌpər‿ən ˌləʊə keɪs ˈletəz] Groß- und Kleinbuchstaben 89
up the hill [ˌʌp ðə ˈhɪl] den Berg hinauf 22
up to date [ˌʌptəˈdeɪt] aktuell 199
urgent [ˈɜːdʒənt] dringend, eilig 147
usage [ˈjuːsɪdʒ] Gepflogenheit, Gewohnheit, (übliche) Praxis 107

V

vacancy [ˈveɪkənsɪ] offene Stelle 207
valid [ˈvælɪd] gültig, bindend, rechtskräftig 126
valid until [ˈvælɪd ʌnˌtɪl] gültig bis 168
valuable [ˈvæljʊəbl] wertvoll 183
van [væn] Kleintransporter 152
variety [vəˈraɪətɪ] Vielfalt 195
VAT (value-added tax) [ˌviːeɪˈtiː (ˌvæljuː‿ˌædɪd‿ˈtæks)] Mehrwertsteuer 163
veal [viːl] Kalbfleisch 26
vegan [ˈviːgən] Veganer/in 25
vegetable(s) [ˈvedʒtəbl(z)] Gemüse 26
veggieburger [ˈvedʒɪˌbɜːgə] Gemüsebratling 25
vehicle [ˈvɪəkl] Fahrzeug 151
venison [ˈvenɪsən] Hirsch, Rotwild (als Fleisch) 25
venue [ˈvenjuː] Treffpunkt, Veranstaltungsort, Gerichtsstand 79
verdant [ˈvɜːdənt] üppig grün 203
vessel [ˈvesl] Schiff 159
via [ˈvaɪə, ˈviːə] über 90
vibrant [ˈvaɪbrənt] lebendig 18
view [vjuː] *(hier:)* Ausblick 46
vinegar [ˈvɪnɪgə] Essig 27
to violate [ˈvaɪəleɪt] verstoßen gegen 223
virtually [ˈvɜːtʃʊəlɪ] fast, so gut wie 66
visible [ˈvɪzəbl] sichtbar 79
visual aids [ˌvɪʒʊəl ˈeɪdz] visuelle Hilfsmittel 89
vocational college [vəʊˈkeɪʃənl ˌkɒlɪdʒ] Berufskolleg, Berufsfachschule 10
vocational school [vəʊˈkeɪʃənl ˌskuːl] Berufsschule 7
volume order [ˌvɒljuːm ˈɔːdə] Großauftrag 120

W

waiter service [ˈweɪtə ˌsɜːvɪs] Bedienung 79
to wait one's turn [ˌweɪt wʌnz ˈtɜːn] warten bis man an die Reihe kommt 25
wall calendar [ˈwɔːl ˌkæləndə] Wandkalender 181
warehouse [ˈweəhaʊs] Lager 196
wastepaper basket [weɪstˈpeɪpə ˌbɑːskɪt] Papierkorb 199
wastepaper bin [weɪstˈpeɪpə ˌbɪn] Papierkorb 44
to watch [wɒtʃ] aufpassen auf 47
to wave your arms around [ˌweɪv jɔːr‿ˈɑːmz əˌraʊnd] mit den Armen herumfuchteln 91
waybill [ˈweɪbɪl] Frachtbrief 158
weather forecast [ˈweðə ˌfɔːkɑːst] Wettervorhersage 19
well-substantiated [ˌwelsʌbˈstænʃieɪtɪd] gut belegt 92
we've already met [wiːv ˌɔːlredɪ ˈmet] wir kennen uns schon 17
whatever the price [wɒtˌevə ðə ˈpraɪs] ganz unabhängig vom Preis 182
What is the weather like? [ˌwɒt ɪz ðə ˈweðə ˌlaɪk] Wie ist das Wetter? 19
whenever [wenˈevə] immer dann, wenn 99
whereas [weəˈræz] wohingegen, dagegen 107
wholesale and export clerk [ˌhəʊlseɪl ənd ˈekspɔːt ˌklɑːk] Kaufmann/-frau im Groß- und Außenhandel 8
wholesaler [ˈhəʊlˌseɪlə] Großhändler 10
wide range [ˌwaɪd ˈreɪndʒ] breite Palette 193
willing [ˈwɪlɪŋ] bereit 194
to withdraw money from an account [wɪðˈdrɔː ˌmʌnɪ frəm ən əˈkaʊnt] Geld von einem Konto abheben 165
with order [wɪð ˈɔːdə] bei Auftragserteilung 167
without engagement [wɪˌðaʊt ɪŋˈgeɪdʒmənt] freibleibend 126

to wonder [ˈwʌndə] sich fragen 55
wooden case [ˌwʊdn ˈkeɪs] Holzkiste 154
wording [ˈwɜːdɪŋ] Formulierung 166
workforce [ˈwɜːkfɔːs] Belegschaft, Gesamtheit der Mitarbeiter 33
to work on one's own [ˌwɜːk ɒn wʌnz ˈəʊn] selbständig arbeiten 12
work-out [ˈwɜːkaʊt] Fitnesstraining 8
to work out [wɜːk ˈaʊt] sich körperlich fit halten, trainieren 7
work placement [ˈwɜːk ˌpleɪsmənt] Praktikum 221
world championship [ˌwɜːld ˈtʃæmpɪənʃɪp] Weltmeisterschaft 33
written order [ˌrɪtn ˈɔːdə] schriftliche Anweisung 165

Bildquellennachweis

6 Corbis RF (Royalty-Free), Düsseldorf; **6** Getty Images RF (Digital Vision), München; **6** Getty Images (PhotoDisc), München; **6** Fotosearch Stock Photography, Waukesha, WI; **7** JupiterImages photos.com (Photos.com), Tucson, AZ; **8** plainpicture GmbH & Co. KG (Maria Simon), Hamburg; **8** Alamy Images (Janine Wiedel Photolibrary), Abingdon, Oxon; **8** iStockphoto (RF/Locke), Calgary, Alberta; **10** Photothek.net Gbr (Ute Grabowsky), Radevormwald; **11** Robert Bosch GmbH, Stuttgart; **11** Imageshop (Imageshop), Düsseldorf; **11** Mauritius Images (Gilsdorf), Mittenwald; **16** www.bilderbox.com, Thening; **16** Corbis (Eric K. K. Yu), Düsseldorf; **16** Joker (Marcus Gloger), Bonn; **16** JupiterImages photos.com (RF/Photos.com), Tucson, AZ; **17** Klett-Archiv (Meyle + Müller/Harter), Stuttgart; **18** Klett-Archiv (Meyle + Müller/Harter), Stuttgart; **19** iStockphoto (RF/artydanmark), Calgary, Alberta; **23** Kartographie Huber, München; **23** images.de digital photo GmbH (Giribas), Berlin; **23** Jahns, Rainer, Siegsdorf; **25** Klett-Archiv (Meyle + Müller/Harter), Stuttgart; **25** iStockphoto (Natasha-R-Graham), Calgary, Alberta; **26** Fotolia LLC (Ralf Beier), New York; **26** StockFood GmbH (Newedel), München; **26** StockFood GmbH (Joff Lee Studios), München; **26** obs (ABCEuroRSCG), Hamburg; **26** Getty Images RF (PhotoDisc), München; **32** Avenue Images GmbH (Corbis RF/Tom Grill), Hamburg; **32** MEV Verlag GmbH, Augsburg; **33** Picture-Alliance (akg), Frankfurt; **33** Picture-Alliance (epa), Frankfurt; **33** Picture-Alliance (Imaginechina), Frankfurt; **33** Klett-Archiv (Meyle + Müller/Harter), Stuttgart; **35** Dreamstime LLC (Maksim Shmeljov), Brentwood, TN; **37** Klett-Archiv (Meyle + Müller/Harter), Stuttgart; **37** Mauritius Images (Pöhlmann), Mittenwald; **37** MEV Verlag GmbH, Augsburg; **37** Avenue Images GmbH (Ingram Publishing), Hamburg; **37** Ingram Publishing, Tattenhall Chester; **38** Fotosearch Stock Photography, Waukesha, WI; **38** Avenue Images GmbH (Image Source), Hamburg; **38** Avenue Images GmbH (Image Source RF), Hamburg; **38** Bananastock, Watlington/Oxon; **38** Imageshop, Düsseldorf; **38** BBC Information and archives, London; **43** shutterstock (Monkey Business Images), New York, NY; **43** Thinkstock (Erik Snyder), München; **43** iStockphoto (Dmitry Kutlayev), Calgary, Alberta; **43** Corbis RF (Image Source), Düsseldorf; **44** Klett-Archiv (Meyle + Müller/Harter), Stuttgart; **45** shutterstock (ArtmannWitte), New York, NY; **46** iStockphoto (Jason Stitt), Calgary, Alberta; **46** iStockphoto (RF/Chen), Calgary, Alberta; **46** iStockphoto (RF/Anna Bryukhanova), Calgary, Alberta; **47** iStockphoto (Anna Bryukhanova), Calgary, Alberta; **47** iStockphoto (Jason Stitt), Calgary, Alberta; **47** iStockphoto (RF/Chen), Calgary, Alberta; **53** Thinkstock (Jupiterimages), München; **53** Avenue Images GmbH (Corbis RF/Jack Hollingsworth), Hamburg; **53** PhotoAlto, Paris; **53** Getty Images RF (Eyewire), München; **55** Klett-Archiv (Meyle + Müller/Harter), Stuttgart; **55** Fotosearch Stock Photography (Banana Stock), Waukesha, WI; **55** Avenue Images GmbH (Image Source), Hamburg; **57** Klett-Archiv (Meyle + Müller/Harter), Stuttgart; **60** iStockphoto (RF/peter chen), Calgary, Alberta; **60** Fotosearch Stock Photography (Banana Stock), Waukesha, WI; **60** MEV Verlag GmbH, Augsburg; **64** BigStockPhoto.com (RF), Davis, CA; **64** Dreamstime LLC (Ronfromyork), Brentwood, TN; **64** iStockphoto (RF), Calgary, Alberta; **66** Thinkstock (Stockbyte), München; **74** Thinkstock (Ryan McVay), München; **75** Klett-Archiv (Meyle + Müller/Harter), Stuttgart; **75** Fotosearch Stock Photography (Banana Stock), Waukesha, WI; **76** Klett-Archiv (Meyle + Müller/Harter), Stuttgart; **76** iStockphoto (RF/Thompson), Calgary, Alberta; **78** Klett-Archiv (Meyle + Müller/Harter), Stuttgart; **81** Klett-Archiv (Meyle + Müller/Harter), Stuttgart; **81** BBC Information and archives, London; **82** Klett-Archiv (Meyle + Müller/Harter), Stuttgart; **82** iStockphoto (RF/Media), Calgary, Alberta; **88** Thinkstock (IT Stock), München; **92** Fotosearch Stock Photography, Waukesha, WI; **92** LinguaTV GmbH, Berlin; **98** iStockphoto (Jill Fromer), Calgary, Alberta; **98** Mauritius Images (B. Lehner), Mittenwald; **98** Thinkstock (Hemera/Keith Bell), München; **99** iStockphoto (RF/Hudson), Calgary, Alberta; **103** Thinkstock (Hemera), München; **116** Düsseldorfer Messeges. mbH, Düsseldorf; **119** iStockphoto (McDonald), Calgary, Alberta; **120** LinguaTV GmbH, Berlin; **126** Corbis (Talaie), Düsseldorf; **131** MEV Verlag GmbH, Augsburg; **132** Thinkstock (Jupiterimages), München; **135** iStockphoto (William Bacon), Calgary, Alberta; **137** shutterstock (Ralf Beier), New York, NY; **137** iStockphoto (Bogdan Lazar), Calgary, Alberta; **137** Avenue Images GmbH (Corbis RF/Jose Luis Pelaez, Inc./Blend Images), Hamburg; **137** Fotosearch Stock Photography (Corbis RF), Waukesha, WI; **141** BLG Logistics Group AG, Bremen; **145** MEV Verlag GmbH, Augsburg; **145** Fotosearch Stock Photography (Digital Vision), Waukesha, WI; **145** Corel Corporation Deutschland, Unterschleissheim; **146** MEV Verlag GmbH, Augsburg; **147** Thomas Gremmelspacher, Stuttgart; **149** BBC Information and archives, London; **151** Corbis (Saloutos), Düsseldorf; **152** Klett-Archiv (Meyle + Müller/Harter), Stuttgart; **152** Fotosearch Stock Photography (PhotoDisc), Waukesha, WI; **152** Flughafen Frankfurt-Hahn, Hahn-Flughafen; **153** iStockphoto (bluenemo), Calgary, Alberta; **153** iStockphoto (RF/Prikhodho), Calgary, Alberta; **153** creativ collection Verlag GmbH, Freiburg; **154** iStockphoto (RF/David Meharey), Calgary, Alberta; **154** iStockphoto (RF/Paul Senyszyn), Calgary, Alberta; **154** iStockphoto (RF/Joe Gough), Calgary, Alberta; **154** iStockphoto (RF/Tschakert), Calgary, Alberta; **154** Thinkstock (Hemera Technologies, Getty Images), München; **154** Klett-Archiv (Ruth Feiertag), Stuttgart; **154** Das Fotoarchiv (Fotoarchiv/Pohl), Essen; **154** Image Source Ltd (Imagesource), Soho, London, W1F 9NZ; **154** Thinkstock (iStockphoto), München; **154** Thinkstock (Hemera), München; **156** iStockphoto (Rohde), Calgary, Alberta; **156** Getty Images RF (Annie Reynolds/PhotoLink), München; **157** Klett-Archiv (Meyle + Müller/Harter), Stuttgart; **159** MEV Verlag GmbH, Augsburg; **162** iStockphoto (RF/Paul Cowan), Calgary, Alberta; **165** iStockphoto (RF/Hudson), Calgary, Alberta; **165** iStockphoto (RF), Calgary, Alberta; **165** MEV Verlag GmbH, Augsburg; **167** iStockphoto (fazon1), Calgary, Alberta; **168** Fotolia LLC (ExQuisine), New York; **168** iStockphoto (RF/Maureen Perez), Calgary, Alberta; **168** iStockphoto (RF/Caspel), Calgary, Alberta; **168** Mauritius Images (Pöhlmann), Mittenwald; **168** creativ collection Verlag GmbH, Freiburg; **172** Thinkstock (iStockphoto), München; **176** Thinkstock (Polka Dot Images), München; **178** Fotolia LLC (Sulamith), New York; **181** Getty Images RF (Photodisc), München; **181** Corel Corporation Deutschland, Unterschleissheim; **182** Klett-Archiv (Meyle + Müller), Stuttgart; **186** iStockphoto (David Hughes), Calgary, Alberta; **188** shutterstock (Iurii Konoval), New York, NY; **193** shutterstock (ary718), New York, NY; **195** MEV Verlag GmbH, Augsburg; **196** Alamy Images (Expuesto - Nicolas Randall), Abingdon, Oxon; **196** Avenue Images GmbH (CorbisRF), Hamburg; **197** iStockphoto (DSGpro), Calgary, Alberta; **198** BBC Information and archives, London; **199** Alamy Images (Adams Picture Library t/a apl), Abingdon, Oxon; **201** Corbis (Harms), Düsseldorf; **203** Corel Corporation Deutschland, Unterschleissheim; **204** MEV Verlag GmbH, Augsburg; **204** shutterstock (Reinhold Foeger), New York, NY; **207** iStockphoto (Zorani), Calgary, Alberta; **208** Mercedes Benz, Niederlassung, Stuttgart; **208** MEV Verlag GmbH, Augsburg; **208** iStockphoto (RF/Maier), Calgary, Alberta; **216** BBC Information and archives, London; **217** Thinkstock (Digital Vision.), München; **218** Klett-Archiv (Meyle + Müller/Harter), Stuttgart; **220** Mauritius Images (Simone Fichtl), Mittenwald; **221** creativ collection Verlag GmbH, Freiburg; **222** Comstock, Luxemburg; **224** iStockphoto (fazon1), Calgary, Alberta; **224** creativ collection Verlag GmbH, Freiburg; **232** Klett-Archiv, Stuttgart; **COVER** iStockphoto (Dominik Pabis), Calgary, Alberta; **COVER** shutterstock (Yuri Arcurs), New York, NY; **COVER** Avenue Images GmbH (Fancy), Hamburg; **Incoterms** iStockphoto (William Bacon), Calgary, Alberta; **Inhaltsverzeichnis** Thinkstock (IT Stock), München; **Inhaltsverzeichnis** shutterstock (ary718), New York, NY; **Inhaltsverzeichnis** www.bilderbox.com, Thening; **Inhaltsverzeichnis** Thinkstock (Hemera/Keith Bell), München

Sollte es in einem Einzelfall nicht gelungen sein, den korrekten Rechteinhaber ausfindig zu machen, so werden berechtigte Ansprüche selbstverständlich im Rahmen der üblichen Regelungen abgegolten.